ESSENTIAL
HUMANITIES

KRISTINA M. JANTZ

SECOND EDITION

Kendall Hunt
publishing company

Cover image © Shutterstock, Inc.

Kendall Hunt
p u b l i s h i n g   c o m p a n y

www.kendallhunt.com
Send all inquiries to:
4050 Westmark Drive
Dubuque, IA 52004-1840

Contents

Prehistory: Cultural Roots from the Stone Age and Monomyth

Fig. 1.1 Callanish stones in Lewis, Scotland

© Swen Stroop/Shutterstock.com

Knowledge Acquisition

◆ *Analyze the unique aspects of prehistoric people and the foundations of culture.*

◆ *Discover what is known about key cultural artifacts, including cave painting and sculptures.*

◆ *Appreciate the role of the monomyth in ancient life.*

SETTING THE SCENE

Fossil records dating to 5.7 million years ago indicates that upright hominins, a group classification including apes, chimpanzees, and humans, roamed the forest regions of Ethiopia. Genetic testing suggests that the San people of Zimbabwe are the most genetically diverse people in Africa, implying that they are the ancestors of modern humans after they spread from Africa to Asia, then Europe, and eventually the Americas and Australia.

The birth of humanity predates written records, but evidence of the earliest humans, *Homo sapiens*, dates to 200,000 BCE as they began to displace *Homo erectus* after 1.6 million years of domination (fig. 1.2). Both species are believed to have originated in Africa and were toolmakers. They wore animal skin clothing, cooked with fire, and possibly performed ritual burials of their dead. Paleolithic people's understanding of their domain is evident in cave paintings. The paintings are located deep within the caves instead of at the opening where people might have lived and where natural light was available. Each artifact expressed the beliefs and values of lithic people.

CULTURAL FOUNDATIONS

The term **culture** represents the shared values and beliefs of a group that developed over time and passed from one generation to another. Culture is seen in artifacts, religious or spiritual beliefs, systems of laws, or the customs comprising the way a group functions. Human culture, under this definition, dates back at least 30,000 years and possibly even earlier. The Paleolithic, or Old Stone Age, cultures of Europe hunted wild game and gathered plants to sustain themselves, and their groups were small in number. As the harsh conditions of the Ice Age began to subside, from 10000 to 8000 BCE, a new lifestyle emerged where humans settled in one location and farmed the newly arable land.

Paleolithic Era

Historically, the **Paleolithic** period corresponds to the Ice Age or Pleistocene. The

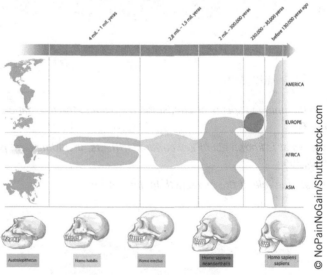

Fig. 1.2 Ancestral linage of modern *Homo sapiens*

first *Homo sapiens* were hunter-gatherers who followed the herds northward in the summer and withdrew to caves in the south during the winter. Their survival hinged on the animals they killed and foods they forged such as nuts, berries, and edible roots. As the ice covering the plains receded further into the upper reaches of the Northern Hemisphere, landmass was exposed. In harsher environs of modern-day Ukraine, Paleolithic people built small village communities with houses made of mammoth bone. The average number of mammoths used to construct one house is between 80 and 100. Houses measured between 13 and 26 feet in diameter, with almost every large bone of the animal used in the construction process.

One innovation that allowed hunters to kill wild game successfully was the bow and arrow due to its longer-range capabilities in the open plains. To help with the hunt, Paleolithic people domesticated dogs around 11000 BCE. Soon afterward, other animals, such as goats and cattle, were domesticated and used to cultivate the fields and as a food source. The transition from the Paleolithic to the Neolithic era was underway.

Neolithic Era

By the end of the last Ice Age and the beginning of the **Neolithic** era, or New Stone Age, around 8000 BCE, new groups of people developed, whose lifestyles became increasingly sedentary, and based on agriculture, quickly replaced nomadic hunting and gathering groups. With the rise of agriculture, complex societies arose throughout the world. They began to plow fields and plant seeds for harvesting crops, which led to the creation of simple millstones to grind wheat and other grains (fig. 1.3). Along with developing a rudimentary system for cultivating the land, they domesticated wild animals, including cattle, goats, pigs, and sheep. Permanent communities began to take shape.

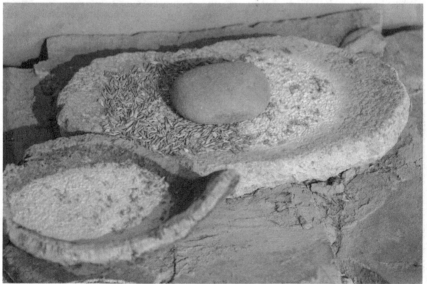

© Juan Aunion/Shutterstock.com

Fig. 1.3 Neolithic hand mill stone for grinding grains

CREATIVE IMPULSE

Prehistoric creation expression was based on primitive motives that ensured their survival or conveyed simplistic messages. Scholars may never unearth their exact meaning or importance for the people who created them. But, ever since their discovery, modern humans have marveled at the skill of prehistoric people in producing such artifacts, given their circumstances.

Cave Paintings

Images found in the Lascaux Cave depict a hunting scene; the hunter's spear pierces the hindquarters of a bison while a rhinoceros moves to the left, but it is unknown if the male image was original in the painting. Other images in the Lascaux Cave show geometric shapes, bulls, horses, and felines. There is speculation about the use of this cave and other caves found throughout Europe. Current belief about the caves includes their possible use as sanctuaries for the performance of sacred rites and ceremonies since there is a sense of power and grandeur elicited when standing in the cave.

Along with the cave images found in Lascaux, France, another 27 caves were discovered along the Ardèche Region on the cliff side. When the Chauvet cave was discovered, the world's belief regarding prehistoric people changed. The caves provided insight into the minds of early humans. Scholars deduced that the images (fig. 1.4) were painted to allow those who come in contact with the images to have a degree of influence over the animal. The belief is that images on cave walls were associated with hunting and conjuring up a successful hunt. However, this is not the case at Chauvet because more than half of the animals painted on the cave walls were either never or seldom hunted.

It is now proposed that cave painting played a role in **rituals,** or performed

Fig. 1.4 Paintings of animal figures on the rock walls of the Chauvet cave, in Vallon Pont d'Arc

© Jeff Pachoud/AFP/Getty Images

actions. These cave rituals are the first recorded evidence of religious ceremonies being practiced by a group of people. The caves may have been used as a gateway to an underworld, and possibly as a connection to death. The cave functioned symbolically as a **womb for birth**, or perhaps as a pathway to the unconscious world of dreams the Paleolithic people would experience in the dark of the night. Such ritual rites were connected with the passage of life and how life may have been conducted.

Most caves had a customary arrangement associated with them, where groups of animals were depicted on the basis of the species and gender. The group arrangement implies that there was some purpose and may have served as a lunar calendar used to predict seasonal migration of animals. No matter the reason for the images on the cave walls around the world, we can safely presume that the development of human culture was underway. There was a clear and decisive movement toward expressing life experiences and recording the world one inhabited.

The longest continuously practiced cave and rock painting by humans (fig. 1.5) stretching from 40000 BCE to the present day are found in Australia and are made by the Aboriginal people. Since these artistic traditions were passed down from generation to generation, we know more about their meaning. For the Aboriginal people, painting is a way to link the past with the present. Each artist firmly believes they are not the creator or inventor of the images, instead the **mimis**, or ancestral spirits, send the designs to them, making the artist simply a means for transmitting the design onto caves, rocks, or flat boards. Artists depict both the external features and the internal anatomy of certain organ structures, showing some degree of primitive dissection on deceased animals (fig. 1.6).

© Ivonne Wierink/Shutterstock.com

Fig. 1.5 Aboriginal Art, Northern territory Australia

© Stanislav Fosenbuaer/Shutterstock.com

Fig. 1.6 Aboriginal rock art paintings in landscape Australia

Sculptures

Depictions of the human form are rare, but some nomadic, hunter-gatherers were interested in creating portable images and carried them from location to location as they searched for food and shelter. In particular, a sculptural figurine referred to as the *Venus of Willendorf* (fig. 1.7), a 4-½-inch statue dating from 24000 to 21000 BCE, depicts a female figure with certain body parts enlarged, including the breasts, abdomen, and genitalia, but other parts are ignored. The figurine may have a connection to human fertility.

The *Venus of Willendorf* is one of a just handful of tiny female figurines found throughout Europe, all of which have similar exaggerations of certain body parts and almost complete denial of other parts. The faint hints of red pigment covering the figurine allude to the female menstrual cycle, a quality highly prized during harsh conditions.

© frantic00/Shutterstock.com

Fig. 1.7 *Venus of Willendorf* figurine, c. 24,000 to 21,000 BCE

These disparities in depicting the female anatomy can easily be understood by using the science of evolutionary psychology to summarize the ideas behind human behavior in terms of sexual selection. According to the English naturalist Charles Darwin's theories, it is understandable to associate the principle of the survival of

Global Focal Point

Cultures around the world have an interconnected history, but the terminology applied to a specific era may differ. In Japan, the Neolithic era is termed the "Jomon period." Jomon period is named after the "cord-marking" style of decoration found on the pottery that emerged (fig. 1.8). The cord was pressed into the damp clay before fired in an outdoor bonfire.

Dr. and Mrs. Roger G. Gerry Collection, Bequest of Dr. and Mrs. Roger G. Gerry, 2000, The Metropolitan Museum of Art

Fig. 1.8 Earthenware with cord-marked and sculpted decoration, Japan, c. 3500 to 2500

the fittest as a prerequisite to fertility, a fundamental principle of a species to its continuation. Males and females within a species that are most likely to survive will be the ones with the ability to successfully reproduce. For example, males were judged by their aptitude for protection and supplying the family with adequate food and shelter. Likewise, successful females were those whose bodily resources allowed them to undergo the ordeals of childbirth and her ability to endure the difficulties associated with feeding a newborn child.

Pottery

Ceramic vessels were heavy and fragile, making them unfit for hunter-gathers. When Neolithic nomadic cultures began transitioning to a more sedentary lifestyle, a new necessity for pottery vessels emerged. Settlements in Japan dating to as early as 10000 BCE show evidence of clay pots capable of performing a number of utilitarian functions

such as cooking, storing, or transporting food and water.

The earliest example of ceramic vessels (fig 1.8) can be traced to the Jomon period (12000 to 300 BCE) in Japan. These vessels were made by women. Women are connected to pottery creation because of their and the vessels' ability to bring forth and sustain life. Vessels were built using the **coiling method**, or long snake-like pieces, from the bottom up on a flat base. Clay was mixed with various materials such as crushed shell, fibers, lead, or mica for better adhesion. Once the vessel was formed, the women used either their hands or flat tools to smooth internal and external surfaces. Lastly, the external surface was decorated by a cord being pressed into the damp clay. In Europe, the development of ceramic vessels lagged and they were not produced until around 3000 BCE. The earliest of these vessels were made by clay being pressed over a rounded stone or by the coiling method.

Innovation and Progress

By 3000 BCE in Egypt, artists were employing the potter's wheel to create symmetrical vessels. The potter's wheel high degree of uniformity facilitated in its spread to the Middle East and China as the preferred method. In many ways, it is considered the first technological innovation in human history and resulted in the first form of human manufacturing as individuals became more skilled.

Architecture

The only prehistoric architecture to survive from the Neolithic period is the form of **megalithic**, or big stone, structures. A lesser-known megalithic structure referred to as the "stone ring of Callanish" is found in Lewis, Scotland (fig. 1.9). Excavations of the site revealed that the stones originally sat atop a cross and aligned with the astronomical constellations of Pleiades, Capella, and Altair through the sites use from 3500 BCE to 1500 BCE. The decline of the sites use is attributed to a cooling event that caused the skies to become clouded and therefore rendering the sites unusable.

Three basic architectural styles exist. The first is the **menhirs**, consisting of long, single stones either alone or in groups. At Carnac in Brittany, France, 13 straight rows cover a stretch of plain for 2 miles (fig. 1.9). The stones are arranged in an east to west direction with the west end being 10 feet taller than the east, which are 3 feet tall. Given the east to west arrangement and height difference, there is a possible connection to the cycle of life from birth through maturity in their arrangement.

The second is **dolmen**, or **post-and-lintel**, formed by two posts topped with a capstone. Evidence suggests that the dolmen was covered with earth to form an enclosed burial chamber called a "cairn." The third is the **cromlech**, meaning place with a circle. Stonehenge, contrasted around 2000 BCE in Wiltshire, England (fig. 1.10), is the most famous example of a cromlech.

MONOMYTHS

Role of Myths

A **myth** is grounded in a culture's observation of a natural phenomenon, which stands outside the realm of scientific explanation. Each culture's myth is a way of conveying the collective beliefs and views it has amassed regarding the world. Myths are the driving forces behind the development of the people's culture and assist in explaining the unknown, including the universe and human origins. Prehistoric myths were passed from generation to generation by oral storytelling. When myths from around the world are analyzed, common

Fig. 1.9 Carnac megaliths alignment in Brittany, France

Fig. 1.10 Aerial photograph of Stonehenge, England

themes emerge, creating a monomyth, or the hero's journey.

The monomyth consists of specific patterned episodes with slight variations the hero of the story will accept in order to fulfill the quest to which he was entrusted. The simplest pattern is departure, initiation, and return, with each phase of the quest defined by particular events. In the departure phase, the hero is called to the adventure but initially refuses the call, then meets with a mentor who helps the hero cross the first threshold, and finally enters into the journey. The initiation phase is marred by trials, meeting the gods/goddess, temptation from the path, atonement, and apotheosis, which is all beneficial to the journey. The final phase, return, begins with a refusal to return. But, this phase results in a mystical travel where a second threshold must be crossed to return home as the one who mastered two worlds and can live in true freedom.

Interpreting Myths

Mythic tell interpretations reveal the intricacy of the people ascribing to the myth.

How the myth is deciphered depends on the message being conveyed. The simplest decoding of a myth is in the form of a story explaining the origins of a civilization such as the founding of Rome in the story of Romulus and Remus. Other decoding forms the bases of a people's belief system and is used to disguise historical events as seen in the myths referring to Zeus's affairs. More complex myths provide either a prescientific or social system explanation for otherwise irreconcilable structural conflicts. Regardless of the intended interpretation of the myths, one fact remains. Myths are prose narratives considered truthful accounts of what happened in the remote past for the society in which they are told.

Creation Myths

The Anasazi, a Navajo word translating to "enemy ancestors," people of the American Southwest, left only ruins and artifacts attesting to their cultural myths. They abandoned their communities such as Mesa Verde sometime in the latter part of

© krayka/Shutterstock.com

Fig. 1.11 Puebloan cave dwelling, Mesa Verde, Arizona, c. 1140 to 1300 CE

the thirteenth century of the current era. Much of our understanding of their beliefs and daily life is found in their descendants, the Hopi and Zuni Pueblo peoples. For the Pueblo people, the village was more than the center of their culture. The village was the center of the entire world, and the **kiva**, or underground chamber, was the cultural center of village life (fig. 1.11).

The construction of the kiva formed a dome with a single access hole, and the roof above was used as common space. Under the roof in the domed kiva was a **sipapu**, or a small, rounded depression, that symbolized the **emergence tale**, or a type of creation myth, of the Anasazi. The creation myth served not only as an explanation for the Anasazi origins from the depths of the Earth but also as a means for the community to understand that everything necessary for their survival would also emerge from Mother Earth. In the Zuni emergence tale, the community learns of the **kachina**, or a deified spirit; kachinas were personalities that number

to roughly 250. The kachina represents a number of both material and nonmaterial objects such as the weather, plants, animals, and ideas such as knowledge (fig. 1.12).

Pueblo emergence tales also emulate early Neolithic beliefs of **animism**, or living spirits in forces of nature, and **anthropomorphism**, or human characteristics and behaviors. One

Gift of Miss Ima Hogg, The Museum of Fine Arts, Houston

Fig. 1.12 Talavai, early morning singer, Kachina; Hopi, ca. 1925; wood, feathers, and string

major feature of both practices was helping ancient people explain the unexplainable, and this provided a general sense of normality in a world that existed before the advent of modern science. Another rationale was in the creed that such communication with nature and the spirits would produce favor with the gods.

Myths and Religion

Much like creation myths, religion within a cultural group attempts to comprehend the divine who resides in an unearthly realm. The **rituals**, or performed actions, practiced by faithful adherents express the stories related to the people. One such example resides in the Shinto religion practiced by indigenous Japanese in Ise, Japan. A principal goddess, Amaterasu, is housed in a shrine complex that dates to prehistoric times. Japanese nobility claim they descend from the goddess after the creation of three female and five male deities.

Every 20 years a ritual renewal ceremony transfers the deity from the existing shrine house (fig. 1.13), which is subsequently destroyed, to a new shrine house. After destruction, the old shrine site remains empty except for a covering of large white stones and a tiny wooden hut enclosing a consecrated wood pole believed to date to the ancient past. Through this ritual of destruction and renewal, the people connect their past with the present along with the gods and their cosmic energies.

PREHISTORIC LEGACY

The beginning of the hominid species, specifically *Homo sapiens*, was distinguished by the widespread use of stone tools, occurring around 120,000 to 100,000 years ago. During the Paleolithic period, humans began to create cave paintings and sculpture figurines around the world. The cave paintings discovered in the Chauvet cave show a degree of artistic skill for rendering subject matter. Such images helped form the realization for human capacity to illustrate their world in naturalistic terms. Paleolithic people's aptitude for creating images showed the earliest signs of the formation of culture, a way of living based on religious, social, and political classifications. Over the next thousands of years what will happen will be the passing of these newly formed culture identities from one generation to the next through mythic storytelling.

© Phuong D. Nguyen/Shutterstock.com

Fig. 1.13 Amaterasu shrine house, Mei, Japan, ca. third century CE

Critical Thinking

Examine the key features characterizing the foundation of human culture.

Describe the transition from the Paleolithic to the Neolithic period.

Analyze the purpose of female figurines such as the *Venus of Willendorf*.

Explore the architectural achievements of the Neolithic period.

Explain the role of myth in prehistoric thinking.

ONLINE RESOURCES

Understanding Paleolithic People

https://www.khanacademy.org/humanities/world-history/world-history-beginnings/
origin-humans-early-societies/a/paleolithic-culture-and-technology

Organization of Paleolithic Societies

https://www.khanacademy.org/humanities/world-history/world-history-beginnings/
origin-humans-early-societies/v/organizing-paleolithic-societies-video

Neolithic Revolution

https://www.history.com/topics/pre-history/neolithic-revolution

Lascaux: Hall of Bulls

https://smarthistory.org/hall-of-bulls-lascaux/

The Story of Aboriginal Art

https://www.aboriginal-art-australia.com/aboriginal-art-library/the-story-of-aboriginal-art/

Story of the Venus of Willendorf

https://www.humanjourney.us/ideas-that-shaped-our-modern-world-section/
paleolithic-beginnings/venus-of-willendorf/

The Mystery of Stonehenge

http://www.britannia.com/history/h7.html

Monomyth: The Hero's Journey

http://www.movieoutline.com/articles/the-hero-journey-mythic-structure-of-joseph-
campbell-monomyth.html

Creation Myths from around the Globe

http://www.crystalinks.com/creationcountries.html

Alcohol's Cultural Use around the Globe: From Neo-Paleolithic to Modern Times

https://www.nationalgeographic.com/magazine/2017/02/alcohol-discovery-addiction-
booze-human-culture/

Mesopotamia: The Rise of Civilization

Fig. 2.1 Hunting relief Ashurbanipal, Nineveh, Assyria. 645 to 635 BCE

© IR Stone/Shutterstock.com

Knowledge Acquisition

◆ *Explore the creation of civilization through urbanization.*

◆ *Discover distinguishing artistic, cultural, and literary works from Mesopotamia.*

◆ *Discuss key historical figures.*

◆ *Appreciate the role of religion in ancient Mesopotamia.*

SETTING THE SCENE

Between 9000 and 3000 BCE, the Mesopotamia regions underwent three significant revolutions in human existence: agricultural cultivation, urbanization, and the invention of writing in the Fertile Crescent, the land between the Euphrates and Tigris Rivers. Agricultural cultivation first developed here around 9000 BCE, and copper mining became an established trade by 6000 BCE. Cuneiform, a standard of writing throughout the region of Mesopotamia, was invented by the Sumerians around 3000 BCE. Mesopotamian history is divided among a variety of the following cultural groups: Sumerian, Akkadian, Babylonian, Assyrian, and Persians (map 2.1). Each was unique but adopted traditions from their predecessors.

INAUGURATION OF CIVILIZATION

The people who settled in the Fertile Crescent were probably wanderers with a root cause for leaving their homelands possibly due to overpopulation or desiccation. In regions without a steady supply of fresh water, drought and desiccation could dramatically and suddenly destroy food supplies and result in the immediate threat of famine. The southern regions of Mesopotamia experienced centuries of drainage from the two great rivers. Annual flooding built up the soil with a tremendous number of nutrients around the deltas, where crops grew if water was continually available. The region flourished because of its ability to grow 32 of the 56 edible grasses, including barley, corn, lentils, onions, peas, and wheat from the wild, whereas in the Americas and Africa, only four species grew, and in Europe, only one grew in the wild, oats. There was also a steady supply of fish from the gulf waters.

The various religious or spiritual beliefs held by this early civilization varied from group to group but had numerous commonalities. Their religious beliefs were central to each civilization's way of life, and the religious practices were not extractable from cultural beliefs or society.

Sumerians

The region of Sumer occupied the southern reaches of Mesopotamia, beginning between 3500 and 3000 BCE and grew to 30 to 40 cities. While Uruk, located on the north side of the Euphrates, is the oldest city in Sumer, it is Ur that holds the most well-maintained and fully restored temple structure known as a "ziggurat" (fig. 2.2). The construction of the ziggurat is thought to remind the Sumerians of the surrounding

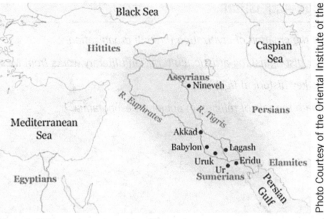

Map 2.1 Map of ancient Mesopotamia

Photo Courtesy of the Oriental Institute of the University of Chicago

Fig. 2.2 Ziggurat at Ur, c. 2100 BCE

mountainous terrain, which was the source of life. The building material for the ziggurat was baked mud bricks instead of stone because stone was scarce. Walls of the temple were **battered**, or sloped inward to provide strength. The temple was topped with a holy sanctuary; only members of the priesthood were permitted entry, symbolizing the passage conduit between the realm of the gods and earth (fig. 2.3).

Visiting priests would climb to the top via stairs to bring offerings to the resident god, including food, animals to be sacrificed, and statues. Each city had a different god in resident that watched over and protected the people

from harm and provided blessings in the form of bountiful harvests. In Ur, the resident god was Nanna or Sin, god of the moon.

Ur and Uruk are widely recognized as major contributors to our understanding of Mesopotamian culture. It is at Ur archeologists found evidence of people digging canals to divert water for irrigating crops. Their ability to grow excessive crops every year allowed them to produce beer. Each city was an independent **city-states**, or an autonomous region, that began to interact more frequently with each other. They traded the extra harvest and beer for commodities, such as metals, stone, and wood, found up river.

Cross-Cultural Connection

Writing as a means of communication and record-keeping led to a major shift within a cultural group. Ancient civilizations first invented pictographic writing to indicate an idea or spoken word. The writing system used in China is well documented at its inception. According to Chinese ledge, Fu Xi, a culture hero in Chinese mythology, was inspired by constellation patterns along with the footprints of birds and animals in the creation of Chinese writing. Between 1400 and 1200 BCE, oracle bone was used to answer the questions of the early Chinese rulers. The bone was heated, which allowed for patterned cracks to form. These cracks were interpreted and the message recorded on the bone.

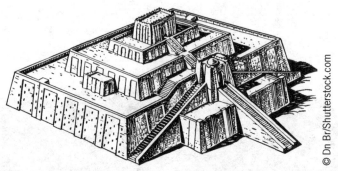

© Dn Br/Shutterstock.com

Fig. 2.3 Illustration of a complete ziggurat

The technology of **metallurgy**, or separation of metal from ore, transformed the region's social structure and initiated an era called the Bronze Age. Skilled metallurgists learned to combine copper and tin to create bronze, a strong and durable metal. Bronze weaponry transformed warfare by creating an elite class of soldiers who helped gain and control valuable trade lands. Each city-state then created governments ruled by a **priest-king**, who was the intermediary between the people and gods along other secular responsibilities. The priest-king's secular duties included establishing laws governing social order needed for the continuation of a successful agricultural society.

In 3500 BCE, Sumerians invented a record-keeping system for agricultural production in the form of **pictograms**, pictures used to represent objects or ideas. For example, the word *belief* would be represented with pictures of a "bee" and a "leaf." Beginning around 2900 BCE, a primitive writing system style known as **cuneiform** emerged (fig. 2.4). A **stylus**, a writing tool made of cut reed, was used to make wedge impressing into wet clay. It was not until 2000 BCE that **phonetic writing** developed.

Akkadians

Few artifacts remain from the Akkadian culture, a people who arrived from the north

© Fedor Selivanov/Shutterstock.com

Fig. 2.4 Sumerian cuneiform

and settled around the modern-day city of Baghdad. Two sculptured artifacts, *Head of an Akkadian Man* (fig. 2.5) and *Stele of Naramsin* (fig. 2.6), provide a glimpse into Akkadian creativity.

The head was made of bronze using what is referred to as the **lost-wax casting** technique. The technique allowed large bronze pieces to be produced with hollow centers, making the pieces economical and lightweight.

Surviving clay tablets describe an account of an illegitimate child named Sargon (r. c. 2332 to 2279) whose mother placed him at the river bank of the Euphrates in a basket.

Fig. 2.5 *Akkadian Head*, bronze, c. 2300 to 2000 BCE

the command of Sargon I, the Akkadians conquered almost all of Mesopotamia. He referred to himself with honor as "King of the Four Quarters of the World" and likened himself to the gods. From the time of Sargon onward, all Akkadian rulers took the same name honor.

The second sculpture artifact is a **stele**, a vertically carved slab of stone depicting a commemorative scene or inscription. The stele depicts the grandson of Sargon, Naramsin, victory over the Lullubi in the Zagros Mountains (fig. 2.6). The belief is during his reign Naramsin became divine, as depicted in the stele by the inclusion of a horned helmet and physical perfection of his body. Notice how he stands atop the mountain with an injured and lifeless Lullubian below him. One Lullubian collapses in front of Naramsin as others plead for his mercy.

Fig. 2.6 *Stele of Naramsin*, c. 2254 to 2218 BCE

A man named Akki, who belongs to Akkad, discovered the boy while fetching water and raised him as his own son. The legend of the mythic hero who was abandoned, orphaned, and then found gives rise to a type of storytelling with a universal theme called a **narrative genre**. The Sargon narrative is a classic "rags-to-riches" story. Under

Fig. 2.7 *Law Code of Hummurabi*, c. 1760 BCE

Babylonians

Mesopotamia was dominated by the Akkadians for roughly 150 years until their rule collapsed around 2200 BCE. No single city-state retained power until Hammurabi of Babylon (r. 1792 to 1750) came into power 400 years later. He introduced order to Babylon at a time when chaos and disorder were the norm. The order he created was recorded on a giant stele called the *Law Code of Hammurabi* (fig. 2.7), it captures the most complete collection of his decisions and decrees. The sculptural relief shows the Shamash, the sun god, with light rays emanating from his shoulder giving Hammurabi his blessing. Notice how large Shamash is compared to Hammurabi, much like ruling figures in Mesopotamia were shown larger than those they ruled. To heighten the sense of masculine propensities of the king, the stele was designed in the shape of a phallus.

The cuneiform writing below the relief records 282 separate declarations, or more pointedly, reforms of existing laws. The law "code" was Hammurabi's way of proclaiming a divine justice on the basis of his rule. The stele created a uniform code followed throughout Mesopotamia for a millennium. The code covered almost every aspect of life with the **talion**, or an eye for an eye and a tooth for a tooth, as a dominant principle. The code also provides a good understanding of daily life within Mesopotamia. Preservation of the family was of utmost importance, with women being the property of their husband, just like slaves, but women were protected from neglect and unjust treatment.

Assyrians

In 1595 BCE, most of the Babylonian-dominated territories fell to the swift invasion of the Hittites from Turkey. The only city managing to retain a distinctive cultural identity was Assur, whose people were known as the Assyrians. The Assyrians slowly gained control over the region until under the reign of Ashurnasirpal II (r. 883 to 859 BCE) they dominated it.

Ashurnasirpal II built his capital at Kalhu, modern-day Minrud, on the banks of the Tigris River surrounded by a 5-mile wall. The wall was 120-feet thick and 42-feet tall with 100,000 residents. The palace walls were adorned with repeated alabaster relief scenes of *Ashurnasirpal II Killing a Lion* (fig. 2.8). The kill ended in the sacrifice of the lion.

As seen at the palace of Ashurbanipal to the north in Nineveh, palace depiction almost 200 years later still favored hunting scenes (fig. 2.1). The hunt changed from a realistic event to a ritual performed in an arena ending with the sacrifice of the lion. As the sacrifice was performed, musicians played, **libation**, liquid offerings to a deity, were poured over the lion, and other offerings were brought to the table by servants. The ritual was viewed as the ruler mastering the cycles of nature, specifically life and death.

Assyrian artists went to great length to ensure that the archer's face was never obscured (fig. 2.9). The archer was never

Innovation and Progress

Sumerians discovered how to ferment baked loaves of bread roughly 8,000 years ago. The process involved crumbling crusty baked bread called "bappir" into water, allowing it to ferment, and then filtering the liquid using baskets. Records indicate almost half of the annual grain harvest was used in the production of beer, including black beer (*kassi*), fine black beer (*kassag*), and the finest premium beer (*kassagsaan*).

Fig. 2.8 *Ashurnasirpal II Killing a Lion*, c. 850 BCE

© Kamira/Shutterstock.com

Fig. 2.9 Ashurnasirpal II Killing a Lion on a Chariot, c. 850 BCE

© Khd/Shutterstock.com

depicted aiming down the shaft of the arrow, as this would cover his eye. Instead, Assyrian artists created an unrealistic representation by showing the string passing behind the archer's head and back. The entire scene creates a **synoptic** view of what is happening, or a scene illustrating multiple actions taking place at once. Later Assyrian kings, such as Sargon II (r. 721 to 705 BCE), used massive gateways to greet, impress, and terrify visitors. The gateway entrance was adorned with **composites**

Image Courtesy of Kristina Jantz

Fig. 2.10 *Human-Headed Winged Bull and Lion*, c. 720 BCE

images that were part human, part eagle, and part bull or lion (fig. 2.10). The bull portion implied that the king was strong, and the eagle suggested that he maintained vigilance over his kingdom.

Neo-Babylonia

Under the rule of Nebuchadnezzar (r. 604 to 562 BCE), two major events occurred. The first was to continue his father Nabopolassar's (r. 626 to 604 BCE) plans to make the

city of Babylon the most beautiful one in the Mesopotamian world. Nebuchadnezzar used the existing Processional Way (fig. 2.11) entrance, referred to as "May the Enemy Not Have Victory," lined with lions and terminated into the Ishtar Gate (fig. 2.12), to accomplish his beautification project.

The gate was a double gate with a second-arched entrance above the lower one dedicated to Babylon's founder god, Marduk. The ziggurat built to honor Marduk is believed to be the Tower of Babel described in the book Genesis of the Jewish and Christian Bible. The gate included an inscription proclaiming the might of Nebuchadnezzar and his want for future generations to maintain or rebuild it, if necessary. When Saddam Hussein (r. 1979 to 2006 CE) ruled over Iraq, he was in the process of rebuilding the gates and surrounding structures until he was deposed and executed. The second major event was the destruction of Jerusalem and conquering of the Hebrews in 587 BCE, discussed in

© Juan Carlos Oller/Shutterstock.com

Fig. 2.11 *Processional Way*, 575 BCE

Fig. 2.12 Ishtar Gate, 575 BCE

Chapter 6. The Hebrews lived in exile for almost 50 years (586 to 538 BCE) when the Persians seized control of Babylonian land in 538 BCE.

Persians

The Persians were formerly nomadic people with tribal roots in the plateau of modern Iran. Slowly, the empire grew to encompass lands from Egypt to Ukraine under the kingship of Darius (r. 522 to 486 BCE). In their capital city, Parsa, artisans and other skilled workers from all over the Persian Empire built a city that reflected King Darius's multicultural empire. **Fluted**, or shallow grooves running vertically, columns point to Egypt's influence (fig. 2.13) and admiration for Assyrian colossal human-headed winged bulls (fig. 2.14) found at the palace of Sargon II.

Building spectacular monuments to display their broad and diverse culture was only one artistic feat. Persian artisans perfected the art of metallurgy. The rhyton, or ritual cup, shown in figure 2.15 was fashioned during the Achaemenid period (539 to 330 BCE). The piece shows a gazelle with a smooth and flared rim and alternating inverted lotus flowers.

CREATIVE IMPULSE

Art

Sumerians fashioned small, handled stone statues (fig. 2.16) for religious or remembrance purposes. The statues are easily recognizable because of key features such as large, wide open eyes, a double-arching, continuous eyebrow, and surprised facial expressions. Scholars believe the statues function was to represent worshipers, or possibly gods. The statue was, in other words, standing in for an "absent" worshiper, both male and female statues were recovered.

Found at Ur were tombs used to bury both the rich and the poor in single coffins. A few contained a burial chamber with more than one body, in certain instances up to 80. These types of burial chambers suggest that more elaborate rituals were conducted for kings and queens. One such chamber discovered by Sir Leonard Wolley was found in the Royal Cemetery and held an artifact in the Royal Tomb of Ur that is still a mystery. The piece is called the *Royal Standard of Ur* with images of "war" and "peace" on opposite sides (fig. 2.18). The object is made of multiple material, shell, lapis lazuli, and red limestone originally on

Fig. 2.13 Columns at Persepolis Temple, c. 519

Fig. 2.14 *Human-headed Winged Bull*, Persepolis temple, c. 519

a wooden frame, and is a little larger than a legal sheet of paper, 8″ × 19″. Each side comprises three **registers**, or horizontal strips with action scenes, being enacted on a **ground-line**, or boundary.

In the "War" panel, three different acts of war are visible. The king, who stands in the middle of the top register, is recognizable because of kings always being the largest figure in images. He calls his men to battle and

Societal Emphasis

The first-known poet was from the Sumerian reaches of Mesopotamia. Her name was Enheduanna, the daughter of Sargon I. She wrote poems to the gods and goddess in the form of hymns. Her most noted poems are dedicated to the Sumerian goddess of love, Inanna. In the following poem, Enheduanna bares her reverence and adoration for goddess Inanna:

> Destroyer of the Foreign Lands,
> You have given wings to the storm,
> Beloved of Enlil—You made the storm blow over the land,
> You carried out the instructions of An.

impresses upon them the reasons for war. In the middle register, the foot soldiers engage in battle. The final register depicts warriors on chariots tramping the enemy. But, notice that the chariots have solid wheel because spoked wheels did not exist until 1800 BCE.

Akkadians used special artifacts to seal business and legal transactions, known as **cylinder seals** (fig. 2.19). Images were engraved into a cylinder and pressed into wet clay creating a signature. Figures on a seal were recognizable as either gods or goddess because of the pointed headdress with multiple horns.

Literature

The oldest story ever recorded is the *Epic of Gilgamesh* dating between 1900 and 1600 BCE. Gilgamesh was the fourth king of Uruk and ruled sometime between 2700 and 2500 BCE. The story survives in fragments on 11 Akkadian clay tablets comprising 2900 lines. It is termed an **epic** because it is a long

Fig. 2.15 *Ram Rhyton*, c. fifth century

Gift of Norbert Schimmel Trust, 1989, The Metropolitan Museum of Art,
© The Trustees of the British Museum

Fig. 2.16 Standing Male worshiper, c. 2900 to 2600 BCE

Fletcher Fund, 1940, The Metropolitan Museum of Art

Global Focal Point

For the Shang Dynasty (c. 1700 to 1045 BCE), the world was shaped upon the bases of the marriage of Qian and Kun, who symbolizes the concept of yin-yang. They form an endless cycle of night and day that balance the five elements (earth, fire, metal, water, and wood) and the five powers of creation (cold, dry, heat, dampness, and wind). Each half encloses a smaller, opposite valued circle, thus revealing an everlasting harmony and shared union.

Fig. 2.17 Yin-yang symbol

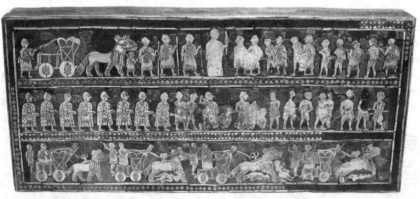

Fig. 2.18 *Royal Standard of Ur*, "War", c. 2600 BCE

poem written in narrative style with raised language following specific characters on a sequence of adventurous events, frequently to the land of the dead.

In the poem, Gilgamesh is an unjust ruler who oppresses his people. His people plead to the gods for relief. In turn, the gods create Enkidu to challenge Gilgamesh. The two are complete opposites. Gilgamesh represents the civilized world and Enkidu the wilderness. After a series of events, Enkidu dies and Gilgamesh departs distraught with a longing for his friend and immortality. Dismayed by the prospect of his own death, Gilgamesh sets out on an expedition to find Utnapishtim, who survived the Great Flood. The journey to find Utnapishtim ends with gaining and losing immortality. In Gilgamesh's adventures, questions regarding human nature, the treatment of the natural world, responsibilities to friends, family, and others, and mortality in general emerge. The

Fig. 2.19 Cylinder seal of the Colony Period, c. 1920 to 1740 BCE

Image Courtesy of Kristina Jantz

poem reveals that Gilgamesh is willing to acknowledge his very own human limitations and powerlessness to overcome death.

Religion

Early Mesopotamia religion was rooted in the fertility of harvests and centered on multiple gods and goddesses, **polytheistic**, who governed every aspect of daily life. These gods and goddesses were **anthropomorphic**, or possessing both human form and personalities but presided over a specific aspect of the natural world.

The Persian culture rose to power between the latter part of the sixth century and developed a **dualist religion**, or one based on opposing ideas. The most prevalent understanding of dualism is the concepts of good and evil. The religion is known as Zoroastrianism and relied the Persian by the prophet Zoroaster. His writings collected in the *Zend-Avesta* reveal the rituals, prayers, and laws of the supreme deity Ahura Mazda

or "the Wise Lord." The religion is only quasi-monotheistic due to the inclusion of lesser gods. There are some ways by which it relates to later monotheistic religions, such as Ahura Mazda stating that it is "left to men's will" to decide to lead a life of "good thoughts, good words, good deeds," thus allowing everyone to choose their own path of good to heaven or evil to hell.

MESOPOTAMIA LEGACY

Between 9000 and 3000 BCE, three important revolutions of humanity occurred: (1) agricultural cultivation, (2) urbanization, and (3) invention of writing. From the beginning of civilization, some 11,000 years ago, structures of administrative, religious, or social importance were erected in urban centers. Mesopotamian history is divided among a variety of the following cultures: Sumerian, Akkadian, Babylonian, Assyrian, Neo-Babylonian, and Persian. Each was unique but adopted traditions from their predecessors. Both the oldest poet and recorded poem emerge in Sumer to portray a people immersed in a life ruled by the gods and goddess. But, as power shifted and empires expanded, newer concepts of what and how to worship appeared and transformed the idea of how individuals lived.

Critical Thinking

Examine the characteristics and development of civilization in Mesopotamia.

Explain the relationship between Sumer, Akkad, Babylon, Assyria, and Persia civilizations.

Analyze the purpose of the *Law Code of Hammurabi*.

Explore the meaning of the *Epic of Gilgamesh*.

Describe the development of religion in Mesopotamia.

ONLINE RESOURCES

What is Civilization?

https://www.nationalgeographic.org/encyclopedia/civilization/

Major Ancient Mesopotamian Civilizations

https://www.khanacademy.org/humanities/world-history/world-history-beginnings/
ancient-mesopotamia/a/mesopotamia-article

First Know Written Language: Cuneiform

https://smarthistory.org/cuneiform/

Role of the Ziggurat

http://www.livius.org/articles/concept/ziggurat/

Law Code of Hammurabi

https://www.louvre.fr/en/oeuvre-notices/law-code-hammurabi-king-babylon

Epic of Gilgamesh

https://www.sparknotes.com/lit/gilgamesh/summary/

Understanding Zoroastrianism

http://www.bbc.co.uk/religion/religions/zoroastrian/

Ancient Egypt: Creating Social Stability

Fig. 3.1 Temple of Horus, Edfu, Egypt. c. 237 to 57 BCE

© Grificam Ahmed Saeed/Shutterstock.com

Knowledge Acquisition

◆ *Analyze distinctive features of ancient Egyptian art form and civilization.*

◆ *Infer differences between the Old, Middle, and New Kingdoms.*

◆ *Evaluate the role of religious ritual and ceremonies in ancient Egypt.*

◆ *Understand the formation of a longstanding social order.*

SETTING THE SCENE

Around 5000 BCE, a vastly different civilization formed in Egypt. While Mesopotamian cultures evolved numerous times throughout its long history, Egypt barely changed over several thousand years. Egypt's geography gave protection, while allowing the culture to develop. The annual floods provided a lush, fertile valley where agriculture was able to flourish.

Unlike Mesopotamia, Egypt created a genuinely united civilization ruled by a single, all-powerful individual. Unification of Egypt occurred around 3100 BCE under the rule of King Narmer. Eventually, the king became an absolute ruler who was considered divine. The king was able to impose his will because of a vast network of priests and bureaucrats, which explains the stability and permanence of Egyptian life. The pyramids found in Egypt tell the stories of not only the culture but also the lives of those entombed in them. Other monumental structures such as the Temple of Horus in Edfu (fig. 3.1) were constructed for elaborate annual festivals to the gods.

CULTURE OF THE NILE

The river Nile was deeply connected to Egyptian kingship and the heart of Egyptian culture. It was the Nile that made this civilization possible. Egypt developed along the last 750 miles of the 4000 miles river originating in the mountains of Ethiopia and Lake Victoria in Uganda. Annual flooding from July to November would deposit silt fertile in nutrients. Flooding that was either too intense or too minimal over a few years might result in famine. These annual cycles of flooding and warmth from the sun led to a highly productive and stable society.

More than 3000 years witnessed a culture with remarkably little change.

Map 3.1 Lower and Upper Egypt

Egypt is divided into three major periods of advancement: Old, Middle, and New Kingdom. Each kingdom is further divided into successive dynasties, or royal houses, that created peace and stability. In between each period, instability occurred during intermediate periods. The continuity of culture enjoyed by Egypt demonstrates how harmony and prosperity are the counter partners to cultural stability. Egyptian society relied on unity for its success, which was unlike warring Mesopotamia.

Old Kingdom

The longest kingdom in Egyptian history occurred during the Old Kingdom and resulted in the formation of the most significant events in Egyptian history. The oldest **mummification,** or the process of preserving the remains of the deceased, dates between 3100 and 2890 BCE and is found at Saqqara. Saqqara is the site where the first great pyramid was constructed, a Stepped Pyramid (fig. 3.2)

Vladimir Wrangel / Shutterstock, Inc.

Fig. 3.2 Stepped Pyramid at Djoser, Saqqara, 2610 BCE

for Djoser (r. c. 2628 to 2609 BCE), predating the Ur ziggurat by 500 years.

Construction of this type of pyramid with a base form by a **mastaba**, or trapezoidal tomb, predates the pyramid of Djoser. Single mastabas were first used for the burial of individuals of lesser importance and were smaller in size. In the Djoser pyramid, no aboveground chamber or rooms are found. Instead, the burial chamber is located roughly 90 feet below the first mastaba.

The inclusion of six stacked mastabas of increasingly smaller size was the innovation of Imhotep, chief architect for Djoser. The importance of his burial design gained him immense fame, as he is the first architect whose name survives in Egyptian history. His fame continued a thousand years after the death of Djoser in graffiti expressing how his building seemed to radiate heaven. The pyramid became a mainstay for distinguishing kings from royal family members and other less important figures within Egypt.

Fifty years after the pioneering of the stacked pyramid, the style was abandoned.

Innovation and Progress

Everyday objects such as the spoon are rarely studied for their origins. In modern society, we take simple innovation toward fundamental progress for granted. While the origins of the first spoon is unknown, archeologists found ornamental and religious spoons around 1000 BCE in Egypt. These ancient spoons were made of a variety of materials, including ivory, slate, and wood with a simple handle of animal bone. Prior to the crafting of the utensil, spoons were seashells or preformed stones. The use of a utensil devoted to food consumption was novel.

Cross-Cultural Connection

Each great ancient civilization leaves behind grand monuments attesting to their engineering abilities and ceremonial practices, but their use may be dissimilar. Unlike the people of ancient Egypt, who began controlling water flow for agricultural purposes, the people of the Indus valley are believed to have created a massive water tank for their ceremonial rituals (fig. 3.3). The tank measured approximately 39 feet by 23 feet with a maximum depth of 8 feet. Descent into the tank was by one of two wide staircases on the north and south sides. The tank was water tight after the fitted bricks were applied with gypsum plaster and a thick layer of bitumen, a natural tar.

© Jawwad Ali/Shutterstock.com

Fig. 3.3 Ancient water storage, possible ritual bathing area, Mohenjo-Daro, Indus valley civiliation, modern day Pakistan, c. 2600-1900 BCE

The replacement pyramids were smooth, triangular slanting sides with a point at the apex of the structure. The most recognizable and stunning examples are found at Giza, consisting of pyramids built for Khufu, Khafre, Menkaure, and six queens (fig. 3.4).

The Khufu pyramid is the oldest and most spectacular of the three largest pyramids at Giza. Archeologists propose that the 2.3-million stones were moved into place by one of two methods: ramps or levers. Both methods would have involved an enormous amount of engineering. Another major shift in the construction of the Giza pyramids is where the burial chamber was located. The Khufu pyramid had a false chamber located directly under the true king's chamber but still below ground level. Two airshafts are also present and coordinate to specific stars, including Sirius, in the night sky.

A second monumental structure at Giza is the Great Sphinx (fig. 3.5) dedicated to

Fig. 3.4 Pyramids of Menkaure (c. 2470 BCE), Khafre (c. 2500 BCE), and Khufu (c. 2530 BCE), front to back, at Giza

Wang Tingxi / Shutterstock, Inc.

Fig. 3.5 Great Sphinx, Giza, Egypt. c. 2500 BCE

Anton_Ivanov/ Shutterstock, Inc.

Khafre, son of Khufu. The Sphinx is the largest statue made in the ancient world. In Egyptian art, gods were depicted with an animal head and a human body. The Sphinx is opposite, human head and animal body.

The reversal of the head and body suggests Khafre association with the gods.

Sculptures during the Old Kingdom set the standard for those poses most often used. Human figures were depicted in one of four poses and were used for different purposes, with a few exceptions: (1) sitting on a block, (2) standing in **contrapposto**, or counterpose, (3) kneeling, and (4) sitting crossed-legged (fig. 3.6). The first three were reserved for kings and important officials, while the fourth was intended for royal scribes. Each pose had fixed principles that survived mainly unchanged for three millennia.

Middle Kingdom

The Middle Kingdom began after 150 years of division between the north and south when Nebhepetre Mentuhotep II (2040 to 1999 BCE) reunited the country. Little change emerged during the Middle Kingdom, except in the form of literary works. Scribes began producing a diverse array of literature. Surviving literary works speak about chance meetings with supernatural powers and were decidedly creative when compared with earlier literature. More importantly, these writings explored daily life in the Middle Kingdom.

Sculptures of the Middle Kingdom continued in the traditional standards set forth during the Old Kingdom. Only one advancement emerged, an altered version of a seated or standing king (fig. 3.7). Traditionally, the king would sit or stand upright, rigid, and frontal with a simple skirt. The newer style placed the king's arms crossed tightly across his chest, much like a mummy. The main cause for this shift was that kingship had long been associated with the embodiment of the gods. The mummy-like pose draws a direct connection between the king and Osiris, god of the underworld, and overseer of the judgment of souls.

Middle Kingdom relief carvings reveal why Egyptian art remained consistent from one period to the next. Reliefs were begun by creating a grid, like graph paper, and then images were drawn over the grid in a systematic manner. Each standing figure was 18 squares from the top of the forehead to the soles of the feet. Knees were 6-squares high, and the waist was 11, elbows were

Vladimir Wrangel / Shutterstock, Inc.

Fig. 3.6 *Scribe*, seated crossed-legged, c. 2400 BCE

Fig. 3.7 Statue of Nebhepetre Mentuhotep II, c. 26.3.29

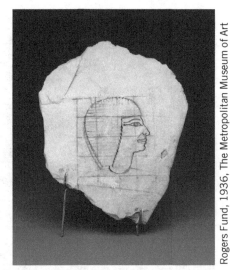

Fig. 3.8 Artist's Gridded Sketch of Senenmut, c. 1479 to 1458 BCE

located 12-square high, and armpits 14. The Egyptians created a measurement system to accurately render the human body, with each square comparable to one clenched fist. Further, the eye was set one-half the distance from the center of a square (fig. 3.8).

During the Twelfth Dynasty of the Middle Kingdom, the worship of Amun-Re, chief deity of all of Egypt, developed. In reliefs, Amun watched as the king was presented an **ankh**, or life, directly to his nose, signifying that the king was breathing in life from the gods (fig. 3.9). The tradition would carry into the New Kingdom.

New Kingdom

Worship of Amun continued into the New Kingdom and expanded under the Eighteenth Dynasty as it sought to align itself more closely with the Middle Kingdom's goals. To accomplish these goals, Egyptian

kings constructed elaborately, magnificent funerary and other temples. The funerary temple for Hatshepsut is a fine example of how the New Kingdom rulers elevated Amun and placed themselves alongside the god.

Hatshepsut ruled Egypt for 20 years after her husband and half-brother's death, Thutmose II, as a result of becoming regent for her son, Thutmose III. Toward the end of her reign, she was increasingly depicted in a less feminine manner with barely visible breasts and false beard of the king (fig. 3.10). The beard was a traditional symbol of the king's power and majesty.

Hatshepsut's reign witnessed the construction of a three-level temple modeled after a Middle Kingdom funerary temple for Nebhepetre Mentuhotep II. The model temple is on the left side in figure 3.11. The temple is both freestanding and cut into the rock cliff of the surrounding hill. The first level is an open plaza with a long **colonnade**, a row of columns supporting a lintel and roof. The second level is accessible via a long ramp leading to shrines dedicated to Anubis, god of embalming, and Hathor, the sky mother.

mountainpix / Shutterstock, Inc.

Fig. 3.9 Thutmose IV receiving the gift of life, c. 1400 to 1390 BCE

Global Focal Point

The Shang Dynasty (c. 1700 to 1045 BCE) was established by King Tang and comprised a collection of villages linked together stretching across the lower Yellow River plains. The first classical Chinese literature was developed and compiled on the basis of ideas from the Shang era. The Chinese share a wisdom commonly associated with the Egyptian—that order derives from balance. Therefore, when the world is out of balance, the Chinese believe that over time, through a series of changes, balance will be restored. An example from the literature of the day is *T'ai*, or "Peace," where the heavens and earth are unified:

Heaven and earth unite: the image is PEACE.
Thus the ruler
Divides and completes the course of heaven and earth,
And so aids the people.

The inclusion of Hathor is a possible reference to Hatshepsut's femininity. A second ramp leads to another colonnade faced with colossal statues of royal figures. A succession of chapels and two more colonnades are reached before entering into the central shrine cut into the cliff dedicated to Amun.

During the New Kingdom, the Egyptian king was known as a **pharaoh**, meaning the house of the king or simply "great house." The king's place of residence was used to refer to the king in a general sense much like we call the presidency merely "the White House." The current use of pharaoh as referring to all

Fig. 3.10 *Kneeling Statue of Hatshepsut*, c. 1479 to 1548 BCE

Egyptian kings can probably be accredited to the Hebrew Bible's use of pharaoh as both earlier and later kings.

Pharaohs of the New Kingdom undertook vast building programs in which equal attention was paid to both temples to the gods and tombs for their burial. Amun remained the focus of temples, but images and dedication to both Amun's wife, Mut, and son, Khonsu, were included. Each temple was unique but shared common architectural features. One feature was a **pylon**, or enormous gateway with sloped walls, seen at the Luxor temple in Thebes built by Ramses II (fig. 3.12).

The temple complex built by Ramses II at Luxor incorporated other architectural features. One feature was a **hypostyle hall** (fig. 3.13), an enormous spaced filled with huge columns intended to support a stone slab roof, and a second was a sanctuary for the deity. The hypostyle hall acted as a means for transporting visitors from the light-filled exterior to the darker interior. As one passed from the exterior to the interior, they moved from a secular to a sacred and more spiritual space. The temple further functioned as a metaphor for birth and creation.

Fig. 3.11 Funerary temple of Hatshepsut, Western Thebes. c. 1460 BCE

Fig. 3.12 Pylon gate of Ramses II, c. 1279 to 1212 BCE

Fig. 3.13 Hypostyle hall, Great Temple of Amun, Thebes. c. 1294 to 1212 BCE

Throughout the Eighteenth Dynasty, the temple of Thebes was added onto in accordance with what each new pharaoh believed would honor the gods, except toward the end of the dynasty. In 1353 BCE, Amenhotep IV (r. 1353 to 1337 BCE) ascended the throne and changed Egyptian religion and artistic expression until his death. Amenhotep IV believed that all gods were inferior to the sun disk Aten and abolished worship of the pantheon of Egyptian gods. The belief in Aten as the only god to be worshiped was so pervasive to Amenhotep IV that he changed his name to Akhenaten, or "The Shining Spirit of Aten." Scholarly consensus attributes the change in worship as an increase in how pharaohs viewed themselves. For Amenhotep IV, the change also signaled a shift in political and cultural thought.

The artistic expression promoted by Amenhotep IV is known as the Amarna Style. The Amarna Style altered the way the human form was depicted, from rectilinear to curvilinear with a more casual posture (fig. 3.14). Prior depictions were highly idealized and perfect in proportion. One image to retain a sense of perfection was a bust of Queen Nefertiti (fig. 3.15), the favorite wife of Amenhotep IV.

The religious revolution began by Amenhotep IV was short-lived as it ceased upon his death in 1336 after his son, Tutankhaten (r. 1336 to 1327 BCE),

Fig. 3.14 *Relief Head of Akhenaten*, c. 1353 to 1336 BCE

Fig. 3.16 Tutankhamun's "Golden Throne" from his tomb, c. 1335 BCE

Fig. 3.15 *Nefertiti*, c. 1348 to 1336 BCE

assumed the throne. The new king abandoned the religion of this father and changed his name to Tutankhamun, signifying a return to the traditional gods. Tutankhamun's fame is partly due to how his royal tomb was discovered, free from the devastation of looters. A golden throne dating from the early time of the king's reign still bears the stamp of the Amarna and curvilinear style (fig. 3.16).

CREATIVE IMPULSE

Literature

Egyptian literature did not fully blossom until the Middle Kingdom when stories, biographies, historical and scientific writings, poems, and satire were recorded by scribes. Much like early Mesopotamian writing, ancient Egyptian writing was based on pictographs called **hieroglyphics**. The glyphs were first believed to be based on whole ideas instead of sounds (fig. 3.17). The discovery of a fragmented black granodiorite stele by French soldiers in 1799 near Rosetta unlocked the mysteries of how to read Egyptian hieroglyphics.

Extensive written genres developed, but one of the most important pieces of literature was the *Book of Going Forth by Day*, or more commonly referred to as *Books of the Dead*. The book was a collection of hymns,

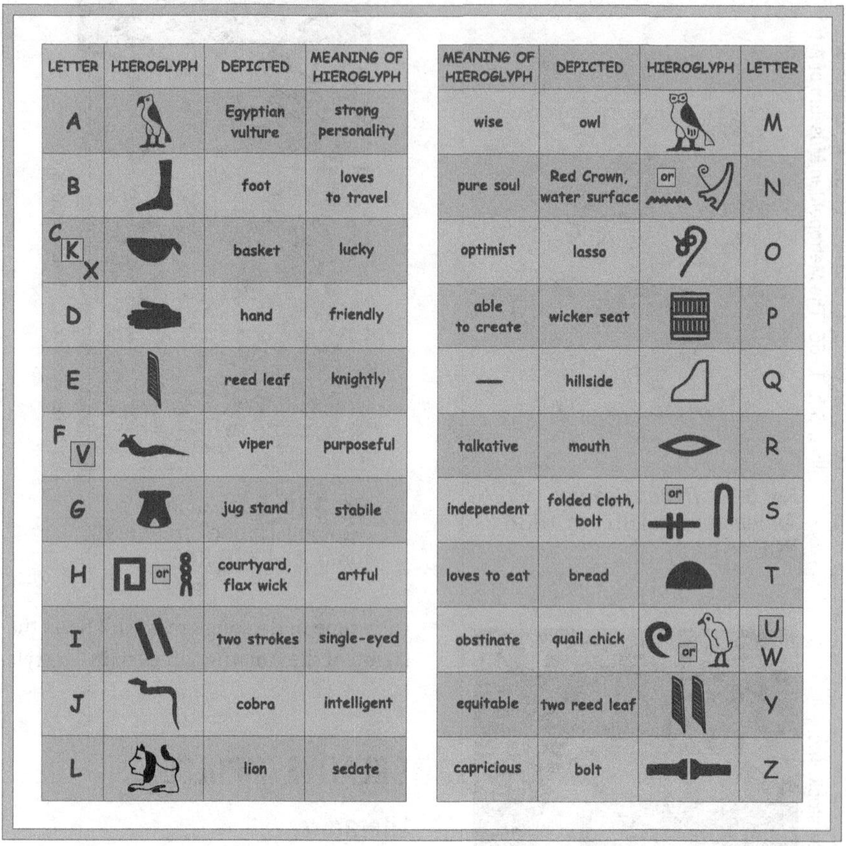

LETTER	HIEROGLYPH	DEPICTED	MEANING OF HIEROGLYPH	MEANING OF HIEROGLYPH	DEPICTED	HIEROGLYPH	LETTER
A		Egyptian vulture	strong personality	wise	owl		M
B		foot	loves to travel	pure soul	Red Crown, water surface		N
C K X		basket	lucky	optimist	lasso		O
D		hand	friendly	able to create	wicker seat		P
E		reed leaf	knightly	—	hillside		Q
F V		viper	purposeful	talkative	mouth		R
G		jug stand	stabile	independent	folded cloth, bolt		S
H		courtyard, flax wick	artful	loves to eat	bread		T
I		two strokes	single-eyed	obstinate	quail chick		U W
J		cobra	intelligent	equitable	two reed leaf		Y
L		lion	sedate	capricious	bolt		Z

© tramway5/Shutterstock.com

Fig. 3.17 Table of Egyptian hieroglyphs

spells, and poems used to aid the deceased through the ritual of the afterlife. In the latter portion of Chapter 183 (*Worshiping Osiris*), the spell reads:

> I have come to you with my hands bearing Truth, and my heart has no lies in it. I place Truth before you, for I know that you live by it. I have done no wrong in this land, and no man will suffer loss of his possessions.

The concept of Truth was vital to Egyptian passage into the afterlife, as seen in *Last Judgment by Osiris* (fig. 3.18). The scene comes from Chapter 125 and unfolds as Hunefer's heart is weighed against an ostrich feather as a symbol for Maat, the goddess of truth, justice, and order. Egyptians believed that the heart was the seat of an individual character, emotions, and intellect. If the deceased heart was unable to balance the feather, were condemned to nonexistence, and the heart was gobbled down by Ammit. The chapter was so important that it was commonly placed at the beginning of the book or tomb entrance.

Mummification

Upon death, an Egyptian's body needed to begin the preservation process, or **mummi-fication** (fig. 3.19) shortly after death. The

Fig. 3.18 *Last Judgment by Osiris*, c. 1285

Fig. 3.19 Egyptian mummy and sarcophagus

need resided in the existence of the **ka**, or life force, and **ba**, or personality, each person possessed. In order for the ka and ba to be reunited in the afterlife, the physical body must be preserved. For the Egyptian rulers, not only was mummification necessary but other worldly essentials such as food and furniture were also buried with them.

From start to finish, the mummification process took 70 days. A full 40 days were reserved for removing the organs, stuffing the body with linens to maintain its shape, and then surrounding it with bags of natron, a mineral salt, for dehydration. After day 40, the body was cleaned with spices and perfumes. Oils were rubbed on the body to aid in restoring the deceased's luster and resin was applied to act as a waterproofing agent. Each nail was sewn to the nailbed and artificial eyes placed in the eye sockets. Ancient forms of cosmetics were applied to the face and a wig placed over the head.

Once these necessary preparations were completed, the body underwent an elaborate wrapping process. While the method of mummification changed over the more than 3000 years it was used, the elaborate, highly ritualized, process never did. Humans were not the only living beings mummified, Egyptians mummified cats, dogs, monkeys, birds, and more (fig. 3.20).

Religion

Polytheism was a mainstay for most of Egyptian history except for the reign of Akhenaten from 1353 to 1337 BCE. During this 16-year period, the religion of Egypt was **monotheistic**, or the belief in one god. Scholars debate the reason for the shift, with some attributing the break as a result of Hebrew influence, others maintaining the conversion was purely political. Regardless of the reason, the Egyptians never truly discarded any god

© Andrea Izzotti/Shutterstock.com

Fig. 3.20 Ancient Egyptian mummified cats

Fig. 3.21 Illustration of Egyptian gods and goddess

Charis Estelle / Shutterstock, Inc.

or belief in favor of another. There were also instances where two deities would merge to form a third.

Their belief in the afterlife was unlike the Mesopotamians. Egyptians reveled in the joys the afterlife held for them, while Mesopotamians viewed their society as dismal and simply a fragment associated with a larger universe governed by the gods.

In Egyptian religion, an ordered universe was reflected when each component, gods, humans, plants, and stars were all part of a larger harmonious design. If each faction did not upset the harmony of the universe, there was no reason to fear death. Each god or goddess represented natural forces and was distinguishable for each other (fig. 3.21). Most were represented with human bodies and animal heads, and they wore a headdress that identified who they were.

EGYPTIAN LEGACY

Ancient Egypt has imprinted itself onto modern civilization much as it did during the time it reigned supreme. Modern society is still captivated by Egyptian pyramids; we place them among some of the most extraordinary places in the world, most notably by architect I. M. Pei's entrance to the Musée du Louvre. The annual cycle of life that comes from the Nile River Valley helped establish a highly stable and prosperous society. The stability within Egypt was so pervasive that only for a short decade and a half did the artistic style and religion ever change.

Societal Emphasis

In Egypt, herds of hippopotamuses devastated crops and continually threatened food shortages. Pharaohs hunted them in the marshes to drive them south into Upper Egypt. Hippos, therefore, became associated with chaos, but the hunts proved the power of the pharaoh to conquer evil. Small sculptures such as figure 3.22 were placed in tombs to remind the deceased of their love for hunting.

Gift of Edward S. Harkness, 1917, The Metropolitan Museum of Art

Fig. 3.22 Hippopotamus, Middle Kingdom, Dynasty 12, c. 1961 to 1878 BCE

Critical Thinking

Explain how the idea of cycles helped shape Egyptian civilization.

Describe the changes in architecture design from the Old to the New Kingdom.

Examine the impact of Amenhotep IV on Egypt.

Explore how the Egyptian creative impulse such as the *Book of Going Forth by Day* connected to its religious ideologies.

ONLINE RESOURCES

Ancient Egypt by Period and Kingdom

https://www.history.com/topics/ancient-history/ancient-egypt

Building an Ancient Egyptian Pyramid Video

https://www.smithsonianmag.com/videos/category/history/what-the-completed-great-pyramid-wouldve-lo/

Discovering Luxor Temple

https://discoveringegypt.com/luxor-temple/

The Queen Who Would be King: Hatshepsut

https://www.smithsonianmag.com/history/the-queen-who-would-be-king-130328511/

Ancient Egyptian Hieroglyphic Writing

https://discoveringegypt.com/egyptian-hieroglyphic-writing/

Standing Hippopotamus **Video**

https://smarthistory.org/standing-hippopotamus/

Ancient Egyptian *Book of the Dead*

https://www.ancient.eu/Egyptian_Book_of_the_Dead/

Mummification Process Video

https://smarthistory.org/the-mummification-process/

Akhenaten and Nefertiti Relief Video

https://smarthistory.org/house-altar-depicting-akhenaten-nefertiti-and-three-of-their-daughters/

Ancient Egyptian Religion

https://courses.lumenlearning.com/suny-hccc-worldcivilization/chapter/ancient-egyptian-religion/

Ancient Greece: Establishing a Democracy

Fig. 4.1 *Porch of the Maidens*, Acropolis, Athens, Greece, 421 to 405 BCE

ariy / Shutterstock.com

Knowledge Acquisition

◆ *Identify individual differences between per-Aegean people, Cycladic, Minoan, and Mycenaean.*

◆ *Describe significant artistic events of Classical Greece including the Acropolis sculptures, vases, and playwrights.*

◆ *Identify and evaluate the political and philosophical thought of Ancient Greek intellectuals such as Socrates, Plato, and Aristotle.*

◆ *Understand the formation of democracy.*

SETTING THE SCENE

The Greek civilization remains one of the most pervasively influential cultural forces in the realms of expression and thought. The historian Jackson Spielvogel asserted that the ancient Greeks represent the "fountain-head of Western culture" as the philosophical, artistic, literary, and political concepts that are familiar features of modern society and reflect the continuing legacy of Greek civilization. Greek culture is divided into two major time frames: people of the Aegean and Ancient Greece.

The people of the Aegean cultures flourished in the areas surrounding the Aegean Sea between 3000 and 1100 BCE. The following three cultural groups dominate this area: the Cyclades, Minoan, and Mycenaean Map 4.1. Ancient Greek history began around 1100 BCE as new civilizations were established and segmented into four historical periods. The geometric period was from the eleventh to the eighth centuries BCE, Archaic period from the seventh to sixth centuries BCE, Classical period from the fifth to fourth centuries BCE, and Hellenistic from 323 BCE to 27 BCE.

BRONZE AGE CULTURE

The Cyclades of the Aegean Sea

Between roughly 2500 and 2000 BCE, the most ancient Greek civilization known as the Cycladic developed on the islands in the Aegean Sea. The culture is known collectively as the Cyclades. Their names derive from the Greek word *kyklos,* meaning circle. Little is known about the people who inhabited these islands, as no written records survive, but artifacts made of marble and wall paintings were recovered from ruin sites. The marble figurines are exceedingly basic with abstractly stylized features (fig. 4.2). Each figurine varies in height from a few inches to life-size, with anatomical details reduced to the fundamentals. Many of the statues are nude females and probably represent the Mother Goddess, a chief deity in the ancient Aegean, and were found in graves. Therefore, they are thought to have played a ritualistic funerary role.

Minoans of Crete

To the south of the Cyclades was the Isle of Crete where a Bronze Age civilization inhabited

Map 4.1 Aegean and Ancient Greece

pavalena / Shutterstock.com

Gift of Christos G. Bastis, 1968, The Metropolitan Museum of Art

Fig. 4.2 Marble Female Figure, Cycladic, attributed to the Bastis Master, Greece. 2600 to 2400 BCE.

the island between 2800 and 1375 BCE. Early settlers of Crete established trade routes near and far with the peoples of Turkey, Egypt, Britain, and Scandinavia to import amber, copper, gold, and lapis lazuli. Tin was imported from Britain to produce bronze once mixed with copper. Around 1900 BCE, a people known as the Minoans flourished. The Minoan culture is named after their legendary king Minos, who built the spectacular palace at Knossos

(c. 1600 to 1400 BCE) which was referred to as the House of Double Axes. In the ancient Greek world, the Minoans are among the most intriguing civilization. The palace was continually added on to until it spanned six acres with more than 1300 rooms. Today, only fragmented ruins remain, attesting to the triumph of the Minoan's palaces' former grandeur (fig. 4.3).

Construction of the palace was with gypsum, mud bricks, and clay reinforced with wood and walls painted with **buon fresco**, where pigment is mixed with water and applied to a wall coated with wet lime plaster. Over 3000 years later, Renaissance artists employed a similar technique. But, what amazed archeologists the most when the frescos were discovered was that they were found not only on the interior but also on the exterior. The entire palace complex was brightly colored. Another intriguing find was in the queen's **antechamber**, or waiting room, located below her private chambers. The find indicates that even over 4000 years ago interiors were renovated as decorative styles changed (fig. 4.4). The antechamber contained two different **motifs**, or decorative designs. The older one was a spiral pattern, probably immolating the ocean waves, while the other was an ornate flower design.

© Timofeev Vladimir/Shutterstock.com

Fig. 4.3 Ruins of the Knossos Palace on the Island of Crete, Greece, 2800 to 1375 BCE

Fig. 4.4 Queen's antechamber, Knossos Palace, c. 1750 to 1500 BCE

© Georgios Tsichlis/Shutterstock.com

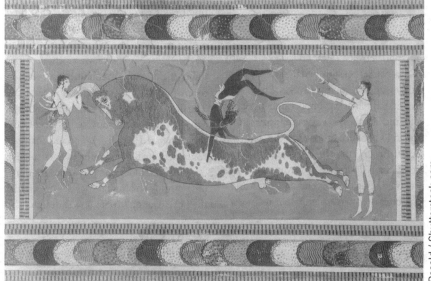

Fig. 4.5 *Bull-Leaping*, from the Palace of Minos, Knossos, Crete, c. 1550 to 1450 BCE

Pecold / Shutterstock.com

Another colorful and naturalistic fresco mural, *Bull-Leaping* (fig. 4.5), shows three individuals engaging in bull vaulting. It is uncertain if this was a ritual activity or maybe a rite of passage. We do know that bulls were routinely sacrificed in Minoan culture and symbolically associated with male virility and strength.

A statue found on the island of Crete is known as the Snake Goddess (fig. 4.6), thought to be associated with fertility, or Mother Goddess. In ancient times, snakes were universal symbols for both rebirth and fertility. Even though little is known about the Snake Goddess or religion of the Minoans, scholars of ancient religion have

Fig. 4.6 Snake goddess, from the Palace of Knossos, Crete, c. 1500 BCE

Anna Pakutina / Shutterstock.com

proposed that the Minoan worship of one or more female deities provides evidence that early culture's principal deity was a goddess rather than a god. After the decline of the Minoans, as a result of either deforestation of the island or a volcanic eruption, Mycenaean, a mainland Greek culture, rapidly began to occupy Crete and became the power in the region.

Minoan culture is the creator of the Greek myth based on the Minotaur who lived in a **labyrinth**, eventually coming to mean maze. In the myth, King Minos prayed for a bull to sacrifice to Poseidon. But, the white bull that emerged from the sea was too lovely to sacrifice. Minos kept the bull for himself and sacrificed a bull from the royal herd. Minos's defiance enraged Poseidon, who exacted revenge by making Pasiphae, Minos's wife, fall in love with the white bull. Pasiphae persuaded the chief craftsman to fashion a hollow, wooden cow. She climbed inside to consummate her lust for the bull. The resulting union produced a ghastly creature, the Minotaur, half man, and half bull with an appetite for human flesh.

The myth continues as a possible explanation for the decline of the Minoan culture and rise of the Athenian's. According to the Athenians, every year they were required to send 14 young women and men to be sacrificed to the Minotaur. One year, King Aegeus's son Theseus set sail with 13 other young souls after vowing to slay the Minotaur and return home victorious under a white flag. Upon arrival at Crete, Theseus enticed Ariadne, King Minos's daughter, to help him. She supplied Theseus with a sword and spool of thread for him to tie at the entrance and then use to guide him back after killing the Minotaur. Once the deed was done, Theseus sailed for Athens but forgot to change the flag from black to white. When King Aegeus saw the flag was not white, he plunged himself into the sea and drown. The sea was subsequently named the Aegean Sea in honor of newly kinged Theseus's father, Aegeus.

Mycenaean of the Mainland

The Mycenae are considered the ancestors of the Ancient Greeks. While Minoan towns were unfortified and battle scenes were scarce, Mycenaeans built fortified, hilltop communities (fig. 4.7) with wall murals dominated by battle and hunting scenes, suggesting that the Mycenaeans lived and died by the sword. Society was **feudal** in nature, or organized around an all-powerful lord, an extensive bureaucracy for collecting taxes, civil servant, and military personnel as trade was an important way of life. The feudal nature of the culture was based on allegiances between the lord and those he protected. The social structure allowed the lords an immense amount of power to accumulate personal wealth.

Mycenae is most famous for its involvement in the Trojan War between King Agamemnon of Mycenae and King Priam of

Global Focal Point

A group known as the Olmec inhabited Veracruz and Tabasco around 1300 BCE. In the center of their communities, they built enormous ceremonial areas with massive pyramid structures. Each pyramid is believed to be either a mimic of the volcanoes dominating Mexico or burial tombs. At one location, La Venta, three colossal stone heads stand, which are considered guardians of the south end of the ceremonial centers. A fourth head stands alone at the north end (fig. 4.9). Each head weighs between 11 and 24 tons with unique features. They are carved of basalt, volcanic rock, quarried from a location 50 miles from where they reside.

Fig. 4.9 Colossal head, La Venta, c. 900 to 500 BCE

© alexandersr/Shutterstock.com

Troy after Helen abandoned her husband, King Menelaus of Sparta. The epic tale became immortalized in Homer's poem the *Iliad*, first written down around 800 BCE.

An important shift in the architecture of burial developed around 1300 BCE. The use of **shaft graves**, or vertical pit up to 25-feet deep, was replaced by **tholos**, or a rounded beehive structure. The most famous of these types of tombs is the Treasury of Atreus, the father of Agamemnon. The burial chamber is accessed via a long passage nearly 115-feet long and 20-feet wide. Above the door is a **relieving triangle**, or an opening designed to relieve weight the lintel must bear (fig. 4.8). A pair of green marble columns topped by two red columns initially enhanced and beautified the entrance to the tholos. The columns were **engaged**, or purely decorative with no structural purpose, with only half the column present.

CLASSICAL GREECE

Classical Greece, often referred to as the "high point of Greek civilization," is characterized by creativity in the arts, literature, and philosophy. The central feature of Classical Greece was the emergence of Athens as the central polis and the pursuit of democracy. From the culture of Classical Greece comes the birth of history from the Greek word

Fig.4.7 Lion Gate, Mycenae, c. 1300 BCE

Constantinos Iliopoulos / Shutterstock.com

Fig. 4.8 Treasury of Arteus Mycenae, c. 1250 BCE

Tatiana Popova / Shutterstock.com

historia, meaning to investigate or research. Two Greek Historians leave an everlasting impression for later generations and the world. Herodotus (c. 484 to 430/420 BCE) was the first, and Thucydides (c. 460 to 400 BCE) the second.

The Greek cultures bequeathed the world with monumental structures. While these legacies are truly awe-inspiring, the genuine vestige of Greece was the spirit it evoked, a spirit rooted in the belief that man was a free being. The prior 3000 years of civilizations including Mesopotamian and Egyptian believed man to be a dismal creature who groveled before, and was governed by, the deities. The Greeks picked humanity up and set us on a path to modernization.

Many battles occurred in Greek history, but only one set the Greeks on the path to a cultural revolution, the Persian Wars. When the wars finally concluded, the Athenians returned to Athens to find their beloved city devastated. Initially, they pledged to preserve the **acropolis** (fig. 4.10), or top of the city, in a state of ruin as a remembrance of the horrific cost of war, but the former general turned statesman Pericles convinced them otherwise, resulting in a decision that ushered in what is known as the "Golden Age of Athens." Under Pericles's guidance, the city promoted new ideas in architecture, sculpture, literature, dance, music, and even government.

Rise of Democracy

Democracy means rule by the people. In ancient Greece, by the people meant two things: the people were directly involved in the state and the people were male citizens of the polis. Essentially, a large minority ruled the state. Rules varied by polis and time, but generally, citizenship required one parent to be a citizen. Naturalization occasionally occurred, granting citizenship to those who were otherwise cut off from democracy. The concept was innovative in the ancient world, and it demonstrates the Greek idea that culture could be universal.

The development of the **polis**, or city-state, allowed for political experimentation during the Archaic period (700 to 480 BCE), a time that would give the West (Europe and European-based cultures) most of its political structures. The polis began as monarchies with a hereditary king, but by the eighth century BCE (799 to 700 BCE), most had been overthrown and a rising merchant class began to make itself heard in the seventh century BCE.

By the late sixth century BCE, most polies were **oligarchs**, or rule by a few, with absolute rulers holding powers similar to those of a king. Many were **totalitarian**, a centralized, dictatorial state requiring complete subservience, since the members were of the same class and shared common interests. Sometimes during unrest or crisis, the oligarchs were overthrown by a **tyrant**,

Fig. 4.10 The Acropolis of Athens and surrounding theater with the Parthenon to the right, Athens, fifth century BCE

alexandersr / Shutterstock.com

an unrestrained, absolute ruler who maintained power by oppressive means. In many cases, tyrants were illegitimate usurpers of political power with widespread support by the people in the name of political reform. Many were brilliant leaders and morally sound reformers who focused on crisis and reform. By 550 BCE, Athens was a democracy and became an important trading and commercial center along with the center for arts, literature, and architecture. Over the next 100 years, Athens would become the dominant political and cultural force in the Greek world.

The development of democracy in Athens was aided by the economic instability of farming combined with social dynamics in the polis during the eighth century. Some farmers became wealthy by investing in the cash crops of olive oil and wine, whereas others grew wheat. Prices for wheat dropped as Athens began importing wheat and exporting olive oil and wine. In the end, wealthy farmers became richer, whereas poor farmers fell deeper into debt and were often forced to sell their families and themselves into slavery to pay off the debt. The situation became so grave that average Athenian farmers prepared for a revolution.

Recognizing the danger, the **Areopagus**, or High Court of Appeal for criminal and civil cases in Athens, attempted political reform. The aim was to end the privatization and exploitation to ensure that it never happened again by installing Solon (630 to 560 BCE), a poet, politician, and lawmaker, into power. He eventually established democracy in Athens around 549 BCE.

Solon's reforms included dismissing outstanding debt; freeing as many of those who had sold themselves into slavery including those abroad; banning loans secured by the promise of slavery, and encouraging the production of olive oil and wine. He also divided the Athenian population into four broad classes of citizens: women, metics (noncitizens but free), and slaves, with each class further subdivided on the basis of wealth and property. All classes participated in government in one form or another. Solon was considered a great hero and his reforms were the basis of Athenian government, but these reforms did not last long. Within a few years, Athens was verging on anarchy, and a nobleman, Peisistratus (r. 560 to 527 BCE), rose into power as a tyrant. But, this new form of tyranny was as critical to the foundation of Athenian democracy as Solon's reforms

Cross-cultural Connection

Greece was not the only place in the world where new ideas were being formed and disseminated. In India, Prince Siddhartha (c. 563 to 483 BCE) became troubled by the suffering of those around him. He abandoned his life and family in search of enlightenment. After 6 years of meditation, he attained a new understanding of how to live and began teaching his Four Noble Truths.

1. Life is suffering.
2. Suffering has a cause, ignorance.
3. Ignorance is removable.
4. Removal of ignorance is accomplished by following the Eight-fold Path of right view, resolve, speech, action, livelihood, effort, mindfulness, and concentration.

were. Peisistratus began a building program in Athens and worked on both cultural and religious reform. He desired to make his city culturally sophisticated and dynamic. He attacked the power of the nobility by shifting some power to the lowest classes. He broke up exiled aristocrats' estates and clipped their powers with traveling judges. He also endeavored to ensure that the Solonian government functioned and regular elections were held.

After Peisistratus's tyranny ended, upon his death, the rule of Cleisthenes initiated (c. 570 to 508 BCE), and Cleisthenes was another influential leader in the development of democracy. Between 527 and 508 BCE, Cleisthenes installed a series of reforms, resulting in what is now considered Athenian democracy. He gave citizenship to all free men in Athens and surrounding locales. An innovative system developed to break the power of aristocratic families with a political realignment of citizenship and citizenry. A new council, the Council of Five Hundred, was introduced, and it was organized by demographics, not by hereditary. The structure of the military was changed from the old tribal system to a general commanded, who was elected on an annual basis from the tribes by popular vote. In time, generals found themselves in situations where they could become leaders in Athenian politics.

The last piece of Athenian democracy was instituted in 487 BCE, long after Cleisthenes's death, in the form of **ostracization**, or the exclusion from society by general consent. The design of ostracism was one where the Assembly voted a citizen into an exile citizen's status. Once exiled, the citizen had 10 days to leave and stay away for 10 years. Most exiled individuals were contemplating seizing power or thought to have dangerous ideas and were removed before they became too powerful.

Golden Age of Greece

By the time the great Athenian leader Pericles (c. 495 to 429 BCE) came to power during a popular democratic movement in 462 BCE, the Areopagus had been stripped of its power, and the city was governed by the council and Assembly. Pericles advanced the legislative process by allowing anyone to serve as an **archon**, one of nine central leaders of the country, despite birth or wealth. The Assembly became the central power of the state as it was given sole approval or **veto**, or rejection, power over every state decision.

Pericles introduced state payment to juries allowing poorer citizens to recover some money when they served as a jury member. A tightening of citizenship requirements now demands both parents to be Athenian citizens. In the past only male citizens participated in government, and

Innovation and Progress

Earthquakes have shaken and surprised the world since ancient times. The use of instruments to detect one is not new. In 132 CE, the Chinese inventor, Zhang Heng, created the first seismoscope. Unlike modern instrumentation, Heng's device is highly ornate. contained 8 dragons holding small bronze balls marking the compass directions and toads with their mouths open beneath to catch a dropped ball. In 2005, a Chinese scientist named Zengshou replicated and tested Zhang's device. The replica of the ancient device was as accurate as the modern-day seismometer.

the great democracy of Periclean Athens was one in which only a very small minority of the people living in Athens ruled. Nonetheless, this is the closest humanity has come to an unadulterated democracy. A wide array of what is presently associated with Greek culture was derived during the period of Pericles's rule. Some of the greater dramatic works of the Greek world were written, and the astonishing monumental architectural achievements were built using the wealth that poured into Athens. Both in wealth and at peace, Athens was able to benefit from its resources by investing in a massive cultural revolution in art, poetry, philosophy, and architecture.

During the Periclean Age, Athens and Sparta entered into the Peloponnesian Wars (431 to 404 BCE). Massive campaigns with fierce fighting took place throughout the Greek world, and the first war was recorded by the historian Thucydides, considered the "Father of History." The Peloponnesian Wars are viewed as archetypal conflicts between the commercial democracy of Athens and the agricultural aristocracy of Sparta. The wars between the maritime superpower, Athens, and continental military machine, Sparta, placed the two city-states at odds. Pericles insisted that the greatness of the state was only a function of the greatness of its individuals. In fact, he felt so strongly about the role of each individual in Athens prosperity as being a link to their individual freedom and a their civic responsibility. For most living in Western culture today, these two sentiments are recognized as the foundation of society and the political system.

Hellenistic Period

The Greek Golden Age was responsible for as much destruction as it was for its greatness. Without this remarkable period, and Pericles as its leader, the Western world would not be as it is today, yet one more step

was necessary to plant the seeds of Western culture and democracy: Hellenism.

Hellene is the Greek word that refers to the "Greek" people. The Hellenistic age was the era when Greek culture and ideas were extended throughout the world it discovered. Hellenism was the act of spreading the culture. Two Macedonian kings, through their conquests, would actively export all aspects of Greek culture. The exportation of such ideas was novel and profoundly shaped subsequent civilizations as they developed.

The Hellenistic world marks the first time in history that a single culture was considered an international culture. Greeks exported all aspects of their culture by altering the cultures and religions of the Mediterranean, Near and Middle East, and northern Africa. A unique aspect of Hellenism was its ability to accept other cultures, bringing non-Greek ideas and people into Greece and Italy, a Greek colony. The process mostly occurred in the city-states, and pragmatically, the Greeks accepted the barbarism of kingship with a compromise of building polies that were not politically independent but had a similar structure. A result of the growth of new polis cities was massive migrations from the Greek mainland. Greeks began settling in these new, far-flung polies as a means of gaining lucrative positions in the military and administration.

Alexander the Great's Empire

Under the rule of Alexander the Great (c. 356 to 323 BCE) and his father, King Phillip (c. 382 to 336 BCE), the world saw the unification of the entire Greek empire, except for Sparta, and gained territory to the Indus River. Alexander stopped only when his army engaged in a fierce battle with King Porus's (c. 340 to 315 BCE) men, who were equipped with 200 elephants in the territory east of Taxila in India. His troops refused to continue only after hearing rumors that the next kingdom was ready to fight with more than 500 elephants in addition to its warriors.

CREATIVE IMPULSE

Architecture

Ancient Greeks believed that all things must be enjoyed in moderation, but this idea did not necessarily extend to their taste for beautiful and elaborate buildings. Architecturally, they gave us the Doric and Ionic orders, which are functional yet elegant, still in use. They also created the more elaborate column order known as Corinthian. Each order was named after the Greek town or people creating the column style. The significant difference between each order can be discerned by identifying the differences in the **platform** and **entablature** (fig. 4.11).

Simple stylistic differences allow for the distinction between each order. The Doric is the oldest and simplest with no actual capital. The Ionic order was most commonly used on administration building during Greek times and is used in modern times. Iconic columns are recognizable because of their scroll capital. The Corinthian order is the most elaborate and expensive to create, with capitals terminating in flowers and acanthus leaves.

At the Erechtheum Temple dedicated to both Athena and Poseidon (fig. 4.1), the architect used columns shaped like women called **caryatids**, named after the young korai (maidens) from Caryae who dance for the goddess Artemis. The maidens were viewed as complements to the male kouros (fig. 4.13). None of the maidens' forearms or hands survive, but scholars believe that each caryatid may have held an offering plate to the gods. Irrespective of their purpose, they are a testament to Greek superior craftsmanship, given that the roof of the porch rests on the slender necks of six maidens.

Under the rule of Pericles, the city of Athens was beautified to a degree rarely seen in ancient times. Building projects were repaired and erected to appease the gods on the Acropolis. A 40-foot tall gold and ivory statue of Athena Parthenos, the main deity worshiped by Athenians, was housed in the

Lefteris Papaulakis / Shutterstock.com

Fig. 4.11 Classical Greek Column Orders, from left to right: Doric, Ionic, and Corinthian.

Parthenon (fig. 4.10). She stood, rather than sat, with shield, spear, and snake to her left symbolizing her eternal power as protector of the city. In her right hand, she holds a mini statue of the winged Goddess of Victory, Nike, to symbolize Athens's victory of others. At the base of the block upon which Athena rests, a 525-foot long frieze depicts a processional ceremony (fig. 4.12).

Sculpture

Along with developments in architecture, the Greeks perfected sculpture with an almost-obsessive desire to show human perfection. The Greeks' celebration of the human body was unique. In particular, the male body was depicted in a typical genre of sculpture known as **kourus**, meaning young man (fig. 4.13a and b). In fact, no other Mediterranean culture emphasized the depiction of the male body as the Greeks did. In the sixth century BCE alone, they created 20,000 male nude statues.

Upon first examination, the Greek obsession with male nudity may appear odd, but such statues were primarily found

Fig. 4.12 Replica of *Athena Parthenos* originally designed by Phidias, c. 440 BCE.

© legacy 1995/Shutterstock.com

in sanctuaries and cemeteries, most often serving as votive offerings to the gods or as commemorative grave markers. Sculptures enjoyed showing the beauty of the human

Fletcher Fund, 1932, The Metropolitan Museum of Art

(a)

© Lefteris Papaulakis/Shutterstock.com

(b)

Fig. 4.13 (a) Marble statue of a Kouros, c. 590 to 580 BCE, **(b)** *Anavysos Kouros*, cemetery near Athens, c. 525 BCE.

form as a nude to emphasize the combination of reality and **idealization**, or perfection.

The statue known as *Kritian Boy*, attributed to the sculpture Kritios, is the image most known for being realistic in its depiction of the human body. There is a subtle balance to the lines of the body, which forms the basis of classical art because of its delicate balance. The style of naturally depicting the human body did not last long. Within a few years of the sculpture's creation, artists no longer made realistic images of the human body. Instead, the artist Polyclitus created an entirely new system of beauty. All of the sculpture's beauty was reflected in a highly mathematical order, an order that embodies the ideal harmony between the natural world and the intellectual or spiritual realm.

In later years, the idea of the male nude body becomes ever increasingly unrealistic to emphasize the perfect male body, which was modeled after the gods. The rationale for this shift from the realistic depiction of the male human body is rooted in the Greek belief that they were modeled after the gods. All sculptural representations of the body had to be perfect in form. Sometime around the sixth century BCE, Athens became a major center for pottery production, which highlights the Athenians' aptitude for painting.

Painting

As with Athenian sculpture, the decorations on Athenian vases grew increasingly naturalistic and detailed until each side of the vase was filled with a scene. In many of the pottery scenes, the artists depict various stories of their gods and heroes. Although the scene in *Amazonomachy* appears quite natural, this is not the reason for its appeal to our emotions. Instead, the vase is valued for its perfectly balanced composition. The tragedy of death

Fig. 4.14 *Amazonomachy*, Attic, c. 450 BCE.

Rogers Fund, 1907, The Metropolitan Museum of Art

is transformed into a rare depiction of death as an occurrence of both dignity and order (fig. 4.14).

Before the more naturalistic depiction on figures of vases, the tenth century witnessed the establishment of ceramic manufactures in Athens at the Kerameikos cemetery. The town was on the outskirts of Athens and provided the sources for the word *ceramics*. These potteries devised newer potter's wheel allowing for faster revolutions with more control when shaping vases. The invention of a new wheel needed a kiln with more heat control to produce richer, more lustrous glazes. At first glance, early Greek vases (fig. 4.15) were simplistic, but the concentric circles were made with a new tool, the compass.

In the ninth century, the more complicated pattern of **geometric style** dominated pottery, referring to the shapes decorating the vase surface. Such pieces (fig. 4.16) are highly stylized and recall the Greek belief of the unity of the whole. The layered bands echo how the Greeks imagined the cosmos

And, Euclid (325 to 250 BCE), a Greek philosopher, devised the definitive geometry of two and three-dimensional space.

Shortly after the creation of geometric ware, Athenians developed two distinctive vase styles on the basis of a relationship between the figures and background colors. **Black-figure** (fig. 4.17) vases employed a technique where a mixture of clay and water, or **slip**, is painted onto the vase and fired. After firing, the slip remained and was highlighted on the bare red clay. The production of **red-figure** (fig. 4.14) vases was the reverse of black-figure but more complicated. The vase background was painted with slip and the figures were outlined, but the process was carried out in stages. Three stages were needed to regulate the amount of oxygen allowed in the kiln.

By the first half of the fifth century, a newer style, **white-ground technique** (fig. 4.18), had been introduced. This technique is similar to the red-figure, with the surface covered with a white slip, creating a dull, matte finish. Figures are then carefully painted onto the vase with a fine brush in a freer manner with fluid lines.

Julie A. Felton / Shutterstock.com

Fig. 4.15 Protogeometric skyphos, tenth century

Rogers Fund, 1948, The Metropolitan Museum of Art

Fig. 4.16 Terracotta pyxis (box with lid), mid-eighth century, Attic.

to be structured. Pythagoras (c. 580 to 500 BCE), a physical philosopher, created his famous theorem that in a right triangle, the square of the hypotenuse is equal to the sum of the squares of the other two sides.

Rogers Fund, 1906, The Metropolitan Museum of Art

Fig. 4.17 Terracotta hydria (water jar), c. 510 to 500 BCE, Attic.

Fig. 4.18 Terracotta pyxis (box), c. 465 to 460 BCE, Attic.

Rogers Fund, 1907, The Metropolitan Museum of Art

Drama and Music

The Greeks invented drama. Many tragedies and comedies, such as Euripides' *Medea*or and Aristophanes' *The Clouds*, are as compelling today as when they were first preformed. To understand Greek theater, however, the audience must have a good imagination. Modern society views the theater as a form of entertainment, but during Greek times, theater was the mechanism for communal expression of the society's religious beliefs accompanied by music, dance, and drama.

The theater was such an integral part of Greek life that three annual religious festivals took place in different cities. Contests were held at these festivals, where three playwright winners were chosen for production. Once the winners were selected, each playwright was assigned a chief actor and a patron who paid all the expenses for the production. The winner, in most cases, functioned as the director, choreographer, and musical composer, and frequently played the leading role as well.

Music in ancient Greece was connected with festivals, both religious and social events, and dramas. Greek dramas such as the Homeric epics consisted of long narratives where stories were told through chants accompanied by a **lyre** (fig. 4.20), a stringed musical instrument. Musicians competed at festivals, much like athletes, for honor and prestige. The ancient Greek philosopher Plato described music as a means of influencing human behavior, character, and emotions. Aristotle espoused his perception of music as having a binding force on the maturity of our inner being.

Literature

Early Greek literature included several epic tales. An **epic** is a long poem where characters are typically high born and experience a series of adventures. The hero may have human faults, but he must possess superhuman courage and strength as well as greatness of character. Many adventures within an epic involve great wars, battles, fighting monsters, and deities who often play a role in the epic. The action, however, cannot be gratuitous: they must be important ones in the history of the rave and the hero must be in some sense a savior of that nation or race. Thus, the hero is not only a great individual but also a cultural icon.

The epics *Iliad* and *Odyssey* mark the beginning of Greek poetry. The original purpose of these two epics was to sing the famous deeds of men and to teach people in a pleasurable way about the great heroes of their culture. Historians call the author of these works Homer, but they know nothing about him. Early Greeks believed he was blind, and scholars believe he lived in Iona, located in Asia Minor, not Greece, but none is proven as factual.

The *Iliad* transmits a fraction of the events that occurred during the 10-year

Societal Emphasis

Socrates (fig. 4.19) is considered the "Father of Ethics," as he pursed wisdom to unearth the good, just, and beautiful of human existence. For this, he was brought to trial in 399 BCE on charges of impropriety against the gods and corrupting the youth. At his trial, he acknowledged causing discontent, but believed that it was his duty to help others and for himself to seek the truth. Modern society is most familiar with his famous adage "Know thyself" as a means for self-examination to attain insight. His method of dialectic inquiry, or "Socratic Method," is widely used to guide others to a more balanced understanding of who they are in relation to the world around them.

© Kamira/Shutterstock.com

Fig. 4.19 Portrait Bust of Socrates. c. 350 BCE

Trojan War. King Agamemnon of Mycenae began the war along with his many allies around 1200 BCE. In the opening lines of the epic, a narration referred to as "the rage of Achilles" conveyed how the troops were already encamped on the shores of Troy. The poem is most notable for painting a fearless verbal account of the realities of war. Greek soldiers were commonly depicted as demonstrating *areté*, or virtue, the most important of all Greek values.

After the fall of Troy to the Greek army via the famous Trojan Horse events, as described in the *Odyssey*, Odysseus leaves Troy to sail for Ithaca, his home. His journey home takes 10 years and along the way he encounters giants, monsters, and seductive enchantresses. While anger and lust are the driving forces in the *Iliad*, it was love and familial attachment that encouraged Odysseus to continue his quest to reunite with his wife, Penelope, and son, Telemachus.

Religion

Many god and goddess ruled over the Greek world, but there are only 12 major

Fletcher Fund, 1956, Metropolitan Museum of Art

Fig. 4.20 Terracotta jar with lyre musician, c. 490 BCE, Attic.

gods believed to live on Mount Olympus. Mount Olympus, in northeastern Greece, is the traditional location where the Greek gods resided. Zeus, the chief god, headed the **pantheon**, or family of gods (chat 4.1). He was viewed as a model for the tyrants who ruled each individual polis. Because of his multiple love affairs, his wife Hera was often mistrustful and sought revenge. In many ways, their marital relationship echoes the inevitable weakness of human relationships. The many jealous fits of rage of the gods and goddesses mirrored the multitude of hostilities seen as impeding civic harmony. These antagonistic behaviors provoked the many wars throughout ancient Greece. No matter what happened between the gods, the Greeks took extra precautions not to overstep their boundaries and compete with the gods. In competing with the gods, a Greek would be demonstrating the sin of **hubris**, or pride, and the gods would not offer protection to them.

Philosophy

Greek philosophy has a long history beginning before Socrates, and these philosophers are known as the **per-Socratics**. These earliest philosophers were mindful in how the natural universe was described. A tradition began by Thales of Miletus who is known for simple questions, such as "What is everything made of? How does it work?" Because of their line of questioning, they were scientists who yearned to investigate the natural world to derive an understanding. Early philosophers included Pythagoras, Leucippus, Democritus of Thrace, and Heraclitus.

A second philosophical tradition known as the **Sophists**, or "wise man," arose during Socrates's time. The Sophists moved from a quest of "What do we know?" to "How do we know what we think we know?" and "How can we trust what we think we know?" Their focus was not on the natural world they lived but on the human mind. For them, the human mind contained weaknesses,

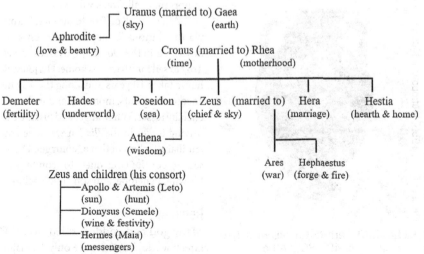

Greek Pantheon

Chart 4.1 Greek Pantheon family tree

they devoted themselves to investigating what we now call **humanism**, or actions of human begins. A general practice of the Sophists was to demand payment for what they taught others.

Socrates (fig. 4.19) had little in common with the Sophists, as he despised almost everything they stood for and did not charge for his teaching. The only common ground the two had was their use of rhetorical debate to resolve questions or disputes. Socrates employed the **dialectic method**, or a process of inquiry using a question-and-answer–style dialogue to disclose unexamined thoughts and solutions. He believed that one's true meaning resided in one's **psyche**, or the seat of both character and intellect, and through **inductive reasoning**, or moving from specific to general to universal truths, one could understand one's ideals and aspirations. The rise of Socrates and the Sophist's intellectual geniuses could have flourished only under the democracy of the polis, as it was a crime of impiety to question openly as they did. Sadly, in 399 BCE, his teachings would end, see Societal Emphasis section.

During his lifetime, Socrates never solidified his ideas in writing. We only know of his thinking through the dialogue writings his greatest student Plato (c. 428 to 347 BCE) gave to the world. The dialogues are presented in a master and pupil format and we learn how the two have much in common regarding how the psyche is immortal and immutable. Plato continued the advancement of these thoughts by setting forth the new concept of **idealism**, or a seeking of pure ideas untainted by material reality, in *The Republic*. The work outlines an ideal state as a reaction to Socrates's death sentence, not because Plato disagreed with Socrates but because he believed that his death was unjust. While *The Republic* was free of sexual acts, *The Symposium* recounts the nature of love,

homoerotic love in particular. Each party guest gave a speech about the nature of love and desire per the god Eros.

A student of Plato's named Aristotle (384 to 322 BCE) would disagree with his teacher's position toward idealism. Reality did exist in the material world itself, and through careful observation, universal truths were discoverable. The observational method Aristotle used is known as **empirical investigation**, a close resemblance to the modern investigational process known as the **scientific method**. His empirical investigation created specific procedures for testing theories about the natural world allowing him to study astronomy, biology, zoology, physics, politics, logic, ethics, and literary expression. By 350 BCE, his observations about lunar eclipses helped him conclude that the Earth was round and motivated Alexander of Macedonia to cross into India. He used the philosophical method of **syllogism**, or a means for drawing a conclusion from two premises, to show unity of action and time as having ethical ramifications:

All men are mortal;
Socrates is a man;
Therefore, Socrates is a mortal.

The *Nicomachean Ethics* was written for and edited by Aristotle's son Nicomachus as an attempt to define Greek society. A definition meant to express what Greek society's purpose was in the creation of polis from the very beginning. For Aristotle, they were striving for the good life. He uses a simple syllogism to find middle ground between two extremes:

The way to happiness is through
the pursuit of moral virtue;
The pursuit of the good life is the
way to happiness;

Therefore, the good life consists in the pursuit of moral virtue.

It was through balance, Aristotle reasoned, that the good life was reached. The Roman poet Horace came to call Aristotle's good life the **Golden Mean**, or middle ground between two extremes.

Greek Legacy

The "Golden Age of Greece" saw much advancement in art, architecture, sculpture, literature, dance, music, and government. Greeks' cultural advancements were pure ingenuity on the part of those who lived within the society. Each member of classical Greek society was propelled to push the limits of creativity and human understanding further than it had even before. Even the Athenians realized the excellence of their sculptures as they were actively striving to create images more naturalistic with an increasingly perfect sense of proportion.

The rise of democracy in Athens is reflected not only in the magnificent ruins of the city but also in the spread of those ideals into other parts of the world. Each aforementioned promoter of democracy—from Solan, who established the thought process from creating democracy, to Alexander the Great, who spread the culture and ideas as he conquered new territories—played a hand in creating a cultural, political, and social structure on the basis of logical and philosophical morals in order to create a world rooted in equality for those living within its society. The ideas and culture created by the Greeks was first transferred to the Romans, who would themselves continue shaping the course of Western culture and history.

Critical Thinking

Examine the three dominant civilizations of the early Aegean period.

Describe the founding myths of the Minoans.

Analyze how the polis contributed to the rise of democracy.

Explain the difference between Classical and Hellenistic Greece eras.

Illustrate how artistic expression transformed Greece into a highly cultured civilization.

Examine how Pericles, Socrates, Plato, and Aristotle contributed to Greek advancements.

Consider how the Greek gods directed actions among the Greeks.

ONLINE RESOURCES

Culture Overview of Ancient Greece

https://www.khanacademy.org/humanities/ancient-art-civilizations/greek-art/beginners-guide-greece/a/ancient-greece-an-introduction

Frescoes at Akrotiri Video

https://smarthistory.org/thera/

Mask of Agamemnon **Video**

https://smarthistory.org/mask-of-agamemnon/

Birth of Democracy

https://www.history.com/topics/ancient-greece/ancient-greece-democracy

The Rise of Pericles as a Leader

https://www.britannica.com/biography/Pericles-Athenian-statesman

Kritios Boy **Video**

https://smarthistory.org/kritios-boy/

Riace Warriors

https://smarthistory.org/riace-warriors/

The Alexander Sarcophagus **Video**

https://smarthistory.org/the-alexander-sarcophagus/

Dying Gaul **and** *Ludovisi Gaul* **Video**

https://smarthistory.org/dying-gaul/

Ancient Greek Architecture

https://www.ancient.eu/Greek_Architecture/

Ancient Greek Pottery

https://www.khanacademy.org/humanities/ancient-art-civilizations/greek-art/greek-pottery/a/greek-vase-painting-an-introduction

Ancient Greek Drama and Theatre

http://www.ancientgreece.com/s/Theatre/

Ancient Greek Literature by Period

https://www.ancient.eu/Greek_Literature/

Greek Gods and Religious Practices

https://www.metmuseum.org/toah/hd/grlg/hd_grlg.htm

Ten Influential Ancient Greek Philosophers

https://www.ancienthistorylists.com/greek-history/top-10-ancient-greek-philosophers/

Ancient Rome: From a Republic to an Empire

Fig. 5.1 Interior of an ancient Etruscan tomb, Cerveteri, Italy, seventh to third century BCE

Michele Alfieri / Shutterstock.com

Knowledge Acquisition

◆ *Appreciate the role of Roman architects, sculptors, painters, dramatists, philosophers, and poets.*

◆ *Evaluate achievements made during the Roman Empire era including the Colosseum, Column of Trajan, Pantheon, Virgil's Aeneid, and wall paintings.*

◆ *Discover insight into key Roman figures, including Augustus, Trajan, Marcus Aurelius, and Constantine along with their historical significance.*

◆ *Discover how Ancient Rome connects humanistic expressions from around the world to its own artistic, cultural, literary, and political interests.*

SETTING THE SCENE

There are difficulties in arguing that the Romans were not profoundly shaped by Greek influences; the Greeks colonized the southern Italian peninsula, transferring their art, literature, philosophy, and religion to the region. Despite the influence of the Greeks, the Romans were their own people, industrious and practical in taking pieces of other cultures around them and changing these to something distinctly Roman. The area occupied by Rome was vast at the height of the Roman Empire (map 5.1) but other people lived in these areas prior to their territories being conquered by the Romans, including the Etruscans, Latins and Celts.

The contributions to Western culture by the Romans are substantial. Numerous scholars believe that their advancements in the fields of politics, law, and engineering are unparalleled. In addition to the arch, Romans invented our modern-day alphabet system with exception to the letters C, G, U, and W, the 12-month calendar, and even the blueprint for Europe's roadways.

ROMAN ORIGINS

In the central part of the Italian peninsula, a group of people whom historians call the Etruscans developed a civilization roughly coinciding with the Greek Archaic period. Little is known about their people, but their influence on the Romans was nearly as profound as the influence of the Greeks on Roman culture and society. They were skilled at working in metals and stone.

Etruscan Civilization

Etruria, corresponding to modern-day Tuscany, was the homeland of the Etruscans. With less than 10,000 surviving texts, it is clear that their language was unique and not linked to any other European language. Most of the words within the texts have yet to be translated, even though scholars know how to pronounce the words. The evidence

Peter Hermes Furian / Shutterstock.com

The Roman Empire
in 117 AD, at its greatest extent

Map 5.1 Ancient Rome at its zenith, second century CE

of who they were is observed in painted pottery, a black ceramic called **bucchero**, bronze and jewelry works, oil, and the wine they exported. The greatest clues to who they are reside in tombs called **tumulus** (fig. 5.1 and fig. 5.2, interior and exterior, respectively), a structure covered with earth patricianly below and aboveground with a rounded shape. The arch appears to have come from the Etruscans; the Romans perfected the arch and developed the dome.

Art

Three primary means for appreciating who the Etruscans are exist in their construction of temples, tombs, and sculptures. Temples closely resembled those of the Greeks with a raised platform consisting of more than three steps only on one side. No intact structures remain, but written description by the ancient Roman Vitruvius, an author and architect, helped explain their formation. The Etruscans' front porch was deep,

whereas the Greeks were shallow. The Greeks surrounded the entire temple with columns in the form of a peristyle hall (similar to the Egyptian hypostyle, fig. 3.12), whereas the Etruscans did not. One advancement was made in the creation of a new column design. The Doric order was transformed into the **Tuscan order** by the inclusion of a base but no fluting on the column (fig. 5.3).

Etruscan tombs reveal most of the clues as to who these ancient ancestors of the Romans were. Tombs for the dead were buried away from the city but laid out in the configuration of a city. Each tomb was rectangular and possibly resembled the common domestic architecture style of an Etruscan home. Walls were decorated with plaster reliefs of everyday items, such as kitchen instruments, tools, and other necessities (fig. 5.1). Their sense of the afterlife was similar to the Egyptians, of whom they traded goods.

Inside many tombs, there are examples of their ability to create unique life-size

francesco de marco / Shutterstock.com

Fig. 5.2 Exterior of an Ancient Etruscan tomb, Cerveteri, Italy, seventh century BCE

Fig. 5.3 Tuscan order, replica

and miniature sculptures made of terracotta. The life-size sculptures are known as **sarcophagi**, or coffins, and the miniatures are called **cinerary urn**, or a container for holding ashes. Sarcophagi show reclining couples where the couples are animated with their hands seeming to be in motion, while other examples are more relaxed. In the cinerary urn (fig. 5.4), there is a single reclining figure with a battle scene depicted below an Etruscan using a plow as a weapon. Scholars believe that the scene is possibly of the Greek hero Echetlos, who aided the Athenians during the Battle of Marathon in 490 BCE. However, no satisfactory rationalization explains why this Greek legend would be so popular in Etruria.

Etruscan Founding Myth

Rome had competing legends of its founding myth. One originates from Etrusia dating to 759 BCE as recorded by Livy (59 BCE to 17 CE) in his *History of Rome*. The legend holds that Romulus and Remus, infant twins, were abandoned on the bank of the Tiber to die but saved by a she-wolf (fig. 5.5) who suckled them and were later raised by a shepherd. Once the twins grew older, they built a city on the Palatine Hill above the spot in which they were found. In time, they feuded over who would rule the city. In a rage of anger and heated passion, Romulus killed Remus. Romulus was the sole ruler and the city was named in his honor as the founder.

ROME'S INAUGURATION

The traditional founding of Rome dates to 753 BCE, but the Etruscan kings were not expelled until 509 BCE by the Latin-speaking Romans. Until the assassination of Julius Caesar by the senators in 44 BCE, the Roman Republic flourished. A 17-year civil war ensued, leaving Augustus to rule over the newly founded Roman Empire. The Empire would reach its greatest height in power during the second century CE as Roman troops conquered vast territories.

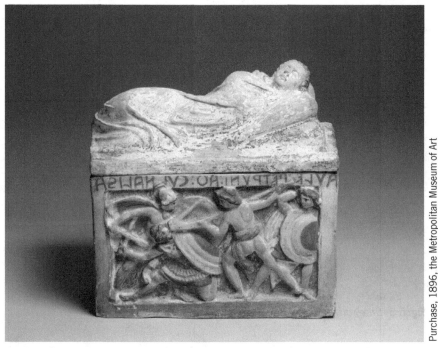

Fig. 5.4 Terracotta cinerary urn, Etruscan, second century BCE.

Roman Republic

The **imperium**, or supreme power, resided with the **patricians**, or landowning aristocrats holding rights and privileges because of being elected to a high Rome office such as judges, lawyers, priests, and magistrates. Another class of citizens was the **plebeians**, who were poor and not only tilled the land and herded the livestock but also worked for wages on the basis of their skills. Because of differences in the social and economic status between the two classes in Rome, plebeians in early Roman period selected a patrician as a patron. A system known as "patronage" developed into a paternalistic relationship between the patricians and plebeians.

In time, the plebeians came to resent the system. In a situation similar to that facing Solon in Greece, Roman peasants were falling into deep debt and were forced to sell their families into slavery. The resulting plebeian protest, called *The Conflict of the Orders,* came when plebeians refused to participate in the military. Rome was at war, and the patricians could not fill the ranks. Between 494 and 287 BCE, plebeians engaged in five separate strikes led by wealthier landowners of their class, slowly earning the right to elect their leaders, called **tribune**, who brought grievances to the consuls and Senate. They could also veto new laws.

Furthermore, by 450 BCE, Roman law was codified and displayed in public. The new governing body was called the 12 Tables; it governed public and private behavior and was seen as the beginning of European law. Among different codes of the 12 Tables, the following governed the actions of Romans: Let them keep the road in order. If they have not paved it, a man may drive his team where he likes. He who commits treason is considered one who shall have roused up a public enemy or

Fig. 5.5 *She-wolf*, c. 50 to 480 BCE, bronze with glass-paste eyes

Ammit Jack / Shutterstock.com

Global Focal Point

Much like the Roman Empire, Chinese emperors as early as the fifth century BCE fortified their territories with walls (fig. 5.6) to protect their people from northern foreign invasions. Wall building reached its peak during the Ming Dynasty. The Great Wall of China stretches more than 4000 miles in total. The wall is 20 to 26 feet tall with towers roughly every 600 feet reaching 40 feet in height with a base width of 13 to 23 feet and a summit road nearly 11.5 feet wide. The wall passes over mountains that ascend to over 4000 feet above sea level and into valleys.

Fig. 5.6 *The Great Wall of China*, North of Peking, c. sixteenth century CE

© Hung Chung Chih/Shutterstock.com

handed over a citizen to a public enemy and must suffer capital punishment. Marriages should not take place between plebeians and patricians. Whatever the people had last ordained should be held as binding by law.

During the early days of the Roman Republic, most wars were considered defensive strategy. Because of experiences with the Etruscans, Rome set out to create a buffer zone. By 265 BCE, they controlled the entire Italian peninsula. Over the next century, from roughly 264 to 146 BCE, Rome and the North African country of Carthage engaged in warfare, referred to as the Punic Wars. Carthage, to the southwest of Rome, was considered a threat as an invasion by sea was possible and Carthage built a powerful Empire extending to Spain. Three separate wars were carried out over more than a century and numerous new territories conquered; Rome emerged victorious from the Punic Wars. Warfare in this manner created a type of cultural class, powerful generals, within Roman society.

The Punic Wars' devastation of the Roman countryside, carried out by Hannibal, had dramatic results in the country. Wealthy patricians remained safe in Rome, whereas plebeians saw their property destroyed. With ravaged land and no work, the plebeians flooded into the major cities. A new type of living space, a multistoried apartment block called an **insulae**, was created to accommodate the overcrowding in major cities. Shops were on the ground floor, with living quarters rising above five or six stories high. Often, construction was not adequate and buildings collapsed or caught fire. Wealthy building dwellers hired slaves to act as private fire brigades. By 6 CE, Augustus created the position of **vigils**, or professional firefighters and policemen, to patrol the city at night.

The entire situation was exacerbated since the wars brought in an abundance of new slaves. Around 200 BCE, most people in Italy were slaves, which eventually caused

a depression of wages and opportunity. The result was a population of free but angry Romans, which erupted in civil war in 133 BCE when a tribune member, Tiberius Gracchus, proposed redistribution of land, a legislation that was blocked by the landowning patricians via the tribune Octavius, whom Tiberius Gracchus promptly removed from office. When Tiberius stood for reelection, noticeably unopposed, he was assassinated by mob senators hired, which was the first political bloodshed in Roman history.

Tiberius Gracchus is among the most important Roman politicians but not for his murder. He sought political change by outside cooperation with the patricians and turned to the masses, creating a new kind of politician known as **populares**, or demagogues and the most populist individual. Traditional politicians became known as **optimates**, meaning best ones or aristocrats, a societal change that would have a lasting impact on the Republic.

In 123 and 122 BCE, Tiberius' brother, Gaius, was elected tribune. Enormously popular among the people, he stabilized grain prices by building storehouses for excess, which kept prices low enough so the poor did not starve but allowed small farmers to continue to sell and survive. In a law provoking the most opposition, he proposed that citizenship be granted to all Italians as a means of increasing his power base. The two laws threatened the power of the patricians; in 121 BCE, Gaius Gracchus was declared an enemy of the state by the Senate. In the final confrontation, Gaius committed suicide rather than allowing to be captured, and many of his followers were executed.

The chaos and murder continued when all four generals, Gaius Marius, Sulla, Crassus, and Pompey, rose to prominence over the next 40 years. The first general who rose to power, Marius, created a new situation for Rome where victorious generals with loyal armies could govern areas of Rome at will. Sulla, on the contrary, was from an old but poor patrician family and was a committed patrician. He eventually defeated Marius on the battlefield in 86 BCE and massacred Marius' supporters. The Senate, fearing a plebian uprising, made Sulla the **dictator**, traditionally a 6-month position where the individual maintained control over all state matters. He alone held the imperium until his death in 78 BCE. Sulla reformed the government by cutting the power of the **assembly**, or the legislative branch, and handed it to the Senate in an effort to restore what he considered the "original" Republic. By the time of his death, the Senate had faced armed rebellion.

The other two generals appeared in history around 70 BCE, and they were Crassus and Pompey. Both were ambitious generals and allied to repeal Sulla's reforms by standing against the Senate, but the alliance was tenuous. Pompey would become the most popular man in Rome because of his military victories and the expansion of territories to the East (70 to 63 BCE). Crassus, a very wealthy man, was universally unpopular. In an effort to gain more power, he allied himself with a brilliant general named Gaius Julius Caesar (fig. 5.7), who used his new ally's money to his advantage.

Caesar came from an old patrician family and had fought extraordinary campaigns in Spain and Gaul (France). Upon his return from Spain, he demanded a **triumph**, or victory parade, but he was refused as the Senate feared his popularity. Caesar's ambitions would not be quashed. He quickly realized that the way to power in Rome was through military conquest providing a general with a loyal army, wealth, and prestige in Rome. Therefore, he took his army to Gaul seeking glory.

Rome had little reason to conquer northern Europe; the people who lived there were tribal, seminomadic, and of no threat. Caesar conquered them anyway, bringing northern France, Belgium, and southern Great Britain into the fold. When he returned to Rome, the **triumvirate** or group of three men holding power was over. Crassus was dead and Pompey had turned the Senate against Caesar and declared him an enemy of the state and was told to hand over his governorship, provinces, and army.

Caesar's troops were intensely loyal to him. In 49 BCE, they crossed the Rubicon River into Italy, breaking the law. War erupted again. Caesar defeated Pompey at Pharsalus in Greece in 48 BCE, and Pompey was assassinated shortly thereafter. Caesar turned his attention to Asia Minor in a conquest so quick that he famously commented, "Vini, vedi, vici" (I came, I saw, I conquered). The civil war continued until 45 BCE.

As populares, Caesar was resented by many in the Senate for his usurpation

Cross-cultural Connection

Roman legion soldiers brought the Persian mystery cult of Mithra to Rome after a long military campaign in Persia. Shrines to Mithra are found as far away as the borders of Scotland to the shores of the Black Sea and the northern frontiers of the Sahara Desert. Soldiers were attracted to the cult because it cheered military virtues, gave merits to self-discipline, abstinence, and restraint against passions, and instilled a sense of brotherhood (chapter 6).

Gift of Joseph H. Durkee, 1899,
The Metropolitan Museum of Art

Fig. 5.7 Gold aureus of Julius
Caesar, 46 BCE, Roman.

Gift of Joseph H. Durkee, 1899,
The Metropolitan Museum of Art

Fig. 5.8 Gold aureus of Mark
Antony, 38 BCE, Roman.

of power and arrogance. Even the greatest Roman orator, Cicero, opposed Caesar. Roughly 2 years before Caesar's death, he reportedly said, "It is more important for Rome than for myself that I should survive. I have long been seated with power and glory; but, should anything happen to me, Rome will enjoy no peace. A new civil war will break out under far worse conditions than the last." He had ruled only 2 years, and his killers believed that the Republic would return, but Caesar's words came to fruition.

Three new men stepped up to form the Second Triumvirate, Marc Antony (fig. 5.8) as consul, Lepidus as a high official, and Octavian as Caesar's grandnephew and general. Civil war again racked Rome. By 37 BCE, what little stability remained was gone. Marc Antony not only married Octavian's sister but also entered into a marriage contract with the Egyptian Queen Cleopatra—an action that dishonored the importance of Roman familial bonds and made a bitter enemy of Octavian. Antony and Cleopatra's navy was defeated in 31 BCE, and the couple committed suicide, forever immortalized by Shakespeare's *Antony and Cleopatra*. Lepidus survived, but as a result of his support for Antony, he was stripped of most of his offices. Octavian stood as the sole master of Rome, and the Republic, for all intents and purposes, was over.

Imperial Rome

Octavian intended to restore order and provide equity to the Empire. Changing his name to Augustus Caesar, Augustus meaning *the exalted or revered one*, in 27 BCE, he (fig. 5.9) began a relentless reform campaign. Ridding the government of "more dubious men," that is, anti-Augustans, Augustus Caesar trimmed the Senate from 1000 to 800 members. He extended citizenship to all Italians. In the elections, the best candidates, often handpicked by him would win. Augustus and his reforms were so popular that he was made **tribunicia potestas**, or tribune for life.

Reforms in Rome after the 17-year civil war did not come easy. Augustus had to compromise between inherited tradition and economic, political, and social realities. The display of typical Roman practicality certainly saved the Empire. Consolidation of border territories was crucial, pulling back in some areas and strengthening what remained. The army's size was shrunk and it was sent to the borders and provinces. Augustus resettled soldiers on farmland and made the army a professional one, doing away with the practice of volunteers being loyal to a single general. Anyone who served more than 20 years in the military received a cash payment from the state.

One area that Augustus was unwilling to compromise was family. The demise of family

Fig. 5.9 Augustus of Primaporta, marble, c. 20 BCE

life was common place because of adultery and divorce along with the cost of living in the city. Quickly, Augustus reacted by criminalizing adultery and passing other laws geared toward promoting the family. New laws required men between 20 and 60 years and women aged 20 to 50 years to marry. Divorced women were required to remarry within 6 months, while widowed women were allowed a year to mourn the loss of their husband. Adults without children were taxed at a higher rate or, possibly, even denied their inheritance. For aristocrats with a large family, political ambitions were almost limitless. To reinforce the importance of the family, Augustus created a large relief monument to commemorate the restoration of peace in Rome.

Each frieze on the alter depicts the values of a Roman family and its celebration. On the east wall (fig. 5.10), a scene depicting human fertility and natural abundance is found. Two infants rest on the lap of the female figure, each tugging at her clothing. Surrounding the central figures is an array of natural abundance from the lands along with the traditional personifications of the land and sea breezes. No matter if the goddess is Tellus or Pax, the theme remains the same, harmony and abundance.

Both were central to Augustus's message for the restoration of a peaceful state for Rome.

The greatest of August's reforms was seen in the massive building project of restoring temples or creating new buildings. He famously said, "I found Rome a city of bricks and left it a city of marble." The result of his efforts would become known as **Pax Romana**, or Roman Peace, which would be the hallmark of the Augustan Age and lasted nearly 200 years despite some emperors who were less than capable of leading.

CREATIVE IMPULSE

Architecture

While the Greeks built sacred buildings, the Romans were more practical. They were among the first to develop city planning on an extensive basis, and their methods of planning were in themselves a significant guide to their values. The perfect Roman city was rectangular and had major streets intersecting at right angles that were coordinated to the cardinal points of a compass. Smaller streets branched off from the main streets, forming a grid pattern, and these grids had different functions of living, marketing, and entertainment. A series of aqueducts fed water to the city, and the center of the town had a forum, initially a place for public speeches, but during Julius Caesar's time, it became a sign of Roman conquest, where law and administrative functions were held.

Romans did not invent concrete, but they made the process for its use better. Of all the buildings in Rome, the Pantheon (fig. 5.11), a huge, circular-domed temple dedicated to "all the gods," exemplifies the Roman ability to manipulate concrete. The dome is 20-feet thick at the base, narrowing to 6 feet and crowned with an **oculus**, or circular opening, 30 feet in diameter. Recessed panels, or **coffers**, were used to provide additional weight relief on the roof. The only light flooding the interior was through

Cortyn / Shutterstock.com

Fig. 5.10 Tellus (or Pax) Panel, east wall of *Ara Pacis Augustae*, Rome, 13 to 9 BCE

Luca Ladi Bucciolini / Shutterstock.com

Fig. 5.11 Pantheon, Rome, c. 118 to 125 CE

the oculus, which reminded Romans of the watchful eye of Jupiter. The Pantheon also offers a perfect example of the Roman's use of post and lintel architectural techniques developed during the prehistoric era.

The arch was employed in every major culture's building projects, but the Romans would perfect it. Aqueduct construction, such as Pont du Gard (fig. 5.12), may be among the most important use of the

Fig. 5.12 Pont du Gard, near Nimes, France, late first century BCE to early first century CE

arch. Some were miles long and spanned great rivers and valleys, went over mountains, and passed underground. In 144 BCE, the first system was built to bring water into Rome, paid for with the spoils of the Carthaginian defeat, and the best preserved is the Pont du Gard in southern France built between the first century BCE and the first century CE. It is based on a series of arches, each arch buttressed by the arches on either side of it. The water channel is at the very top and is lined with cement. Flat stone slabs were placed over the top to keep out leaves and debris. More remarkable, however, is that the aqueducts were constructed using gravity to move the water. The slope typically had a gradient with astonishing accuracy.

Romans built baths, theaters, and arenas. The Colosseum (fig. 5.13) is one of the most famous amphitheaters, where gladiatorial fights and other spectacles took place. The Colosseum's construction was formed via a

Fig. 5.13 Detailed view of an outer wall, Rome, c. 72 to 80 CE

series of groin and barrel vaults on thick walls supporting row seating for as many as 50,000

Societal Emphasis

Portrait busts from the second and first century BCE help place a context around the Roman virtue of **verism**, or truth. Busts during this period were lifelike with a high level of naturalism (fig. 5.14). Romans preferred an extraordinary degree of reality when creating a representation of people. The ideas of *gravitas* (weight), *dignitas* (character), and *fides* (honesty) were encapsulated in such busts. If a person was wrinkled with age or had warts, these were to be shown.

Rogers Fund, 1912, The Metropolitan Museum of Art

Fig. 5.14 Marble bust of a Roman man, mid-first-century CE

with no blocked views and passageways for a quick exit. The exterior columns were decorative rather than functional, emphasizing the scale and height of the structure. A movable roof made of cloth was maneuverable by Roman sailors to provide shade from the sun. An extensive plumbing system allowed the floor to be flooded with water for the reenactment of naval battles. Beneath the main floor was a series of passageways in intricate, movable lifts, and trap doors that allowed wild animals to appear before the audience.

Sculpture

Romans created a sculpture style that was realistic where people and places were represented accurately. They emphasized accomplishments of Roman leaders and heroes, rather than the gods and goddesses.

In Prima Porta, a statue was found depicting Augustus (fig. 5.9) exemplifying the Roman idea and the very embodiment of a ruler as presented in Book 6 of the *Aeneid* by Virgil. Augustus is shown with a sense of **pietas**, or duty-bound obligation, devotion, and respect for family and country. In fact, the emperor was declared the **pater patriate**, or father of the fatherland, by the end of the first century BCE.

Other monumental structures created to personify greatness within Rome were triumphal arches and columns. In 70 CE, Titus (r. 79 to 81 CE) squashed a rebellion that took place in Palestine by the Jews. Titus's army sacked the Second Temple of Jerusalem. After his death and to honor his victory against the Jews, the Arch of Titus (fig. 5.15) was constructed of concrete

Fig. 5.15 Interior details of the Arch of Titus, spoils from the Temple of Jerusalem, c. 81 CE

and faced with marble. On the interior of the arch, soldiers are shown carrying the Ark of the Covenant, a menorah, and other artifacts from the temple.

Trajan's column (fig. 5.16) was another favored monumental structure by the Romans with two types of symbolism: power and male virility. The column, like a triumphal arch, was made of a masonry and concrete platform depicting 150 narrative marble relief scenes of Trajan's two military conquests against the Dacians. Standing 125-feet tall, the complete narrative, if laid end to end, would be 625-feet long. Bands at the bottom are 36-inch wide, whereas at the top they are 50-inch wide. The difference in width was to allow for scenes at the top to be more easily seen from the ground. In total, the column has 2500 figures, with more than three-quarters of the scenes concentrating on harvesting crops, religious celebrations, and building fortifications (fig. 5.17).

Painting

Most examples of Roman paintings are from the cities of Pompeii and Herculaneum, as many were preserved because of the eruption of Mount Vesuvius in 79 CE. August Mau, a German historian, classified the wall paintings into four types in 1882. The **First Style,** a coating or "masonry" style, was popular from the second century to roughly 80 BCE because of the way it imitated colored marble slabs. A wall was first divided into squares and rectangles then painted to resemble marble with no figures or depth of space (fig. 5.18). The purpose was to create an expensive decorative look using inexpensive materials.

The **Second Style,** an "illusionistic style" with architectural features, dates from roughly 80 to 25 BCE. At the Villas of Mysteries, a beautiful mural was painted onto the wall in the dining room possibly depicting an initiation scene of brides into the cult of Dionysus (fig. 5.19). The cult was popular in Pompeii as it was associated with orgies. The novelty of the imagery is in how the figures seem to act and react to each other, just as a living figure would.

The **Third Style,** reflecting "ornamental" or "candelabra" stylization, dates from the end of the first century BCE to 62 CE and

Fig. 5.16 Trajan's Column, Rome, 106 to 113 CE

Fig.5.17 Details of Trajan's Column, Rome, 106 to 113 CE

Fig. 5.18 First Style, Pompeii, first century BCE

coincides with the reign of Augustus. The Third Style (fig. 5.20) reverts to the simple interior decoration seen in the First Style. Most wall colorings are monochromatic red, black, and white with particular attention given to delicate details.

S-F / Shutterstock.com

Fig. 5.19 Second Style, Pompeii, first century BCE

duchy / Shutterstock.com

Fig. 5.20 Third Style, Pompeii, first century CE

The **Fourth Style**, a "composite," "fantasy," or "intricate style," dates from 62 CE to 79 CE when Vesuvius erupted. This style includes elements of the previous three styles by having simulated marble, illusionistic architecture, and large areas of solid color (fig. 5.21). Of all the mural decorations at Pompeii and Herculean, the erotic scenes

Fig. 5.21 Fourth Style, Pompeii, first century CE

are the most eye-catching for the forthright depiction of human relations. Until 2000, all erotic scenes from Pompeii and Herculean at the Naples National Archeological Museum had been accessible only with written permission, which is still the case for minors.

Music

Scholars speculate that the Romans adopted much of the Greek musical traditions. Various mosaics, sculptures, and remains of brass instruments found at battlefields inform little of what the Romans accomplished in regard to music. Romans seemed to use music not as much for plays and dramas but for the backdrop of open-air games, festivals, and military campaigns.

Brass instruments such as the cornu, a "G"-shape instrument, and tube, a long-straight trumpet, were the main sources of music. On the battlefield, musical instruments were used to communicate field orders or as a means for announcing notable visitors. Events at the **Circus Maximus**, chariot racing stadium, and the Colosseum used

a hydraulos to create excitement with the crowd or announced when certain events were about to take place, much like modern-day sporting events.

Literature

Roman writers developed rare examples of unique literary advancements. Most Roman poets used Greek stylization, except for the invention of **satire**, or dramas exposing and ridiculing an individual's idiocy. A prime example is the dramas by Petronius (c. 22 to 66 CE), who presented a critically realistic view of events during the reign of Nero (r. 54 to 68 CE). His *Satyricon* is witty parody denouncing imperial depravities mocking Tigellinus, an adviser to Nero. Fearing retaliation and feeling hopeless as Tigellinus spread unfounded rumors, Petronius committed suicide.

A few lyrical poets, Catullus (84 to 54 BCE) and Ovid (43 BCE to 17 CE), were active. Catullus wrote passionate love poems. The poems reveal an affair with a woman named Lesbia and how love creates a lifestyle rather than a lust-filled, madding state of existence. In *Familiarity: to Lesbia*, we can begin to discern Catullus' perception of love:

> *Once you said you*
> *preferred Catullus*
> *alone,*
> *Lesbia: would not*
> *have Jupiter before*
> *me.*
> *I prized you then not*
> *like an ordinary lover,*
> *but as a father prizes*
> *his children, his*
> *family.*
> *Now I know you: so,*
> *though I burn more*
> *fiercely,*
> *yet you're worth*
> *much less to me, and*
> *slighter.*

How is that, you ask?
The pain of such love
makes a lover love
more, but like less.

Ovid in a similar fashion wrote poems of eroticism, but his works were written in open defiance of Augustus's reforms on adultery. His poems satisfied the loose morals of the Roman aristocrats as found in *Ars Amatoria* (The Art of Love). In the poem, Ovid describes actions one needed to take to gain knowledge about love.

One of the greatest Roman poets was Virgil (70 to 19 BCE), and his *Aeneid* was also one of the greatest. The poem is an epic created to rival the Greek poet Homer's the *Iliad* and *Odyssey* about the founding of Rome by the Trojan prince Aeneas. The actual theme was to demonstrate Rome's greatness during the Augustan Age, to

exemplify the Roman values of *pietas*, "devotion to country and family with a sense of duty"; **virtus**, "fortitude in the face of adversity"; and **officium**, "service and courtesy." Where Achilles and Odysseus were individuals, Aeneas embodies cultural values. Augustus, grandnephew of Julius Caesar, probably commissioned the work as a means of instilling the importance of the reforms he was instituting and to establish the new direction of Rome. Although the poem is similar to Homer's, it is completely Roman and saturated with Roman traditions and marked at every turn by its respect for family and country.

Aeneas represents Roman Stoicism, suffering to achieve a better life, and a parallel is drawn to Augustus' own inclination to surrender himself to the greater good of his people. He clearly wanted to instill a feeling of patriotism into every Roman.

Innovation and Progress

A first-century Greek mathematician and engineer, Heron Alexandrinus, invented the first steam engine. He called the device the aeolipile named after the God of wind, Aiolos. The overall design of the device is simplistic by today's standards (fig. 5.22) with a rotation of 1500 revolutions per minute. Heron's invention was lost to history until 1577, when an Ottoman Turk philosopher, astronomer, and engineer, Taqu al-Din, reinvented the steam engine as a way to automatically rotate roasting meat. Then, in 1769, James Watt built an improved version of the steam engine designed by Thomas Savery and Thomas Newcomen that led to the Industrial Revolution.

Fig. 5.22 Illustration of Heron's steam engine

© Fouad A. Saad/Shutterstock.com

The poem was an epic that came during a time when Augustus was using propaganda to its maximum in Rome. The *Aeneid* shows how Romans were conscious of their own intellect; it was not in individualism but in the art of administrating and ruling that they excelled.

Religion

Roman and Greek gods were essentially the same but with different names. The assimilation of Greek ideas into Roman life provides an understanding that no matter how mighty the Greeks once were they were eventually conquered by the Romans. A major difference lies in how Roman gods were viewed more through a political than a spiritual lens.

Christianity would spread into Roman territories rapidly beginning in 200 CE. Over the next century, the Empire's leaders openly resisted the new religion. Emperor Diocletian (r. 284 to 305 CE) unleashed a passionate persecution of Christians lasting 8 years. An era of instability ensued under the watchful eyes of Constantine I (r. 307 to 337 CE), known as "Constantine the Great" in 306 CE. A decisive battle at Milvain Bridge on October 28, 312 firmly established him as emperor. In 313 CE, Constantine openly tolerated Christianity with the Edict of Milan. By 380 CE, Theodosius I (r. 379 to 395) recognized Christianity as the official religion of Rome and ordered the closure of all pagan temples within the Empire.

Philosophy

Two philosophies were at odds with each other in Rome: chance and reason. Epicureanism is based on the teachings of the Greek philosopher Epicurus (341 to 270 BCE) and promoted in Rome by the poet Lucretius (c. 99 to 55 BCE) in his work *On the Nature of Things*. Epicurus believed that fear was at the heart of human actions, especially the fear of death, which caused all human misery. He espoused that the gods played no part in human interactions and argued all things were propelled by arbitrary movements of atoms as they swirled in space. The philosophy was rejected by most Romans, given its indulgence in bodily pleasure to find clarity.

Stoicism, or willingly enduring agony without feelings, was far more popular. Self-indulgence and debauchery were viewed as easy ways for ridding oneself of discomforting situations. This philosophy was promoted by Epictetus (c. 60 to 110 CE) and then by his follower Marcus Aurelius (121 to 180 CE), who became the ruler of Rome in the second century. In placing one's emotions aside, one could reach what Lucius Annaeus Seneca (c. 8 BCE to 65 CE) referred to as "tranquility of mind."

The emperor Marcus Aurelius (r. 161 to 180 CE) was popular and had influence beyond his ability to guide the Empire through stability and prosperity. His words in *The Meditations* seem to still resonate with humanity today because of his notions of how to live. In Book 7, he wrote, "My only fear is doing something contrary to human nature -the wrong thing, the wrong way, or at the wrong time." His astute understanding of evil was articulated in a manner similar to that of Stoic ideas. Individuals and possessions were not important; what mattered most, according to Aurelius, was one's inner self.

Roman Legacy

Given the scope of the Empire, the legacy of Rome remains relevant. During the early founding of Rome, the governing body consisted of two consuls, patricians, and a member of the aristocracy elite in early Republic, elected for 1 year. The Romans dismantled the monarchy, giving the power to the Senate and Assembly, thus creating the Republic. Two consuls were given the supreme power, or imperium. Consuls also initiated legislation, were head of the judiciary and military, and acted as chief priests. Because of the fact that there were two consuls, the imperium was limited; either could block the other with a veto.

In addition, a consul served on the Senate after his elected term ended, leading to greater cooperation with the governing body. These limitations, however, stifled creativity. Early Republican government was conservative and careful. In 325 BCE, proconsuls, consuls whose terms were extended usually because of warfare, were added.

Rome did not destroy most conquered cities; the destruction of Carthage was an exception. They gave some people limited Roman rights; others received complete autonomy, while still others became allies. All newly conquered territories were required to send troops to satisfy the voracious appetite of the Roman army. Roman soldiers were settled on land in conquered territories, thus providing a local army still loyal to Rome. Any revolt was met with a swift, harsh response. In addition, Rome built high-quality roads to move soldiers and supplies quickly from one place to another—hence the saying "All roads lead to Rome."

One of the everlasting impacts Rome had on future civilizations was the spread of multiple languages, known as the Romance languages—Italian, Spanish, French, and Portuguese, which all stem from Latin. There are countless examples of modern architecture and engineering styles that are directly derived from the monumental accomplishments of Rome. And, legal traditions, like trial by jury, continue to exist and are considered universal norms.

Critical Thinking

Examine what influence the Etruscans had on Rome.

Describe the founding myths of the Etruscans.

Consider the significance of historical events leading to the development of the Roman Republic and Imperial Rome.

Analyze Roman engineering monuments including the aqueducts, triumphal arches, Colosseum, Pantheon, and Trajan's Column.

Describe the variances in Roman wall paintings found at Herculaneum and Pompeii.

Explore the differences between the Roman poetic styles of Catullus, Ovid, and Virgil.

Discuss the two contrasting philosophies of Rome.

ONLINE RESOURCES

Ancestors to the Romans: The Etruscans
https://smarthistory.org/the-etruscans-an-introduction/
Sarcophagus of the Spouses, **Etruscan Video**
https://smarthistory.org/sarcophagus-of-the-spouses-rome/
Etruscan Tomb of the Reliefs Video
https://smarthistory.org/tomb-of-the-reliefs/
Ancient Rome: Romulus and Remus
https://www.ancient.eu/Romulus_and_Remus/
Ancient Roman Domestic Architecture: The Insula
https://smarthistory.org/roman-domestic-architecture-insula/
Ancient Roman Social Classes
http://www.vroma.org/~bmcmanus/socialclass.html
Trajan's Column Video
https://smarthistory.org/column-of-trajan/
Ancient Roman Aqueducts: Quenching Rome's Thirst
https://www.romae-vitam.com/ancient-roman-aqueducts.html
Four Ancient Roman Painting Styles at Pompeii
https://www.khanacademy.org/humanities/ancient-art-civilizations/roman/wall-painting/a/
roman-wall-painting-styles
Hadrian Wall Video
https://smarthistory.org/hadrian-building-the-wall/
The Colossus of Constantine Video
https://smarthistory.org/the-colossus-of-constantine/
Five Key Literary Figures of Ancient Rome
https://www.historyhit.com/key-works-of-roman-literature/
Ancient Roman Religion: A Pantheon of Gods
https://www.ancient.eu/Roman_Religion/

Judaism, Christianity, and Islam: Monotheistic Developments

Fig. 6.1 San Vitale dome interior, c. 547 CE, Ravenna, Italy

Rovenko Photo / Shutterstock.com

Knowledge Acquisition

◆ Grasp the philosophies central to the ideologies of Judaism, Christianity, and Islam.

◆ Evaluate how works of art relate to the literature and are inspired by and reflected in these three monotheistic religions.

◆ Consider the key religious leaders of Judaism, Christianity, and Islam with a keen awareness of their importance.

◆ Discover how Judaism, Christianity, and Islam connect works of art from around the world to their own artistic, cultural, literary, and political interests.

SETTING THE SCENE

Humankind has a fascinating and persistent preoccupation with the origins of our existence and the creatures living among us. Many scholars of art history believe cave paintings are rooted in the earliest forms of religious ceremonies and festivals. Inevitably, questions prompt many individuals to search for the origins of religion.

The origins of monotheistic religion are traceable to the ancient Near East. Even though Hinduism is the oldest written and continually practiced religion, it is believed to have been brought to India by a nomadic people of the Vedic civilization, possibly more than 8000 years ago. The early Vedic religious practices have similar aspects seen in the religious practices of many other cultures. For instance, the practice of performing sacrificial rituals seen in Greece with the sacrificial offerings of a bull to the gods, and also in the Old Testament, there are many descriptions of burned offerings of animals to God.

For the purposes of clarification, we must discuss the three classification categories of religion: polytheistic, pantheistic, and monotheistic, which all date to ancient times. **Polytheism** is the belief in many gods who control natural events such as rain, lightning, harvests, or fertility. **Pantheism** is the belief in the idea that god is in everything, and everything is god. In pantheism, mankind is no different than any other animal. The last religious category is **monotheism**, or the belief in the one and only God.

Vedic traditions are little known today outside of India and the Indian culture. When most people think of religion and religious practices, they are referring to Judaism, Christianity, and Islam. All three of these religions origins are traced to one man named Abraham living around 2000 BCE and are referred to as "religions of the book."

Judaism and Christianity are rooted in the Bible, Hebrew Scriptures for Judaism, and the New Testament for Christianity. Islamic practices are based on the Koran (Qur'an).

JUDAIC DEVELOPMENTS

Along the delta river banks of the Tigris and Euphrates, a group of people religiously different from other Near Eastern cultures thrived. Their religious difference was in the worship of a single god. It is here that God, or Yahweh, created Adam and Eve in the Garden of Eden. After Noah survived the great flood, the same one Utnapishtim survived in the *Epic of Gilgamesh*; God made a **covenant**, or agreement, with him that was renewed with later **patriarchs**, or scriptural fathers, such as Abraham, who is considered the first patriarch. In Genesis 35: 11–12, God outlines his plan for the descendants of Abraham with the understanding that multiple nations would spring from his descendants. The covenant is reinforced throughout the first five books, the Christian Holy Bible, or Torah for Judaism, and forms the laws the Hebrews followed.

Initially, the people of Judaism lived in the hills between the Jordan River and Mediterranean coast until they were forced from their homeland around 2000 BCE. Abraham led his people from Ur into Canaan to escape the Akkadians and Babylonians. During this time, they became known as the **Hebrews**, meaning outcast or nomad. Through their sacred scriptures in the Hebrew Bible, or the Old Testament to Christians, their history and unique relationship with their God is revealed. God refers to the Hebrews as his "Chosen People" as they agreed to obey God's will. A common misunderstanding of the phrase "chosen people" resides in the fact that they were chosen not out of favor but instead to set an example of a higher moral standard that humanity should follow.

Through a series of historical events, the Hebrews are enslaved in Egypt until the patriarch Moses defied the pharaoh and led his people out of Egypt around 1250 BCE into the Sinai Desert. On Mount Sinai, God gave Moses the **Decalogue**, or Ten Commandments. Subsequently, Moses's disobedience to God caused the Hebrews to wander in the desert for 40 years until the patriarch Joshua delivered them into the "Promised Land." The next 200 years were marked with terrestrial gains until they controlled the entire region. The Hebrews now called themselves Israelites, in honor of the patriarch Joshua who renamed himself Israel, and from his 12 sons Israel will arise.

Holy Texts

The Hebrew Bible was originally composed in Hebrew, and some Aramaic, over a 1200-year span. The current Bible was influenced by multiple languages from its origins through the seventeenth century, under the reign of King James I, and the scriptures profoundly influenced English and American literature. The Hebrew Bible comprises three main literary groupings: the Law, the Prophets, and the Writings.

The first five books, *Genesis, Exodus, Leviticus, Numbers,* and *Deuteronomy,* are attributed to the authorship of Moses. Each book provides a historical account of the Hebrew people and their laws. The remaining 32 books are dedicated to the prophets and the narrative, poetic, and wisdom books. Israel's **prophets** were not individuals who foretold their future, instead each served as mouthpieces for God to communicate with the people through visions or ecstasy. Their contribution to Hebrew society was to remind them of straying from any wrongdoing. Traditionally, the holy texts were inscribed on a scroll and placed in a case. While read during ceremonies, the reader wore the **kippah**, or head covering, and tallit, or cloak, and use the **yad** to point at the scriptures being read (fig. 6.2).

Hebrew Kings

In the eleventh century BCE, the Israelites established a kingdom under their first king, Saul (r. 1040 to 1000 BCE). During the reign of Saul, the Israelites were threatened by a group of people called the Philistines. The first book of Samuel describes how young David slayed the giant Goliath with a stone launched from his slingshot. David (r. 1000 to 961 BCE) would become Israel's greatest king after capturing Jerusalem and making it the capital of his kingdom. The Hebrews will later become known as the Jews, as they originate from the area around Jerusalem known as Judea.

David composed music and poetry and is believed to be the author of the Psalms, making him the most complex and interesting person in ancient literature. In the Bible, he is portrayed as an imperfect man who commits transgressions but is then remorseful for his actions. The most famous of his sins was sending Bathsheba's husband, Uriah, to the frontline where he would surely be killed so David could then take the widowed Bathsheba as his wife. The books of Samuel further describe civic deception and familial intricacies observed in modern times.

Fig. 6.2 Torah with kippah, tallit, and yad

Oleg Ivanov IL / Shutterstock.com

King Solomon (r. 961 to 922 BCE) was the last influential king of Israel. Like his father, David, Solomon was the poet who espoused his wisdom within his writings. He is most famous for the Temple he built in Jerusalem and his authorship of the Biblical book *Song of Songs*. The stories are saturated with sexual escapades, secret rendezvouses, and extramarital affairs, as perceived in *Song of Songs* 2:16–14:

*My lover is mine and
I am his; he browses
among the lilies.
Until the day breaks
and the shadows flee,
turn, my lover, and
be like a gazelle or a
young stag on the rug-
ged hills.*

After David's death, Israel split into two kingdoms: the kingdom of Israel in the north and Judah in the south. By 722 BCE, Assyria had taken control of Israel, leading to the beginning of the **Diaspora**, or dispersion. Babylonia conquered Judah 140 years later in 587 BCE. Solomon's temple was destroyed, and the Hebrews were exiled from Judah for nearly 60 years. In 539 BCE, the Persians, whom they believed were sent by Yahweh, invaded and freed the Hebrews from Babylonian control. Upon their return, the Hebrews began refereeing themselves as the Jews.

CREATIVE IMPULSE OF THE HEBREWS

Ancient artistic expression by the Hebrews was limited to their belief in following the commandment of not making engraved images. Some engraved images were made, either to hold religious objects or for ceremonial purposes. In the second century CE, more openly outward displays of Judaism's creativity were established within the **synagogue**, or meeting place. In 1932, an intact early example of a synagogue was unearthed in Dura-Europos, Syria. The synagogue endured because of being buried, as the entire area was, when the Romans created a ramp to attack the Persians. The frescos inside depict various scenes from the Old Testament, including Moses leading his people out of Egypt. Most scholars believe that the synagogues were created with images to compete with local religious temples as a means of attracting potential converts.

In later examples from an early-sixth-century CE synagogue at Gaza, images of an influential founding leader, King David of Israel, are depicted. Much like the Dura Europos synagogue, the Gaza synagogue was unearthed in 1965 after centuries of concealment, not under soil but at the seashore. Highly damaged mosaic images illustrate David playing a harp with images of a suckling lion and a leaping tigress

Societal Emphasis

Hebrew people hold moral beliefs about fornication not only in the context of marriage and for procreation but also as a means for ensuring a sense of commitment and responsibility. The primary purpose of sexual relations is to reinforce the loving marital bond between husband and wife because marriage is foremost about companionship. But, it must also be noted that sexual relations are the right of the woman, not of the man. The practice called **onah** specifically sets aside time for positive conjugal relations that are separate from procreation.

Alexander Sviridov / Shutterstock.com

Fig. 6.3 King David, Gaza, Israel, 508 BCE

(fig. 6.3). An inscription reads: "Menahem and Yeshua, sons of the late Jesse, wood traders, as a sign of respect for a most holy place, donated this mosaic in the month of Louos 569."

CHRISTIAN DEVELOPMENTS

Christianity flowered from the practices and teaching of the Hebrew Bible, given the fact that most founding figures of the religion were Hebrew. Occurrences within Christianity can be understood only when placed in context to its Jewish history. In 80 CE, Josephus (c. 37 to 100 CE), a Jewish historian, wrote *Jewish War's* that outlined the events from the Maccabees revolt ending in 142 BCE to the second Diaspora in 70 CE. In the first part of the first century CE, various people claimed to be the Messiah and preached the apocalypse. Three **sects**, or small groups who separated themselves from the larger religious establishment, rose into prominence: the Pharisees, Sadducees,

and Essences. The Pharisees were associated with the masses, the Sadducees contained the aristocracy, and the Essences were mainly confined to Qumran and associated with writing the Dead Sea Scrolls. When the Romans conquered Judah, they installed Herod as king. As a result of these developments, Judaism would primarily operate in a sectarian manner, which allowed Christianity to flourish after the death of Jesus.

Emergence of Christianity

Jesus of Nazareth was born to Mary and Joseph of Judea, a land controlled by Rome, in about 4 BCE. Around the age of 30, he began to live an itinerant rabbi life and performed his first miracle of turning water into wine. He preached the love of God and neighbor, compassion for the poor, repentance, and what he called "the coming of the kingdom of God," or **apocalypse**. Through his teachings, the foundation of Christian beliefs and values was formed. These teachings were in the form of **parables**, or relatable stories with a moral lesson, such as the Good Samaritan. His followers, who were the first Christians, identified him as **Christ**, or Messiah/Anointed One. They believed that it was their responsibility to spread the word of his life and resurrection by becoming his **evangelists**, or bearers of good news. In time, **apostles**, or those sent by God, would witness as a means of spreading the words of Jesus.

Pagan Cults and God's Influence

Teachings espoused by Jesus were not cemented into a cohesive message after his death. Three centuries passed before a unified understanding of Christianity would emerge. As a result, the religion was highly influenced by various **pagan**, or a term originally meaning non-combatant villager, and Jewish rituals along with Greek philosophies.

Even though Christians did not recognize pagan practices, pagan elements were absorbed into Christianity via **syncretism**, or reconciliation of different practices into a single philosophy. In a pagan ceremony called the **taurobolium**, or bull sacrifice, bull's blood ran over a person beneath the sacrificial altar. The individual was considered "reborn for eternity" in a ceremony that was performed annually on March 24. The pagan taurobolium that echoes the practice of **Eucharist**, a ceremony celebrating the Last Supper, roughly corresponds to the Christian holy day of Easter. The pagan cult of Isis possibly influenced the emergence of the Virgin and Child theme within Christian art. In Egyptian images (fig. 6.4), Isis is shown suckling Horus in the same way Mary will be depicted beginning in the fourth to the fifteenth century CE.

The mystery-cult of Mithra, traced back to Neolithic times, is viewed as a reverse understanding of Jesus and God. The most popular understanding is Mithra kills his father

Purchase, Joseph Pulitxer Bequest Fund, 1955, The Metropolitan Museum of Art

Fig. 6.4 *Isis Lactans*, Isis giving her breast to the infant Horus, 332 to 30 BCE.

to create life. The cult had seven stages of initiation, with baptism being one. The most striking similarity between the two religions is the December 25 birthday of Mithra. In 350 CE, when the date was adopted as Jesus's birth date, it is likely Christian leaders were trying to attract Mithraic cult members to Christianity (fig. 6.5).

Gnosticism Rejection

In 1945, Gnostic Gospels were found by Arabic peasants buried in jar dates to the fourth century CE. The texts are referred to as **Gnostic**, or knowledge, and written by Christians claiming to have secret wisdom and knowledge of Jesus's life. There are the Gospel of Thomas who claimed that Jesus was a twin, the Gospel of Philip insinuating that Jesus was intimate with Mary Magdalene, and the Gospel of Judas attesting to the fact that Jesus asked Judas to betray him. Gnostic writings were banned by the Orthodox Church as **heresy**, or opinions at odds with traditional beliefs.

Fig. 6.5 Mithras slaying the bull, mid-second to early third century CE.

Rome and Early Christians

Christians refused to worship Roman gods or participate in the annual celebration known as the Cult of the Emperor. Successive Roman emperors were unpleased with the new religions strict adherence to its faith. Shortly after Paul's execution, in 64 CE, the Emperor Nero blamed Christians for a fire that burned down a portion of Rome. Over the next 200 years, various atrocities were enacted by Roman rulers to curb the spread of Christianity. Under the rule of Constantine I, in 313 CE, Christianity was officially tolerated and recognized as one of many religions within Rome. Not until the reign of Theodosius I, in 380 CE, was Christianity the official religion of Rome.

Paul's Martyrdom

One of the most influential early martyrs of Christianity was Paul, originally named Saul. Paul assiduously preached the beliefs of Christianity after his conversion in 35 CE to his execution in 62 CE. He brought about a proficient and unified **doctrine**, or teaching, of what it meant to be a Christian. He wrote letters and traveled widely as a missionary, which is recorded in the *Acts of the Apostles* book in the New Testament of the Christian Bible.

The Nicene Creed

Once Christianity was officially tolerated by Rome, the religion needed a unified **dogma**, or a set of principles. Constantine I convened the first **ecumenical**, or worldwide, **council** to produce a document targeted at creating an **orthodox**, or a traditionally accepted, faith. The Creed is not an article of rational observation, but instead an article representing a spiritual belief. Most importantly, the Nicene Creed established a united church on the basis of the teaching of the apostles and was further organized into a hierarchy.

Cross-cultural Connection

Five hundred years prior to the life and teachings of Jesus of Nazareth (Christ), a prince named Siddhartha Gautama was born to a war-king in Nepal. The prince lived a sheltered life of opulence until he fled the palace at the age of 29 to begin his spiritual quest. Under a Bodhi tree he became a Buddha, a Sanskrit word meaning "a person who is awake." The sayings and teachings of Buddha are recorded in the Dhammapada. A number of the Buddha's and Christ's sayings are similar. For example, in Dhammapada 2:21-23, Buddha says "nirvana is deathless" and in I John 3:5, Jesus states "That God gave us everlasting life."

To solidify the religion, the Hebrew Bible and Greek texts of the New Testament were translated into Latin by Saint Jerome becoming the **Vulgate**, or common Bible.

CREATIVE IMPULSE OF THE CHRISTIANS

Architecture

Christian architecture was derived from the designs of earlier Roman buildings. **Basilicas**, a structure as long and wide as tall, were the first physical church structures where Christians worshiped. Before entering the church, visitors passed through a tripled-arched gateway that opened onto an open **atrium**, or rectangular courtyard, with a fountain in the center. The church (fig. 6.6) itself consisted of a **narthex**, or entrance hall, and a **nave**, or central portion, with two side aisles. Toward the rear, a **transept**, or transverse aisle, was used to cross between the nave and **apse**, or semicircular recessed area housing an altar. The apse was where Holy Communion (Eucharist) was performed. The nave was two stories tall and the aisles one story, permitting a **clerestory**, or a series of windows for illuminating the interior space.

A second church design emerged in 350 CE. Constantine's daughter, Constantia, was a devout Christian. Upon her early death, Constantine had a **central-planned church**, or a circular design with a dome, erected as a mausoleum. An **ambulatory**, or walkway enclosing the domed interior, was elaborately decorated with mosaics with vine patterns intermingled with winemaking scenes (fig. 6.7). The imagery clearly symbolizes the wine-drinking ritual of Eucharist, but a connection to Dionysian practices is evident.

Sculpture and Painting

Few free-standing sculptures were made during the early Christian era. *Jonah Swallowed by the Big Fish* (fig. 6.8) was a favored Biblical story. The story reads from right to left:

Fig. 6.6 Etching of the interior of St. Paul's, Rome, 386 CE

© Alexander Sviridov/Shutterstock.com

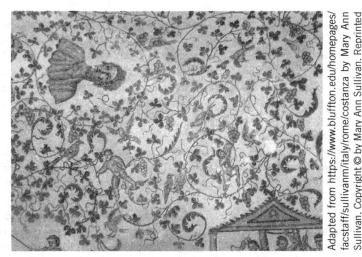

Fig. 6.7 Ambulatory mosaic, Church of Santa Costanza, Rome. c.350 CE

Fig. 6.8 *Jonah Swallowed by the Big Fish*, Asia Minor, early 300s CE.

Jonah is thrown overboard into the mouth of a whale, but she emerges from the whale and rests on dry land. A closer inspection of the whale reveals that it is more serpent like, indicating that the sculptor had no visual reference for the resemblance of a whale.

Christian burial differed from pagan practices because of the Christian belief in the resurrection of the soul upon Judgment Day. To accommodate this belief, Christians buried their dead in **catacombs**, or underground cemeteries found outside Rome and other locations. Miles of corridors with tiers creating recesses were cut into the rock to hold sarcophagi. Ceiling and walls were painted with scenes eluding to the afterlife, in a similar fashion to Egyptian wall carvings. Christianity promised an enjoyable afterlife that accounted for its appeal to people. The message in early Christian imagery was overwhelming positive. Many scenes were either Biblical based or from the life of Jesus and the saints. *Scenes from the Lives of Saint Peter and Christ* (Fig. 6.9) portrayed both the deeds of Jesus and Peter but more importantly reveals a beginning of the abandonment of classicism in art. The work does not provide any real sense of illusionistic space. All figures are arranged linearly with frontal poses with clothes rendered as mere lines cut into the stone surface. Each figure is the same height, even the ones in the background.

Mosaic

Mosaics became the favored media in the Byzantine portion of the Roman Empire. Small cubes of glass, stone, and occasional gold were embedded into wet plaster after it was coated on a wall, ceiling, or floor. Once the cubes were set, space between each cube were filled with mortar. In honor of Justinian's reign (r.527 to 565 CE), Ravenna's Bishop Maximianus and donors constructed a magnificent basilica to honor him, his wife, and the patron saint and martyr of Ravenna, Saint Vitale (fig. 6.1). A unique aspect of the basilica is the apse mosaic depicting Jesus (fig. 6.10). The uniqueness rests in how

Jesus is depicted as a young, beardless youth who rests on an orb, a symbol showing his dominance of the entire world. On either side, angels separate him from the world while he hands a crown to San Vitale and holds the book of the Holy Seal in his left hand.

Music

Early Christian music was founded on Jewish customs but quickly evolved into distinctive traditions. Jewish tradition held that sacred texts were chanted as rituals and were performed with an instrumental harp or lyre backdrop. Choirs would sing the more complex portions and the congregation would sing either "Alleluia" or "Amen" in response. Church leaders such as St. Augustine (354 to 430 CE) and Ambrose (339 to 397 CE) declared singing to be an integral part of worship and helped comfort the faithful by bringing harmony to the congregation. Ambrose composed simple one-syllable hymns for common people to sing.

Literature

Literary works within early Christianity primarily consisted of the scriptures of the New Testament and the writings of Augustine of Hippo. St. Augustine's words are usually classified more as the philosophical fulcrum of Christianity. The New Testament consists of four individual writing styles: The first one is the **gospels**, or narratives dedicated

Fig. 6.9 *Scenes from the Lives of Saint Peter and Christ*, sarcophagus, early third century.

Roman Sigaev / Shutterstock.com

Fig. 6.10 *Beardless Jesus Blessing San Vitale*, traditional standards of beauty were replaced by an abstract standard of beauty, c. 547 CE, mosaic, Ravenna.

Global Focal Point

Irish Celtic culture was transferred when Christianity was introduced to the island by Saint Patrick in 432 CE. Later monks and missionaries drew on the native talents of the Celtics to create an entirely new form of religious artifacts. Tradition holds that Patrick created the Celtic Cross (fig. 6.11) by extending the length of the existing Celtic sun symbol downward.

© spectrumblue/Shutterstock.com

Fig. 6.11 West High Cross, Monasterboice, Ireland, tenth century CE.

to the life and ministry of Jesus, written by evangelists, Matthew, Mark, Luke, and John. Each gospel contains similar narratives while detailing individual experiences regarding Jesus. The **epistles**, or letters to churches, were mostly written by Paul, who was a convert to Christianity a year after Jesus was crucified. The letters were fundamental to establishing Christian doctrine. Acts of the Apostles, the third style, recount the chronological spread of Christianity 30 years after Jesus's death. These works provide an interpretation of who the apostles were. The final book of the Bible, the Book of Revelation by John, is referred to as an apocalyptic writing style. It focuses on detailing the concerns of the end of the world.

Philosophy

Augustine of Hippo wrote two influential prosed works, *Confession* and *The City of God*, that amalgamated Plato's philosophy with the revelation understood by Judeo–Christian society. *Confession* is the first autobiography in Western civilization. In the work, he admits to being a wild adolescence who "longed to be satisfied with worldly things." Much like Plato, Augustine refers to sexual activity as an inferior state where carnal pleasure triumphs over spiritual sensations. *Confessions* highly influenced Medieval thought on morality. *The City of God* written between 413 and 425 argues that it was not the Christians who caused the fall of Rome to the Visigoths. Instead, it was their pagan practices, philosophies, and especially the hubris of the emperors believing they were divine that were responsible for the fall.

ISLAMIC DEVELOPMENTS

The youngest of the three monotheistic religions, Islam is rooted in the revelation of the prophet Muhammad (c. 570 to 632) from Mecca. Muhammad's family traced its ancestry back to Ismael, first born son of Abraham. He was orphaned at six and worked for his uncle as a camel driver for his caravan trade. At 25, he married a wealthy widow 15 years older than himself. When he was 40, in 610, he began a 22-year long period of receiving **recitation**, or the act of repeating from memory, from God through the Archangel Gabriel. He memorized and recited them to scribes, who created the collection of scriptures forming the Islamic **Qur'an** (or Koran), which translates to mean "continuous recitations in Arabic."

A series of events caused Muhammad to flee Mecca for Medina where he united the tribes. After several years, in 630, he returned to Mecca and conquered the city. Two years later, Muhammad would deliver his farewell sermon in March 632, the same year he died. The core of his revelation message was submission to God; in fact, the word *Islam* means to "surrender" or "submit." Muslims, followers of Islam, like Christians, believe humans have immortal souls and that they must accept and surrender to God.

The faith has central beliefs such as God is called Allah, meaning "the One God" and Muhammad is a prophet, who is considered the last prophet in a long line of prophetic traditions extending back to Abraham. The faith does not deny that Jesus existed but considers him a prophet instead of a messiah. The Muslim calendar does not follow the Judeo–Christian calendar, instead it begins in the year 622 when the Muhammad migrated to Medina, which is year 1 for Muslims.

Asiatic nomads, now known as Ottoman Turks, in the thirteenth century converted to Islam and expanded the reach of the religion. By 1453, because of a series of powerful sultan leaders, the Ottoman Turks had conquered Constantinople. Between the seventieth and eightieth centuries, the Turks lost control of Egypt, Lebanon, Serbia, and Greece along with the Balkan states.

Five Pillars of Islam

A tenant of a faithful Muslim lies in the practice of fulfilling the five pillars of Islam by witnessing, prayer, alms, fasting, and pilgrimage. **Shahadah**, or witnessing, is in repeating a single sentence, "There is no God but Allah; Muhammad is the messenger of Allah." **Salat**, or prayer, is recited in the direction of Mecca five times a day and at noon on Friday for men. **Zakat**, or alms, is in giving one-fortieth of one's assets and income to the poor. **Sawm**, or fasting, is a ritual obligation performed during Ramadan. **Hajj**, or pilgrimage, is a journey to Mecca completed once in an individual's life during the 12th month of the Muslim calendar.

Sufism

Sufis' and Sufi orders found around the world play an intricate role not only in the believer's personal life but also in the community's culture as a whole. **Sufis**, or "woolen," is the mystical aspect of Islam. Sufism owes its beginning to the elite spiritual preoccupation started within the realm of institutional Islam, not necessarily by free-thinking Sufis. In the eleventh century, Ghazālī (d. 1111) established an order open to and representing all different classes of society. Institutional expressions employ many of the same "rites of passage" found in later Sufi orders. For instance, even before Sufi orders were created, there was a **shaykh**, or master, and **murīd**, or disciple, relationship. Their relationship was one where an intoxicating spiritual personality attracted disciples from all over.

Another commonality found among Sufis is their gift of **ta'wīl**, or the ability to cleverly convey messages through allegory or symbolism from God to his people. A Sufi is said to act as a messenger on God's behalf for those not able to adequately fulfill the principle of **dhikr al-awqāt**, or to become intimate with God on an intermediate world level. Their goal is to practice **dhikr**, or

remembrance of God, as their central means of worshiping to help invoke the presence of God. While Sufis believe that they are messengers on God's behalf, tradition holds that Muhammad is the last messenger. The practice of Sufism is strictly forbidden in Saudi Arabia as the notion of additional messengers negates the core belief in Muhammad as the last messenger.

CREATIVE IMPULSE OF ISLAM

Architecture

Mosques, or places of proportion, are the houses for worshiping Allah. Originally, mosques were constructed on the basis of the house Muhammad built in Median. Typically, mosques were a rectangular walled plan with an open courtyard for communal gatherings and multiple columns holding a roof.

The back wall has a **qibla**, or a wall indicating the direction of Mecca, a **minbar**, or a stepped pulpit for preaching, and a **mihrab**, or a prayer niche (fig. 6.12).

Fig. 6.12 Prayer Niche from Isfahan, Iran, c. 755 CE.

Innovation and Progress

In 100 BCE, paper, a thin material produced from pulp, was abundant in China but was not mass-produced until 105 CE after Ts'ai Lun was declared the first man to start the paper-making industry. Starting in the eighth century, Muslim Arabs' rediscovery of the paper and its subsequence was a major factor behind the prosperity and the creative fever experienced during Islam's golden age. Paper became the primary medium for calligraphers and artists, who created not only scholarly treatises but also romances, epics, and lyric poetry.

Mihrabs commemorate the spot where Muhammad planted his lance in Medina to indicate the direction Muslims were to pray.

Music

Muhammad and his followers originally viewed music with skepticism since it was associated with carnal pleasures and luxury. Much like the infusion of songs into Christian worship, music became a central practice in Islamic culture during the Umayyad dynasty (611 to 750). Both Arabic and Persian music influenced later Islamic traditions. When Muslims are called to prayer, the **adhan** melodious voice resembles a musical tone. Music is used for chanting Qur'an verses and singing hymns on holy days.

Literature

Like Judaism and Christianity, Islam's holy texts are considered the religion's major literary work. The Qur'an is a book of poetry containing 114 **surahs**, or chapters, arranged with the longest first and shortest last. Each surah begins with the **bismillah**, or sacred invocation, translated to "In the name of Allah, the Beneficent, Ever-Merciful." Muslims are commanded, in the Qur'an, not to create images of people, God, or angels as this competes with Allah's right to create. Instead, artists create decorative designs using **calligraphy**, or a fine art handwriting style (fig. 6.13).

While the Qur'an is the main source of Islamic tradition, the **hadith**, or report, contains the sayings of Muhammad throughout his life. Originally, the hadith stories were handed down orally until his followers began writing them down 100 years after his death.

Poetry as a whole was popular throughout the Arabic world beginning around 700. Poems were chanted by professional reciters known as **rawi**. The poetry of Persia was more lyrical and referenced to love. The premise behind these love poems was to illustrate in a metaphorical way the relationship between a believer and God and was less about human relationships. Persian poems are a commemoration of renewal and hope. In fact, the inclusion of spring flowers symbolized the welcoming attitude between the hot day and cold night climates of the desert.

The most famous Arabic literary work is *The Thousand and One Nights*, which is influenced by a combination of Arabic, Indian, and Persian ethic rituals and beliefs. It mostly reflects the cultural and artistic traditions of Arabic Islam. The stories were aggrandized after they were introduced in the tenth century. The tale is based on stories the Indian wife, Scheherazade, narrates to

Fig. 6.13 Ornamental Style Calligraphy, c. 1285, Iran.

her Persian husband, King Shahryar, night after night. After 250 stories, over 1,000 nights, the king appreciates her cleverness and loveliness. Through Scheherazade's storytelling, her life was extended and her husband's animosity toward women was lessened.

Philosophy

Islamic philosophers, Avicenna (980 to 1037) and Averroes (1126 to 1198), drew their inspiration about the existence of God from Plato and Aristotle's writings. Each argued that the existence of God was logical and provable by revelation. Avicenna's viewpoints married the two Greek philosophers' works with Islamic beliefs. Averroes's perceptions helped join Islamic thought with Greek rationalization. For the medieval Catholic theologian Thomas Aquinas, Averroes's philosophy will pave the way for Aquinas to prove to the Christian world that God is found through reason. Without either

philosopher, our modern world would be drastically different.

MONOTHEISTIC LEGACY

The "Children of Israel," a tribe of Hebrews, later known as Jews, founded the Hebrew spiritual and mystical traditions. The Hebrew Bible illustrates how these people were driven out of their homeland to settle in Canaan, the "promised land." They believed that the Yahweh created a "covenant" with them if they agreed to be his people and follow his will. After being enslaved in Egypt, it was in the Sinai desert that God is said to have given Moses the Ten Commandments found in the Hebrew Bible, which contain the Laws, the Prophets, and the Writings.

Christianity flourished in the first century CE, as Christians began spreading the word of Jesus being the son of God and the world's Savior. As a result, he was crucified by the Romans and rose from the death, according to Christian doctrine. The first Christians were Jewish, just like Jesus. Christianity acquired followers slowly over the first 250 years until Constantine I, in 313 CE, tolerated the religion, and by 380 CE, Theodosius I had made it the official religion of Rome. New Testament gospel writings illuminate the life and words of Jesus, and the remaining portion of the New Testament includes the Letters to the Churches, Acts of the Apostles, and Apocalyptical writings.

Muslims are followers of Islam and believe that their faith is a continuation of Judaism and Christianity, but call God "Allah." They submit themselves to Muhammad and through him to Allah. The Qur'an is their holy scripture, as it is the word of God given to Muhammad by Gabriel. Faithful Muslims must follow the "five pillars" of Islam. Of all the Islamic thinkers, Avicenna and Averroes united Greek philosophy with Islamic belief and thought and paved the way for the Catholic theologian Thomas Aquinas.

Critical Thinking

Discuss how the Hebrews were different from people of other cultures in the ancient Near East.

Examine what influences Judaism had on the subsequent Western civilization.

Describe how the Hebrew Bible helps direct the lives of Hebrews and later Christians.

Explore the events leading to the rise of Christianity.

Describe the Romans' reaction to Christians in the first through the fourth centuries.

Explain the importance and later impact of the writing by Augustine of Hippo.

Assess the similarities and differences between Christianity and Islam.

Describe the tenet of the Islamic belief system.

Explore the distinguishing characteristics of Islamic creativity.

ONLINE RESOURCES

Judaism Overview

http://www.bbc.co.uk/religion/religions/judaism/

Christianity Overview

http://www.bbc.co.uk/religion/religions/christianity/

Islam Overview

http://www.bbc.co.uk/religion/religions/islam/

Middle Ages: Fiefdom to Florence

Fig. 7.1 Mont Saint Michel, Normandy, France. c. 966 to 1523

Martin Froyda/Shutterstock.com

Knowledge Acquisition

◆ *Recognize the artistic and cultural importance made by artists, writers, and composers during the Middle Ages.*

◆ *Evaluate major achievements advanced during the Middle Ages including the rise of monasticism, development of feudalism, cathedral architecture, music, troubadour poetry, and Dante Alighieri's Divine Comedy.*

◆ *Discover insight into key figures of the Middle Ages including Charlemagne, Peter Abelard, and Thomas Aquinas.*

◆ *Assess the role of women during the Middle Ages.*

◆ *Explore the advancements made in painting including Cimabue, Duccio, and Giotto.*

SETTING THE SCENE

The Middle Ages span the fall of Rome in the late fifth century until the mid-fifteenth century in Northern European areas. Often called the *Medieval Era,* the Middle Ages are divided into early, high, and later periods. Early Middle Ages (550 to 1000) are characterized by sparse populations and basic agricultural cultivations. In contrast, the High Middle Ages (1000 to 1300) witnessed population growth, urbanization, and commercial expansion. Finally, the Later Middle Ages (1300 to 1450) were viewed as perilous times as the spread of the Black Plague devastated many regions in the fourteenth century, resulting in the loss of between one-quarter and one-half of the population of Europe.

EARLY MIDDLE AGES

As Rome withdrew its stronghold, many of the areas it dominated returned to their **pagan practices**, or those against established Christian practices, as seen at Sutton Hoo in England, which offers a unique glimpse into Anglo-Saxon artistry and culture in the 600s. As time progressed, the "Dark Ages" took hold from the sixth to eighth centuries, only to pave way for the Carolingian Renaissance under the rule of Charlemagne in the late 700s. By 843, the empire Charlemagne created had dissolved, and the Ottonian Empire emerged.

ANGLO-SAXON CULTURE

A burial mound at Sutton Hoo and jewelry made in Kent provide some of the best-preserved understandings of life after Roman powers diminished in the region. Artifacts unearthed at Sutton Hoo show evidence of a chief or lord and the use of **feudalism**, or a loyalty system between a nobleman and people who worked their land. Feudalism was based on the Roman custom of patronage but evolved into an economic and political system that encased the cultural ebbs and flows. A nobleman controlled a **fiefdom**, or large parcels of land, and each tenant worked a **fief**, or a piece of land, in exchange for protection.

At Kent, in southeastern England, exquisite jewelry was made using a technique called **cloisonné**. The technique used colored enamel and slices of semiprecious stone set in gold cells (fig. 7.2). The brooch was delicately crafted with gold filigree and polished garnets. Anglo-Saxon jewelry pieces were symmetrical in design with an interwoven spontaneity and highly patterned geometric shapes.

Dark Ages

The time from roughly 550 to 750 is referred to as the "Dark Ages" because of a lack of documentation, denoting the various activities during this time. While little narrative literature is known, **manuscripts**, or handwritten documents (fig. 7.3), have

---

Global Focal Point

Farming practices vary widely depending on the environment a people lived. In Mesoamerican, two drastically different practices were used. In the Mayan lowlands, farmers employed a "slash-and-burn" method. First, the dense jungle was cut, allowed to dry, and then burned to enrich the soil. The newly created field produced crops for about 3 years and then remained uncultivated for 8 years. In the highlands, the technique of terraces cut into the hillsides took advantage of the mineral-rich soil.

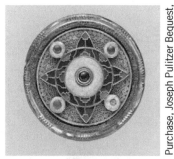

Purchase, Joseph Pulitzer Bequest, 1987, The Metropolitan Museum of Art

Fig. 7.2 Disk Brooch, early 600s.

Purchase, The Cloisters Collection, Rogers and Harris Brisbane Dick Funds, and Joseph Pulitzer Bequest, 1991, The Metropolitan Museum of Art

Fig. 7.3 Illuminate manuscript, tempera, gold, and ink on parchment, Spanish, c. 1180.

been discovered. A considerable amount of care was taken in the preparation and creation of these works.

A division within the Church caused a considerable amount of fracturing. The division was between **monks**, or those who chose to live behind walls confined from the world, and secular clergy such as the pope, bishops, and parish priests. In many respects, both withdrew from the world, leaving very few Church representatives to reduce the isolation and ignorance of their

followers. It seemed as though everyone was withdrawing behind wherever they found comfort. The impact this withdrawal had on society and education remained with Europe for almost 300 years.

In 590, after the death of Pope Pelagius II, Gregory was elected pope. The new pope, Pope Gregory I, the Great, believed that the world was coming to an end, and quickly. For this reason, he did not foresee his decisions affecting the distant future, instead only the immediate. Many scholars agree that Rome was rescued by Pope Gregory I as a result of this shortsightedness. His single most important act was in sponsoring Augustine on his mission to Britain in 597. Augustine helped continue re-spread of the word of God, according to the Holy Bible, back into lands once occupied by Rome. Conversion of pagans to Christianity by Augustine created a unique form of Christianity in Britain, the British Isles, Scotland, and Ireland. In fact, Pope Gregory I urged Augustine not to eliminate pagan traditions instead they needed to incorporate some of the pagan practices into their Christian practices. The idea of combining both pagan and Christian practices was first established under Pope Julius I from 337 to 352 CE. For example, the Christian celebration day of Easter is named after the pagan goddess Eostre, an Anglo-Saxon maiden-goddess of fertility who is celebrated in late March.

During the Dark Ages, Vikings, originally meaning "raiding seafarers from Vik," began invading the British Isles. The term gradually morphed to include all Scandinavian seafarers, Norseman, who raided or not. Vikings used long, sleek intricately carved boats (fig. 7.4) to carry them long distances. The Vikings mainly targeted their attacks on isolated, wealthy monasteries but would devastate and plunder any settlement. Their attacks caused everyone from nobility to peasants an increased need to attach themselves to

Fig. 7.4 Viking boat replica

a powerful lord for military protection. As a result, the feudal system became a fixture in medieval society.

Carolingian Culture

Anglo-Saxons in England were slow to convert to Christianity. This was not the case on the European continent. By 711, the Muslim army had entered Spain and continued to advance until it encountered the king of the Franks, Charles Martel (r. 714 to 741). After the defeat of the Muslim advances, the king confiscated Church land and bestowed it to the landed gentry. The Church was unable to protest since it relied on the Franks for protection. In 768, Martel's grandson, Charlemagne, ascended the throne and expanded the Franks' kingdom. His ambitions for terrestrial conquest were soon realized as he brought the pagan tribes in France, Belgium, most of Germany, Holland, northern Italy, Spain, and Switzerland under his domain. On Christmas Day in 800, Pope Leo III crowned Charlemagne

emperor and created what would be known as the Holy Roman Empire.

Charlemagne created a working model of government to oversee his vast territories. He appointed individuals to govern specific regions, calling them **counts**. Each count was given a tremendous amount of independence and authority. The counts were responsible for raising revenues and maintaining the military in their locales. Charlemagne soon realized this was too much power for one person to have in one's region; in many respects the counts were acting like minor kings themselves; therefore, the two responsibilities were split. Counts were still responsible for collecting revenue, but **dukes** maintained the military.

The death of Charlemagne in 814 transformed the Holy Roman Empire as his son and grandson were not robust enough to hold the empire together. After 200 years of family feuds, two monarchies emerged from Huge Capet (c. 936 to 996) and the Duke of Normandy, William

(c. 1027 to 1087) to rule France. The Capetian Dynasty ruled France and lasted almost 350 years. During this time, the Capetians built a vast administrative bureaucracy. William, a Norman, invaded and conquered England in 1066, which united England and France as one country for the first time. Between 1066 and 1086, Normans built roughly 500 **motte and bailey**, or raised and enclosed, castles to defend themselves from the Saxons. Originally, the fortifications were made of wood and could be built in 8 days, but due to their susceptibility to fire, wood was replaced with stone. The Duffus Castle in Scotland (fig. 7.5) is a perfect example of motte-and-bailey castle built around 1140 and used until roughly 1705.

Ottonian Culture

In German reaches of Charlemagne's vast empire, Duke Otto I (r. 936 to 73) rescued Pope John XII in 961, who in return crowned Otto emperor in 962. Showing once again, the Church needed earthly rulers for its military support. Otto envisioned unifying the Church and State as Charlemagne had. But he and his successor's efforts failed by the eleventh century when the Church rejected secular power.

Monastic Culture

Beginning in the third century, a new type of communal living unfolded, allowing men and women the opportunity to seek a vocation. Monasticism across Europe developed quickly, and each monastery was connected with a particular order such as the Benedictine and Cluniac orders. Monks were to live a life in one location in the pursuit of spiritual perfection. The Benedictine order was founded by Benedict of Nursia (c. 480 to 547). Those who entered into the monastery adhered to four vows: poverty, chastity, obedience, and stability. Their days were divided into eight **horarium**, or hours, with a daily schedule based on the **Divine Office**, or heavenly duty. Each horarium was marked by specific recitations of psalms and chanting of hymns. The order's motto was "Pray and work." The dukes of Normandy from the tenth century onward, and latter French kings, support the development of a major Benedictine abbey such as the one at Mont-Saint Michel (fig. 7.1)

While the Benedictine order was highly structured and devoted to its religious duties, other orders were not very strict. The Cluniac order was established in Cluny, France. Cluniac monasteries became popular withdraw locations for the nobility in France once they reached a certain age or a noble girl was disgraced. The Church encouraged this practice because of the vast donations the nobles gifted to the Church. The Cistercian order viewed the wealth and luxury at Cluniac monasteries against the vows of faithful monks and nuns. In response, they rebelled by simplifying their religious services to the most basic rules and removed most religious artistic expressions.

Innovation and Progress

The first mention of gunpowder in human history was in the Chinese Han Dynasty by a man named Wei Boyang in the second century. But, it was not until 850 CE that gunpowder was formally invented by the Chinese. As the Mongols spread the new substance through Eurasia, it was not long until the powder revolutionized warfare with the use of cannons, rifles, and grenades.

© johnbraid/Shutterstock.com

Fig. 7.5 Duffus Castle ruins, Scotland

Monastic life for women was an alternative to being a housewife or worker but typically was available only to daughters of the nobility. Benedict's sister, Scholastica (c. 480 to 543), was head of a monastery not far from Benedict. Hild (614 to 680), abbess of Whitby, was the first woman to rise to an important position in a mostly male-dominated medieval Church. She hosted a council to help reconcile the fracture between Celtic and Latin factions of the Church in England. Roswitha of Gandersheim (c. 935 to 75) was mostly forgotten until the late fifteenth century when her plays of female heroism resurfaced.

Of all the women who lived a monastic life, it was Hildegard of Bingen (1098 to 1179) who was the most famous. She became abbess of a German monastery after entering the convent at the age of eight. Her accomplishments ranged from writing on natural science, disease treatment, dialogues on vices and virtues, and composing devotional songs. She was the first woman

in a long line of female visionaries and mystics. Pope Eugenius II at the Synod of Trier endorsed Hildegard's visions, which authorized her to write and publish every vision she received. Official recognition from the pope made her vision divinely inspired and thus gave her permission to criticize both secular and religious superiors, even the pope. Completed in 1151, the *Scivias*, or Latin for "know the ways of the Lord," contains the visions she experienced in 1141 at the age of 42.

HIGH MIDDLE AGES

A unique aspect to emerge in Christianity was the concept of the Christian pilgrimage during the High Middle Ages. To a faithful person, prayers were a way of asking for forgiveness, healing, fertility, or anything else. In medieval minds, prayer was more likely to being fulfilled if a person praying was in closer proximity to a holy object, person, or site. Along with a new style of devotion came a new architectural style for devotees to feel closer to God. New churches began appearing all over the Christian world with an emphasis on lifting the Christian soul to the heavens.

Pilgrimage Churches

A way to be closer to **holy relics**, or objects and bones considered blessed, was through the pilgrimage route, such as the one leading to Santiago de Compostela, a destination favored by Europeans since it was closer than Rome or Jerusalem. Pamphlet guides (map 7.1) were created, describing and illustrating various towns and monuments a pilgrim would pass as he or she traveled to Santiago de Compostela.

Romanesque Style

The new frenzy of the faithful going on pilgrimages created a new type of business for the Church while creating some problems for the monks. The difficulty that arose was how to accommodate a large number of visitors to existing abbeys and allow the monks to perform their daily activities at

the main altar. The problem was resolved by a new style of architecture known as **Romanesque**, or in the manner of the Romans, which included the construction of new pilgrim churches on the basis of the original Roman basilica.

Instead of a simple large rectangular building, the new style included an ambulatory that extended out and around the main altar in the choir, the transept, and apse (Chapter 6). The new pathway allowed the pilgrims to walk on the outskirts of the main areas of the abbey and not disturb the monks' daily ceremonies. The newer abbey design, termed a cathedral, started to resemble a **Latin cross plan** (fig. 7.7) instead of a **Greek cross plan**. The difference was in the arms of the design, with the Latin style having one long arm and the Greek style having arms of equal length.

The original design of the Roman basilica was changed since it was still controversial to use Roman ingenuity because Christians had a long-standing aversion to using any style created by the pagan Romans. However, the revival of architectural traditions,

Map 7.1 Way of St. James, ancient pilgrimage path to the Santiago de Compostela, Spain

© Lora Sutyagina/Shutterstock.com.

Cross-cultural Connection

Journeying to a holy location to perform rituals is not unique to Christianity. Buddhists visit stupas such as the Great Stupa of Sanchi to realize Buddha's teaching known as the Four Noble Truths (fig. 7.6). The truths allowed the deceased to cease the endless cycle of birth and death, **samsara.**

Four Noble Truths:

1. Life is suffering
2. The cause of suffering is desire
3. The cause of desire must be overcome
4. When desire is overcome, there is no more suffering

Fig. 7.6 Great Stupa of Sanchi, Sanchi, Madhya Pradesh, India, third century BCE

© DR Travel Photo and Video/Shutterstock.com

reaching back almost an entire millennium, represents in part a lack of technological innovation rather than a philosophical return to Roman traditions. The earliest example of a pilgrimage church made in the new Romanesque style is the Abbey Church of Sainte-Foy at Conques (fig. 7.8), the second church on the route to Santiago de Compostela that began in Le-Puy.

In France at Toulouse, Saint-Sernin exemplifies the new Romanesque style with its enormous size, bulky walls, emphasis on horizontal and vertical space, semicircular arches, petite windows, and dim interior space. The nave of Saint-Sernin (fig. 7.9) was constructed using **barrel vaults,** or rounded arches. The vaults served in creating superior acoustics and reduced the

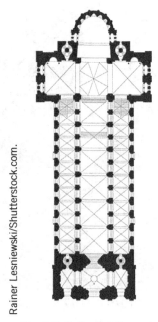

Fig. 7.7 Cathedral floor plan

threat of fire since stone was used instead of wood. The lateral thrust generated by using

stone was balanced by buttresses. This was accomplished by reducing the number of windows, which resulted in darker interiors.

Normandy and England were politically aligned in 1066 when William the Conqueror became king of England. The Romanesque style in England was referred to as the "Norman Style" and drew its inspiration from Roman interior spaces using **groin vaults**, or the merging of two barrel vaults. The **complex rib vault**, or a modified groin vault, creates a rectangular bay with seven-part ribbed vaults (fig. 7.10). A result of the use of complex rib vaults was higher ceilings and spaces flooded with more sunlight, creating a truly awe-inspiring and spiritual sensation.

Crusades

A **crusade**, or holy war, was a military campaign launched against the Muslims in Palestine to recover the Holy Land. The word *crusade* originates from the Latin word *crux* and translates to "cross." For this reason, those who went on crusade referred to it as

Fig. 7.8 Conques medieval village and Stain Foy Abbey, France, c. 1050 to 1130

Anibal Trejo/Shutterstock.com.

Fig. 7.9 Interior of Saint-Sernin, Toulose, begun in c. 1070 or 1077

PHB.cz (Richard Semik)/Shutterstock.com.

Fig. 7.10 Interior of Bayeux Cathedral, Normandy, begun in c. 1077

"taking up the cross" and wore clothes with a cross on their backs. While the long-standing theory is that the Crusades occurred for religious reasons, other reasons factored into medieval motives which included commerce and the opportunity to travel to a faraway, exotic location.

The first crusade commenced in 1095 by Pope Urban II under the guise of calling Christian soldiers into action to regain the Holy Land from the Ottoman Turks. An unorganized army comprised of knights and peasants departed for Palestine without a concrete plan or enough weapons. They were unsuccessful in their attempt and met huge defeat. The second crusade was more organized and left for Palestine in 1099 and captured Jerusalem. By 1187, the Muslims had regained control of Jerusalem under the leadership of Saladin. Several unsuccessful Crusades occurred thereafter with their primary outcome of pillage along the way.

mountainpix/Shutterstock.com

Fig. 7.11 Tomb of Eleanor of Aquitaine, Fontevard Abbey, c.1204

While the Crusades are viewed as military failures, the Crusades had the positive effect of jump-starting trade and the exchange of ideas between Muslims and European thinkers.

Courtly Love

Another tradition that developed in the High Middle was courtly love. If feudalism is considered the masculine code of behavior, then chivalry and courtly traditions must be regarded as emerging from a feminine point of view rooted in the ethics of personal conduct. One woman stands out during this time, Eleanor of Aquitaine (1122 to 1204, fig. 7.11). In one of her first of many examples of selflessness, during the Second Crusade to the Middle East, she and 300 other women dressed in armor, accompanied her husband King Louis VII of France into battle, with the intention of caring for the sick and wounded. Her actions

were viewed as uncommon for her personal sacrifice and social bravery.

It was when Elenore of Aquitaine married King Henry II of England, and reigned as queen, that the notion of chivalry and courtly traditions truly flourished. It was during this time in her life that she was considered the most intriguing woman of her time and the most powerful and enlightened woman of her age. Women were becoming literate, which promoted the growth of **troubadour**, or lyrical poetry composed and sung. Women poets, or **trobairitz**, also emerged. Troubadour poetry was a style originating in the south of France with very characteristic features that included the following:

- A feeling of longing
- Suffering for love
- Wandering aimlessly
- Unable to concentrate on anything but your beloved's image

Societal Emphasis

Hunting parties routinely assembled for sport that allowed young unmarried nobles to mingle. *Panel with Hunting Scenes* (fig. 7.12) depicts a hunt. On the left, hounds and the hunting party depart the castle. Next, women lure falcons as hunters prepare to descend on a stag. In the final portion of the scene, the hunter kills the stag. Secular scenes like this one were particularly popular as they were allegories for a successful hunt for love.

The Cloister Collection, 2003,
The Metropolitan Museum of Art

Fig. 7.12 *Panel with Hunting Scenes*, ivory, French, c. 1350.

- Losing one's appetite
- Lying awake unable to sleep
- Willing to perform any deed to win your love's favor
- Feudal-style loyalty for one's king getting transferred to the lady
- A quasi-religious element resulting from resisting your desires and rising above human nature

Beatriz de Dia, a female troubadour, expressed her regret for remaining faithful to her husband and not taking her knight as her lover, in the following poem:

Cruel are the pains
I've suffered
For a certain cavalier
Whom I have had. I
declare
I love him – let it be
known forever.

But now I see that I
was deceived;
When I'm dressed or
when I languish
In bed, I suffer a great
anguish –
I should have given
him my love.
One night I'd like to
take my swain
To bed and hug him,
wearing no clothes-
I'd give him reason to
suppose
He was in heaven, if I
deigned
To be his pillow! For
I've been more
In love with him than
Floris was
With Blanchefleur:
my mind, my eyes

I give to him; my life,
my heart.
When will I have you
in my power,
Dearest friend,
charming and good?
Lying with you one
night I would
Kiss you so you could
feel my ardor.
I want to have you in
my husband's
Place, of that you can
rest assured
Provided you give
your solemn word
That you'll obey my
every command.

Not only did courtly love have a profound impact on society but it also had an important impact on religious philosophy. For the Church to remain relevant, it needed to harness these newer, warmer feelings to create a new model of compassionate motherly love, and Mary, mother of Jesus, would serve as the focal point. Mary's new role would be seen in much of the art of the High and Late Middle Ages with a plethora of images collectively referred to as "Madonna enthroned."

LATE MIDDLE AGES

Imagine an illness so powerful that people who go to bed healthy do not live until dawn. The disease killed most of the people exposed to it, depending on the particular strain. Imagine a plague that kills an estimated one-third of the entire population of Europe in a matter of three short years. Now imagine that you are living in the Late Middle Ages. Modern medicine had yet to develop, and scientific processes that could explain where the disease came from and

how it was transmitted were well beyond the horizon. This was the world that the people of Europe found themselves in the mid-1300s, as the Bubonic Plague swept through Europe.

From late 1347 until 1350, the Black Death ravaged Europe. It was most active in the spring, summer, and fall months and less active in the cold winter months, but all individuals were at risk of infection. The plague took the lives of more than half of the inhabitants of some cities. Peasants were found dead along roadsides, and ships were washed ashore after their crews perished at sea. Entire streets or families would succumb to the illness seemingly overnight.

Historical records from the time are not complete, so determining an exact number of victims is impossible. Many estimations put the death toll at or above 25 percent of the European population during the height of the plague years alone. All of Europe was impacted. No one could be assured of being spared. Much of this was because people did not know how the disease was spread, nor did they take basic precautions encouraged in modern society to stop or slow the spread of disease.

The Black Death was carried by rats and transmitted when fleas bit the rat. Although rats and fleas are not part of modern daily life, in the fourteenth century, these creatures were part of day-to-day existence. Records show that there had been rumors of a plague sweeping through areas to the east in the years before it came to the European continent, but relatively little attention was paid to these tales.

The idea of isolating oneself from the general public or large gatherings during times of a disease outbreak was an unknown practice. Likewise, isolating the ill from the well, and ensuring that the well did not come in contact with the bodily fluids of the ill, was not a common practice. The treatment of the dead and the handling of corpses were also different from modern practices. The lack of knowledge about how disease was transmitted and what could be done to slow or stop its spread contributed to a significant number of deaths.

The effects of the Black Death were many and varied. The initial human population decrease resulted in scare availability of food at markets. Records show that animals were affected by the plague too. Some reports note entire flocks of dead sheep in the fields. Economically, the Black Death hurt the nobles the most. Nobles were accustomed to collecting large sums of income in the form of either crops or cash payments, but eventually, there were fewer serfs they depended on for payments. In turn, this reduced the power the nobility had in demanding payment for the privilege of working in their lands. Eventually, serfdom was replaced by a system in which the landowners paid those who worked in their lands. The sociopolitical structure that existed before the plague underwent momentous changes.

Another effect of the Black Death was an increase in university enrollments at institutions where medicine was a field of study. Students who had seen the effects of the plague and survived brought new ideas about how diseases could spread or how it

might be treated. At this time, there was also push for the translation of medical texts into vernacular languages from the more traditional Greek or Latin presentations.

Île-de-France: Late Middle Ages

No other region was more advanced in the development of a new architectural style or intellectual inquiry than Île-de-France was. Architecturally, the new style during the Later Middle Ages was referred to as **opus modernum**, or modern work, and **opus francigenum**, or French work. The new modern and French style in the sixteenth century would become known as **Gothic**, a derogatory term used to describe the abandonment of classical traditions as the Goths took power.

Gothic architecture has seven defining characteristics: emphasis of vertical space, large windows, interior spaces filled with stain glass that filtered in colored light (fig. 7.14), pointed arches, slender proportions, flying buttresses (fig. 7.13), and thin walls. The stylistic changes within the Gothic architecture are classified as either early, high, Rayonnant, or Flamboyant.

Abbot Suger (1081 to 1151) of the Abbey Saint-Denis is credited with inaugurating the new Gothic style of architecture as a means for the installation of large-stained glass windows. Suger wrote how "the whole would shine with the miraculous and un-interrupted light" as he believed were the original plans of Saint-Denis. He further produced the elements ascribed to the typical façade of Gothic cathedral: a three-portal entrance, two towers, and one rose window (figs. 7.15 and 7.16).

The third Gothic style, Rayonnant (fig. 7.17), is French meaning to shine or radiate. Saint-Chapelle (Holy Chapel) was constructed under the influence of Louis IX (r. 1226 to 70) to house the holy relics of what was believed to be a part of Jesus's crown of thorns. The architect was Pierre de Montreuil who built the chapel in a smaller size, thus eliminating the need for flying buttresses. Saint-Chapelle has two distinct areas, an upper chapel, for the king, and a lower open space, for lower-ranking members of the court. When the king stepped into the upper chapel area, he was at eye level with the stained glass. Those on the ground were made to turn their gaze upper toward both the king and God.

Courtesy Kristina Jantz.

Fig. 7.13 Flying buttresses of Notre Dame de Paris, c. 1250 to 1345.

Renata Sedmakova/Shutterstock.com.

Fig. 7.14 Interior of Saint-Denis, Paris, begun in c. 1137

Courtesy Kristina Jantz.

Fig. 7.15 Entrance of Notre Dame de Paris, c. 1250 to 1345

Courtesy Kristina Jantz.

Fig. 7.16 Rose window of Norte Dame de Paris, c. 1250 to 1260

Siena and Florence: Late Middle Ages

Italy was not notably influenced by the Gothic style created in France. Instead, two Italian cities, Siena and Florence, were locked in a perpetual rivalry for supremacy dating to the time of Charlemagne. Two political groups, Ghibellines and Guelph, sided with either the pope or the emperor, respectively. Typically, Siena sided with the Guelphs and Florence with the Ghibellines. At the end of the thirteenth century, the pope retaliated against Siena and annulled the city's papal banking and bestowed it to Florence.

Before the rift between the papal powers and Siena, the city had established a free **commune**, or a collective gathering of people for a common interest, in 1125. In doing so, Siena crafted a momentum in the exchange of ideas and goods unlike any other in the region. A common saying of the time was "Town air brings freedom," a freedom to prosper was what attracted a large number of people to Siena.

Siena was divided into three neighborhoods on the basis of the three hillsides within the city. Three consuls were established to govern over the city, one from each neighborhood. Other divisions of social class existed too. **Guilds**, or associations of like-minded people, were founded and their power increased until the merchant guild was organized in 1192. By 1280,

Zabotnova Inna/Shutterstock.com.

Fig. 7.17 Interior of Saint-Chapelle, Paris, begun in c.1241/1243

the merchant guild had gained control of the government and in 1355, other guilds gathered at the Palazzo Pubblico to force its resignation. As a result of infighting for power, the government disintegrated in 1368. Commune life was a thing of the past.

Florence, like Siena, relied on its extensive trade system for prosperity. It was the center for textile production in the West and, therefore, had a pivotal part to play in trade markets. The dyeing industry that Florence created was unsurpassed. Unique to its banking and moneylending were the inventions of checks, credit, and life insurance. In 1252, most significantly, a single currency, the gold *florin*, was created.

CREATIVE IMPULSE

The symbolism that we now associate with the devil started to take fashion after Rome, the Imperial power of the civilized world, had fallen. In the minds of medieval people, the devil was the one who created the darkness and evil around them. The Church would use these growing feelings toward the devil to manipulate the fears of the faithful and convert pagans. People were reminded on a daily bases about the promise waiting for them in heaven and the fiery pits of hell in many different forms of art, from the architecture discussed throughout the chapter to frescos, literature, and other forms of creativity.

Sculpture

There were two main attractions of any abbey: the exterior decorations and the relics they housed. One account by the French Benedictine monk Raoul Glaber explains how the lavish décor is found, "throughout the world, especially in Italy and Gaul, a rebuilding of Church basilicas . . . each Christian people striving against the others to erect nobler ones."

The detail of the **tympanum**, or semicircular section, above the west portal of Sainte-Foy at Conques was filled with images of the *Last Judgment* (fig. 7.18 and 7.19) and divided into two parts: one with angles welcoming the saved and one with demons shoving the damned into hell.

Fig. 7.18 *Last Judgment*, west tympanum (portal arch), Sainte-Foy at Conques, ca. 1065

Weskerbe/Shutterstock.com.

Fig. 7.19 Detail of *Last Judgment*, damned souls, Sainte-Foy at Conques, ca. 1065

Images like these were used to serve as a reminder of the wretchedness of humankind and our perpetual state of weakness, folly, selfishness, and vileness. Jesus is depicted in the center within a **mandorla**, or an oval shape illustrating the glory of his light. In a sermon written by Pope Innocent III (papacy 1198 to 1216), he lists the outcome of a sinful life:

> There shall be weeping and gnashing of teeth, there shall be groaning, wailing, shrieking and flailing of arms and screaming, screeching, and shouting; there shall be fear and trembling, toil and trouble, holocaust and dreadful stench, and everywhere darkness and anguish; there shall be asperity, cruelty, calamity, poverty, distress, and utter wretchedness; they will feel an oblivion of loneliness and namelessness; there shall be twisting and piercing, bitterness, terror, hunger, thirst, cold and hot, brimstone and fire burning, forever and ever world without end . . .

Sainte-Foy at Conques also housed the relics of Sainte-Foy, a martyred child who in 303 refused to worship Roman pagan gods. The saints' bones were enclosed in a **reliquary**, or a container used to house and display relics. In the case of the reliquary for Sainte-Foy, a seated, enthroned female encrusted with jewels, many of the precious stones were gifts provided by pilgrims.

Painting

Manuscripts were handmade with care usually by monks in monasteries. Images within the works are called **illuminations**, or an image with intellectual or spiritual enlightenment, instead of illustrations. Each manuscript was a collaboration between a scribe and an illuminator. The scribe would write text on **parchment** and **vellum**, or animal skin, and leave room for the illuminator to include images. Paint pigment was derived from animal, vegetable, and mineral sources and bound to the surface with egg white or other binders.

Three artists are considered the preeminent figures of the Middle Ages, Cimabue (fig. 7.20), Duccio, and Giotto (fig. 7.22). Each helped the Church showcase the new role of women by painting religious scenes on **tempera panels**, or gesso-covered,

Fig. 7.20 *Crucifixion*, Cimabue, c. 1271

engraved and painted wood, and **frescos secco** (dry) or **buono** (good), especially the role of Mary as the warm, compassionate motherly figure. Each artist executed many Madonna images to capture the essence of Mary's motherly love and compassion. It is Duccio who turned Mary's icy stare in *Madonna and Child* (fig. 7.21) into a woman on the verge of tears with an ever so tender touch from Jesus, giving his work the feeling of humanity.

Music

Medieval music was inextricably associated with religion. **Plainchant** was the prevailing form of musical expression during the Middle Ages. The expression was in singing Latin liturgical texts with a **monophony**, or single melody, without accompanying instruments. The most popular form was the **Gregorian chant**. Other more complex chant forms emerged, leading to the development of **polyphony** involving two or more voices singing in unison.

Literature

Beowulf is the greatest Anglo-Saxon Germanic epic poem recording the deeds and values of King Beowulf set in Denmark. His duty is to care for this loyal **thanes**, or nobleman.

Fig. 7.21 *Madonna and Child*, Duccio, c. 1290 to 1300.
Purchase, Rogers Fund, Walter and Leonore Annenberg and The Annenberg Foundation Gift, Lila Acheson Wallace Gift, Annette de la Renta Gift, Harris Brisbane Dick, Fletcher, Louis V. Bell and Dodge Funds, Joseph Pulitzer Bequest, several members of the Chairman's Council Gifts, Elaine L. Rosenberg and Stephenson Family Foundation Gifts, 2003 Benefit Fund, and other gifts and funds from various donors, 2004, The Metropolitan Museum of Art

The poem reveals a mixing of pagan and Christian ideas. His actions are those of a moral Christian soldier willing to generously

Fig. 7.22 *The Adoration of the Magi*, Giotto, c. 1320.

John Steward Kennedy Fund, 1911, The Metropolitan Museum of Art

give to create unity and brotherhood. His funeral and immortality are pagan.

During the Carolingian Renaissance, the development of Latin literacy was greatly promoted. Although reading and writing were skills some people had, literacy was not widespread until after this time. Literacy was in Latin and was limited to people of the upper classes and members of the clergy.

The poem *Song of Roland* exemplifies ideas of both feudal and chivalric values created during Charlemagne's rule. The poem expresses the values of feudalism, by celebrating the main character's courage and loyalty to his ruler and no one else. The events within the poem are based on actual events that happened when Roland, Charlemagne's nephew, and others were returning from Spain. The story is quite simple: Roland's army is betrayed by Ganelon after he tells

the Saracen Muslim the route the French will take through Roncevaux. As the Muslim army approaches, Roland sounds his ivory horn, informing Charlemagne of its presence. Charlemagne discovers Roland and his army dead and executes Ganelon for his traitor action. Charlemagne and the Muslims fight in an epic battle where Charlemagne is victorious, only after receiving divine intervention, by not allowing the sun to set and providing his army time to defeat the Saracens.

In the story, there is an understanding that it is out of duty Roland will turn and fight the Saracens, the duty to his lord, Charlemagne, and the Christian God. Roland would inevitability sacrifice his life for his king, making him an ideal feudal hero. The *Song of Roland* also prompted the unwritten chivalric code between knights. This code of conduct was courage in battle, loyalty to his lord and peers, and a courtesy verging on reverence toward women. Even though this chivalric code was often broken, both feudalism and chivalry were useful devices for preserving social order and political harmony throughout medieval Europe.

Dante's *Divine Comedy* was the most celebrated literary work during the Middle Ages. Dante Alighieri (1265 to 1321) was an Italian poet who presented a work that he divided into three parts: Inferno (Hell), Purgatorio (Purgatory), and Paradiso (Heaven). In medieval theology, these were three places souls can be sent after death. Dante guided by Virgil, who represents human reason, will narrate his ascent from hell into purgatory. His dead beloved, Beatrice, will guide him through heaven because Virgil was a pagan and, therefore, is not allowed into heaven.

The poem contains 100 **cantos**, or songs, with the first serving as a preface to the entire poem and each part having 33 cantos dedicated to describing Dante's journey. The poem employs a stanza verse known as **terza rima**, or an interlocking rhyme pattern of ABA, BCB, CDC, and so on. Canto one:

*Midway upon the
journey of our life
I found myself within
a forest dark,
For the straightfor-
ward pathway had
been lost.
Ah me! how hard a
thing it is to say
What was this forest
savage, rough, and
stern,
Which in the very
thought renews the
fear.*

*So bitter is it, death is
little more;
But of the good to
treat, which there I
found,
Speak will I of the
other things I saw
there.
I cannot well repeat
how there I entered,
So full was I of slum-
ber at the moment
In which I had aban-
doned the true way.
But after I had
reached a mountain's
foot,
At that point where
the valley terminated,
Which had with con-
sternation pierced my
heart,
Upward I looked, and
I beheld its shoulders,
Vested already with
that planet's rays
Which leadeth others
right by every road.*

Two features are prominently displayed in the poem. The first was a real sense of chivalric duty, much like an epic love story, but not necessarily for a woman; instead it was for God. Second, the poem was written with a political slant as the politics of the day had severely influenced Dante's life and writings. The *Inferno* is where Dante exacts his revenge on his political enemies by populating hell with them according to how they sinned in life. He further argues for the separation of Church and State.

Giovanni Boccaccio (1313 to 1375) and Geoffrey Chaucer (1342 to 1400) straddle the line between Medieval and Renaissance thought. Boccaccio lived during the ravages of the Black Death that profoundly influenced his greatest work *Decameron*, or *Work of Ten Days*. The **novella**, or a collection of short stories, is told by 10 Florentine youth, 7 women, and 3 men, while the retreat to the countryside to escape plague infected Florence.

Chaucer's *Canterbury Tales* was written in English as he began to understand the usefulness of writing in the language the people spoke. Some of the tales and the underlying narrative of the book were derived from Boccaccio's *Decameron*. The book is a collection of tales told by a group of pilgrims as they travel to St. Thomas Becket's shrine from London to Canterbury. Chaucer brings the book to life by including characters from all walks of medieval life, lowest to highest classes. The narrator of the poem helps develop the sense of ironic and satiric portraits of each pilgrim. The narrator does not establish a moral sense of good and evil regarding human motives and behavior. In doing this, Chaucer was able to capture a complex visual narrative, nuanced between elegance and spiritual zest, thus proving he was moving literature beyond the medieval concepts of storytelling.

Christine de Pizan (1364-c. 1430) was an early female feminist who out of necessity became the first female professional writer in European history. She first criticized the favored thirteenth-century poem *Romance of the Rose* as being misogynistic and demeaning to women. Two years later, she wrote a biography of King Charles V at the request of his brother, Duke of Burgundy, but it was in the *Book of the City of Ladies* she actualized the accomplishments of women. In the book, Pizan created an allegorical debate that questions why men demean women and built an Ideal City.

Pizan's greatest literary triumph was in glorifying Joan of Arc in a 61-stanza poem. After almost 100 years of the English and French warfare and thousands dead, a 17-year old peasant girl begged the king for permission to obey the voices ordering her to expel the English from France. Stanzas 35 and 36 describe the joy Pizan felt for Joan's accomplishments:

XXXV

A girl of only sixteen
years
(Does this not outdo
Nature's skill?)
Who lightly heavy
weapons bears,
Of strong and hard
food takes her fill,
And thus is like it.
And God's foes
Before her swiftly flee-
ing run,
She did this in the
public eye.
There tarried not a
single one.

XXXVI

She frees France from
its enemies,
Recovering citadels
and castles.
No army ever did so
much,
Not even a hundred
thousand vassals!
And of our brave and
able folk,
She is the chief and
first commander.
God makes it so; not
even Hector
Nor Achilles could
withstand her.

Education

Bologna founded the first university in 1158, but it was the popularity of the University of

Paris that led to the expansion of cathedral schools and the growth of educational institutions in Oxford and Cambridge in England. By the end of the Middle Ages, eight higher learning institutions had existed throughout Europe. At university, students studied the *trivium* (grammar, logic, and rhetoric) and the *quadrivium* (arithmetic, geometry, music, and astronomy). Degrees in civil and canon law, medicine, and theology were also awarded. In Paris, students were grouped together into a house or college system to help them focus their study efforts.

Philosophy

Peter Abelard (1079-c.1144) was the most brilliant lecturer at the University of Paris who authored the treaties *Yes and No*. The treaties, much like his lectures, used the **dialectical method**, or a presentation of opposing views to reconcile them, of teaching. No question was closed, even in regard to the Church and Bible. He believed, "by doubting we come to inquire, and by inquiring we arrive at truth." A relationship with a private student, Heloise, drove him to seek the protection of Abbot Suger at Saint-Denis. Heloise joined a convent, and in time she served as the abbess of Paraclete, a chapel and oratory founded by Abelard. So great was their love affair that it was celebrated in the *Romance of the Rose*.

Thomas Aquinas (1225 to 1274), a monk from the Dominican order, arrived in Paris from Italy at the age of 20. His first taste of university life was from a 100-year-old debate between Abelard and Bernard regarding the nature of how one knows God. Aquinas took the question head-on, eventually becoming the most distinguished student and lecturer. Like Abelard, Aquinas based his theological inquiry on the dialectic method but referred to it as **Scholasticism**. Faith and reason were in conflict, but most theologians argued that they were from God, and the conflict was a misunderstanding.

Scholastics sought to reunite the two by using Aristotelian observation and logic, not holy scriptures. Aquinas's greatest effort, *Summa Theologica*, written in 1265, took on every theological issue from the cause of evil to selling items for more than they were worth to the place of women. A total of 518 questions with 3,652 responses took 7 years to complete.

John Duns Scotus (1265 to 1308) and William of Ockham (1285 to 1349) vehemently opposed Aquinas's amalgamation of faith and reason. Duns Scotus underscored the concept and importance of free will. He further rebuffed the notion that man could look into the "mirror of nature" and determine God's ideas, purposes, or designs. Duns Scotus believed that man did not have the ability to infer certainties of religions from observing the natural universe. Ockham pressed harder to separate the notion that man could understand God through reason, an idea he believed demystified God. His principle of "Ockham's razor" was a famous doctrine stating that the plainest rationalization was the most sound. Ockham's philosophy would pave the way for later thinkers such as Sir Frances Bacon and René Descartes.

MIDDLE AGES LEGACY

The Early Middle Ages was a time of reestablishment after the fall of the Roman Empire. After almost 300 years of medieval people feeling as if "darkness and evil" surrounded them, and the Church using this fear as a way to manipulate the faithful and to convert pagans, Charlemagne and the Carolingian Renaissance arose to give them hope. The rebirth of creative thought allowed people the freedom of learning not experienced since the fall of the Roman Empire, it was limited, but it existed again. Other political and social changes such as feudal and chivalric values occurred during the Early Middle Ages because of the rule of Charlemagne. However, because of Norman invasion, feudalism would eventually be built around a lordship—political, economic, and cultural powers given to a particular nobility rather than the king.

The High Middle Ages appears in history at a time when rulers, both secular and religious, were focused on building cities, elevating a middle-class society, monarchies, and universities. A way to accomplish this was through the construction of pilgrimage churches and Christians going on pilgrimages. The idea and religious experience of pilgrimage was strong in medieval Europe, as it fueled the imagination and forged the need to travel. It was Europe's need to feel connected with its inherited faith that started to pull it out of the misery and darkness that many felt surrounded them on a daily basis. Profound social changes occurred and contributed to the involvement of the Church. Hiding behind the safety of a monastery wall

as witnessed during the Early Middle Ages was no longer necessary. In many ways, the pilgrim's route was instrumental in reconnecting the whole of Europe. The routes allowed for population growth, urbanization, and commercial expansion.

The greatest advancement that the Late Middle Ages witnessed was human ingenuity. They were marked with change in every sense of the word and would give way to the Renaissance. Black Death, in essence, helped fuel much of the social, political, and economic changes seen in later years. In many towns, traditional burial services were not performed and the dead were buried in mass graves. During this time, **humanists**, or individuals interested in the recovery, study, and spread of art and literature of Greece and Rome, emerged. These people would start to rebuild and revolutionize the Western course of history and change social behaviors to the greatest degree ever seen in the Western civilization.

Critical Thinking

Discuss distinguishing characteristics between the Early, High, and Later Middle Ages.

Describe how Europe transitioned from Early to High Middle Ages.

Explore the architectural changes of the Church and their reasons.

Examine the elements of feudalism.

Consider the role of monasticism, pilgrimage, and the Crusades in the development of art from the Early Middle Ages to the Romanesque.

Explain the impact Medieval thinkers and writers had on secular and Christian thought.

Explore the uniqueness of Siena and Florence during the Later Middle Ages

Discuss how the Black Death affected Medieval thought and daily life.

ONLINE RESOURCES

Middle Ages Overview

https://www.khanacademy.org/humanities/ap-art-history/early-europe-and-colonial-americas/
medieval-europe-islamic-world/a/introduction-to-the-middle-ages

Medieval Architecture and Liturgy

https://www.khanacademy.org/humanities/ap-art-history/early-europe-and-colonial-americas/
medieval-europe-islamic-world/a/architecture-and-liturgy

San Vitale Basilica Video

https://www.khanacademy.org/humanities/ap-art-history/early-europe-and-colonial-americas/
medieval-europe-islamic-world/v/justinian-and-his-attendants-6th-century-ravenna

Hagia Sophia (former Greek Orthodox Cathedral) Video

https://www.khanacademy.org/humanities/ap-art-history/early-europe-and-colonial-americas/
medieval-europe-islamic-world/v/hagia-sophia-istanbul

The Lindisfarne Gospels

https://www.khanacademy.org/humanities/ap-art-history/early-europe-and-colonial-americas/
medieval-europe-islamic-world/a/the-lindisfarne-gospels

The Bayeux Tapestry Video

https://www.khanacademy.org/humanities/ap-art-history/early-europe-and-colonial-americas/
medieval-europe-islamic-world/v/bayeux-tapestry

Sainte-Foy Church and Reliquary

https://www.khanacademy.org/humanities/ap-art-history/early-europe-and-colonial-americas/
medieval-europe-islamic-world/a/church-and-reliquary-of-saintefoy-france

Chartres Cathedral Video

https://www.khanacademy.org/humanities/ap-art-history/early-europe-and-colonial-americas/
medieval-europe-islamic-world/v/chartres-cathedral

Röttgen Pietá Video

https://www.khanacademy.org/humanities/ap-art-history/early-europe-and-colonial-americas/
medieval-europe-islamic-world/v/roettgen-pieta

Giotto's Arena (Scrovegni) Chapel, Part 1

https://www.khanacademy.org/humanities/ap-art-history/early-europe-and-colonial-americas/
medieval-europe-islamic-world/v/giotto-arena-scrovegni-chapel-padua-c-1305-part-1-of-4

Saint Louis Bible

https://www.khanacademy.org/humanities/ap-art-history/early-europe-and-colonial-americas/
medieval-europe-islamic-world/a/blanche-of-castile-and-king-louis-ix-of-france

***Beowulf* Plot Overview**

https://www.sparknotes.com/lit/beowulf/summary/

Dante's *Divine Comedy*

https://www.khanacademy.org/humanities/renaissance-reformation/late-gothic-italy/
  florence-late-gothic/a/dantes-divine-comedy-in-late-medieval-and-early-renaissance-art

Chaucer's *The Canterbury Tales* Plot Overview

https://www.sparknotes.com/lit/canterbury/summary/

The Plague: Origins and Devastation

http://www.eyewitnesstohistory.com/plague.htm

Cross-Cultural Encounters: Indigenous People

© Phattana Stock/Shutterstock.com

Fig. 8.1 Matsumoto Castle; Marunouchi, Matsumoto, Japan; 1504 CE

Knowledge Acquisition

◆ *Examine the artistic and cultural achievements of non-Western civilizations.*

◆ *Evaluate the principal accomplishments made during each culture's expanse history with a specific emphasis on the Western cultures encountered.*

◆ *Assess the impact of key artistic, historical, and philosophical figures.*

◆ *Discover how this era of global connective motivated creative expression for both the explorers and the native people.*

SETTING THE SCENE

Cross-cultural encounters, during and after the Renaissance, gave Europe exhilarating possibilities for prosperity and new advancements in innovation, creativity, and thought. Such encounters allowed both peoples the ability to explore new lands and meet new people. The lands of China, India, The Americas, both north and south, and West Africa fulfilled their insatiable appetite for discovery fueled by their curiosity to know more about the wider reaches of the world. European exploration endeavors did not always bode well for the indigenous people. The previous harmony and cultural uniqueness of these regions was lost, in some cases forever.

A great emphasis in Europe was placed on patronage of the arts and support of the science starting in the Renaissance thru the Enlightenment. The nobility and ruling elite were integral part of this process, but the cost of supporting the explorations was high. There was competition among nations, each vying to support the best craftsmen and innovators. Growing nationalistic pride and increasing interest in religious agendas of the Reformation and the Counter-Reformation (Chapter 10) required new revenue streams. Europe also demanded access to the luxury goods found in Asia that were otherwise unavailable. Spices, objects of art, and other goods considered exotic to Europeans were highly prized and spoke to the overall status of its owner. The exploitation of newly encountered lands provided the necessary funds to support these diverse agendas.

European encounters shared little commonalities with peoples of these cultural groups they viewed as *others*. Viewing people of different cultures as *others* served to objectify them. Rather than being considered individuals, they were treated as commodities to be bought, sold, or discarded. Scholarly debate suggests that slavery resulted, in part, from this commoditization of human beings. Another resulting factor of this thinking was the use of the term **savage,** meaning wild or of the woods.

INDIGENOUS PEOPLE

A group of people rooted in a region are referred to as **indigenous**. The word also infers that these people are "digging" into the ground to create long-lasting, permanent connections between themselves and their surroundings. The term also refers to a group of people who are *original* to a given area. Many times such groups are titled first nations, native peoples, or tribal peoples, but collectively they are indigenous peoples. There are over 5,000 different groups of indigenous peoples living in more than 70 countries worldwide with more than 4,000 distinct languages. While no standard definition of who an indigenous people are exists, these people share commonalities of congregating in small groups, have a unique language, have distinct cultural traditions, and are tied to the land for cultural, religious, and ethnic reasons.

SOCIAL STRUCTURES

No matter the culture an individual is born into, there are spoken or unspoken social structures with children immediately given the same social status as their parents. At first glance, the social structure of Western civilization appears similar to that of non-Western cultures, but upon closer examination, differences are evident. Each person born is similarly given the culture they must grow up in and learn to navigate. In Western civilization, however, changing social status occurs once an individual establishes a life and career on their own. Western social structure is not primarily based on a clan, tribe, or caste system like many non-Western cultures.

Western Structure

Social structure in Westernized cultures is definable to an extent. People tend to partake in social events with like-minded individuals on the basis of their personal interests on any given subject matter, but this social stratification is a choice unlike the social system seen in many non-Westernized cultures. For example, Karl Marx believed that a person's social class was an outcome of their relationship to the labor they performed. The product a person created was how society judged their worth. And, most people identify more with people they have something in common or with someone they share a common experience and interest.

In many Western societies, the complexity of dealing with social issues became harder than in non-Western cultures. In a Western society, individuals in one social group tend to believe that everyone lives, acts, or thinks as they do because they are less aware of the fact that social classes exist. In non-Western cultures, the class and/or caste system is apparent from birth onward.

There are a number of ways to study social stratification, but psychology seems to be the most comprehensive. But, even psychologists cannot decide how an individual eventually ends up being categorized in one social group over another. Currently, there are two models, cognitive idealist model and materialist model, for the creation of Western social structures.

The first model, cognitive idealist (fig. 8.2), refers to structure as the religion, rules, values, accepted norms, scientific understandings, and symbols used to identify a person within its society. The model assumes that society is formulated and based on a number of influences, with religion comprising the largest difference. Another influencing factor taken into consideration when applying the model to social structure is that people ultimately think differently and therefore they live differently on the basis of varying culturally imbedded ideas.

The second model, materialist (fig. 8.3), refers to the way society maintains itself by producing goods and services and in accordance will organize itself to accomplish these production outcomes. The model further suggests that society is based on how a culture provides for itself and, in turn, this provides the defining circumstances of its social structure. Therefore, an individual's identity is a consequence of that culture's

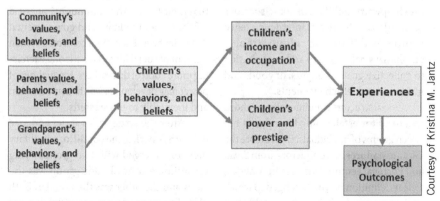

Fig. 8.2 Cogitative Idealist Model of Western social structure

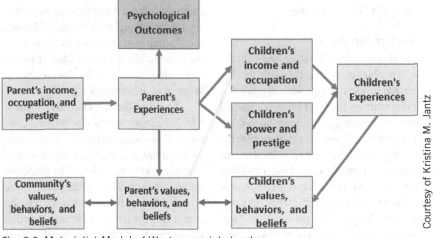

Fig. 8.3 Materialist Model of Western social structure

ideas about lifestyle choices because each group within a larger cultural context will live life differently on the basis of its needs.

Non-Western Structure

A number of non-Western cultures, those not having primary roots linked to ancient Greek or Roman thought, reside around the world. Individuals belonging to these cultures purposefully divide themselves into groups. A common feature of these groups is how they establish their social hierarchy, which tends to be based on a birth status or class-color/class-caste system without much upward mobility. In some societies such as Japan, the idea of interdependence is promoted. Japanese culture strongly emphasizes belonging to and contributing to collective goals, thoughts, or goods and not to individual achievements.

Social structure is additionally grounded in a need for establishing boundaries between groups of individuals. Even before the **Conquistadores**, or conquerors, from Spain and Portugal ventured into South America, a clear definition of who belonged to which social group and subgroup was established

by the Aztecs, Inca, and Maya cultures. Each group had 4 social classes, with the ruler, his family, and nobles at the top.

The term **complex society** addresses the social classes of people in a specified region and the role of power in controlling that region. In South America, *social hierarchy* was often dependent on skin pigmentation and origin of birth (fig. 8.4). But, another powerful concept, *social stratification*, played an active role in determining a person's place in society. Stratification refers to the layering of people within a society or social unit operating in accordance with the influences that their family, the community, political affiliation, and military and governmental dynamics have. Each *strata* controls a certain amount of social identity, with one exercising more control than others. Inequalities of power may develop, leading to confrontation and inevitably to power shifts.

After the struggle for independence in South America, the **caudillo**, or military dictator, emerged with two groups vying for ultimate control. One group was the elites and the other was the popular. Both played a pivotal role to usher in stability and

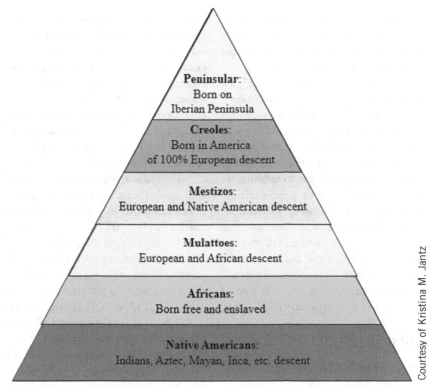

Peninsular:
Born on
Iberian Peninsula

Creoles:
Born in America
of 100% European descent

Mestizos:
European and Native American descent

Mulattoes:
European and African descent

Africans:
Born free and enslaved

Native Americans:
Indians, Aztec, Mayan, Inca, etc. descent

Courtesy of Kristina M. Jantz

Fig. 8.4 Social hierarchy of South American societies during colonization

prevented further disintegration of the state. Each encouraged and enabled the building of infrastructure and legitimatized its rule through the endorsement of the military, landowning aristocracy, and the Roman Catholic Church. In fact, many caudillos had served in the army and understood the importance of the institution to either enforce or destroy a ruler.

The elites, the Peninsular and Creoles, were those who enjoyed social, economic, and political control. Within the elite strata, two political attitudes prevailed, liberalism and conservatism, much like the United States. The liberals mirrored progressive attitudes, while the conservatives held fast to traditional values. Neither group was interested in the problems of the commoners or in the redistribution or restructuring of the social, land, and labor system. The **mestizos**, or a person of mixed Spanish and Native American ancestry, and **mulattoes**, a person of mixed European and African ancestry, formed the largest social classes. But, it was not until the latter decades of the nineteenth century that they were able to seize power.

While the growth and social structure of Latin America was shaped by the elites, they failed to understand the underlying global forces at work. For example, many miles of railroads were constructed but not linked to principal cities within the nations. The possibility of a unified nation was eliminated along with the prospect of a change in the nation's social structure.

To correct the problem, loans were made to fund other "modernization" advancements and the government was forced to budget even greater sums to pay the interest.

Loans made by the elites eventually led to the destabilization of many South American nations and resulted in the problems witnessed in South America and its social structure well into the twenty-first century. Larger South American nations such as Brazil were stabilized and began to industrialize by forming industries to support internal demands. The establishment of industries enabled the development of a better balanced economy base on a multitude of products and protected Brazil from the fluctuation in European markets. These advancements also helped mestizos and mulattoes rise into a new social strata, a very small middle class.

WORLDWIDE CONTACT

China's Limited Encounters

Over more than a 1,000-year period from 618 to 1644 CE, the Chinese isolated and resisted influence from foreigners but did not completely remove themselves from the world stage as they continued trade and economic growth. Four dynasties, Tang, Song, Yuan, and Ming, played a role in shaping cultural thought and progress inside China. But, as one dynasty ascended to dominance, others were thriving in one form or another even if the newer dynasty was considered the prominent force in China.

By the last half of the first millennium, the Tang Dynasty (614 to 907 CE) had produced the largest and best organized government in the world. Under the Tang Dynasty, the Silk Road trade route between the East and the West was restored. The Silk Road ended in the capital Tang Dynasty of Chang'an, "City of Enduring Peace," which was also the largest city in the world at the time. The city was laid out in a carefully

conceived grid that dramatized the Tang commitment to social order and mirrored what they believed to be the order of the cosmos. Along with reestablishing and re-creating the Silk Road and Chang'an capital, respectively, the Tang Dynasty also valued education. Chang'an boasted of an imperial college where all civil servants, except women, were trained and where intellectual abilities were of high value.

Toward the beginning of the Tang Dynasty, two poets rose to prominence, the Daoist Li Bai (701–62 CE) and the Confucian Du Fu (712–70 CE); both poets based their writing on early philosophies found in either Daoism or Confucianism. Both poets belonged to the Eight Immortals of the Wine Cup, who gathered on moonlit nights to drink wine to unbridle their poetic musings. The poems of each artist personify the multifaceted features of the Tang culture. The dynasty was durable and dynamic as well as obsessive and compassionate, simultaneously sensible and romantic, intensely individualistic, while having great dedication to public duties. The following poem is by Li Bai:

"In the Mountain on a Summer Day"
Gently I stir a white feather fan,
With open shirt, sitting in a green wood.
I take off my cap and hang it on a jutting stone:
A wind from the pine-trees trickles on my bare head.

By far the most spirited interactions to occur between the East and the West were during the Song Dynasty (1127 to 1279 CE) when Marco Polo (1254 to 1324 CE) traveled over land in 1271 CE to the capital city of Hangzhou. Polo was the first Westerner to see Hangzhou and referred to the city as the "grandest city in the world." Another city named Kinsai, or City of the Heavens, amazed Polo. Being a native a Venice, it reminded him of home because it had an elaborate system of canals and was crisscrossed by thousands of bridges with floating teahouses.

The citizens of the Song Dynasty and the capital of Hangzhou were familiar with living well. Polo even claimed that the houses of the citizens are well built and elaborately finished with delightful detail to decoration. He asserted that the cost of their paintings and architectural design must have been a huge sum. These and other explanations provided by Polo of the Hangzhou way of life lead scholars to believe that Hangzhou was the cultural center of Asia during this time. Polo's account exceeded any ideas the West had of how those in the East lived.

The Yuan dynasty (1271 to 1368 CE) was created by Mongol Kublai Khan (r. 1260 to 1294 CE), who conquered the Song dynasty, which was overthrown by the Ming Dynasty (1368 to 1644 CE). The transition from Yuan to Ming dynasty marked a time when China was once again ruled by Chinese after almost 100 years of Mongol rule. Under the Ming Dynasty's Emperor Zhu Yuanzhang (r. 1368 to 1398 CE), the

Forbidden Palace (fig. 8.5) was constructed at the Imperial Palace compound in Beijing. The palace's name was derived from the fact that only those on official imperial business were allowed entry through the gates. The Forbidden City was laid out on a grid. The city covered 240 acres and was fortified with 15 miles of wall. The city contained 9,999 buildings, and the rooms were constructed with a traditional post-and-lintel design with each having nine nails per row. The words "nine" and "everlasting" sound similar in Mandarin, the language of the Chinese people. Nine was connected to extreme positivity; therefore, the use of nine was reserved for the emperor alone.

Daoists believed that certain forces called *dragon lines* form energy that flows through the earth, through natural formations including along mountains and ridges, and down streams and rivers that influence the lives of nearby inhabitants. Forces of evil were said to flow from the north; therefore, the city opened to the south. The entire design of the city was constructed around the principles of *feng shui* because the emperor was considered divine. The overall purpose of the construction of the palace was to create balance and harmony for emperors and their families, as it was designed to mirror the harmony of the universe. The architecture was a representation of the emperor's reign and obligation to preserve order, stability, and the accord of his land as the Son of Heaven.

Fig. 8.5 Forbidden City, in modern Beijing, 1406 to 1420 CE

© Brian Kinney/Shutterstock.com

India under Islamic Rule

By the seventeenth and eighteenth centuries, India had Muslim rulers not Hindu, the original religion of the indigenous people of the country. As early as the eleventh century, a variety of Islamic groups moved across the Hindu Kush mountain range through the northern passage and by the early part of the thirteenth century Muslims had established a foothold in Delhi. A group referred to as the Turko-Mongol Sunni Muslims, more recognizably known as Moguls, had established a permanent empire in northern India in parts of Delhi and Agar by the sixteenth century. Such footholds and establishments were tolerated and even welcomed by the native people of India. However, between 1540 and 1555, Hindus rose up to exile the Moguls.

During this time of Mongol exile, from India, the great Persian leader, Shah Tahmasp Safavi (r. 1524 to 1576 CE), in Tabriz, accepted these Islamic Moguls into his court. Safavi was a patron of the arts and his love of the arts would make an impression on Abu'l-Fath Jalal-ud-din Muhammad Akbar (r. 1556 to 1605), who eventually ruled India as Akbar I after the Moguls reconquered the country 15 years later.

In 1556, the new ruler was quick to establish a school dedicated to painting and open to both Hindu and Islamic artists, but taught by Persian masters introduced from Tabriz. Akbar also encouraged artists to learn Western styles of art brought to the East by Portuguese traders. Records from the period state that more than 1,000 artists were needed to create a library containing more than 24,000 illuminated manuscripts. In fig 8.6, created posthumously, Akbar I is placed between a lion and a calf. Both animals became a common motif during the Elizabethan era to symbolize peace under the reign of Akbar I. Lions were commonly

Fig. 8.6 *Akbar with Lion and Calf*, ink, opaque watercolor, and gold on paper, Govardhan, c. 1530 to 1550 CE.

used to instill a feeling of protection. The calf, however, has a modest and uneasy disposition probably because of its close proximity to the lion. Likewise, Akbar's people should fear and love for the peace he brought to their land.

The rule of Akbar I was one in which he recognized the diversity of the people he reigned over. For this reason, he welcomed Christians, Jews, Hindu, Buddhists, and others to his court to debate the most prominent Muslim scholars of the day living under his rule. By the time Akbar's son, Jahangir (r. 1605 to 1627 CE), had become ruler, the court's taste for art had switched from Persian influence to a British-Dutch style.

In 1599, King James I of England awarded the British East India Company exclusive trading rights to the East Indies.

Jahangir's growing interest to English life is most visible in image *Jahangir Seated on an Allegorical Throne*. Even though Jahangir assumes the typical profile pose of the Mogul court, the inclusion of two putti, or cherubs, flying across the top of the composition was a new Westernized introduction. The background is similar to those seen in images from the Netherlands, which were popular.

In other renditions of where putti are included, specifically during the reign of Jahangir, they are in the act of shooting arrows, alluding to the importance of loving the world, while others cover their faces in the act of contemplation, possibly of worldly power. Still other images incorporate putti at the bottom of an image in the act of inscribing the importance of a central figure within the image. The most prominent Western influence seen in Indian works of art is a decorative flower border with the outer Western-style flower border in stark contrast to traditional Turkish flower border pattern.

Jahangir's son, Shah Jahan (r. 1628 to 1658 CE, fig. 8.7), did not embrace the art of painting nearly as much as his father and grandfather did. However, he would become a patron of architecture, with his most significant contribution to Indian art being the construction of the Taj Mahal. The Taj Mahal (fig. 8.8) is more than a mere architectural structure, it is a mausoleum Jahan had constructed for his favorite wife, Mumtaz Mahal (1593 to 1631 CE), whose name means "Light of the Palace." Mahal died while giving birth to their 14th child.

The overall look of the tomb combines Islamic with Indian architecture. The white marble tomb is set on a broad marble platform with minarets at each corner. And at the top of these minarets are **chattri**, or small pavilions that are traditional embellishments

of Indian palaces. The minarets also act as a location where the muezzin announces the call to worship for Muslims. The main structure has an identical facade with a central **iwan**, or a traditional Islamic architectural feature consisting of a vaulted opening with an arched portal, flanked by two stories of smaller *iwans*. The open vaulted facades contribute to the Taj Mahal's overall feeling of weightlessness.

Sadly though, by 1658, Shah Jahan had fallen ill and his more conservative son Aurangzeb had won power and confined his father to the Red Fort on the Jumna River. Aurangzeb would reinstitute traditional forms of Islamic law and worship, ending the pluralism that had defined the Mogul court under his father, grandfather, and even his great-grandfather. However, from the

Fig. 8.7 *Shah Jahan on a Terrace, Holding a Pendant set with his Portrait*, ink, opaque watercolor, and gold on paper, Chitarman, c. 1627 to 1628 CE.

Purchase, Rogers Fund and The Kevorkian Foundation Gift, 1955, The Metropolitan Museum of Art

© YURY TARANIK/Shutterstock.com

Fig. 8.8 Taj Mahal, Agra, India. Mogul Period, c. 1632 to 1648

Red Fort, Jahan was able to look out over the Jumna River and see the Taj Mahal and re-create in poetry the paradise where his beloved wife rested.

Originally, Shah Jahan intended to build a matching tomb across the river in black marble and connect it via an open air bridge. Sadly, he never built his own magnificent tomb and was interned next to Mumtaz Mahal in a tomb slightly taller than hers.

Japan's Foreign Influences

Around 550 CE, Japanese culture was comprised of three clans, the Soga, Mononobe, and Nakatomi, with each clan having ties to the imperial family through royal marriages. Each clan also performed a specific duty. The Mononobe clan was responsible for maintaining the emperor's military, while the Nakatomi clan was charged with overseeing the national rituals associated with Shinto, the indigenous spirituality practiced by the people of Japan. Shinto is not necessarily a

faith, instead it is more of a way of life. Both the Mononobe and Nakatomi clans opposed the practice of Buddhism in Japan. The Soga clan supervised the management of the emperor's trade and estates with Korea and China. They would be the clan to introduce Buddhism to the island. Through the Soga contact with these two other cultures they were introduced to Buddhism and were intensely attracted to the Buddhist way of life. For this reason, the emperor allowed the Soga clan to practice the Buddhist faith.

Japan's relative isolation from the rest of Asia caused the nation to develop slowly and it was more susceptible to the influences of the more advanced cultures it encountered. Even though the initial reaction to the infusion of Buddhism into Japanese culture was not welcomed, by the early seventh century, the ideologies of Buddhism and Shintoism had been influencing each other. The two ways of life eventually intertwined so much so that the *Great Buddha of Nara* (fig. 8.9)

Fig. 8.9 *Great Buddha of Nara*, gilt bronze, 743 to 751 CE

became synonymous with the Shinto goddess Amaterasu, and Buddhist ceremonies were incorporated into Shinto court rituals.

In the eighth century, Japan was afflicted with social unrest as a result of the frequent political changes and revolts. Emperor Shomu (r. 724 to 749) believed that the power of Buddhism would protect the nation. Instead of requiring Buddhism to become the national religion, he promoted the construction of Buddha statues. In 741, the emperor issued an imperial decree for the construction of 62 provincial temples specially designed to enshrine statues of Buddha. The Nara temple (fig 8.10) is a seven-story pagoda structure that was ceremoniously consecrated by an officiating monk in 752 CE. Records indicate more than 2.5 million people helped in the building of both the statue and the temple.

Because of the close relationship between Buddhism and Shintoism sometime between 784 and 794 CE, the capital was moved to Heian-kyō. Records from the period indicate that the relocation of the capital arose out of a need for the secular court to separate itself from the sway of the Buddhist monks at Nara.

The move of the capital created a fracture within the religious and secular communities, but the arts were able to flourish in the Heian Period (794 to 1185 CE). Japanese court life was determined and, therefore, dominated by gender. The lives of men were public, while women lived concealed, private lives. Women rarely ventured into public life; if they did, it was usually to a Buddhist temple. While Japanese women lived lives out of the public domain, they were highly educated. Women did gather at court for poetry reading, where "poems were generally composed for a single recipient—a friend or lover—and a reply was expected". Much of the daily activities of court life were captured in *nikki*, or diaries. Such diaries give us an idea of what Heian court life was like.

Yury Zap/Shutterstock.com

Fig. 8.10 Nara pagoda housing the *Great Buddha of Nara*, 743 to 751 CE

The Heian Period was considered a time when the Japanese people witnessed courtly refinement, while the Kamakura Period (1185 to 1333 CE) endured intense rivalry and warfare. Many Japanese felt that the widespread warfare across the country announced the coming of *Mappo*, or the Third Age of Buddha, proposed to begin 2,000 years about the death of Buddha and last for 10,000 years. The time came to be understood as one when Dharma declined and people were unable to obtain enlightenment. Pure Land Buddhist artists emerged and appeared to extend an alternate way out of this degenerate third age. An attractive alternate method for the Japanese people was in chanting the phrase *Namu Amida Bustu,* meaning "Hail to the Buddha Amida." The faithful believed that by repeating this chant their next life would begin in the Pure Land of Ultimate Bliss, a place where enlightenment might be attainable.

The Muromachi Period (1392 to 1573) witnessed the building of Japan's most complete and beautiful castle, Matsumoto Castle (fig. 8.1). A unique aspect of this castle is that it was built on flat land rather than on a hilltop or near a river. Like many Western culture castles, Matsumoto has a vast network of adjoined walls, a moat, and a gatehouse. Such similarities in architecture showcase the increasing influence that Western culture had on the Japanese during that period.

Muromachi rulers, as a result of prior experiences, reinstituted the indigenous cultural patronage of Zen Gardens (fig. 8.11). The influence of Zen Gardens became a way for Japanese artists to express long-held traditions of water features along with other aspects of nature. Many of the Zen Gardens are best appreciated when viewed as whole, much like a narrative that incorporates the passage of time. The passage of time is an

Fig. 8.11 Zen Garden at Kennin-ji Temple, Kyoto, Japan. Muromachi Period, c. late-fifteenth to mid-seventeenth century

allegory for the cycle of life itself—a cycle where the convoluted and perplexing facets of human life become cleaner as we age.

Zen Buddhism aesthetic additionally influenced Japanese paintings as the artists believed that a tranquil artistic mind revealed the genuine essence of an object or idea, which is derived from prehistoric Japanese Shintoist. Unlike the earlier Shinto artistic expression of ink on paper of *Shakyamuni Triad with the Sixteen Protectors of the Great Wisdom Sutra* (fig. 8.12), Zen ink required the viewer to use his or her own imagination to apply color to a monochromatic drawing, as in *Dwelling in the Qingbian Mountains* (fig. 8.13). The style is a strong contrast to that of esoteric Buddhist painting with its high complexity and ritualistic geometric designs symbolic of the universe and that of the Amida Buddhist who strives to illustrate a dramatic scene between heaven and hell.

As a result of the aesthetic qualities of Zen creativity, little change in Japanese art occurred since the fifteenth century.

The last major period of foreign influence occurred during the Azuchi-Momoyama Period (1573 to 1600). Even though the country was culturally thriving, civil war ripped it apart for 24 years. This war ended with political unification after a leader, Nobunaga (1534 to 182), was introduced to gunpowder by Portuguese traders. Once the warring subsided, foreign trades, mainly the Dutch and Portuguese, were used as an inspiration in Japanese paintings. A new genre of painting known as **namban**, or "southern barbarian", a term *namban* used to refer to the Westerns, was developed during this period. Images from this period are highly engaging with people from every social class enjoying the outdoors (fig. 8.14). Other images depict ships with their crews

Fig. 8.12 *Shakyamuni Triad with the 16 Protectors of the Great Wisdom Sutra,* Nanboku-chō Period, c. late fourteenth century.

Fig. 8.13 *Dwelling in the Qingbian Mountains,* ink on paper, Ming Dynasty, Qichang, 1617.

Fig. 8.14 *Amusements at Higashiyama in Kyoto,* details of six-panel screen, ink, color, mica, and gold leaf on paper, Kano School, c. 1620s.

Fig. 8.15 *Woodcutters and Fishermen*, ink and color on paper, Edo Period, Goshun, c. 1790 to 1975.

unloading goods and priests converting the Japanese to Christianity.

No matter what experience Nobunaga had with Western people, his successor, Hideyoshi, would become very suspicious of Christianity. Around 1587, Hideyoshi would disallow the practice of the Christian faith within Japan, and in 1597, he had 26 Spanish and Japanese Jesuits executed. Later rulers would forbid Japanese to travel in 1635, and by 1641, there had been limited trade between Japan and the Dutch. Japan would remain sealed off from the Western world until 1854 after being urged by the president of the United States to receive American sailors.

Japanese art movement after the sixteenth century veered away from the reliance of religion and became one that also merged with outside influences, much like the Chinese. But the art works still relied on the beauty of simple aesthetics. A significant school of thought that arose in the early Edo Period (1603 to 1868) was the Rinpa school. The school used classical themes, but presented them in a bold and lavishly decorative format. Two artists who accomplished a high level of this school's style were Matsumura Goshun

(fig. 8.15) and Itō Jakuchū (fig. 8.16). Both helped advance this decorative style by re-creating themes from classical literature,

Fig. 8.16 *Hen and Rooster with Grapevine*, ink and color on silk, Edo Period, Jakuchū, 1972.

using brilliantly colored figures and motifs from the natural world.

During the same time as the Impressionists' movement, a Japanese artist, Kuroda Seiki (1866 to 1924), who originally studied law, arrived in France to follow the traditional course of study in Academic Art and discovered painting. In two of his paintings, *Lakeside* and *Withered Field*, he illustrates the combination of traditional Japanese painting while using the *plein-air* technique he learned while in Paris. Paintings of later centuries were more vivid in color yet stayed in the custom of combining nature with tradition, a style that has carried through to contemporary times.

Spain in Latin America

Using modern technology, archeologist Anna C. Roosevelt (b. 1946) and a team of anthropologists argued that a prehistoric society predated Andean societies located in eastern Marajó, a low-lying area around the Amazon in the modern-day State of Pará in Brazil. The Marajoara people, named after Marajó Island where they flourished, were a large civilization numbering 100,000 or more. The discovery developed a new picture of prehistoric Latin America where people settled at rivers and estuaries to exploit the natural food sources. Pottery (fig. 8.17) dates to between 1,400 and 3,000 years prior to the first appearance of pottery in the Andes Mountains or in the coastal areas of Peru. The Marajó culture developed into chiefdom society, but the people disappeared mysteriously before 1300 CE. By the first written accounts, a different culture existed in the savannas of the Marajó.

The Spaniards, known as the Iberians, first encountered the indigenous peoples of the New World and hoped to trade with them. The Indians, as they were known because of their similar pigmentation to those

in the country India, were not interested in commercial associations. In response, the Iberians began to settle and colonize "their" new territories. Social hierarchies based on land ownership were slowly put into place by Iberian settlers. Although many settlers sought gold, others focused on agricultural development. For the purpose of stabilizing the colonies and make each more self-sufficient, skilled craftsmen and farmers were encouraged to migrate to the New World.

The Indian empires were conquered, their opulence seized, and the inhabitants became subjects of the Castilian crown. Although the Spaniards were outnumbered, European innovations such as steel, gunpowder, the domestication of the horse, effective military tactics, crossbows, and desire helped facilitate their victories. Another aspect that helping to insure European domination over the natives was through the spread of European diseases, against which the natives had no immunities.

The Iberians exploited all of the natural resources found and cultivated in the New World. Eventually, this rich land of resources and wealth drew the attention of the French, Dutch, and English. The abundance of gold and silver mined in Peru, Brazil, and Mexico helped stimulate the European economy and funded revolution. Even though the Indians were exploited as slave labor, the Iberians learned much from their subjects about how to survive in their new environment. Through intermarriage, the settlers and subjects were irrevocably linked together creating a new social class structure (fig. 8.4).

The Latin America of today, and historically, is economically dependent on the export of agricultural and mineral commodities. Early trade attitudes were initially defined by the **physiocratic doctrine**, or national wealth derived exclusively from land agriculture, with regard to competition.

(a)

(b)

Gift of David Bernstein and Family, in Memory of Jean Eugene Lions, 2005, The Metropolitan Museum of Art

Fig. 8.17 (a) plate front and (b) plate back, ceramic, Marajó culture, eighth to twelfth century.

Observing the wealth accumulated by trade in economic markets, countries began to vie for free trading privileges. Unfortunately, they competed against each other and flooded the market, causing prices and profits for farmers to fall.

Several attempts were made to form trading coalitions within Latin America. The goals were to unify the countries and protect the markets from outside competition and to form larger internal markets. In 1960, a trade association known as the Latin American Free Trade Association, now known as the Latin American Integration Association, was developed to encourage trade within Latin America. Fostering trade between the countries was believed to eliminate some of the dependency incurred by separate nations trading outside the continent with foreign competitors. In 1969, the Andean Pact was signed with a similar goal in mind. In 1992, the North American Free Trade Agreement was signed by the leaders of three countries: George H. W. Bush of the United States, Brian Mulroney of Canada, and Carlos Salinas de Gortari of Mexico. Finally, a trade agreement was promoted by Brazil on the basis of the North Atlantic

Free Trade Organization and was called the South American Free Trade Area.

West Africa and the Portuguese

Portuguese explorers were shocked to discover indigenous people already living on the coast of West Africa when they arrived. To their amazement the region contained several large kingdoms, in particular the Yoruba people of Ife and Owo and the kingdom of Benin, both located in modern day Nigeria. The Yoruba culture developed sometime around the eighth century on the bank of the Niger River in West Africa. The people began creating exceedingly realistic sculptures as a form of commemoration in clay, stone, and ivory. When an elephant was killed the **Oba**, or ruler, was always given one tusk with the option to purchase the second. If the Oba did not purchase the second tusk only members of the royal family could making ivory a royal object.

An ivory bracelet from the Owo group of the Yoruba peoples celebrates the origins of the kingdom at Ife. On either side of the bracelet (fig. 8.18a) are two chiefs with a short robe, beaded necklace, and characteristic **coiffure**, or person and elaborate hairstyle, surrounded by smaller figures. The figures are both right-side-up and upside-down so that the wearer of the bracelet and viewer can "interpret" their meaning properly. Figures incorporated into the bracelet are flute players, observers, foot soldiers, animals, and bound captives (fig. 8.18b). The message of the bracelet illustrates the chiefs duties by suggesting he leads a good life due to his military achievements and political authority. The inclusion of two crocodiles and fish -legged humans underscores the ruler's connection to Olokun, the god of the sea who gives his faithful wealth and fertility.

The Yoruba people are a cultural tribe still thriving today who can trace their ancestral linage to the people of Ife. The culture revolves around the king because he serves as a linkage to the two cosmic worlds the Yoruba believe exist. The two cosmic worlds contain the world of the living and the realm of the gods. The realm of the gods further comprises two groups: the primordial deities and ancestral heroes. Therefore, the king's head is considered sacred as he will one day reside with the ancestral heroes in the realm of the gods.

Once the people living at Ife mastered how to manipulate clay and stone, they developed the metallurgy of brass to create bronze. The bronze works created comprise a large number of sculptural portraits probably of deceased and living rulers. The **ooni**, or the king of the Ife, was the only one who could commission such images. One *Ife Head* (fig. 8.19) shows the decorative feature of scarification and a number of holes on the mouth area and the neck region with a large hole at the base. The hole at the base of the neck was used for placing the head on a wooden mannequin. An Ife court robe was attached to the mannequin by the smaller holes around the neck. The symbolism for this action was to represent a deceased leader or a leader unable to attend the gathering. The smaller holes on the mouth, and head in some sculptures, were perhaps used for veiling purposes. The veil may denote the king's aptitude for organizing the world and prosperity. However, the Ife left no written record of their cultural beliefs and we can understand their traditions only by observing the descendants of the Ife, such as the Yoruba.

Another pervasive characteristic of Yoruba culture is the highly stylized **Ade**, or beaded crown (fig. 8.20). The head is not only the resting place for a crown but also the

(a)

(b)

Fig. 8.18 (a) bracelet viewpoint one and (b) bracelet viewpoint two, ivory, word or coconet shell inlay, Yoruba peoples, Owo group, seventeenth to nineteenth.

Fig. 8.19 *Ife Head*, brass, Yoruba people, Ife group, fourteenth to fifteenth century.

Fig. 8.20 *Ade*, Glass and jasper beads, cotton cloth, raffia cloth, cane, and iron, Yoruba peoples, c. 1900 to 1940.

seat of intelligence. The king's crown rises high above his head to also symbolize his majesty and authority. A row of short and long beads wrap around the bottom of the crown resembling fringe finish. The shorter beads fall over king's face to shield the viewers from the power of his gaze.

Another cultural group known as the Kingdom of Benin thrived roughly 150 miles south of Ife. The kingdom was founded around 1170 when the Edo people living in the region asked the Ife ooni for a new ruler. The region was troubled with political disorder. Prince Oranmiyan was sent to rule, establishing a new dynasty and the **oba**, or leader of the Benin. When Oranmiyan first arrived, he was vexed by the conditions of the people and called the region **ibini**, meaning "the land of vexation." Only after Oranmiyan impregnated the Benin princess did he return to Ife. His son, Eweka (r. 1180 to 1246), became the first oba. The capital city, Benin City, would gain a massive system of walls and moats with 10,000 miles of walls, roughly 4.5 times longer than the Great Wall of China. The Benin also created head sculptures (fig 8.21) of their leaders similar to those found in Ife but in brass with its own unique stylization. The use was also similar to the Ife. Instead of standing in for a deceased oba, the succeeding oba commissioned the head

upon the death of his predecessor to retain influence over the community.

The Court of Benin first encountered the Portuguese in 1486 under the rule of Ozolua the Conqueror (r. 1481 to 1505). Much of the first encounters between the Benin and Portuguese were harmonious, with the Benin people remaining culturally intact. Initially, the goods traded were gold, ivory, rubber, salt, and forest commodities for beads and brass. The Benin additionally created ivory court art to denote the two cultures' relationship. One commodity that was particularly important was salt for its ability to preserve meat for the winter months. Benin court artists created a set of four **saltcellar**, or objects for holding or dispensing salt, possibly at the behest of the oba as a gift to his patrons. The saltcellars (fig. 8.22) show four male figures in traditional Portuguese dress, two are richly adorned. The richly adorned figures are front facing, while the other two, probably attendants, are in profile.

The Michael C. Rockefeller Memorial Collection, Bequest of Nelson A. Rockefeller, 1979, The Metropolitan Museum of Art

Fig. 8.21 *Head of an Oba*, brass, Court of Benin; Edo people. c. 1550 to 1680.

Louis V. Bell and Roger's Funds, 1972, The Metropolitan Museum of Art

Fig. 8.22 *Saltcellar: Portuguese Figures*, ivory, Court of Benin, Edo people, c. 1525 to 1600.

Eventually, the Portuguese and West African trade turned to human exports, or slaves. Many African tribes had been selling those they captured in war to Muslim traders for more than three centuries. Under later trade agreements, however, the Portuguese greatly expanded the practice. By the end of the fifteenth century, around 150,000 African slaves had been in Europe. By the mid-sixteenth century, the Portuguese had turned their efforts to shipping hundreds of thousands of slaves to Brazil. The demand for slaves ultimately outnumbered the amount of men captured during wars between native African tribes. The Portuguese turned their attention to simply capturing and shipping anyone they found to the Americas.

Further, the Portuguese treated their slaves more harshly than the Muslims did. In order to insure that the captives did not escape, the Portuguese chained, branded, and often worked them to death. In the end, the Portuguese initiated a practice of **cultural hegemony**, or cultural domination, that set the stage for the racial exploitation that has haunted the Western world ever since.

IMPACTS OF ENCOUNTER

Under the Tang Dynasty, the trade route known as the Silk Road between the East and the West would be reestablished. The Silk Road ended in the Tang Dynasty capital city of Chang'an, "City of Enduring Peace", which was also the largest city in the world at the time. Two influential poets flourished, Li Bai and Du Fu, and left their poetic mark on history. The journals of Marco Polo paint a picture of cities vibrating with life and culture that like West had never encountered. Under the Ming Dynasty, the Mongols of the Yuan dynasty would be overthrown in 1368, marking a return of China to Chinese rule.

Unlike the people of China, the Indian people were more tolerant of outside forces and, in most cases, welcomed explorers. As early as the eleventh century, a variety of Islamic groups moved across the Hindu Kush mountain range. By the early part of the thirteenth century, Muslims had established a foothold in Delhi. It was not until the sixteenth that the Moguls established a permanent empire in northern India. By the seventeenth century, Muslim had ruled over native Hindus.

From the sixteenth century onward, a number of Mogul rulers, from Akbar I to his grandson Shah Jahan imparted their love of both Non-western and Western art on the Indian culture and its landscape. In the earlier years of the Mogul rule, the love of art was in the form of establishing artistic school. However, in later years, portraiture creation in the English style was popular. Eventually, their love of art was seen in the combining of Indian and Islamic architecture, in the Taj Mahal.

Japanese culture is defined by the three major periods of Heian, Kamakura, and Muromachi before Japan closed itself off to Western influence again in 1587 during the Azuchi-Momoyama Period, which would end abruptly in 1635. In the early formation of Japanese culture, the culture was comprised of three clans, the Soga, Mononobe, and Nakatomi, with each clan having ties to the imperial family through royal marriages and performance of specific duties. The Heian Period witnessed the influx of Buddhism into Japan from China. During the Muromachi Period, the Japanese people reinstituted their indigenous cultural patronage of Zen Gardens and the formality of tea ceremonies.

The last major period of foreign influence was in the Azuchi-Momoyama Period. Japanese culture was thriving, but civil war ripped the country apart. Records from this time witnessed the introduction of gunpowder by Portuguese traders. After warring between the clan died down, the Dutch and Portuguese were able to begin trading with the Japanese. Because of these trading encounters, a new genre of painting known as namban developed.

Trade, eventually, would end under the reign of Hideyoshi, who becamehis suspicious about Christianity. Later rulers forbid the Japanese to travel in 1635 and by 1641 there was limited trade. Japan would remain sealed off from the Western world until 1854 after being urged by the President of the United States to receive American sailors.

In Latin America, industrialization and modernization accompanied the growth of cities in size, number, and population. Cities became increasingly more important in each nation as the "hub" of cultural activity, government, commerce, transportation, communication, and education. Job opportunities and housing were among the many lures that encouraged the migration of peoples to the developing cities. Some cities experienced population migrations that they were unable to support.

Overpopulation led to more competition for job opportunities, less housing, poverty, increased crime, the rapid spread of illness and disease, and the breakdown of the family unit. Cities also provided the opportunity for upward mobility, job training, job opportunities for women, and participation in commercial activity and trading.

In West Africa, the Portuguese were interested in fostering trade prospects. Many explores ventured into the uncharted lands to the south searching for not only people to trade with but also new territories to claim. Two main indigenous cultures were discovered, the Ife and Benin. However, it did not take either the European and African trades long to extend their trading practices into human exploitation.

Critical Thinking

Explain the effects social hierarchy on a people.

Examine the difference between Western and indigenous people social structure.

Discuss distinguishing characteristics denoting the indigenous people and the explorers.

Describe how each encountered affected the creative mindset of the indigenous people.

Explore the historical roots of each culture and it developed.

Examine the positive impacts of the explorers.

Consider the negative impact of the indigenous people.

Explore the uniqueness of cultural artifacts prior to encounters with the Western world.

ONLINE RESOURCES

Neo-Confucianism and Fan Kuan
https://smarthistory.org/neo-confucianism-fan-kuan-travelers-by-streams-and-mountains/
The Forbidden City Video
https://smarthistory.org/the-forbidden-city/
The Taj Mahal
https://smarthistory.org/the-taj-mahal-2/
Jahangir Preferring a Sufi Shaikh to Kings
https://smarthistory.org/bichtir-jahangir-preferring-a-sufi-shaikh-to-kings-2/
Todai-Ji, *Great Buddha at Nara*
https://smarthistory.org/todai-ji/
Zen Buddhism and the Rock Garden Video
https://smarthistory.org/ryoanji-peaceful-dragon-temple/
Olmec Mask Video
https://smarthistory.org/olmec-mask-met/
Teotihuacan City Video
https://smarthistory.org/teotihuacan-2/
Palenque (Mayan)
https://smarthistory.org/palenque/
Codex Borgia (Aztec)
https://smarthistory.org/codex-borgia/
Seated Figure (Djenné peoples) Video
https://smarthistory.org/seated-figure/
Queen Mother Pendant Mask (Edo peoples)
https://smarthistory.org/queen-mother-pendant-mask-iyoba/

Renaissance: Florence and World Exploration

Fig. 9.1 The Duomo. Florence, Italy. 1296 to 1436

© nattee Chalemtiragool/Shutterstock.com

Knowledge Acquisition

◆ Assess significant achievements of the Renaissance, especially in the developing secular idea of humanism with an emphasis on the individual experience.

◆ Examine how the "rebirth" evolved from earlier Greco-Roman ideas.

◆ Survey works by key figures including Brunelleschi, Donatello, Ghiberti, Leonardo da Vinci, Masaccio, Michelangelo, and Petrach.

◆ Explore the contribution of an influential Florentine family and its influence on art, literature, and politics.

◆ Grasp the key concepts central to the philosophical and religious ideas developed by Pico della Mirandola and Machiavelli.

◆ Discover how the Renaissance connects works of art from around the world to its own artistic, cultural, literary, and political interests.

SETTING THE SCENE

Following the deterioration of societal structure witnessed by the spread of the Black Death in the mid-fourteenth century, Europe experienced a remarkable resurgence characterized by the flourishing of cultural, economic, and political expansion. The **Renaissance**, or rebirth, was centered in Florence, Italy and then spread to the rest of Europe from the late-fifteenth through the early-sixteenth centuries. The innovations developed in the Renaissance resulted in an astonishing transformation of Western culture, producing global exploration and expansion by the late fifteenth century.

Throughout the whole of the Renaissance, this time was seen as a reawakening of our perception of humanities' social and creative essence. Nicolaus Copernicus (1473 to 1543) discovered that the Sun was indeed the center of the solar system and that the planets, including the Earth, orbited the Sun. Exploration of new trade routes gained the support of ruling families. The long-standing authority of the Catholic Church was challenged by Martin Luther (1483 to 1546), resulting in considerable changes to Christian theology. Works of one of the best-known writers, William Shakespeare, were composed and performed in England. The Renaissance was a time in which the limitless possibilities of human expression and discovery throughout the world were investigated.

Proto-Renaissance

The intellectual movement of the Renaissance is **humanism**, or a focus on the actions of human begins rather than the divine, that began during the first quarter of the fourteenth century. The purpose of humanism was to study the classical authors of antiquity. Latin and Greek classics were known in the Early Middle Ages, but studying the works was secondary to rebuilding society after the fall of Rome. In the 1300s, reading the classics became common among the educated individuals throughout Europe. Medieval people studied the manuscripts for their own sake, for the beauty of their style, and the ideas of human life. Monastic libraries were scoured for their copies of Virgil, Cicero, and Horace.

A new intellectual group, known as the humanists, believed that through training in the classical literature of the Greco-Romans they could form a more perfect human being. Humanism was less a philosophy and more a method of learning. In contrast to the medieval scholastic mode, which focused on resolving contradictions between authors, humanists would study ancient texts in their original context and evaluate them through a combination of reasoning and empirical evidence. A humanist education was based on the study of poetry, grammar, ethics, and rhetoric. For this reason, historians have struggled with a precise definition for humanism. Most have settled on a compromised distinction that is summarized as a movement to recover, interpret, and assimilate the language, literature, learning, and values of ancient Greece and Rome.

Above all, humanists asserted the genius of man and the greatness of human reason, thus putting man on a central plane or pedestal. The central feature of humanism in this period was the commitment to the idea that the ancient Greco-Roman world was the pinnacle of human achievement, especially intellectual achievement, and should be taken as a model by contemporary Europeans. According to this view of history, the fall of Rome to Germanic invaders, in the fifth century, led to the dissolution and decline of a remarkable culture. The intellectual heritage of the ancient world was lost with many of its most important

Global Focal Point

The Chinese are credited with inventing the printing press, but no evidence remains of when or by whom. The oldest surviving printed book, *The Diamond Sutra*, dates to around 886 CE during the Tang Dynasty. Printing the book employed hand-carved wood blocks in reverse. Given the fact that the blocks were hand cut, each new page was labor intensive and required a skilled cutter. In 1297, Wang Chen (1271 to 1368) advanced the efficiency of using the press by creating a revolving table for typesetters. Over 150 years later, Johannes Gutenberg (1398 to 1468), a German goldsmith, used metal to created movable type. Letters were created in brass in reverse. In 1452, Gutenberg borrowed money from Johannes Fust (1400 to 1466), who became Gutenberg's partner, to print calendars, pamphlets, and the only book produced from his workshop, the *Gutenberg Bible*.

books destroyed or dispersed, and a thousand years later, Europeans were still living a miserable existence. Europeans needed to propel themselves forward into a new intellectual awareness.

As the focus on the individual rose into prominence, thoughts centered on religion, and living an exclusively religious life was slowly replaced with secular activities. Humanists shifted their thoughts and writings away from the sacred, otherworldly concerns of God to those centered on humankind living in this world. The quest for understanding divine intervention was replaced by a preoccupation with daily human actions. Once again, humans were viewed as the measure of all things to be celebrated for our rationalization, determination, and carnal beauty.

Early Renaissance

Florence was at the center for these new innovations and thoughts because of the Medici family. In particular, Cosimo de' Medici (1389 to 1464) and his grandson, Lorenzo (1449 to 1492), nicknamed "The Magnificent" for the grand lifestyle, employed countless scores of artists from all type of backgrounds to produce revolutionary new

understandings of their craft. The Medici also established a banking system that funded many kingdoms and the papacy. Other influential families were scattered throughout the Italian city-states of Naples, the Papal State, duchy of Milan, the republic of Venice, and the courts of Urbino and Ferrara. Each city-state, republic, or court had its own centers dedicated to artistic creativity.

As for the Florentine banker, Cosimo de' Medici, he would be the man who added fuel to the flaming embers created by Petrarch. Cosimo welcomed a flood of scholars into Florence after the fall of Constantinople to the Ottoman Turks in 1453. Many of these scholars would carry precious ancient manuscripts with them to the Neo-Platonic Academy founded by Cosimo. The Academy was a direct reflection of Plato's Platonic Academy he founded around 387 BCE. These scholars gathered to study of Greek literature, language, and philosophy, especially the works by, or related to, Plato.

The Early Renaissance was undoubtedly a time when an extraordinary amount of creative activity was pouring out and into the homes, public spaces, and religious worship houses in Florence. In retrospective, the modern world has the luxury of speculating on whether this time is more than simply a Renaissance. We can examine changes that occurred in how people lived, in the way the political maps emerged, and in how people went about daily life and the exploration of the world. The sheer amount of activities and connections made during this time is astonishing. Scholars, and eventually artists, from all over the known world flocked to Florence to study art and literature directly from the writing of ancient Greek and Roman philosophers. In due time, they began to apply these principles to education, politics, social life, and the arts in general.

Northern Renaissance

Locals to the north such as France, Germany, and England experienced the Renaissance at roughly the same time as Italy. In Belgium and the Netherland, the circumstance of this artist revolution was controlled more by immensely wealthy Dukes of Burgundy and private citizens who acquired their wealth through trade than through the Catholic Church. Both parties began commissioning meditation and prayer works of art for personal use. Unlike artists in Italy with easy access to classical examples of proportion and beauty, Northern European artists drew their inspiration from medieval traditions found in illuminated manuscripts. The difference in inspiration created a uniquely different appearance to northern works of art. In both cases, north and Italy, a vast amount of emphasis was placed on the individual identity of both the artists and the patron.

Bruges, a Flemish City, was the Medici banking city of the north with a strong merchant class. The city's access to the North Sea provided a means for mercantile activities, given that the waterway terminated in the heart of the city. While the city was notorious for its cloth trade, paintings were

its second major commodity. In May, every year, the city sponsored a bazaar where artists of all backgrounds could sell their goods in rented stall on the grounds of a Franciscan monastery. Crafted items were inexpensive, especially oil paintings, making the event popular.

The enjoyed use of oil paint in the North was no coincidence considering that Dutch painters are credited with "inventing" it before it spread south to Italy. The growth of oil painting was a direct result of the development of pressing linseed oil from the seeds of the flax plant. This process was believed to be created by the Flemish van Eyck brothers but was highly debated after the discovery of twelfth-century treatise writings by Theophilus.

High Renaissance

The High Renaissance, unlike the Early Renaissance, was a time of exploration, as well as a time for some of the greatest artists, writers, and musicians humanity has produced. Just as the Medieval Ages gave humanity the feudal system, the Renaissance give birth to a new economic system called **capitalism**, or an economic and political system controlled by trade and private ownership for profit. A new economic system offered each individual a reasonable degree of freedom to pursue a better material standard of living to the extent of his or her wits and abilities. Capitalism, furthermore, advocated a new system where both men and women could pursue their personal goals of wealth and happiness.

By the time the High Renaissance had occurred, exploration was considered the means by which new markets were created to supply the goods needed to support a **capitalist**, or a business owner, lifestyle. Scholars, to this day, debate over whether the capitalist economic system is better

Cross-cultural Connection

Exploration and discovery of new tradable goods were a driving force for the Spanish to explore Hernàn Cortés along with an eagerness to gain fame. In 1519, Cortés was sent to colonize the new territory of Mexico and he personally wanted to convert the native to Christianity. When Cortés arrived at the capital of the Aztecs, Tenochtitlàn, he was greeted with curiosity for his light skin and men on horseback. His arrival also coincided with the prophesized return of Quetzalcoatl, an Aztec god credited with creating humans, to Earth. After a series of events, the Aztec would contract smallpox from the Spanish. The disease inundated the people and killed more than 3 million because they had no immunity to it. The weakened Aztec population was no match for the Spanish, who easily took control of the area. Cortés built Mexico City from the ruins of Tenochtitlàn, with this place becoming a prominent Spanish colony. By 1529, Cortés had been given the noble title *don*.

than the other two main economic systems of socialism or communism (Chapter 12). The capitalism created during the High Renaissance brought about the expansion of trade and high prosperity to four locations in Western Europe, in particular northern Italy, southern Germany, the Low Countries (now Belgium and the Netherlands), and England.

As with all cultural advancements, artistic creativity played a pivotal role. The High Renaissance witnessed some of the most exceptional achievements in painting, literature, and scientific breakthroughs by Michelangelo, Machiavelli, and Leonardo da Vinci. At the same time the aforementioned renowned thinkers were exploring their artistic creativity, the theologian Martin Luther began his endeavors to reform the Roman Catholic Church. The result was the founding of Protestantism and a complete break from the Church.

Mannerism

The style of painting that follows the High Renaissance was known as **Mannerism**, or in the manner of another artist. Mannerist painters departed from the precision, balanced proportion with scientific arrangement, and normal body ratios of the High Renaissance. These artists preferred to exaggerate and distort figures and objects. They favored confused and uneven imagery as the period from which they emerged overlapped that of both political and religious upheaval. The simplicity and certainty of the High Renaissance was replaced with an air of uncertainty and gloom.

CREATIVE IMPULSE

Scholars recognize the city of Florence as a carefully constructed work of art, after it emerged from the ravage of the Black Death in 1348 that killed almost four-fifths of the city-state's population and in 1400 when one-fifth or 12,000 Florentines died. At the same time, to the north, Milan laid siege to the city by blocking its trade with the seaport of Pisa, which threatened famine. In 1401, the Cloth Merchants Guild held a competition to decide who would design a pair of bronze doors for the north entrance of the city's **baptistery**, or a building used

Fig. 9.3 Florence Baptistery, south portal door, bronze, Pisano. Florence, Italy. 1336.

Fig. 9.2 Florence Baptistery of San Giovanni adjacent to the Florence Cathedral, Florence, Italy, c. 1059 to 1452.

for Christian baptismal ceremonies. The Baptistery (fig. 9.2), according to legend, was located on the site of a Roman temple to Mars that was later dedicated to Saint John the Baptist. The Florentine people hoped that a renovation to the Baptistery might bring contentment to an otherwise revengeful God.

When the competition concluded in the summer of 1402, the siege ended after the Duke of Milan died in his encampment outside the city walls. The city received seven entries, but only two entries were selected by the unknown goldsmiths, Filippo Brunelleschi (1377 to 1446) and Lorenzo Ghiberti (1378 to 1455). The subject matter was the Sacrifice of Isaac, where God tested the patriarch Abraham to sacrifice his only son Isaac in the wilderness, made in **quatrefoil**, or a four-leaf clover shape set on a diamond (fig. 9.3). While both goldsmiths depicted

the exactly same scene, it was Ghiberti who achieved a greater sense of gracefulness and heightened drama simultaneously. Even the angle in Ghiberti's panel seemed more dramatic as a result of **foreshortening**, or a technique suggesting that forms are sharply receding into deep space.

No matter their artistic differences, the competition rested on two facts for the Cloth Merchants Guild, economics and reputation. Brunelleschi was a full-fledged member of the guild, but Ghiberti was not, meaning the latter artist was ineligible to receive a commission. While capitalism would become fully developed in Florence by the High Renaissance, the Early Renaissance relied on the Medieval Guild System. The system was an important facet of city life. Each guild was exclusive and helped preserve the rights and privileges of its member.

In Florence, at the time of the competition, there were 7 major, 5 middle, and 9 minor guilds. To become a member, young males had to undertake a long process that began with an apprentice. Apprentices lived with a master's family, starting at the age of 12 to 14, with their parents paying for the master to be taken in and taught by him. They were not allowed to marry and usually endured a 2 to 7-year learning period. The training included the fundamentals of the trade and concluded with him becoming a journeyman. Once the appreciate was elevated to journeyman status, he could earn a wage, but become a master of the craft only after producing a work worthy to be called a masterpiece. The task of becoming a master was not accomplished easily. Journeymen work from dawn to dusk every day expect Sunday. All tools and materials were their responsibility to purchase, which were expensive. Once a work was produced, the members of the guild voted. In some cases, if too many masters were already members, the journeyman would be denied membership on those grounds alone. Once accepted, however, the journeyman became a master with full privileges and protected rights.

Brunelleschi refused to be named on a commission with an apprentice, which Ghiberti was. Scholars speculate Brunelleschi was originally included as a "winner" to allow Ghiberti to work on the project. This is a fact that is evident in his first five contacts including his father, a member of the guild, until he himself was accepted as a full member. As a consequence, Brunelleschi turned down the commission, gave up sculpture entirely, and decided to travel the Roman countryside for several years surveying ancient Roman architecture. The result of this so-called feud allowed Brunelleschi to return to Florence victorious in solving a 100-year problem of how to place a high, elegant dome for Florence's cathedral (fig. 9.1). Thus, it appears individuality was born from a feud that sparked the Renaissance.

Architecture

Much of the information about Greco-Roman architecture was transmitted to Renaissance architects from the ancient Roman architect Vitruvius, who described the façades, moldings, and trim of the ancient buildings in his Treatise on Architecture (*De Architectura*, c. 15 BCE). Architects incorporated these ancient motifs into the interiors of Renaissance churches such as San Lorenzo, Pazzi Chapel, and San Andrea. Ancient motifs appeared in the exterior of numerous other buildings, including Tiempetto (fig. 9.4) by Donato Bramante (1444 to 1514), where one can see the Corinthian capitals and classical shafts with **stylobates**, or continuous base supported by columns with classical Greek architecture. The interior of San Lorenzo in Florence has **coffered**, or recessed, ceilings typical of ancient Greek temples (fig. 9.5).

Fig. 9.4 Tempietto, courtyard of San Pietro in Montorio, Bramante. Rome, Italy. c. 1502 to 1510

© siete_vidas/Shutterstock.com

Fig. 9.5 San Lorenzo, interior, Brunelleschi. Florence, Italy. c. 1420 to 1470

Perhaps as important as the interior/ exterior moldings and shapes of buildings was the fact that architects insisted that church buildings be designed with ancient ideas of mathematical proportion. Filippo Brunelleschi produced a floor plan of San Lorenzo designed in **space-block planning**, or a single geometrical unit, which became the basic shape for subsequent floor plans (fig. 9.6). His action showed a keen interest not only in Christian architectural traditions, but also in the potential mathematical beauty of a building. He is also credited with inventing **one-point perspective**, or a method for representing depth on a flat surface. This three-dimensional graphic technique is frequently cited as a principal achievement of the Renaissance.

Andrea Palladio (1508 to 1580) imitated many features of ancient Roman buildings and used them in numerous villas he built for wealthy patrons in northern Italy. One of his most celebrated buildings, the Villa Rotunda, was based on the Pantheon and was a daring achievement for its time because it represented for the first time that a dome had been mounted upon a secular building (fig. 9.7). Domes were previously reserved only for churches. Like Brunelleschi before him, Palladio also insisted on the use of space-block planning and was then repeated in arithmetic multiples.

Sculptures

The creation of the east doors to Florence's Baptistery by Ghiberti was a significant advancement in art. The artist was able to depict a perspective more naturalistically. When Michelangelo saw the doors for the first time, he reportedly remarked that the doors were worthy to be the "Gates of Paradise", and the name stuck. Ghiberti treats each of the 10 sculpted squares as if he was freely painting on a canvased surface. Each panel is a **continuous narration,** or multiple scenes shown in one image, and employed a **linear perspective,** or the illusion of depth on a flat surface.

Ghiberti arranged the episodes of the story around a vanishing point framed by the central arch of a Renaissance loggia. In

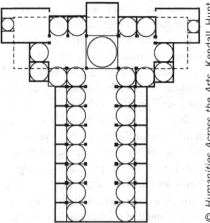

Fig. 9.6 San Lorenzo, floor plan, Brunelleschi, Florence, Italy. c. 1420 to 147.

Fig. 9.7 Villa Capra "La Rotonda", Palladio. Vicenza, Italy. 1566 to 1571

© PHOTOMDP/Shutterstock.com

Isaac with Esau and Jacob (fig. 9.8), a nearly three-dimensional foreground depicts figures rendered masterfully using this newly created scientific perspective. Architecture within the image is impressively illustrated and presents the artist as the one at the forefront of Florentine illusionism and storytelling. In the panel, Jacob obtains the birthright of his elder brother, Esau, and the blessing of their father, Isaac. In this action he becomes the founder of the Israelites. Rebekah, the boy's mother, is shown giving birth to the twins beneath the arcade on the far left. On the rooftop in the upper right, Ghiberti depicts her receiving the prophecy of her sons' future conflict.

Another well-known master to emerge during the Early Renaissance was Donato di Niccoló di Betto Bardi (1386 to 1466), better known as Donatello, a student of Ghiberti, who sculpted in marble. Early in his career he became fascinated by the optical qualities of form and by the intense inner life of his subjects. By 1430, Donatello had developed a refined style of sculpting with his most magnificent refinement showcased in his work titled

David. The work, commissioned by Cosimo de Medici, was the first freestanding nude since classical times. The sculpture exhibits a return to the classical **contrapposto**, or counter-pose, stance. The work is highly refined in symbolizing the story of both David and Goliath in the Old Testament of the Christian Bible, Christ's triumph over Satan, and the pagan mythology of the god Mercury. The sculpture, like Masaccio's *The Tribute Money* (fig. 9.10) fresco, had a double meaning. The Medici family and Florence lived in an age when kings and emperors ruled, but the city of Florence and its surrounding territory was a rare place, it was a republic. The people of Florence, furthermore, likened themselves to a political David pitted against a host of royal Goliaths.

Michelangelo di Lodovico Buonarroti Simoni (1475 to 1564), or simply Michelangelo, was a master of both sculpture and painting, his crowning achievement in sculpture being his rendition of *David* (fig. 9.9). The figure's contrapposto stance was a direct reflection of the de Medici family's revitalization of all

Fig. 9.8 *Isaac with Esau and Jacob*, "Gates of Paradise" on Florence Baptistery, bronze, Ghiberti, c. 1402 to 1424.

Fig. 9.9 *David*, marble, Michelangelo, Florence, Italy, 1501 to 1504.

things Greek and Roman. *David's* stance embodies a self-contained, heroic individualism by capturing perfectly the humanist spirit. Regardless of what impact the sculpture has on modern viewers, contemporary viewers knew both the political and moral implications of the work. The de Medici family had been exiled from Florence and many citizens saw *David* as a symbol of the city's willingness to stand up to any and all tyrannical rule, including the Medicis themselves.

Michelangelo's sculpture is often compared to Donatello's treatment of the same subject matter in bronze. In Michelangelo's piece, he allowed David to appear introspective before battle. In Donatello's piece, the viewer sees David after the fight that God alone allowed him to win, similarly to how the Medici viewed themselves. However, there was a shift in symbolism between the older and newer versions of David. By the 1500s, the people of Florence had grown tired of the Medici family. A new David arose to displace the old one (metaphorically, of course). Michelangelo's contemporaries did not need a lengthy explanation of the history behind the sculpture or its signifigance. The Biblical story of David and Goliath was well-known and the sculptures original placement was of utmost importance to the people of Florence. David was to be placed at entrance to the Town Hall, in a place of prominence, were the Signoria of Florence, the town's medieval governing body, would assembly to discuss crucial matters. The Signoria were entrusted to enter and exit the building to perform their duties for the city and not themselves. The sculpture placement would have been a continual and forceful reminder of their heavy obligation. It was almost as if David was warning them to not follow in the footsteps of Medici's.

During the later nineteenth century, Queen Victoria's reaction to the statue's nudity was typical of the Victoria Age (chapter 12). Before it was exhibited at the Victoria and Albert Museum in London, Queen Victoria ordered a plaster fig leaf be fashioned to spare the general public from any offense of *David's* nudity.

Painting

The prominence that painting holds today was unheard of during the Middle Ages.

Painting was not included among the liberal arts of the ancient Greeks, where broad intellectual capacity was thought to develop. Only rhetoric, arithmetic, astrology, and music were accepted and believed to encompass inspirational and creative imagination. Painting was believed to be a mere form of imitation, a notion perpetuated by Plato in *The Republic*. He argued how inadequately poetry and painting manage to comprehend and convey learned knowledge. Painting, therefore, was considered a mechanical skill used primarily for copying objects. It was not until the early fifteenth century that Italian painters made painting a cultured art form. Once painting was established as a respectable genre of art, it grew and changed with definitive results.

During the Early Renaissance, Tommaso di Ser Giovanni di Simone (1401 to c. 1429), or Masaccio, developed a new style of painting with the inspiration of Brunelleschi's newly discovered ancient Roman concept that allowed a painter to imply deep space and **foreshortening**, or a correct perspective, to figures. One of his most famous images is *The Tribute Money* (fig. 9.10), part of a collection of murals painted in the Brancacci Chapel in the Santa Maria del Carmine church. In the work, he added another quality so that figures had anatomically correct weight distribution, making them seem grounded and not as if

© Isogood patrick/Shutterstock.com

Fig. 9.10 *The Tribute Money*, fresco in Santa Maria del Carmine, Masaccio, Florence, Italy, c. 1427

Societal Emphasis

Images merging Roman mythology, especially the Trojan war, with heritage and Christian beliefs were popular in Italy. In 1519, Duke Alfonso d'Este (1476 to 1534), husband to Lucrezia Borgia (1498 to 1519), the daughter of Pope Alexander VI (1431 to 1503), of Ferrara commissioned Dosso Dossi to paint decorative illustrations from each book of the *Aeneid*. The painting was installed in Alfonso's private chambers. *Aeneas and Achates on the Libyan Coast* (fig 9.13) is believed to illustrate book one. In combining the past with Dossi's day, he clothes the Trojans in modern dress. The figure, therefore, resembles explorers about to undertake an expedition to the New World. An alternate motive, possibly requested by Alfonso, may have been to link himself directly to the goddess Venus through her mortal son, Aeneas, or to imply he was endowed with certain powers of amorous romps. The true meaning of the painting may be lost entirely, given it was cut to accommodate a smaller frame, a fairly common occurrence.

Courtesy National Gallery of Art, Washington

Fig. 9.13 *Aeneas and Achates on the Libyan Coast*, oil on canvas, Dossi, National Gallery of Art. c. 1520.

they were floating in midair, which is especially apparent in the contrapposto stance of the Roman tax collector.

At first glance, the image appears as just another scene from the New Testament in the *Holy Bible*. However, when Masaccio painted the fresco, there was a debate over taxation roaring in Florence. Therefore, many scholars interpret the fresco as an instruction to Florentine people, including the clerics, to pay taxes to earthly rules in support of their military defenses. Paintings such as this one illustrate a newly found independence offered to artists.

Scenes depicting the holy family and other saints were popular from the Middle Ages onward; in the Renaissance, painters created images with a one-point perspective.

Fig. 9.11 *The Annunciation,* tempera and gold on wood, Botticelli, MET, NYC, New York. c. 1485 to 1492.

The resulting imagery was one that included the illusion of depth. In Sandro Botticelli's *The Annunciation* (fig. 9.11), the artist not only produces depth but also divides the space between the holy agent, the Archangel Gabriel, and Mary to heighten the unfolding events. Gabriel's wings are still open, a sign he recently arrived to Mary's bed chamber, holding white lilies. Lilies traditionally symbolize the restoration of the soul, upon death, to the state of innocence. In Mary's case, they symbolize her virginity and purity. Mary, in turn, kneels in humility before the handmaiden of God, as she receives his divine message. Pieces such as this one were more than likely used in private devotion to the virgin.

Another major artistic achievement was by Michelangelo in the painting of the Sistine Chapel. Even though the entirety of the Sistine Chapel is a phenomenal accomplishment, one section stands out and truly captivates viewers, the central panel referred to as the *Creation of Adam* (fig. 9.12). In this work, one could feel

the tension between the spiritual and the material realm. Adam seems lethargic, inert, barely concerned with the events about to unfold, while God glides through the heavens clutching a bulging red drapery behind him. The drapery suggests both a womb and a brain, as a possible reference to creativity and reason. The association within the scene is one of how a single moment changes the course of human history. God will infuse Adam with more than energy but a soul, not just life but the future of humanity.

A discussion regarding Renaissance painters would be incomplete without mention of the most multifaceted man of the Renaissance, Leonardo di ser Piero da Vinci (1452 to 1519), a painter, architect, inventor, poet, engineer, sculptor, musician, and author. While he is remembered for his famous inventions of the tank, parachute, and bicycle, we must remember him for his medical illustrations. His illustrations were considered classics of American medicine until the early twentieth century.

Fig. 9.13 *Creation of Adam*, fresco on the ceiling of Sistine Chapel, Michelangelo, Vatican, Rome, Italy, c. 1510.

Fig. 9.14 *Mona Lisa*, oil on canvas, Da Vinci, Louvre, France. c. 1503 to 1506

Madonna Lisa, or more popularly known as *Mona Lisa,* is the subject of endless research and has probably received more attention than any other European painting (fig. 9.14). Leonardo portrays the sitter with a diffusion of lines called sfumato, or a smoky graduations, giving a special attractive quality to human flesh in portraits. But there is more to this painting than simply portraiture. Giorgio Vasari, the first art historian, wrote that Leonardo was dissatisfied with the expression on the lips of La Gioconda (Mona Lisa) and he hired musicians to perform while he painted in order to get a proper smile on her face.

Another innovation of Leonardo's was the use of parabolas, which appear widely in his paintings. Parabolic shapes appear over Mona Lisa's shoulder, in the mountainous landscape, and even in the smile on her lips, a smile that can be inscribed perfectly in the vertex of a parabola. Recent X-ray photographs of the painting show that Leonardo expanded the left shoulder of Mona Lisa's garment and enlarged it, so that it would fit into a large parabolic curve.

The geometry in Leonardo's painting style evolved over the course of his career. In the early 1480s, he left Florence to accept a position at the Sforza court in Milan, resulting in a 20-year investigation of science, mathematics, and art. He was surrounded by distinguished figures in the arts and sciences. Luca Pacioli (1447 to 1517), the father of modern accounting, asked him to do designs for a book on Euclidian geometry entitled *De Divina Proportione* (ca. 1497). Leonardo's interest in the formal subject of mathematics increased through their friendship. He devoted considerably space to geometry in his manuscripts, and even dedicated a hundred pages to the study of Euclid's Elements.

One of Leonardo's paintings from Milan, Portrait of the Lady with the Ermine (fig. 9.15a), used parabolic shapes to showcase the main motif of the painting, the inclination of the lady. Other curves in the painting such as the body of the

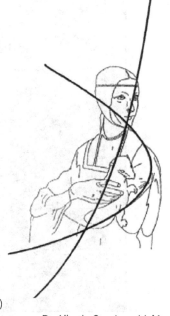

© *Humanities Across the Arts*, Kendall Hunt Publishing Company

(a)   (b)

Fig. 9.15 (a) Lady with the Ermine, oil on canvas, Da Vinci. Czartoryski Museum, Kraków, Poland. 1489 to 1490. (b) Analysis, Lady with the Ermine, Da Vinci.

animal and the necklace worn by the sitter are also parabolic. These characteristics are not immediately recognizable unless one traces the curves over the figure (fig. 9.15b).

One of the most skilled northern painters was Jan van Eyck, with works ranging from massive altarpieces to small private portraits and personal devotion imagery. He created **triptych**, or three-panels, **diptych**, or two-panels, and **polyptych**, or more than three panels, pieces depending on the scene commissioned. In *The Crucifixion; The Last Judgement* (fig. 9.16), a devotion piece commissioned by Philip the Good (1419 to 1467), Van Eyck used a diptych to highlight two important events, those of Jesus' crucifixion and the Day of Judgment. In 1426, Van Eyck traveled on a diplomatic mission to Italy and the Holy Land. But, *The*

Crucifixion scene shows little evidence of his travels, given the inclusion of European-style castles, snow-covered mountains, and Dutch windmills. Only one large, round building with multiple towers, to Jesus' left, resembles Holy Land architecture.

In *The Crucifixion* panel, in traditional fashion, Van Eyck displays Jesus with his arms wide open on a taller cross but with an array of Flemish-looking figures on horseback. In the foreground, Mary has collapsed, with her face barely visible beneath her thick blue mantle. By Mary's side are John the Baptist, even though he was deceased, and Mary Magdalene, in green, on her knees. One of the most remarkable aspects of Van Eyck's crucifix image is the moon. He is credited with painting the surface of the moon accurately for the first time.

Fletcher Fund, 1933, The Metropolitan Museum of Art

Fig. 9.16 *The Crucifixion; The Last Judgement*, oil on canvas, transferred from wood, Van Eyck, MET, New York, New York. c. 1440 to 1441.

In *The Last Judgement* image, the mood of the painting turns to one of rejoice and terror. At the top, Jesus holds out his hands to show the stigmata and the piercing on his left ribs. Both the stigmata and piercing emit golden rays of light, signifying his holiness. A host of faith individuals are greeted by angles and led into the presence of Jesus with Mary to his right and John the Baptist to the left. Michael straddles Death, represented as winged skeleton, a reference to the **memento mori**, or a warning of death. Underneath Death, sinners become enveloped by the depths of hell, a jumbled array of chaos in contrast to the uniformity of heaven. Another difference between Van Eyck's heaven and hell is the absence of clothes in hell. Sinners' naked bodies are plunged into the pits of hell where fanged beasts await their meal. To emphasize that hell does not discriminate between secular individuals and clerics, Van Eyck includes corrupt priests.

Jacopo Tintoretto (1518 to 1594) was a Mannerist who celebrated the Anti-Classical Style of painting as seen in his *The Miracle of the Loaves and Fishes* (fig. 9.17). The proportion of the figures is elongated, imitating gracefulness beyond that which is natural. The stance and gestures of Jesus and Andrew, the central figures, emulate those found in court dance. Areas within the scene are almost empty, while others are overcrowded. Later painters of the Baroque and Rocco seem to mimic Tintoretto, in both the treatment of the oil and figure configuration.

Music

The Renaissance was a youthful period in which high value was placed on beauty. Painters made youthful portraits of aristocrats and sometimes painted children holding their deceased favorite pets such as stuffed birds. Even musical scores had a humorous artistic design with some manuscripts in the shape of a **cordiform**, or heart, with notation distributed around the edges. Some composers made music so that the notes would create hidden messages or shapes in the score called **augenmusik**, or eye music, where the notes spelled out words of objects being represented in the music.

The Renaissance also produced the first systematic grouping of instruments into families or bands called "consorts." There were the instruments **bas**, or soft, consisting of flutes, recorders, and other indoor-type

Fig. 9.17 *The Miracle of the Loaves and Fishes*, oil on canvas, Tintoretto, MET, NYC, New York. c. 1545 to 1550.

Francis L. Leland Fund, 1913, The Metropolitan Museum of Art instruments and instruments **haute**, or loud, intended for outdoors, such as the cornet, sackbut, and other brass instruments. These two families of instruments, loud or soft, could be combined to produce a full consort of instruments. Michael Praetorius (1571 to 1621), a well-known composer, rendered many compositions in his *Syntagma Musica* (1550) that employed these instrumental combinations. Some of the pieces were "foot stompers", while others were stylized courtly dances. Musicians also doubled as servants, cooks, valets, and ground keepers and performed their pieces at palace functions.

Composers were no longer anonymous in the Renaissance and a few names stand out, such as Josquin des Prez (c. 1450 to 1521), Michael Praetorius (1571 to 1621), Giovanni Gabrieli (c.1555 to 1621), and Giovanni Pierluigi da Palestrina (1525 to 1594). During the latter part of the Renaissance, complicated musical forms evolved with special types of **cadences**, or chord formulas, developed to close off sections of music. A major expressive development occurred when the rhythm of church music was allowed to subdivide into sets of twos, instead of three, a former symbolic reference to the Father, Son, and Holy Spirit. One of the principal features of Renaissance music was the overlapping of voice parts, something akin to singing rounds and referred to as "points of imitation." The voices do not all sing together, but enter at staggered time intervals. The effect was somewhat like the sound of a camp song such as "Row, row, row, your boat...."

Although opera is often construed as an invention of the Baroque, it was actually developed during the late Renaissance as a revival of ancient Greek theater. Florentine intellectuals met at Count Bardi's palace in Florence to create a modern counterpart of ancient Greek music. They succeeded in developing **recitative**, or music that is half sung and half spoken. Recitative was linked with songs called **arias**, or music with an expressive melody, thus setting the stage for the production of opera in the late 1500s. Aria and recitative became the principal pair among the various numbers of opera. Representative of the Greek revival spirit, the earliest operas by Jacopo Peri (1561 to 1633), Giulio Caccini (1551 to 1618), and Claudio Monteverdi (1567 to 1643) were based upon ancient Greek mythology, rather than Christian subjects. In opera, one needs songs, recitative, instruments, and staging. All of these were inventions of the Renaissance and brought together in the 1590s.

Since there were no musical models to imitate from the ancient world, composers had to find ways to create parallel musical styles in the Renaissance. In essence, opera was a Renaissance update of ancient Greek drama. Everything found in an ancient Greek drama such as action, musical delivery, instrumental accompaniment, and staging were now found in Renaissance opera. Most of these elements came together in a production of *Oedipus Rex* (1585) at the Teatro Olympico in Vincenzo, Italy (Fig. 9.18). Combined with the illusory effects provided by the Scammozzi multiple point perspective stage, the total effect on the audience at the time was compelling.

Literature

Petrarch's (1304 to 1374) passion for the classical Greco-Roman culture revived the forgotten works of the Roman orator and statesman Cicero, thus igniting a flame that grew into a blazing fire of ideas 50 years after his death. The ideas found in his writings prompted the renewal of the Sophist's concept of humanism. As the "Father of Humanism," Petrarch acted as a pivotal figure in turning literature from medieval to Renaissance thinking with the resurgence, analysis, and

Fig. 9.18 Teatro Olympico with Vincenzo Scammozzi perspective stage design, Palladio, Vicenza, Italy, 1580 to 1585.

expansion of Greek and Roman thought. In his writings, he espoused the application of these cultures' principles to education, politics, social life, art, and literature in general. His body of work alone prompted a renewal in the value of the individual, leading to the idea of self-determination.

Much of Petrarch's poems were written in a style similar to that of the troubadours of the High Middle Ages. His poems are about love and longing for a maiden named Laura. For example, take sonnet 338:

Death, you have left the world
without a sun
dark and cold, Love blind and
unarmed,
Graciousness naked, and Beauty
ill,
me disconsolate, with my heavy
burden,
Courtesy banned, and Honesty in
the deep.

I alone grieve, but not only I have
cause,
that the brightest seed of virtue's
gone:
with the first value quenched,
where is there another?
The air, and earth, and sea should
weep
for the human race, that without
her
is a field without flowers, a ring
with no gem.
The world did not know her while
she lived:
I knew, I who am left to my
weeping,
and Heaven, so beautified by her
I weep for.

Unlike the poems of the High Middle Ages, Petrarch has a stylistic sophistication and endeavors for the perfection of arrangement found in the classical works by Ovid,

Virgil, and Horace. The Petrarch sonnet would eventually be imported to England, where Shakespeare adopted it to create Shakespearean sonnets over 200 years later.

Philosophy

As the Renaissance's Neo-Platonism replaced the Aristotelianism of St. Thomas Aquinas, attempts were made to join the great works of Antiquity with Christian values in a syncretic Christian humanism, as seen in the writings of Marsilio Ficino (1433 to 1499) and Pico della Mirandola (1463 to 1494). Ethics was taught independently of theology, and the authority of the Church was tacitly transferred to the reasoning logic of the educated individual. Thus, humanists were placing human reason above the teachings of the Church, and they constantly skirted the dangers of being branded as heretics. Although Renaissance humanists were more accepting of pagan philosophy than their scholastic contemporaries, they did not necessarily object to the idea that Christian understanding should be dominant over other modes of thought. As humanists increasingly opposed the strict Catholic orthodoxy of scholastic philosophy, some began to intermingle pagan virtues with Christian virtues and revive religious ideas from the late-classical Greek world, and some risked being declared heretics for distancing themselves from the Church.

Beginning in 1453, a young priest named Marsilio Ficino, under the support of Cosimo de' Medici, translated and interpreted the works of Plato and subsequent Platonic philosophers. Using Plato's thoughts on the sphere of being in an eternal, unchanging space and our world as continually altering, Ficino promoted the idea that human reason was in the realm of the eternal. Through the realization of mathematics and our moral compass, humans can commune with the eternal sphere of the being. His notion of the Great Chain of Being was a ladder where the creations of God stepped up stairs with nonliving objects at the bottom and God at the top. Ficino's model of the order of the universe resided in an entities relationship with God. In time, this idea led him to coin the term **Platonic love**, or an idyllic physical relationship, found between two people who, like Plato, strove to find the virtuous, the genuine, and the beauty in life.

While at the Neo-Platonic Academy, a student of Ficino's named Pico della Mirandola wrote one of the most influence documents about humanist thoughts, *Oration on the Dignity of Man*, in 1486. The oration contained 900 theses pertaining to ancient and medieval paganism, and writing by Christian, Jewish, and Muslim authorities. According to Mirandola:

> The nature of all other creatures is defined and restricted within laws which We have laid down; you, by contrast, impeded by no such restrictions, may, by your own free will, to whose custody We have assigned you, trace for yourself the lineaments of your own nature.

Mirandola's writing reinforces the idea that man has considerable amounts of freedom. He was, in essence, arguing that humankind is completely free to exercise free will and how this gift of free will makes humans the most fortunate of all living creatures.

For Mirandola, there was a hierarchical universe with humans residing just beneath angles and above animals with God at the top. He believed humans had the ability to become divine if they used their free will and reason properly. His writings, not surprisingly, were condemned as heretical and Pico was labeled a heretic. When Pope Alexander VI ascended the papal thrown in 1493, he reversed the charges against Pico. Sadly, Mirandola died the following year, never able to fully expand his thoughts.

If Michelangelo was the quintessential artist of the High Renaissance, Niccolò Machiavelli was his equivalent in all matters related to political philosophy. To modern, nongoverning individuals, his most famous work, *The Prince*, may seem at odds with our sensibilities of charity, compassion, and self-respect. *The Prince* comments at length about the responsibilities of a leader to their people, saying:

> A Prince ... should have no care or thought but for war ... for war is the sole art looked for in one who rules ... we often see that when Princes devote themselves rather to pleasure than to arms, they lose their dominions ... need never hesitate ... to incur the reproach of those vices without which his authority can hardly be preserved; for if he will consider the whole matter, he will find that there may be a line of conduct having the appearance of virtue, to follow which would be his

ruin, and that there may be another course having the appearance of vice, by following which his safety and well-being are secured.

To fully understand the meaning of *The Prince*, a reader must not approach these writings with modern sensibilities or the entire message will be lost. In the aforementioned passage, Machiavelli suggests that the well-being of the prince is synonymous with the well-being of the state. These words, more than likely, served as a warning for the absentee Medici popes who were far away in Rome not tending to business in Florence. Additionally, the lessons were drawn from Roman history and intended as a guide to aid Italy in rebuffing the French invasion.

These ideas of humanism demonstrated the pride and confidence in the human mind and value on human accomplishments, which was almost like worshiping man and human nature rather than God. Of these two directions, the first mostly dissipated as an intellectual trend, later leading to movements in Western esotericism such as Theosophy and New Age thinking, while the second has had the great continuing influence on Western thought.

Innovation and Progress

Superior weaponry allows for military triumph, as was the case when the Ottoman Turks laid siege to Constantinople in 1453. The use of **mortars**, or a portable, short-barreled, muzzle-loading artillery piece, for the first time in recorded history provided the Ottomans the ability to fire explosive projectiles at lower velocity with higher, arcing trajectory toward the city's fortification. Mortars are a military advancement over the use of the cannons, which were first used in the late twelfth or early thirtieth century in China. Mortars offered their holder the capability of a lighter weight weapon for attacking from a distance. The mortars worked and Constantinople fell for the first time into non-Christian hands in over 1,000 years.

Technology

One important item manufactured during the Renaissance, books, came as a direct result of the invention of movable type for the printing press (fig. 9.19). The tradition of using parchment as a writing surface carried into the Renaissance, with the first Gutenberg Bibles being printed on parchment. In time, printing costs created serious financial problems as print runs ran into the hundreds and thousands. Three thousand copies of Martin Luther's New Testament, for example, were published in 1522. Paper, introduced a few centuries earlier, solved the economic problem and production of this material developed as a result of the growth in the cottage industry in the fifteenth century. In fact, paper became a useful product for a variety of trades, including the graphic arts and music. Some of the greatest drawings were created on paper during the Renaissance.

Originally, manuscripts were copied by hand by scribes in monasteries. One of the earliest uses of paper for printing was for music composition The invention of the movable type allowed for musical manuscripts to be duplicated and circulated easier and more quickly. Ottaviano Petrucci (1466 to 1539), one of the earliest publishers of sheet music, produced instrumental catalogs and composition books, *Harmonice Musices Odhecaton*, that remain the classic source for Renaissance music. Print shops divided up labor between the type casters, woodcutters, who created the illustrations, paper makers, bookbinders, and printers.

The printing press made possible a whole new culture that opened up a world of communication about the past and speculation about the future. In Enchiridion's *Handbook of a Christian Knight* of 1503, he celebrated the Dutch Christian traditionalist Erasmus, who recommended the study of ancient writings. Studying the ancients was

Fig. 9.19 Replica of a Renaissance printing press.

a radical suggestion for the time. Though almost nothing is known of his work today, Enchiridion was widely read and circulated at the time because of the invention of the movable type for the printing press.

Publication allowed other forms of literature to develop including criticism and art history; the translation of the Bible into English, now known as the King James Bible. Writers gained fame by publishing personal essays using the personal pronoun "I." Giorgio Vasari (1511 to 1574), the first art historian in the West, produced his biographical book, *Lives of the Artists*, and Machiavelli wrote *The Prince*, a book that offered leaders advice on how to obtain and maintain power and control. Machiavelli advised rulers to learn "how not to be good" in order to promote the welfare of the state. Renaissance playwrights such as William Shakespeare (1564 to 1616) popularized a Greco-Roman revival in the north. Shakespeare adopted not only the concept of the tragedy as seen in "Romeo and Juliet" but also famous characters from the past such as "Julius Caesar". His poetry possesses the highly ordered character of ancient lyrics, deriving from the Italian conceit, and originating in the ancient Roman love poetry of Ovid.

RENAISSANCE LEGACY

During the sixteenth century, people across Europe began to explore the globe. They recognized their technological advancement when encountering cultures in the areas they explored. The peoples of China, Japan, and the Islamic world were less advanced compared with those of sixteenth-century Europe, but many innovations originated from these regions. Western progress and dominance was due to the rise of capitalism. The growth of capitalism was the result of many European cities' faith in reason. Reason would impact the development of Europe in providing a distinct cultural identity through the Christian faith. Christianity embraced reason and logic as the primary way to religious truth, as is evident in

Renaissance art. Christian faith in reason was influenced by Greek philosophy as it helped preserve the rational Greco-Roman thought.

As discovered in pervious chapters, many other cultures' religions placed a greater emphasis on myths, mystery, and intuition. From the early Christian fathers onward, the Church taught that reason was created by God and given to man. Mankind was destined to employ human reason and it was a means to progressively increase man's understanding. Renaissance thinkers began to orient their selves toward the future. They used logic to understand nature in a rational manner and create a better material, earthly life. The scholastics and the great medieval universities of Europe which were founded by the Church fostered faith in the power of reason to penetrate Western culture, which stimulated the pursuit of science and the evolution of democratic theory and practice. Reason inspired by the Church led to the rise of capitalism.

Critical Thinking

Examine how Florence came to embody the rebirth of human consciousness.

Describe how humanism is more than a philosophy.

Analyze how the Medici family influenced the Renaissance.

Explore the significance of both Donatello and Michelangelo's *David*.

Explain which Renaissance values were reflected in all forms of art.

Examine how literature and philosophy were interconnected.

ONLINE RESOURCES

Recognizing Italian Renaissance Art Video
https://smarthistory.org/how-to-recognize-italian-renaissance-art/
Ghiberti's *Gates of Paradise* **Video**
https://smarthistory.org/lorenzo-ghiberti-gates-of-paradise-east-doors-of-the-florence-baptistery/
Brunelleschi's Dome of the Florence Cathedral Video
https://smarthistory.org/brunelleschi-dome-of-the-cathedral-of-florence/
Donatello's *Mary Magdalene* **Video**
https://smarthistory.org/donatello-mary-magdalene/
Masaccio's *Expulsion of Adam and Eve from Eden* **Video**
https://smarthistory.org/masaccio-expulsion-of-adam-and-eve-from-eden/
Botticelli's *La Primavera* **Video**
https://smarthistory.org/sandro-botticelli-la-primavera-spring/
Galileo and Renaissance Art
https://smarthistory.org/galileo-and-renaissance-art/
Leonardo's *The Virgin of the Rocks* **Video**
https://smarthistory.org/leonardo-virgin-of-the-rocks/
Michelangelo's Ceiling of the Sistine Chapel Video
https://smarthistory.org/michelangelo-ceiling-of-the-sistine-chapel/
Michelangelo's *Pietà* **Video**
https://smarthistory.org/michelangelo-pieta/
Northern Renaissance
https://smarthistory.org/an-introduction-to-the-northern-renaissance-in-the-fifteenth-century/
Bosch's *The Garden of Earthly Delights*
https://smarthistory.org/bosch-the-garden-of-earthly-delights/
Dürer's *The Four Apostles* **Video**
https://smarthistory.org/albrecht-durer-the-four-apostles/
Renaissance Humanism Philosophy and Literature
https://www.thoughtco.com/renaissance-humanism-248119
Mannerism Overview
https://smarthistory.org/a-beginners-guide-to-mannerism/
Parmigianino's *Madonna of the Long Neck* **Video**
https://smarthistory.org/parmigianino-madonna-of-the-long-neck/
Sofonisba Anguissola
https://smarthistory.org/sofonisba-anguissola/

Reformation and Baroque: An Examination of Christian Faith

Fig. 10.1 *The Elevation of the Cross*, oil on wood, Ruben, center alter panel in The Cathedral of Our Lady, Antwerp, Belgium. 1609.

Knowledge Acquisition

◆ *Examine the artistic and cultural shifts made in architecture, sculpture, painting, music, theater, literature, and philosophy during the Reformation and Baroque.*

◆ *Evaluate the principal accomplishments by Bernini, Borromini, Caravaggio, Dürer, Poussin, Rembrandt, Rubens, Shakespeare, Velázquez, and Vermeer.*

◆ *Discover how the Baroque era connects works of art from around the world to its own artistic, cultural, literary, and political interests.*

SETTING THE SCENE

During the Early Renaissance, Petrarch promoted the revival of classical learning and literature referred to as humanism. The humanists wanted to extend quality education to laypeople by investigating natural phenomena without religious bias and logically scrutinizing philosophical and theological teachings. Contrary to popular understanding, the rise of humanism was not intended to signify a decline in the importance of Christian values, as most art in Europe still contained an intense Christian spirituality. However, there was growing skepticism about the Western Church in the minds of Renaissance thinkers. As a result, just as the Renaissance was reaching the northern boundaries of Europe and into England, so was a new way of thinking about religious and secular duties of those in positions of authority. A movement known as the Protestant Reformation questioned the Catholic Church's understanding of the Bible and the use of imagery.

The Roman Catholic Church launched the largest building and decoration campaign in the history of the West to bring back parishioners who had strayed to Protestantism. The movement became known as the Baroque, and like the term Gothic, Baroque is a judgmental term used to describe the Church's efforts. It derives from the Portuguese word **barocco** meaning "imperfect." Portuguese pearl divers who brought up oysters with misshaped pearls often exclaimed them to be "barocco" since they were unsellable. Nineteenth-century art historians used the French version of this word *baroque* to describe the art and architecture immediately following the Renaissance that they viewed as overly embellished and excessively theatrical.

REFORMATION

Throughout the fourteenth and early fifteenth centuries in Europe, a new religious movement, referred to as **modern devotion**, or renewal through genuine pious practices, rose to prominence. The movement was one where untrained biblical individuals gathered and organized themselves in households to encourage a lifestyle comparable to that of monks and nuns. They did not take monastic vows and, therefore, continued to marry and have children. The modern devotion movement ended shortly after the Protestant Reformation began, creating a historical division between religious and secular life.

Global Focal Point

In 1587, Hideyoshi (r. 1585 to 1591) prohibited the Japanese people from practicing Christianity as he was deeply suspicious of the religion. By 1597, 26 individuals had been executed for disobeying the order and in 1603 foreigners living in Japan were banned from participating in the faith. Instead, the people were encouraged to rely on the philosophy of Confucius to bring about individual happiness and to define their roles in society. The Japanese were forbidden to travel abroad in 1635 and trade was further limited to the Dutch in 1641, who were confined to a specific area within the city of Nagasaki. Japan remained closed off to the West until American commodore Matthew Perry (1794 to 1858) presented a letter from the president of the United States. Japan opened its ports to the world the following year.

Three individuals are considered central reformer figures of the Protestant Reformation movement, Martin Luther (1483 to 1546), Ulrich Zwingli (1484 to 1531), and John Calvin (1509 to 1564). A number of issues led to the formal break from the Roman Catholic Church by faithful individuals, beginning around 1050 CE of the High Middle Ages. Among those issues were the sale of **indulgences**, or a paid remission for sins, differences in biblical rituals and practices, the body and spirit relationship, and the concepts of grace, predestination, and transubstantiation. Each reformer used variations of these basic criticisms against the Catholic Church, ending in different outcomes on the basis of the society in which they lived.

The most successful, and therefore prominent, reformer of the Protestant movement was Martin Luther, a German Catholic monk of the Augustinian order. His significant contribution to the protest was in speaking out against the sale of indulgences by the Catholic Church. Selling indulgences was a very lucrative business where Catholic Church officials believed they had amassed a "surplus of merits" or good deeds. These merits, according to the Catholic Church, were sellable to a truly penitent person, in order to liberate them from their obligatory penance for their sins in purgatory. For Luther, there was no need to purchase good deeds in order to obtain favor with God and, therefore, salvation from Jesus.

Luther started to formulate an opposition to the sale of indulgences on the basis of biblical facts and not on clerical teaching. From Luther's understanding of the Bible, Jesus atoned for humankind's sins, otherwise what was the point of his sacrifice. Jesus alone provided the faithful with the assurance of their salvation. Luther's major complaint against the sale of indulgences was directed at the Catholic Church taking away money from the poor in return for atonement for sins and then using the money to beautify Rome with extravagant works of art. In 1510, he began teaching the doctrine of salvation by faith alone rather than through one's deeds.

In addition, England would make a full break from the Catholic Church under King Henry VIII (r. 1509 to 1547). Without the earlier reformers of the Reformation on the Continent, England's departure from the Church would have proven near impossible. Once the flood gates were open, a great deal of free thinking flowed out of England in the form of its musicians, artists, and most celebrated playwright of the day William Shakespeare (1564 to 1616).

BAROQUE (OR COUNTER-REFORMATION)

By the mid-sixteenth century, the Catholic Church underwent an internal reform centered on a desire to revive the spirituality of the faithful. The Counter-Reformation, also known as the Baroque, was led by Pope Paul III (r. 1534 to 1549) and was designed as a direct attack and in opposition to the Protestant Reformation preached by Martin Luther and other reformers, in both doctrine and practices. Faithful Catholics wanted the Catholic Church to provide a constructive impact on the newer contemporary times. Pope Paul III delivered on the wants of faithful Catholics who opposed Protestantism and sought a faith more in line with everyday life. As early as the writings of the Catholic theologians St. Augustine and St. Thomas, a push existed to reconcile the authority of God with the free will of humankind.

As time passed, gaps between these two issues continued to widen until open conflict occurred in the 1550s aided by the Reformation movement in Northern Europe, where Catholics were mixing the two doctrines of Protestantism and

Catholicism together. In delineating the differences between Catholics and Protestants, many characteristics of traditional Catholicism were removed. All of the major reforms of the Church took place in the city of Trent by the Council of Trent from 1545 to 1562, and over these 17 years, a number of issues were decided upon. The most striking difference between Protestantism and Catholicism was that Protestants put individual conscience and the Bible first. Faithful Catholics maintained that human consciousness and Scriptures must be interpreted by the Church in consideration of the faith's traditional arrangement. The Baroque era also boasted of profound thinkers such as Francis Bacon (1561 to 1626), Nicolas Copernicus (1473 to 1543), Galileo Galilei (1564 to 1642), and William Harvey (1562 to 1626),

CREATIVE IMPULSE

After years of religious warring between Catholic supporters and Protestant reformers, two styles of art emerged in the seventeenth century. Catholics turned to creating highly ornate works on the basis of the lives of saints with recurring motifs. Protestants favored a simpler style including portraits with a single light source as a reflection of Jesus. An accurate understanding of their stylistic differences is discerned when appreciating them side-by-side.

Architecture

Saint Carl of the Four Fountain (fig. 10.3), named for the four corner fountains, designed by Francesco Borromini (1599 to 1667), is a small but symmetrical church built on an irregular street intersection. The exterior of the church has repeated patterns creating an unusually, non-Roman, structure. The stone façade appears elastic and dynamic as it curves undulated up and down. The reason for this unconventional façade was a brilliant solution to a problem with the church's position on a narrow street. His solution was to break the viewpoint in two, with an elaborate balcony uniting the two smaller façade arrangements.

Cross-cultural Connection

Almost a century before San Carlo alle Quattro Fontane was constructed, Russia built Saint Basil's Cathedral (fig. 10.2) for Tsar Ivan IV (r. 1547 to 1584). The cathedral does not follow the traditional look as it has of seven churches around the central church; instead the architects designed an eight-sided symmetrical floor plan. A tenth, much smaller church dedicated to Saint Basil was added in 1588. Each compass point of the church is decided to a different saint. The vivid color of the cathedral developed over time beginning in the 1680s.

© Mary_Photo/Shutterstock.com

Fig. 10.2 Saint Basil's Cathedral, white stone and red brick, Barma and Postnik Yakovel, Moscow, Russia. 1555 to 1561.

Baroque interior design was as unique as their exteriors and included endless repetition patters appearing both orderly and natural in formation. The presence of repetition gives these structures the additional appearance of an ornate quality. The *Baldacchino, Canopy* (fig. 10.4), in St. Peter's Basilica in Rome is an exquisite example of Gian Lorenzo Bernini's (1598 to 1680) effect of extensive architectural trim. There are dozens of repeated leaves wrapping around the spiral columns. The arms and legs of the dozens of putti figures that surround the stained glass window, *Gloria,* above the Chair of St. Peter's Basilica (fig. 10.5), add to the spectacle.

Sculptures

Just as Baroque sculptural decoration is replete with repetition of shapes, so are the freestanding figures. The exuberance of a Baroque figure such as Bernini's self-portrait

Fig. 10.3 San Carlo alle Quattro Fontane, façade, Borromini, Rome, Italy. c. 1638 to 1667.

© Khirman Vladimir/Shutterstock.com

© grafxart/Shutterstock.com

Fig. 10.4 *Baldacchino, Canopy*, St. Peter's Basilica, Rome. Bernini, 1623 to 1624.

© vvoe/Shutterstock.com

Fig. 10.5 *Gloria and Chair of St. Peter*, Bernini, St. Peter's Basilica, Rome, Italy. 1657 to 1666.

in David (fig. 10.6) shows an attention to organic shapes in the muscles, cloth, and hair that contrasts sharply with Michelangelo's Renaissance version (fig. 9.9). Michelangelo's David appears as cool, calm, and collected, a person thinking about what he must do in order to conquer Goliath. By contrast, Bernini shows David inscribed within a parabolic curve in the act of actually throwing the stone at the giant.

Another of Bernini's imaginative installation, *The Ecstasy of Saint Teresa* (fig. 10.7), forms the central sculptural piece in the Cornaro Chapel in Santa Maria della Vittoria in Rome. Saint Theresa is the focal point of the chapel and was made in the image of Saint Theresa of Avila, a popular saint of the Baroque. She was known to have been visited by an angel who thrust his spear into her, which led to her claiming that "the pain was so great that I screamed aloud, but simultaneously I felt such infinite sweetness that

Fig. 10.6 *David*, marble, Bernini, Galleria Borghese, Rome, Italy. 1623 to 1624.

I wished the pain to last eternally." Bernini depicted the moment of religious mysticism as described by Theresa of Avila and created a sense of transcendence. Theresa had just been pierced by the arrow of the angel and was literally rising to be at one with God. However, Bernini represented an angel who, instead of plunging the arrow into her heart, is actually pulling it out, and the euphoric relief can be seen on her face.

Painting

A painter associated with the ornate Catholic style was Peter Paul Rubens (1557 to 1640), who generated a plethora of works from his studio in Antwerp. His efforts were aided by a large group of aspiring studio assistants who helped him produce massively imposing and remarkable paintings. Rubens drew out his own designs, but his studio assistants transferred them to large canvases and partially completed them by showcasing each student's specialty. But, Rubens was there to oversee the final details.

The Elevation of the Cross (fig. 10.1) is a triptych high altarpiece original installed in the Church of St. Walpurgis in Antwerp until it was demolished in 1817. It now resides at the Cathedral of Our Lady in Antwerp. Repeated organic shapes in the muscles of the depicted figures and the leaves of vegetation in this painting create a compelling and dramatic visual display. In this painting, and others, Rubens uses nudes in a densely textured pattern surrounded by people of importance such as saints, martyrs, and those well connected with the traditional church.

The central panel depicts the Baroque sense of heightened drama. Rubens has painted the moment when Christ's crucifixion cross was raised into its upright position. A strong diagonal emphasis was created by Rubens placing the base of the cross at the far right of the canvas and the

Fig. 10.7 *The Ecstasy of Saint Teresa*, marble, Bernini, Cornaro Chapel in Santa Maria della Vittoria, Rome, Italy. 1647 to 1652.

top of the cross in the upper left. The angular configuration of Jesus's body causes it to be the main focal point and creates a sense of this event unfolding before the viewer. The viewer is now in the midst of watching the overly muscular men struggle to lift Jesus's weight, a burden the viewer shares.

In 1500, the most astonishing artist in Rome was Michelangelo. A century later, in 1600, the artist who intrigued Rome was also named Michelangelo, better known by his last name Caravaggio (1571 to 1610). Caravaggio was also Rubens's counterpart in Italy which was to the south of Belgium. In 1599, he received a prized commission to paint two massive works for the Contarelli Chapel in the Church of San Luigi dei Francesi portraying pivotal moments in the life of Saint Matthew. Until this commission, Caravaggio painted only enchanted genre scenes and still life's (fig. 10.8).

In the gospel of Matthew (Matt. 9:9), readers learn about the moment when Christ stopped at the place where tax collectors gathered to count their daily collections. Matthew was counting his receipts and Jesus said, "Follow me." Instantly, Matthew left his bags of coins, tax ledgers, and joined the handful of men who became known as the Twelve Apostles.

Caravaggio depicted the moment of the Matthew's call in *The Calling of Saint* (fig. 10.9). Jesus is off-center and is obscured by a shadow in the grungy counting house. Two of Matthew's fellow tax collectors do not even lift their eyes from the pile of coins to see who has entered the room. As for Matthew, his expression betrays his astonishment—eyes wide, finger pointing to his chest, you can almost hear him answer, "Who? Me?" Notice Jesus's outstretched arm, the index finger pointing at Matthew; it is the

Fig. 10.8 *The Musicians*, oil on canvas, Caravaggio, MET, NYC, New York. c. 1597

Fig. 10.9 *Calling of Saint Matthew*, oil on canvas, Caravaggio, San Luigi dei Francesi, Rome, Italy. 1599–1600.

mirror image of God gesturing to Adam at the moment he infused him with life in the iconic scene from the Sistine Chapel ceiling (fig. 9.12, in Chapter 9). With the same gesture, Jesus, Son of God, makes Matthew a man infused with a new life. Caravaggio was not accidently in Jesus' gesture, the pointing of his finger and outreached hand mirrored that of Michelangelo's *Creation of Adam* on the ceiling of the Sistine chapel. And, is viewed by scholars as a tribute from one Michelangelo to another.

An increase in the business class of the Protestant Dutch supported the contrasting style of paintings found in both Rembrandt Harmenszoon van Rijn (1606 to 1699) and his younger contemporary, Johannes Vermeer (1632 to 1675). Protestants wanted their life

reflected in the paintings they purchased, which consisted of restrained posture and mundane activities (fig. 10.11). These **genre**, or common settings of everyday life, designs appealed to the individual taste of the commissioner rather than the fulfillment of commissions to a Catholic church.

Rembrandt was the most accomplished of all the Dutch Baroque painters, his works varying from a single sitter to groups either

Societal Emphasis

The tulip is a mysterious, drama-filled flower only revealing its beauty, or the lack thereof, after months or even years of anticipation. Ogier de Busbecq (1522 to 1591), ambassador of the Holy Roman Emperor to Turkey, is credited with introducing Europe to the flower in 1554. Bulbs were sent to Vienna and then to Augsburg, Antwerp, and Amsterdam. As Dutch merchants grew in wealth in the 1600s, so did the rest of Dutch society. The tulip became the ultimate status symbol of wealth between 1634 and 1637, a period

Fig. 10.10 *Still Life of Flowers in a Glass Vase*, oil on copper, Van der Ast, The Museum of Fine Art, Houston, Houston, Texas. c. 1624.

Source: Sarah Campbell Blaffer Foundation, Houston, The Museum of Fine Art, Houston

known as Tulip Mania. If a Dutchman could not afford a tulip bulb, he commissioned artists to paint them one. While the finest tulip painters such as Balthasar van der Ast (1593 to 1657) and his *Still Life of Flowers in a Glass Vase* (fig. 10.10) could command thousands of guilders for a single painting, a single bulb of "Admiral Liefkens'" fetched more than 4,000 guilders at an auction on February 5, 1637 and "Admiral van Enkhuijsen" almost 5,500 guilders, the peak of Tulip Mania. A single bulb at the peak of the mania cost 10 times more than the annual income of a skilled craftsman. But, by May 1637, the mania had collapsed.

Fig. 10.11 *Herman Doomer*, oil on wood, Rembrandt, MET, NYC, New York. 1640.

seemingly motionless or in action. When he married Saskia van Uylenburgh (1612 to 1642) in 1634, she was from a wealthy family and often his model. Her early death in 1642 saw a devastating turn of events. The same year he painted the *Night Watch* (fig. 10.12) and began having financial difficulties as his style became more personal and difficult for patrons to comprehend.

The painting is a large group portrait of Captain Cocq and his men opening the gates. The images were first thought to portray the men going into the night to watch over the city. Once cleaned and historical records scoured, it was soon realized that the men were opening the gate to welcome Marie de' Medici, queen of France. In true Baroque fashion, Rembrandt created a composition in action with multiple diagonals cutting across the surface. While the captain and

Fig. 10.12 *Captain Cocq Mustering His Company (Night Watch)*, oil on canvas, Rembrandt, Rijksmuseum, Amsterdam. c. 1642.

his lieutenant was the main focal point, they were not yet at the center of the image but instead were walking toward it. The act of walking was a means of implying movement, a convention hard to discern after the painting was cut to accommodate a smaller space for display. The second, and probably, more prominent focal point was the small angelic figure to the right of Captain Cocq. The figure was believed to be Saskia, painted as a memorial to her.

Vermeer avoided the use of heightened drama to offer his private patrons more realistic images with a near photographic quality. Much evidence suggests that Vermeer used a **camera obscure**, or a means of projecting an image onto a screen inside a darkened box, to aid in attaining a photographic image on canvas. Under conventional setting, the human eye cannot detect the thin white line surrounding objects. The addition of this minute but significant element within the painting gave his works an amplified sense of photographic reality.

Vermeer worked both as an artist and as a frame maker in Delft, painting business class people in genre painting. In *The Milkmaid* (fig. 10.13), a piercing ray hits the window and light streaks across the objects of the painting. In turn, this creates a pattern of light and dark shapes, a chief trademark of similar Dutch paintings.

Spain was blessed to have a skilled Baroque painter in Diego Velázquez (1599 to 1660), who began painting flawless images at the age of 20. He was heavily influenced by the works of Caravaggio in his earlier works, with a keen interest in dramatic lighting, focus on people, and presenting the figures close to the picture plane. His techniques would lead the viewers' eyes into the picture and around the canvas to take it all in at once. In 1623, the same year he completed *The Supper at Emmaus* (fig. 10.14), he was appointed

Fig. 10.13 *The Milkmaid*, oil on canvas, Vermeer, Rijks Museum, Amsterdam, Netherlands. 1660.

© Everett-Art/Shutterstock.com

court painter by King Philip IV of Spain (r. 1621 to 1665). In *The Supper*, he employs realism in his figures, a strong sense of dramatic lighting, and a keen attention to still life detailing.

His most celebrated work, *Maid of Honor* (*La Meninas*), is of Princess Margarita painted in 1656 where he combines group portraiture with everyday life on a larger-than-life scale. The painting includes a host of royal attendants from the princesses maid of honors to a nun and dwarf, and Velázquez, himself, is posed painting. In the background, the reflection of the king and the queen are seen in a mirror on the back wall. Velázquez, in effect, created three viewpoints. The first viewpoint was in sharing the space with the king and the queen. The second was with the princess and Velázquez, while the third, and final, space resided in the doorway as the man exits the room.

France became the cultural center of Europe at the beginning of the seventeenth century. Nicholas Poussin (1594 to 1665) cultivated a healthy appreciation for the

Bequest of Benjamin Altman, 1913, The Metropolitan Museum of Art

Fig. 10.14 *The Supper at Emmaus*, oil on canvas, Velázquez, MET, NYC, New York. c. 1622 to 1623.

classical approach to painting as he spent a good portion of his career around or in Rome. His painting varied from religious scenes to both Greek and Roman mythology. Throughout his career Poussin returned to the subject matter of the Holy Family. In *The Holy Family with Saint John the Baptist* (fig. 10.15), he depicts the family sitting under an apple tree with lovely rendered **putti**, or naked cherubs, picking apples and presenting them to Mary. In the foreground, a single apple sits on a blanket linking Jesus to Adam as the salvation of his fall and mankind's. Poussin also includes a grape vine twisting around the apple tree and a lamb, a symbol of Eucharist and redemption.

In other images such as *The Abduction of the Sabine Women* (fig. 10.16), he invokes stories found in Roman mythology. The myth tells the account of when the Romans invited their neighbors, the Sabines, to a festival with the intent of keeping the women in Rome by force. Romulus, in the red cloak, signals his men to seize the women by raising his cloak. Poussin also used the painting to showcase his knowledge of ancient sculpture and architecture along with his ability to convey action through gestures and poses.

Printmaking

The ideas of the Protestant Reformation would eventually find their way into the art world, especially in works by the German painter and printmaker Albrecht Dürer. Prints are of three types: woodcuts, engraving, and etching. **Woodcuts** are the oldest and originate from China. The artist cuts images into the wood block, leaving raised lines that are printed. Ink is applied to the surface of the wood, paper is immersed in water. The paper is placed on the printing press with the woodcut block on top. Pressure is applied to transfer the image to the paper in reverse. **Engravings** use metal to

Bequest of Lore Heinemann, in memory of her husband, Dr. Rudolf J. Heinemann, 1996, The Metropolitan Museum of Art

Fig. 10.15 *The Holy Family with Saint John the Baptist*, oil on canvas, Poussin, MET, NYC, New York. c. 1627.

Harris Brisbane Dick Fund, 1946, The Metropolitan Museum of Art

Fig. 10.16 *The Abduction of the Sabine Women*, oil on canvas, Poussin, MET, NYC, New York. c. 1633 to 1634.

cut the image into the surface of a plate. Ink is pressed into the cavities and the surface is whipped clean. Dampened paper is placed on the printing press and the pressure from the press transfers to the image to the paper in reverse. **Etchings** are similar to the engraving technique but less labor intensive. A waxy coating is used to coat the metal place and a pointed tool draws the image onto the plate, exposing the metal. A weak acid is used to "bite" away the exposed metal and then the wax is removed. Printing occurs in a manner similar to that of engraving, but the image is not in reverse.

The art of Albrecht Dürer attests to the social changes witnessed throughout Northern Europe. In the print called *Knight, Death, and the Devil* (fig. 10.17), one can observe the reversal of years of Church domination. No longer were the faithful being extorted by the Church for their favor with God. Dürer also does not include the normal biblical cast of characters such as Jesus, Mary, and John the Baptist to emphasize how one obtains salvation. Instead, it is through diligent belief and faithfulness one will be taken into the "Kingdom of Heaven."

According to the *Heilbrunn Timeline of Art History* at The Metropolitan Museum of Art, the work is described as a rider on a dark Nordic gorge who rides past Death on a Pale Horse, holding an hourglass to remind

Fig. 10.17 *Knight, Death, and the Devil*, engraving print, Dürer, NYC, New York. 1513.

us of the shortness of life, and is followed directly to his rear by a pig-snouted Devil. The rider is viewed as the personification of moral virtue and is undeterred by his true mission. The print is a testament to the Latin expression *vita activa*, or active life.

Music and Dance

Luther supported the concept of the faithful praying directly to God and during worshiping speaking in one's own **vernacular**, or common language. He modified the music of the Catholic Church, substituting German for Latin. Luther felt that music was a very important part of worship, so he encouraged congregational participation in the Protestant service, a practice that had been abandoned by the Catholic Church. There was also the development of the **chorale**, or choir piece sung in four parts. Chorales are usually sung by congregations or a choir. Music of this sort became popular, especially in Germany and during the time of Johann Sebastian Bach, when he wrote chorales for Lutheran church services during the Baroque period.

In England, composers produced **madrigals**, or compositions for smaller groups of singers, to accentuate and honor their countrymen. Thomas Morley (1557 to 1603) and Thomas Weelkes (1575 to 1623) were the best-known composers of madrigals. One of Morley's more famous **homophonic melody**, or the use of a single melody to support harmony, was "As Vest Was Descending", which included a tribute to Queen Elizabeth I (r. 1558 to 1603). In contrast, Weelkes composed madrigals about English heroic figures from legends and the works of Shakespeare.

Theater

The year 1599 proved to be William Shakespeare's "make it or break it" year, the year he completed *Henry the Fifth*, wrote *Julius Caesar* and *As You Like It* back to back, and

then drafted *Hamlet*. On a frigid night in December 1598, the Chamberlin's Men, the theatrical company he belonged, gathered to dismantle a nearby playhouse called the Theater. The move was risky but necessary. The Theater was on land owned by Giles Allen, but the playhouse was owned by Richard and Cuthbert Burbage, father and son. The father was deceased and the lease expired. Legally, there was a case for the building to be no longer in the ownership of Burbage. The plot succeeded.

Shakespeare's abilities to write plays were unique. He wrote parts for specific actors in his company by drawing inspiration from their natural talents. In total, he wrote 37 plays ranging from romantic comedies resulting in mistaken identities, battle of the sexes, ill-placed judgment, and more. In his tragedy play, heroes such as Hamlet, King Lear, Othello, or Macbeth employed a sidebar **soliloquy**, or a private reflection of a character unheard by other characters, to address the audience directly. Shakespeare's tragedies were also known as **revenge plays**, or plays revolving around avenging a loved one's murder. The plot unfolds as the murdered person requests for the main character to seek revenge for him.

Little is known of his private life outside of his public marriage to Anne Hathaway (1556 to 1623) in 1582 and their three children. His oldest child was Susanna (1583 to 1649) and the two youngest, Hamnet (1585 to 1596) and Judith (1585 to 1662), were twins. Once he left Stratford-upon-Avon, sometime around 1590, to become an actor, little evidence shows he returned until 1613 when he retired.

Literature

Two Frenchmen rose to the humanist call in espousing their thoughts, François Rabelais (c. 1494 to 1553) and Michel de Montaigne (1533 to 1592) (fig. 10.18).

Harris Brisbane Dick Fund, 1917, The Metropolitan Museum of Art

Fig. 10.18 *Portrait of Michel de Montaigne,* etching and engraving print, Augustin de Saint-Aubin, NYC, New York. 1513.

The ease of acquiring books for one's personal library and the ability to disseminate one's thoughts across the entire Continent at rapid speed was transformative. Rabelais was a former monk of the Benedictine and Franciscan order, who left monastic life to study and then practice medicine in Lyon, France. When not attending to his patients, he composed and circulated entertaining pamphlets judgmental of the conventional powers lording over ordinary French citizens.

Rabelais's writings stressed the important of personal liberty. Over a 32-year period, he wrote five connected novels, collective titled *Gargantua and Pantagruel,* about the travels and adventures of father and son that ridicule their stupidities and delusions. In the second book, Gargantua is compared to King Francis I (r. 1515 to 1547). In the book, Gargantua is likened to an old-fashioned scholastic fearful of

giving in to the humanist ideal held by King Frances I. Rabelais was highly objective of the "dark" Middle Age thinking still persuasive in France. The dogmas and sacraments the Church upheld and its inability to see the Reformation as a liberating force for the faithful troubled Rabelais.

Montaigne was a generation younger than Rabelais but realized that the deep divide between Catholics and Protestants was disturbing. He was born to a wealthy merchant, the mayor of Bordeaux, but remitted to the care of a peasant woman for him to foster a deep adoration and appreciation for commoners. By 21, he had completed law school and within 4 years he became magistrate for the king to enforce the laws in Bordeaux. Over a 13-year period, before he retired to the family estate, he witnessed violent attacks of the Huguenots, who were condemned as "heretics" by the Church.

Innovation and Progress

In 1668, Francesco Redi (1626 to 1697) decided to challenge Spontaneous Generation Theory, a doctrine articulately complied by Aristotle explaining the growth of
living organisms without originating from a similar organism. The theory was used
to explain how maggots could grow on meat. Redi designed the first experiment to
test the more than 2,000-year-old theory. He placed meat in jars, allowed one jar
to be exposed to the air, and covered the other with Naples veil cloth. In time the
jar exposed to air grew maggots and the one covered remained maggot free. He
instantaneously disproved Spontaneous Generation Theory but could not explain
why maggots appeared on the covered meat. Not until Pasture was the mechanism
of maggot growth fully understood. But, Redi set the scientific world on the path
toward grasping the concept of a control (open air jar) and variable (covered jar)
that forms the bases of modern scientific experimentation.

Through these attacks he acquired an aversion to the inhumaneness that one human can enact on another because of their personal beliefs.

In the sanctuary of his library, Montaigne conceived a new form of writing, the personal essay he referred to as an **essai**, meaning to "attempt" in French. He tested out his ideas and wrote what occurred, much like a scientist performing experiments. His writings were the first of their kind to record what he read, saw, heard, and experienced on a daily basis. He was engaging his own mind with a critical analysis of what those events that shaped him emotionally, physically, and mentally. His greatest innovation was to write about himself, as he knew himself better than anything or anyone else.

Montaigne's essays range in subject matter from those "Of Fear" to "That Men by Various Ways Arrive at the Same End" and "Of the Vanity of Words" to "Of Thumbs" in 3 books and 107 chapters. The chapter titled "Of Thumbs" from the second book seems nothing more than musing on the importance of one's own thumbs. But, in his reflections, Montaigne outlines a long history of both peaceful and malicious use.

In fact, kings would "join their right hands ... intertwist their thumbs ... lightly pricked them ... and mutually sucked them" as a way to create a blood obligation to the other. During the time of Augustus, "a Roman knight ... cut off the thumbs of two young children," without their thumbs the children could not serve the army. "Of Thumbs" was one of Montaigne's shorter essays and seems a bit trivial but is packed with historical and scholarly references.

Desiderius Erasmus (1466 to 1536), a Dutch humanist and scholar, would influence the Luther's antipapal feeling, in part. In 1509, he attacked the depravities of church clergy in a lighthearted satire, *In Praise of Folly*. Four years later, he anonymously published another satiric dialogue attacking Pope Julius II (p. 1503 to 1513), in which the pope encounters Saint Peter at the gates of heaven. By the end of the play, Erasmus had outlined the misconception that "good works" had the ability to "open" the gates of heaven. He helped promote the Protestant reformers' belief that salvation alone helps one enter the gates of heaven.

In England, Sir Thomas More (1478 to 1535, fig. 10.19) was a Christian scholar

© Kiev Victor/Shutterstock.com

Fig. 10.19 *Statue of Sir Thomas More,* bronze on stone base, Leslie Cubitt Bevis, Chelsea Old Church, Long England. 1969.

who rose to importance during the reign of King Henry the VIII. He published *Utopia*, or Greek for "good place", in 1516 to extoll a comparison between the world he lived in and an ideal society. His idea of an idyllic world was inspired by the accounts of explorers from the New World. In the narration, More is an explorer himself who discovers a new land, an island culture, where everyone shares their goods and property. More explained how these people all worked for the common good, each took personal responsibility for their actions, and treated one another with kindness. His utopia was not the world he lived. In 1535, More was executed for not supporting Henry's want to break with the Catholic Church.

Science

Francis Bacon, Nicolas Copernicus, Galileo Galilei, and William Harvey discovered life-changing advancement in how people thought of the world they inhabited. Bacon is considered the "Father of Empiricism"; he promoted the use of **scientific rationalism**, or valid knowledge. Valid knowledge was a based on inductive reasoning and careful observations to inform a rational explanation of events far removed from any nonrational sources such as intuition or supernatural revelation. It was logical reason that would determine knowledge by testing and confirming, instead of guessing, personal or cultural preferences. In England, Harvey determined that blood flowed through the human body. In Germany, Copernicus profoundly argued against an earth-centered obit, but for a heliocentric planetary existence. His body of work would influence Johannes Kepler, another German astronomer. While still in Italy, the astronomer, physicist, and mathematician, Galileo, would study speed, velocity, and free fall associated with gravity and create the principle of relativity that was later advanced by Isaac Newton and Albert Einstein.

Technology

Vermeer's use of a camera obscura to create photographic quality images was not serendipitous. Dutch spectacle makers Hans Jansen, Zacharias Jansen (1585 to 1632), and Hans Lippershey (1570 to 1619) are credited with inventing the compound microscope around 1590. Ground lenses were able to amplify objects, in particular microscopic objects. In 1663, the Englishman Robert Hooke (1635 to 1703) published a collection of microscopic illustrations of fleas, lice, and nettles using the device. In the book, *Micrographia*, he coined the term **cell** to describe the space between the solid walls of the corked he saw under the microscope.

REFORMATION AND BAROQUE LEGACY

The Catholic Church formulated a strategy to counter the Protestant Reformation with the new Baroque style. The calm stylization found in the Renaissance was replaced with style that appealed to the range of human emotions and feelings, not just the intellect. In the beginning, Baroque style wanted to champion all of the theology and teachings that Protestants rejected, such as mass, sacraments, veneration of saints, magnificently decorated churches, and majestic ceremonies. And, in doing so, the Church created theatrical church interiors with staged scenes to constantly direct the eyes of the faithful to the high altar. Society in the Baroque age was changing for everyone but most of all for those in the northern parts of Europe. Science too progressed into a new and rational thought process involving the scientific method as a way of validating new discoveries.

Critical Thinking

Describe how the Reformation began and who were its major influencers.

Examine the importance of Martin Luther's *Ninety-Five*.

Analyze how the Reformation spread and changed artistic expression in Northern Europe.

Explain what the Counter-Reformation was and how it transformed artistic expression.

Describe how the literature of the period added fuel to the Reformation.

ONLINE RESOURCES

The Protestant Reformation Overview
https://smarthistory.org/the-protestant-reformation/
Protestant Reformation, Setting the Stage Video
https://smarthistory.org/protestant-reformation-part-1-of-4/
Protestant Reformation, Martin Luther's Influence
https://smarthistory.org/protestant-reformation-part-2-of-4/
Variations within Protestantism
https://smarthistory.org/protestant-reformation-part-3-of-4/
The Counter-Reformation or Baroque
https://smarthistory.org/protestant-reformation-part-4-of-4/
How to Recognize Baroque Art Video
https://smarthistory.org/how-to-recognize-baroque-art/
Bernini's *David* Video
https://smarthistory.org/bernini-david-2/
Bernini's *Ecstasy of Saint Teresa* Video
https://smarthistory.org/bernini-ecstasy-of-st-teresa/
Caravaggio's *Calling of St. Matthew* Video
https://smarthistory.org/caravaggio-calling-of-st-matthew/
Rembrandt's *The Anatomy Lesson of Dr. Tulp* Video
https://smarthistory.org/rembrandt-anatomy-lesson-of-dr-tulp/
Ruysch *Fruit and Insects* Video
https://smarthistory.org/rachel-ruysch-fruit-and-insects/
Velázquez *Las Meninas* Video
https://smarthistory.org/diego-velazquez-las-meninas/
Francis Bacon and the Scientific Revolution
https://smarthistory.org/francis-bacon-and-the-scientific-revolution/
Thomas More and Henry VIII
https://www.britannica.com/biography/Thomas-More-English-humanist-and-statesman

Enlightenment: The Age of Reason

Fig. 11.1 Chateau de Versailles, rear view, Rigaud Versailles, France. c. 1661 to 1715

Knowledge Acquisition

◆ *Examine the artistic and cultural shifts made in architecture, sculpture, painting, music, drama, philosophy, and poetry.*

◆ *Evaluate the principal accomplishments made by Beethoven, Boyle and Kent, Canova, David, Fragonard, Houdon, Jefferson, Mozart, Rigaud, Swift, and Wedgwood.*

◆ *Explore key figures such as King Louis IVX and their impact on historical events.*

◆ *Assess the philosophical thoughts of Hobbes, Locke, Rousseau, and Voltaire in prompting the American and French Revolutions, scientific discoveries, the Industrial Revolution, and rationalism.*

◆ *Discover how the Enlightenment connects works of art from around the world to its own artistic, cultural, literary, and political interests.*

SETTING THE SCENE

A new period of human development took shape during the latter years of the Baroque that placed a greater importance on humankind's intellectual abilities. Human creativity played a central and active role in promoting social change, leading to more social diversity. Artists helped society fully understand past experiences that would lead to specific social changes. The following sections try to chart the early roots of the **Enlightenment**, or the Age of Reason, by examining the **Rococo**, or a florid art style, period in France during the 72-year reign of King Louis XIV (b. 1638 to1715, r. 1646 to 1715) to the French Revolution's Neoclassical style. Louis's reign witnessed the most extensively centralized monarchy in France history. The king commissioned the construction of a palace at Versailles, now referred to as Chateau du Versailles, as a means to house his entire court. In true privilege fashion, a number of **salons**, or reception rooms, were on the first floor. Salons were used for the scores of permanent house guests to gather, socialize, and play games and carry on, all under the watchful eye of the king. Each salon's ceiling (fig. 11.2) in the palace was painted with mythological characters and their accompanying story by René-Antoine Houasse (1645 to 1710).

INDUSTRIALIZATION

The mid-1700s witnessed inquiry into science, medicine, and technology, creating a demand for new instrumentation to conduct experiments and take measurements. As the demand for precision instruments increased, so did specialized craft shops. New craftsmen, who would become highly skilled technicians, were able to create a comfortable life as business owners and inventors.

The creation of specialized craftsmen advanced the thought process of seventeenth century scientists. And, as these scientists created specialized tools the need for general craftsmen diminished in the production of goods. **Cams**, or pieces used to transform rotary motion into linear motion, and

Image Courtesy of Kristina M. Jantz

Fig. 11.2 *Figure of the Royal Magnificence, Immortality, and Progress in the Fine Arts* (detail) fresco, Houasse, Chateau de Versailles ceiling, Versailles, France. 1683.

lathes, or pieces used to rotate an object in a fixed location, along with a number of other mechanical devices, were be invented. James Watt (1736 to 1819) patented his idea for the steam engine in 1769. The patent paved the way for the birth of the **Industrial Revolution,** or a change from an agrarian and handicraft economy to one dominated by industry and machine. The first steam engine was not built until after his patent expired in 1800. By 1820, the steam engine had generated an estimated 1,000 horsepower, signaling the beginning of the Industrial Revolution.

While the steam engine transformed manufacturing, other inventors such as Josiah Wedgwood (1730 to 1795) designed new techniques for producing highly durable earthenware. England's Queen Charlotte (r. 1761 to 1818) preferred his work above other artisans and as a result he was appointed the royal supplier of dinnerware. Wedgwood's dinnerware was only one example of the many innovations in manufactured goods. All over England and Europe new machinery was created to manufacture an unprecedented amount of consumer goods from toys, furniture, kitchen utensils, and china, to silverware, watches, and candlesticks. For the first time in recorded history, every day, ordinary people could purchase items usually produced in small quantities only for the very wealthy.

As the years progressed, new innovations in machinery created an easier, faster, and cheaper means for producing goods. Each new invention helped drive society toward modernization. But, no matter how easy these new inventions made life or how cheap the produces were to purchase, they caused a number of problems for workers. Factory workers were made to work long hours, sometimes 15 hours a day standing in one location all day running the same machine. Most workers' health would suffer from continually ringing of the ears from the noise created by the machines they operated. Young people's lungs grew weak from stale air they breathed for hours. Many factory workers suffered from respiratory diseases. Workplace accidents were common because the machinery did not have any safety measures built into them. Oftentimes, women with long hair, or their dresses, would get caught in the machines. Losing a finger or hand was not uncommon. Missing a day's work could result in not only lost wages but also a monetary penalty, and being late to work could result in the loss of a quarter of pay.

Child labor was even worse. Many children started working in a factory at the age of five. They were more desired by factory owners because they were paid less than adults for the same job. Children were expected to work long hours, between 12 and 16 hours a day. Many times children performed the most dangerous and difficult jobs because of their size. Boys were usually expected to work in the mines where they guided the donkeys; a particularly dangerous job due to the risk of floods, cave-ins, and black lung. Girls usually worked in textile factories. At the start of, and well into, the Industrial Revolution, children did not receive an education nor were they offered many opportunities to play with other children.

Artistic Movements

Two countries, in particular, played a pivotal role in advancing the intellectual thoughts of the Enlightenment, and these were England and France. Individuals in other countries were naturally making significant contributions, as well. By far, the English underscored the best and the worst of the new "Age of Reason." The English monarchy would champion individual liberties and English artists were by far the most critical of the new progressive age. In reaction to the divide between the lives of the wealth and commoners, they produced some of the best satires attesting to the horrors of this era.

ROCOCO

Rococo style is an ornamental and directly associated with French court life. The works possess intricate details and textures. The narratives of its paintings often describe the escapades of courtiers in their playgrounds, engaged in pleasantries, entertainments, fête, or festival, and various intrigues. The characteristics of the period were costumes, settings, and freedom from economic worries. Rococo works document the life of the carefree upper class. Paintings often involve a so-called intrigued subject matter with a titillating narrative or slightly suggestive themes such as in Fragonard's *The Love Letter* (fig. 11.3). The woman seems to try to sneakily conceal the sender of the flowers and letter from the viewers.

Fig. 11.3 *The Love Letter*, oil on canvas, David, MET, NYC, New York. c. 1770s.

ENLIGHTENMENT

The "**Enlightenment**," or Age of Reason, grew out of the excessive privilege witnessed during the Rococo period. The extravagant lifestyles of the monarchs, aristocrats, and wealthy class in both England and France would lead to a revolution in the American colonies and France. Human creativity and ingenuity on multiple levels helped lead to social change.

In England, King William III (r. 1689 to 1702) and Queen Mary (r. 1689 to 1694) replaced the turmoil of the previous century with relative stability by restoring the Habeas Corpus Act of 1679. The act was passed during the reign of King Charles II (r. 1660 to 1685), requiring all arrested individuals be presented with a document detailing the cause for their seizure and their right to a speedy trail. Pervious kings such as Henry VIII imprisoned anyone who disagreed with them for extended periods of time without any cause. As a result of improper treat of action by the monarchy, a number of other laws and acts were passed, including a Bill of Rights, Toleration Act, and Settlement Act. Each act passed insured certain civil rights for English commoners.

In France, after the French Revolution, the frivolous aristocratic life faded away and **Neoclassicism**, or a style reverting back to classical Greek and Rome, dominated the arts and philosophy. The style was polished with compositional linearity and highly academic, the use of figures from antiquity being its subject matter. The hidden message of this art was essentially political—the state was to be respected and citizens should be willing to die for worthy political causes.

CREATIVE IMPULSE

No matter how tranquil a scene of London life seemed as portrayed by artists Julius

Global Focal Point

The road to revolution began with the Stamp Act of 1765 when exceedingly high taxes were placed on certain professions and college students. British authorities believed that by placing high taxes on the professional classes they could stop any funding for a revolt. In 1768, the British crown sent troops to protect the tax collectors. By 1770, the colonists had grown tired of paying the taxes without representation. On the evening of March 5, 1770, a mob attacked a small band of British troops who opened fire on the mob, killing five. Soon after the event, Paul Revere Jr. (1760 to 1813) captured the scene in an engraving called *The Bloody Massacre* (fig. 11.4). The engraving was widely distributed throughout the colonies and created more defiance among the colonists.

Fig. 11.4 *The Boston Massacre*, engraving and etching, hand colored, Revere Jr., MET, NYC, New York. 1770.

Gift of Mrs. Russell Sage, 1910, The Metropolitan Museum of Art

---

Caesar Ibbetson (1759 to 1817), the images did not showcase the reality of London life (fig. 11.5). By the end of the eighteenth century, the wealthy and the middle class had mostly abandoned the city by moving west or even into distant villages. Villages that were once primarily meadows were becoming an ever-growing urban sprawl. The poor, on the contrary, who were usually countryside immigrants, flooded the city and lived in areas with narrow, shoddily paved streets and decrepit houses on the brink of collapsing. Assaults, robbery, drunkenness, pickpocketing, and prostitutions were part of daily life.

The English Enlightenment artists showcased the worst of the worst to bring about social change. In France, around the same time, artists were working at the pleasure of the aristocracy to create images highlighting the finer aspects of life such as love and excess in all forms. Artists produced some of the most beautiful, yet frivolous works of art. The creativity of early-eighteenth-century French artists was less critical of the society's need for change than its latter-established idea of equality. The task of being critical about the French monarchy was left to the philosophers and writers; eventually, painters such as Jacques-Louis David (1748 to 1825) brought the need for change in French life to the forefront.

Architecture and Design

Perhaps nowhere was the ornate Rococo style better represented than at Louis XIV's estate at Versailles, southwest of Paris. A painting (fig. 11.6) of Louis XIV (b. 1601 to 1643, r. 1610 to 1643) by Rigaud shows the king in full regalia with his foot turned

Fig. 11.5 *View of London with St. Paul's in the Distance: Woman and Children with a Baby Carriage*, pen, ink, and watercolor, Ibbetson, MET, NYC, New York. 1787.

out in a position to show he knew **presente la jambe**, or steps within ballet, an art to which he was deeply devoted. Louis valued self-gratification, vanity, pleasure, ceremony, prestige, manners, glory, power, pomp, and position in social order. According to the French, the sun rose and set in Louis and he was often referred to as "le Roi Soleil," the Sun King. The motif of Apollo, the Sun God, appears throughout the decorations of his estate at Versailles, as Louis felt himself synonymous with the god Apollo.

Louis was not the longest-reigning monarch in all of Europe by coincidence. Instead, he devised a method for controlling his citizens, specifically his court, using the arts and entertainment. He lured aristocrats to Versailles by providing food, housing, and entertainment. In this way, he was able to keep an eye on them and prevent any political misconduct such as revolt or plot to overthrow his rule. Versailles was,

in essence, a public housing project for the rich, designed to glorify Louis and help him maintain his position of power. Louis was an absolute ruler who ruled without legal constraints. There were, of course, practical constraints to his power. He could not go out on the street and rob a local peasant, for example, but he had the final word in all matters of the law. If a decision was made, Louis made it or he sat on the committee deciding the outcome. He once said, "The State? It's me. I am the state," indicating that he was the center of French life and government. His system of government is labeled an autocratic **theocracy**, or rule by one person through divine right and sanction.

Ceremonies of "waking up of the god" and the "putting to sleep of the god" in ancient Greek temples were applied to Louis' daily routine. Louis was awakened with a ceremony called "**Le leve du roi**," or the getting up of the king, and was put to sleep in a comparable ceremony at the end of the day. His application of pagan temple ceremonies was a fusion of the Greco-Roman and Judeo-Christian worlds that prevailed after the Renaissance.

Louis added gardens (fig. 11.7) and buildings to the existing hunting lodge that his father Louis XIII had already erected at Versailles. Since Louis provided all the entertainments and activities, both indoors and outdoors, at Versailles, the interiors of the buildings, gardens, decorations, fountains, ceremonies, fashion, and dress that accompanied his lifestyle must be considered (figs. 11.1, 11.8, 11.9), so that their implications could be understood. A father and son duo, Jean Berain the Elder (1638 to 1711) and Younger (1678 to 1726), were responsible for creating the unity of style in the tapestries, costumes, woodcarvings, furniture, and embroidery found at the Chateau de Versailles.

Versailles's interior designs were innovative, as Louis understood the significance of maintaining a delightful, almost enchanting, internal atmosphere that complemented the external building design. Lavish use of precious metals, inlaid woods, and intricate patterns required skilled labors many hours to complete. Multileveled chandeliers with sparkling crystal pendants replaced the traditional singular candelabras. Elaborate fireplaces (fig. 11.10) able to hold entire tree trunks replaced their simple counterparts. The

Fig. 11.6 *Louis XIV King of France*, oil on canvas, Rigaud, Louver, Paris, France. 1701

Fig. 11.7 Royal fireplace, marble, gold, and wood inlay, Chateau de Versailles, Rigaud, Versailles, France. 1683

Fig. 11.8 Chateau de Versailles, back overlooking reflecting ponds, Rigaud, Versailles, France. c. 1661 to 1715

© Sean Pavone/Shutterstock.com

Fig. 11.9 Chateau de Versailles, entrance, Rigaud, Versailles, France. c. 1661 to 1715

© YURY TARANIK/Shutterstock.com

interior and exterior was wrought in gold. In fig. 11.9, the exterior surfaces, traditionally painted with color, had gold-leafing applied to them. While the application of gold may seem extravagant and expensive, gold fades slower and, therefore, lasts longer. A new coat of paint must be applied every 5 to 10 years, while reapplication of gold is every 25 to 30 years. The use of gold then and now is a cost savings measure in both material and man hours.

The interiors of Versailles were designed by the architect Louis Le Vau (1612 to 1670) and completed by Le Vau's successor Jules Hardouin-Mansart (1646 to 1708). The decoration ranged from sculpture with pedestals to framed paintings and mirrors to vast amounts of wall hangings. Materials for completing the Versailles were costly and included crystal, marble, wood, bronze, and inlaid semiprecious stones were present everywhere as seen in the Hall of Mirrors

Fig. 11.10 Royal fireplace, marble, gold, and wood inlay, Rigaud, Chateau de Versailles, Versailles, France 1683

Fig. 11.11 Hall of Mirrors, marble, crystal, gold, and wood inlay, Le Vau and Hardouin-Mansart, Chateau de Versailles, Versailles, France. 1678 to 1684

(fig. 11.11). Duplication of moldings and trim as repeatable "figures" required mass production techniques that helped develop cottage industries in carving and casting. The creation of some pieces was completed at the work site, while other decorations were produced in workshops where the castings were stored until they were needed for installation. The new emphasis on interiors during the Baroque resulted in churches and chateaux, with chandeliers containing a myriad of crystal pendants and many **tromp l'oeil**, or trick of the eye, decorations painted onto ceilings.

Louis's residential bedchambers (fig. 11.12) were lined with framed mirrors, upholstered walls, and floor tiles laid so evenly that they look like linoleum to the modern-day visitor. Much of the king's furniture and the palace's decorations were designed by the sculpture Jacques Verbeckt (1704 to 1771) and included chairs, tables, jewelry boxes, beds, dressers, commodes, stools, and throne. The writing desk (fig. 11.13) that Louis used was designed by Verbeckt in 1760 and completed 9 years later by Jean-Henri Riesener (1734 to 1806). His desk was a first of its kind; the designed allowed Louis to leave his paper out but away from curious onlookers. Another remarkable innovation was the lock mechanism, it allowed the king to quickly lock and unlock the lid and all drawers with a quarter-turn of the key. Today the desk is valued at over a million dollars because of the amount of man hours and technical skill it would take to duplicate the intricate inlay in the wood called "parquetry."

Fig. 11.12 King Louis XIV's private bedroom chamber, Chateau de Versailles, Versailles, France, Verbeckt. 1678 to 1684

Fig. 11.13 King Louis XIV's writing desk, Chateau de Versailles, Versailles, France, Verbeckt and Riesener. 1678 to 1684

Many of the buildings erected by Louis XIV used French pavilion style, similar to an ancient Greek temple with wings; the central chateau was laid out in a symmetrical plan with all roads leading to the palace. The palace was capable to housing up to 20,000 people in 2,300 rooms with more than 2,000 windows, 1,250 chimneys, and 67 stair cases. Rooms were apartment-style housing complexes, including apartments for the king and queen, accommodations for aristocrats, the chapel, an opera house, **a salon de la guerre**, or war room, for official state audiences, a hall of mirrors for parties, and other buildings including the Grand Trianon for Louis's mistress and the Orangerie for raising oranges and other citrus fruits. The building project itself took years to complete, especially the construction of reservoirs for water that came from a nearby river for the fountains.

The gardens, like the palace, were laid out in a symmetrical plan to create symmetry, even in the cuttings of hedges into geometrical shapes. The fountains and gardens were further laid out in a terrace style with each a few steps below the previous one. In total, the gardens boast over 1,200 fountains and use an extensive pumping system. There was never a sufficient water supply to provide water for all fountains at once. Palace engineers devised a clever method for turning, allowing water to flow through them in the presence of Louis when the king a tour. Then, once the guests passed, the fountain was turned off to give his guests the impression that water flowed endlessly from all fountains at once. The fountains of Versailles such as Latona Fountain (fig. 11.14) designed by Andre Le Nôtre (1613 to 1700) in 1665 and embellished by Hardouin-Mansart are imitated in location around the world such as Chicago, Illinois (fig. 11.15).

Rococo style architecture gave way to Neoclassical notions of proportion, and an emphasis on classical Greek and

© Mistervlad/Shutterstock.com

Fig. 11.14 *Le Bassin d'Apollon, Apollo Fountain*, bronze, Tuby, Versailles, France. 1668 to 1671

© Richard Cavalleri/Shutterstock.com

Fig. 11.15 *Buckingham Fountain*, modeled after Latona Fountain at Chateau de Versailles, Loyau, Chicago, Illinois. 1927

Roman styles. England, France, and the United States beckoned back to the clean and simple-domed structures with Greek columns. Chiswick House (fig. 11.16) in west London was designed by William Kent (1685 to 1748) and Richard Boyle, the third Earl of Burlington, (1694 to 1753) to exemplify the Neoclassical concepts of symmetry with the use of geometric shapes to present a stately appearance. The house was to provide an attractive setting for Burlington's collection of architectural drawings and paintings in addition to gathering places for family and social events. The house influenced later building constructions of Georgian England.

Cross Cultural Connection

Japanese Kabuki Theater dates to 1603 when Izumo no Okuni (1572 to 1613) a **miko**, or Shinto shrine maiden, began combining acting, dance, and music as a new of performance. The entertainment style was designed for the common people. Characters within the dramas performed sensuous dances on the verge of sexual indecency. In 1629, the government banned women performers but young boys were allowed to dress as women until 1652. The concern for the nation's morals prompted older men to take over the roles, and this is the version of Kabuki that endured.

In the United States, Thomas Jefferson (1473 to 1826) employed the style when he designed his country home Monticello (fig. 11.17) in Charlottesville, Virginia in 1769. Jefferson was a forward-thinking individual, who promoted the Neoclassical ideas within the country. In many ways, he was breaking ties with former Rococo styles for both political and economic reasons. The decadence and extravagance of the Rococo was contradictory to the newly forged colonies and the later development of the United States of America. Monticello was adopted from the design of Chiswick House with a centrally planned rotunda, much like the Roman Pantheon. Unlike both Chiswick House and the Pantheon, Monticello was not built of stone and concrete. Instead, Jefferson used brick and wood-building material, as they were more readily available.

Fig. 11.16 Chiswick House, Boyle and Kent. 1726 to 1729

© Anthony Shaw Photography/Shutterstock.com

Monticello is considered a stately home with almost perfect proportions, with each of the four sides having deep porticos to protect the entrances from the elements.

Sculpture

The process for producing dinnerware was unique. Traditionally, each ceramic ware piece was shaped individually by hand on the potter's wheel. In 1768, Josiah Wedgwood's right leg was amputated. His ability to "throw" pottery was lost, but his insight into other potter's crafts was gained. He began experimenting with the modeler craft of casting pots. Through his experiments he eventually developed the liquid clay cast in molds that were then fired. He opened a factory in June of 1769. He also developed a means of mechanically applying decorative decal patterns rather than

Fig. 11.17 Monticello, Jefferson, designed 1769, built 1770 to 178 and 1796 to 1806

Fig. 11.18 Platter, creamware with transfer-printed decoration in black, Wedgwood, MET, NYC, New York. 1780.

hand-painted images to the finished china. These two technical advancements significantly sped up production. The Wedgwood catalog described the dinnerware as being manufactured with ease and expedition. As a consequence, the dinnerware was more affordable.

The same year the Platter (fig. 11.18) was produced, Wedgwood's longtime business partner died. He invited Erasmus Darwin (1732 to 1802), a natural philosopher and physiologist, for financial assistance. Wedgwood's daughter and Darwin's son married in 1796. They were the parents of Charles Darwin (1809 to 1882), the naturalist who articulated the Theory of Evolution (Chapter 12).

Like Neoclassical paintings, sculpture subject matter includes myths from the Greeks and Romans, but the traditional canons of proportion found in antiquity figures are absent. Neoclassical artists aimed to produce works with technical precision when rendering historical heroes and mythological stories in portraying smooth skin, supple bodies, and appealing fabric displays.

The French sculptor Jean-Antoine Houdon (1741 to 1828) created a statue of *George Washington* (fig. 11.19). In the sculpture, Washington was compared to an ancient Roman emperor. His feet were carefully positioned. He held a staff that helped resonate dignity, and wore gentlemen clothing to indicate his station in life. His pose was naturalistic and not canonical. The most famous Italian Neoclassical sculptor was Antonio Canova (1757 to 1822). He sculpted a beautiful rendition of the mythical tale of *Cupid and Psyche* (fig. 11.20), when Psyche was revived by Cupid's gentle kiss, originally a touch by his arrow. The figures imbue the subject of ancient art with sensuous qualities such images never had in antiquity with a purposeful avoidance of mathematical proportion.

Fig. 11.19 *George Washington,* marble, Houdon, State Capitol, Richmond, Virginia. 1791 to 1792

© Nagel Photography/Shutterstock.com

Canova's use of the Roman myth pertaining to Psyche may have been by chance, but Enlightened people would have understood the message. Psyche was the youngest and most beautiful of her father's daughters. She was adored like a goddess, which maddened Venus with jealousy. Venus sent Cupid to avenge her, but Cupid instead fell in love with her. After years of her father seeing his most beautiful daughter unmarried, he consulted the oracle. The oracle foresaw ruin if Psyche was not deserted on a rock and taken by a monster. Cupid, not a monster, carried her away. The night he visited her they made love, but he forbid her from looking at him. One night, after Cupid was fast asleep, she resolved herself to see who her lover was. She lit an oil lamp, saw Cupid, dropped a speck of oil on him, and he fled feeling betrayed. Desperately, Psyche departed to find Cupid. Along the way, Venus exacted

Fig. 11.20 *Cupid and Psyche*, marble, Canova, Louver, Paris, France. 1787 to 1793

horrific trials on her in order to reunite with Cupid. One such trail was for Psyche to bring back a flask from the goddess of the Underworld, Proserpina, but under no circumstances should she open it. Falling victim to her own curiosity, she opened the flask and inhaled the vile fumes. At once she fell into a deathly sleep. A single touch by Cupid's arrow restored her. The gods were moved by Cupid's affection for Psyche and they allowed them to unite. She was also given immortality and proclaimed the goddess of the Soul. The myth of Psyche was meant to symbolize the sufferings the soul must endure to attain happiness and progress.

Painting and Printmaking

Fragonard exemplified the concepts of the Rococo style within his painting and illuminated the aristocracies disregard for customary public morality. The theme of *The Stolen Kiss* (fig. 11.21) was common throughout the career of Fragonard before

the French Revolution. In true fashion, the theme revealed was one of a secret romance, a passionate touch between lovers in a fleeting moment away from prying eyes. These types of semi-erotic themes were exceedingly popular as they brought to life the gossip of their romantic interludes.

Fragonard's most famous set of paintings were commissioned by Madame Du Barry (1743 to 1793), last mistress of King Louis XV (r. 1715 to 1774), to be situated in her pavilion at Louveciennes in France designed by the architect Claude-Nicholas Leoux (1736 to 1806). The pavilion was more commonly referred to as the Pleasure Palace because of the nature of its use, romantic rendezvous between Du Barry and the king. The commission was for 4 scenes depicting The *Progress of Love* including *The Pursuit, The Meeting* (fig. 11.22), *The Lover Crowned,* and *Love Letters.* In each painting, Fragonard used overtly sexual symbols to underscore chronological order passion.

Fig. 11.21 *The Stolen Kiss*, oil on canvas, Fragonard, State Hermitage Museum, St. Petersburg, Russia. 1788

Fig. 11.22 *The Meeting*, oil on canvas, Fragonard, The Frick Collection, NYC, New York. 1771 to 1772.

The Meeting played out like a scene from a planned tryst within a lush, overflowing garden terrace. The woman holds a piece of paper in her right hand, presumably a letter indicating the arranged meeting time and place. The garment colors, white on her and red on the man, may imply her purity and his passion. The man scales the wall, similar to a knight storming a castle to rescue his maiden, only to find her hesitant for his advancement. Her expression further discloses that their tryst might be interrupted and the risqué nature of their meeting. Venus, in the background, is chastising Cupid for his involvement in the amorous love affair and reinforces her hesitancy for the couple by disarming Cupid of his arrows.

While Fragonard's *The Stolen Kiss* and *Progress of Love* illustrate most of what the French Revolution stood against, *The Oath*

of the Horatii (fig. 11.23) by Jacques-Louis David's (1748 to 1825), purchased before the French Revolution by Louis XVI, celebrated those who pledged allegiance to the people and died for their political beliefs. David used classical Roman themes to define the space and simplified the overall composition to relay the intended message. He also separated the scene into two main groups. The sons on the left were strong with outstretched arms that appear muscular and posed for action, while the women on the right are limply displayed and weeping for their potential lose. According to the legend, one of the brothers was married to a Curatii, the women in the center, while one of the sisters, far left, was engaged to a Curatii. Therefore, the conflict the Horatti felt was out of love for the Curatii they were to fight against. The message David conveyed

Fig. 11.23 *The Oath of the Horatii*, oil on canvas, David, Louver, Paris, France. 1784. *Humanities Across the Arts*, Husarik

was one of civic responsibility eclipsing the joy of domestic life, that sacrifice was the price of citizenship. In 1785, when David completed the painting, the country was primed for a revolution.

As much as David promoted the war, Angelic Kauffmann (1741 to 1807) elevated the reality of who the war was being fought on behalf, future generations. Even though Kauffmann was Swiss-born, her image *Cornelia, Mother of the Gracchi, Pointing to Her Children as Her Treasures* (fig. 11.24) stood in glaring contrast to Elisabeth Louise Vigèe Le Brun's (1755 to 1842) image *Marie Antoinette and Her Children* painted 2 year later. Le Brun staged the ill-favored queen to resemble the embodiment of mother-hood and family virtue. She painted Marie Antoinette's son pointing to an empty bas-sinet to draw attention to the recent death of her fourth child. A main issue with the painting was the fact that it was executed in the Rococo style, which fell out of fashion in the early 1780s.

Kaufmann's painting was executed in the new style of Neoclassicism. The main character was Cornelia, daughter of the Roman general who defeated Hannibal in 202 BCE, being visited by the lady seated next to her. As the two women talk, the seated lady shows Cornelia her jewels and asks to see Cornelia's jewels. Cornelia responded as she points to her two sons, "There are my most precious jewels." Her sons, Tiberius and Gaius, grew up to be great Roman re-public reformers, who led the efforts behind redistribution of public lands to the poor (Chapter 5). There was a clear indication that children represented the future of the state and the French people's care for them was their greatest civic responsibility.

Printmaking

Regardless of the promises this era might offer by the establishment of a new "social order," a sincerely enlightened individual was able to see beneath English society and recognize the depravity within the

Fig. 11.24 *Cornelia, Mother of the Gracchi, Pointing to Her Children as Her Treasures*, oil on canvas, Kauffman, Virginia Museum of Fine Arts, Richmond, Virginia. c. 1785.

Virginia Museum of Fine Arts, Richmond. Adolph D. and Wilkins C. Williams Fund. Photo: Travis Fullerton © Virginia Museum of Fine Arts

social agitation and moral bankruptcy of those around them. A number of artists such as William Hogarth (1697 to 1764) used their talents to expose the irony of the "dark side" of the Enlightenment and try to steer England back in the direction of decent ethics. Hogarth's efforts were in the creation of a number of works emphasizing what had been accomplished in the name of "progress", or Enlightenment. In one such image, *Gin Lane* (fig. 11.25), Hogarth turns his attention, not to the promise of the English Enlightenment, but to the reality of London at its worst.

In his *Autobiographical Notes*, Hogarth wrote, "In gin lane every circumstance of its horrid effects are brought to view; nothing but Idleness, Poverty, misery and ruin are to be seen ... not a house in tolerable condition but Pawnbroker and the Gin shop." Looking closely at the print, Hogarth highlighted a

man so drunk that he appears as a skeleton, a woman oblivious to her child falling over the railing, a women being placed in a coffin, a man who has hung himself, and buildings tumbling to the ground—all while the gin shop and pawn brokers are in good condition.

Hogarth was also critical of the founding of the more socially acceptable "drinking clubs" that arose around London in the early eighteenth century catering to middle and professional class males. In *A Midnight Modern Conversation* (fig. 11.26), he created a humorous satire of the follies of overindulging in liquor from an enormous punch bowl. Each of the 11 men is in varying states of inebriation, with possibly the drunkest man the soldier in the center foreground. A doctor, to the soldier's right, tries to alleviate his want for more alcohol by pouring liquor onto his head. An animated man, in the background, sings a toast while a man

Fig. 11.25 *Gin Lane*, ink on paper, Hogarth, British Museum, London, England, 1751.

© The British Museum Company Limited

Fig. 11.26 *A Midnight Modern Conversation*, etching and engraving, Hogarth, MET, NYC, New York, 1732.

to the far right tries to reignite his pipe but has caught his shirt sleeve ablaze as the man behind him vomits unbeknownst to everyone. Hogarth creation captures individuals from multiple professions, a clergyman, physician, lawyer, soldier, and politician, all partaking in debauchery. The scene is a realistic depiction of London professional life after business hours.

Music

Enlightenment composers succeeded in creating a new musical genre with the fundamental values heard within the Greco-Roman stylistic patterns containing numerical proportions. The verbiage of calling a musical piece "classical" was first applied in the early nineteenth century to denote and advertise works by the deceased Ludwig van Beethoven (1770 to 1827). The term "classical" itself gives clear reference to an even earlier style of music called **gallant**, or

melodic "sentences" of rhetoric within which a musical idea was stated, that was repeated in the same length, and then doubled into lengths called "periods." By multiplying these periods up into the larger levels of musical form, the music easily achieves numerical proportions. Phrases combine to form periods, periods combine to form sections, and sections combine into whole movements.

During the Enlightenment, people knew their social position and behaved accordingly. Aristocrats donned powdered wigs and wore well-tailored, brightly colored clothes made from fine fabrics. In certain towns it was illegal to wear such clothing if you were not a member of the nobility. The rationale was that you could be misunderstood as impersonating the upper classes, a serious offense. In public, the upper classes had expectations when walking on sidewalks; they were given priority and the lower classes had to step aside for them.

Ludwig van Beethoven refused to accommodate aristocrats in this manner, instead he walked directly through the middle of a group as he approached them. He later became a symbol of the rebellion of the lower classes against the upper classes. Unlike other musicians who accepted their roles as servants, Beethoven wore no wig and expected to be treated as an equal to the aristocracy. He was famous for having asserted, "If I can't come through the front door along with the aristocrats then I won't come in at all." He was a true symbol of social revolution.

While Beethoven was labeled a classical composer, he was a revolutionary composer, a destroyer of tradition. Audiences for his music also included the new rising middle class that linked him to the notion of a hero who stood up for their causes of liberty, fraternity, and equality. One of the concepts Beethoven revolutionized was "sonata form." He expanded the length of sections, avoided putting in the second themes, or manipulated the form to create surprise in the audience.

The composer Franz Josef Haydn (1732 to 1809) is often called the "Father of Classical Compositions". He obtained an appointment with Austrian Esterhazy family and lived a life of relative stability, traveling between their two castles in Eisenstadt, Austria, and Fertod, Hungary, and the city of Vienna. He happily served his noble patrons and proudly wore a court outfit indicating his rank as an officer in charge of music and musicians. As a result of living far from Vienna in castles owned by his patrons, Haydn claimed he was "forced to become original" and essentially standardized the form of the symphony and the string quartet. His hymn "Gott erhalte Franz den Kaiser" remains the

Austrian National Anthem since he wrote it in 1797. He, additionally, composed over 100 symphonies, many string quartets, piano sonatas, cantatas, and operas.

Another Viennese musician, Wolfgang Amadeus Mozart (1756 to 1791), was born in Salzburg, Austria. He was the son of a talented musician who wanted to profit from his son's extraordinary talent. At a very early age, Mozart was trained as an entrepreneur and traveled from and to the estates of the wealthy and the highest circles of the church to perform as a child prodigy. His gifts were extraordinary; he could remember anything he ever heard and reproduce it precisely. Mozart played compositions backward and forward and had the capacity to compose large compositions in his head and wait for weeks before writing down the completed works. As a teenager, he visited the Sistine Chapel and heard Antonio Allegri's famous Misère. He immediately wrote it down, even though it had never been shown as a full score to anyone before.

Opera

The orderliness of the society in which Mozart lived was reflected in his music, which was regular, periodic, and balanced. While Mozart's music was restrained, he was rather liberal in his social views. His attitude was also reflected in his choice of librettos for operas, a good example being Mozart's use of the libretto written by Lorenzo Da Ponte (1749 to 1838), a Roman Catholic priest, in his opera *Don Giovanni*. Da Ponte's libretto points out that there were responsibilities that go with privilege and those in the upper classes who grossly violated their social positions should be criticized. As seen in the Medieval Era, each member of the social order retained certain privileges and responsibilities. In the eighteenth century, the social order was still taken seriously and came though *Don Giovanni,* composed just before the French Revolution.

Don Giovanni translates from Italian into Spanish as "Don Juan." Don means "Sir" in English and Juan means "John." The title of this opera translates as "Sir John." Don Juan or Sir John was a **chevalier knight**, or horse owner who practices chivalry. In the medieval hierarchy, a knight swears an oath of allegiance to the king who rules by divine right. The knights promise to protect women and, in a sense, were agents of God who have certain rights and behavioral responsibilities. "Sir John" was a title applied to a knight, or an agent of God; however, Don Juan was a knight who was also famous for his philandering misconduct.

The plot of *Don Giovanni* had serious implications for the people of the eighteenth century and probably stirred unpleasant reactions in the aristocratic audience. The party-loving, misbehaving aristocrats of the time did not react well to the opera message that everyone, from top to bottom, in the social order must accept the responsibilities of their social position and act accordingly. The opera suggested that those who evade their responsibilities should be subject to a cruel fate.

Literature

A talented critic of the "progress" created by the Enlightenment was Jonathan Swift (1667 to 1745). Swift wrote at length about the conditions in England, as well as Ireland. In *Gulliver's Travels,* Swift routinely used simple examples to reduce the politics of the day to a level of triviality. In many instances, he was mocking the monarchy and making connections between the horror of the day and the reasons for their cause.

Even though reading was more common in eighteenth-century England than ever before, with as much as 60 percent of men and 45 percent of women able to read, literacy was still connected to social class. The middle class and city dwellers were more literate than the working class and rural areas. The literate poor were usually unable to purchase books and newspapers because of the cost, nor could they gain entrance into the library. Instead, they relied on an informal network of trading books and newspapers. Shared reading material became so commonplace that it was estimated that every paper sold was read by 20 people.

John Milton (1608 to 1674) wrote a fair-minded essay on the possibilities of liberty and justice in the form of a poem. *Paradise Lost* depicts the debate between absolutism and liberalism in a narration and was written when many people in England were of the Judeo-Christian faith. **Absolutism** refers to a powerful, centralized monarchy with divine right to exercise royal power over the people within its domain. **Liberalism**, on the contrary, argues the opposite that all people are free, equal, and independent and only give consent to a government for protection and, therefore, do not surrender sovereignty to a ruler. The poem struck a chord because of its analogy of Adam and Eve's loss of Paradise and the debate of absolute rule and freedom between Hobbes and Locke, respectively. In the biblical account, Satan rebelled against God by trying to destroy God's beloved creation, humanity.

God was seen as the absolute ruler in *Paradise Lost,* as the royal authority found in Hobbes' publication, while the Archangel Lucifer took on the role of the freedom-seeking spirit found in Locke's publications. According to Milton, God sent the Archangel Raphael to warn Adam about Lucifer and God's fallout, and that Lucifer was now God's enemy. In the poem, Raphael tells Adam how God tells the angels about his son, Jesus, and how his son has supreme authority as a hereditary ruler. In doing so, Lucifer became upset as his position as favorite in God's eyes was replaced by humanity.

Philosophy

Two philosophies regarding the governance of people were solidified at the beginning of the Enlightenment. Each was championed by influential philosophers who supported opposing ideas of rule between absolutism and liberalism. In 1651, after the English Civil War concluded, one question remained, what was the best way to govern over a nation and the people who lived within it? Thomas Hobbes (1588 to 1679) published *Leviathan: On the Matter, Forme, and Power of a Common-Wealth, Ecclesiastical and Civil* in 1651. He was convinced that two factors drove humankind: their fear of dying at the hands of someone else and their desire for

power. Hobbes, additionally, believed that geometry and Galileo's description of the plants revolving around the Sun could be used to explain the relationship between people and their ruler. Just as the planets orbited the Sun, so did people orbit their ruler. If these two factors were controlled, then anarchy could be controlled as well. After almost a decade of Civil War in England, it came as no surprise as to why Hobbes decided to take this position.

The French printmaker Abraham Bosse (1603 to 1676) created the cover image of *Leviathan* (fig. 11.27) to provide a good visual understanding of Hobbes' attitude toward governing. The image showed a king with his body comprised of hundreds of his subjects. In each hand, he holds a sword and scepter used as references to the king's ability to fashion a world on the basis of order and peace. Hobbes acknowledged that humanity

© Morphart Creation/Shutterstock.com

Fig. 11.27 Frontispiece of Hobbes' *Leviathan*, engraving on paper, Bosse, 1651

recognized its own degeneracy and was consequently willing to submit to the king's governance. In this way, the people under the king's rule accept the **social contract**, or a voluntary agreement to give up their sovereignty to their ruler.

When Hobbes published *Leviathan*, the **antiroyalist**, or those against a monarchy rule, had beheaded King Charles I (r. 1625 to 1649) only 2 years earlier. Many of Hobbes' contemporary thinkers were shocked when they read *Leviathan*. One such individual was John Locke (1632 to 1704), who would construct a very different theory about how people should be governed. Locke outrightly disagreed with Hobbes.

In 1690, Locke would anonymously publish two rebuttals known as *Treaties of Government* and *Essay on Human Understanding*. The first treatise argued against the theory of the divine right of kings; the

second constructed a model for popular self-government. Locke's ideal government was one with limited power, governed by the will of the people, and one that protected life and property.

Locke rejected all notions that people should revoke their sovereignty to an absolute ruler. Instead, he argued that humans were reasonable by nature and should maintain their basic rights, which included their rights to life and property, and enter into contracts with each other to create a limited form of government that had no other purpose than the protection of life and property. Additionally, he stated that no one person or rule should have absolute power. Instead, Locke insisted in the creation of a government held in check, having separation of powers and a series of balances. Locke's writings were to become the cornerstone of the formation of the United States government less than

Societal Emphasis

In the aftermath of both the American and French revolutionary wars, women began realizing that their rights were ignored, while the rights of men were to be forcibly declared. Women such as Abigail Adams expressed their feeling privately to their husbands, but other women, like Olympe de Gouges, asserted their viewpoints in the open. De Gouges moved to Paris after the death of her husband and began writing essays, manifestos, and plays regarding social injustices. In 1791, she joined a woman's advocate group and wrote *Declaration of the Rights of Woman and the Female Citizen*. The group advocated for women to plead for more open-minded divorce laws granting them the equivalent rights to sue for divorce and modification to inheritance laws that granted them a comparable right to inherit family property. However, it was her *Declaration of the Rights of Woman and the Female Citizen* that furthered the women rights movement more than anything else. De Gouges lobbied in vain to the Constitutional Convention for passage of her *Declaration* and by 1793 the convention had banned women's clubs from assembling. The banning was for a variety of reasons, but was known to be a reaction to the widespread distaste for a woman's involvement in politics. Four days after the ban was instituted, the French government guillotined de Gouges for being counterrevolutionary. In her last act, she authored a pamphlet that argued for future government decision to be determined by popular referendum, not by the National Convention.

a century after he wrote them. In his essay, Locke argued that people are completely adept at governing themselves:

> If man in the state of nature be so free, as has been said, if he be absolute lord of his own person and possessions, equal to the greatest, and subject to nobody, why will he part with his freedom, why will he give up his empire and subject himself to the dominion and control of any other power?

In short, Locke stated that humankind can obtain true social diversity and development only within a society that is free from any and all unnatural constraints placed upon it.

Versailles was a symbol of the French monarchy through the years starting with reign of Louis the XIV in 1662 until the beginning of the French Revolution in 1788. During this time, the pomp of the monarchy grew and many additions were made to the palace. Marie Antoinette would even have a 5-acre "country" home built on the palace grounds, so she could retreat to the peacefulness of the "country." Because of the royal court's extravagant lifestyle, however, the French people, aided by several prominent philosophers, revolted once the throne's debts tripled in 1774 and by 1788 when more than one-half of state revenues had been dedicated to paying interest on debt already held.

The first great French Enlightenment philosopher was Jean-Jacques Rousseau (1712 to 1778). He too created a "social contract" describing how an ideal state should govern over the people. In the opening lines of the first book, Rousseau famously wrote, "MAN is born free; and everywhere he is in chains." The line refers to the fact that Rousseau believed humankind had essentially enslaved

itself and therefore relinquished the right of its own humanity to a sovereign king. He furthermore believed that the rational thinking of the Enlightenment was causing humankind to become more enslaved than it previously was.

At first glance, Rousseau seemed to argue in favor of monarchies. His earlier writing *Discourse on the Origin of Inequality among Men* of 1755 alluded to very different sentiments. In *Discourse*, he believed that man was better off alone, possibly without a supreme ruler, and only after man decided to help others did he begin his fall into depravity, which is evident in the following passage:

> ... equality disappeared, property was introduced, work became necessary, and vast forests were transformed into pleasant field which had to be watered with the sweat of man, and where slavery and misery were soon seen in germination and flourish with the crops.

In this way, there is a sense that Rousseau believed man was happiest when free of all ties that bound him.

Another influential French Enlightenment writer was François-Marie Arouet, who wrote by the pen name Voltaire (1694 to 1778). Unlike other thinkers of the Enlightenment, he saw the value of other, non-Western cultures and traditions, and believed in an Enlightenment monarchy. At various episodes in Voltaire's life, he was employed by the French and Prussian monarchies, but this relationship did not hinder him from criticizing them by creating satires in play, poem, or novel forms about them. For this reason, he spent time in the Bastille prison from 1717 to 1718 and in 1726 he was exiled to England for a year. While in England he learned of the British governmental system and came to prefer it to the tyrannical French monarchy.

In 1734, Voltaire published his feelings about the French court in the *Philosophical Letters*. The letters were, in many ways, written to praise the English middle class. Some parts read as a historical account, but in between the lines a reader realizes that the *Philosophical Letters* resounded deeply within the consciousness of Europe for many decades to come. Voltaire noted the difference in commerce between England and France, explaining how in France merchants spoke of themselves without respect, but in England merchants were proud of who they were.

One of Voltaire's most profound theories in the *Philosophical Letters* was found in the section called "On the Presbyterians." In this section of the *Letters*, Voltaire argued against homogeny of values, since this was what most often leads to conflicts and religious wars. In many ways he was stating that stagnant and morally corrupt societies were a result of centrally planned and strictly enforced values. These societies were ones where questioning authority or disagreeing was not permissible. In order to avoid stagnation and moral corruption, societies needed diversity and freedom in order to create a peaceful society. In essence, if only one religion were allowed in England, the government would very possibly become arbitrary; if there were but two, the people would cut one another's throats; but as there are such a multitude, they all lived happily and in peace.

A French man of the letters and philosopher, Denis Diderot (1713 to 1784), was a chief editor the *Encyclopédie* that took over 20 years to compile. The men of letters gleaned understanding from significant written works and rendered them into plain language for lay readers. The *Encyclopédie* included a collection of scientific, technical, and historical knowledge with contribution by Rousseau and Voltaire. The collection of

ideas in lay terms, however, was unpopular in France where Louis XV alleged it was doing "irreparable damage to morality and religion" and banned it from print twice. To this, Diderot protested his position on both kings and the clergy in his famous quote, "Men will not be free until the last king is strangled with the entrails of the last priest." The monarchy clearly understood the dangers of the *Encyclopédie* as it was funded by 4,000 subscribers and read by more who rented it from private libraries.

The first German Idealist to appear and produce a cohesive philosophy was Immanuel Kant (1724 to 1804). His notion of **categorical imperative**, or a belief in a binding, unconditional moral obligation that is applied to everyone equally, sought to abandon an individual's selfish, guilt-ridden, or compassionate motivations. In *Critique of Prue Reason*, he delineated two kinds of judgment as being analytic ad synthetic. Analytical judgment determined truth by the definition of the words used. Words have inherent and understood meanings. Synthetic judgment required an examination of the object. For example, all black cats are cats is true by definition, but the cat is black must be examined by action to know if the statement about the cat is true.

In Kant's *Critique of Pure Reason*, he expresses the Enlightenment's commitment to an individual's sovereign right to reason:

Our age is, in especial degree, the age of criticism, and to which everything must submit. Religion through its sanctity, and law-giving through its majesty, may seek to exempt themselves from it. But in this way they awaken just suspicion, and cannot claim the sincere respect which reason accords only to that which has been able to sustain the test of free and open examination.

The ideas expressed here were only a sampling of the emotional outpouring he developed during the Romantic Age (Chapter 12). Other artists revealed the beauty of changing landscapes in their works. They also tried to capture the feelings of undiscovered locations, nostalgic pasts, or tumultuous events.

In Scotland, the social philosopher and political economist Adam Smith (1723 to 1790) argued for a **laissez-faire**, or no interference by governments in free markets, approach to economic activities. In his most influential 1776 book, *An Inquiry into the Nature and Causes of the Wealth of Nation*, he implored governments to discard their domineering regulations over entrepreneurial individuals. The idea was built upon a keen awareness that human labor was at the heart of producing goods. Smith believed that individuals were self-sufficient with the ability to arouse in themselves the means for producing wealth on an unprecedented scale.

Science

Science was the place where true enlightenment was being discovered. In 1687, Isaac Newton (1642 to 1727) published *Mathematical Principles of Natural Philosophy* and demonstrated to the satisfaction of almost everyone that the universe was an intelligible system, well ordered in its operations and guiding principles. Newton's most profound discovery pertained to the law of universal gravitation, in which systems work on each other. In a brilliant mathematical equation, he revealed how all objects were more or less exerting an attraction to and on one another, the Sun to the planets around it and vice versa and the planets to their moons and vice versa. In all these systems of attraction formed functioning units, which allowed the universe to flow in an efficient and precise manner. These concepts that Newton formulated during

the early parts of the Enlightenment would go unchallenged for almost 250 years, until Albert Einstein and others would bring about more comprehensive understandings of our physical world.

The origin behind the science of color, a tool extensively used by artists, is based on experiments carried out by Newton in the 1660s. Newton's experiments were basic in nature and explanation. They not only laid the foundation for the characteristics of color formation, but also how complementary colors are accomplished, which utilizes opposite colors, such as blue and orange, to create aesthetically pleasing works of art. Newton, in many ways, can be credited with establishing the scientific understanding of color theory in a 13-part doctrine about rays. His article states that there are "two sorts of Colours ... one original and simple ..." and the other "... an indefinite variety of Intermediate gradations." This basic, yet highly scientific understanding about color eventually led Johann Wolfgang von Goethe and Michel Eugène Chevreul to outline their ideas and personal opinions about color theory in two founding documents *Theory of Colours* of 1840 and *The Law of Simultaneous Color Contrast* of 1839, respectively.

Antivaccination sentiments are not a modern concept. When Edward Jenner (1749 to 1823) introduced the British people to the idea of inoculating them against the smallpox virus with a dose of cowpox, he was ridiculed. The clergy declared the action ungodly and simply repulsive. The satirical cartoonist James Gillray (1756 to 1815) produced a hand-colored etching with people sprouting cows from every part of the body titled *The Cox Pox or the Wonderful Effects of the New Inoculation!* (fig. 11.28). Jenner discovered the idea behind inoculating people as a result of testing his theory derived from country folklore. The folklore held that milkmaids

Fig. 11.28 *The Cox Pox or the Wonderful Effects of the New Inoculation!*, hand-colored etching, Gillray, British Museum, London, England. 1802.

who experienced the mild disease of cowpox never contracted smallpox, one of the greatest killers through human history and particularly of children.

In 1797, Jenner presented his finds to the Royal Society in a paper detailing his experiment but was rejected for lack of evidence and being too progressive. Over the next year, he experimented on several children including his own son. The same year he published his findings and coined the term vaccine from the Latin "vacca" for cow. His radical idea soon changed the world and he is called the Father of Immunology.

Technology

Long before Wedgwood's techniques for producing inexpensive dinnerware, John Kay (1704 to 1779) was working in the textile industry when he invented the flying shuttle in 1733. The flying shuttle (fig. 11.29) replaced handlooms and spinning wheels. Using the device, a weaver propelled the shuttle carrying yarn that forms the weft through the fibers of the warp, beyond the weaver's reach. This meant that the weavers could make wider cloths much faster. In 1764, the spinning jenny was invented by James Hargreaves (1721 to 1778), allowing one person to spin eight threads at the same time.

Innovation and Progress

Polish-born Dutch physicist Daniel Fahrenheit (1686 to 1736) transformed the medical world's ability to accurately determine body temperature. In 1709, he invented the alcohol thermometer and then, in 1714, the mercury thermometer. He also devised the Fahrenheit temperature scale with below 32°F freezing and 212°F boiling. Shortly later, Andres Celsius (1701 to 1744), a Swedish astronomer, established the centigrade scale with 0°C freezing and 100° the boiling point. The scale was not officially named in Celsius' honor until 1948.

Fig. 11.29 Kay's flying shuttle, 1733

Not until the techniques of iron-casting were fully developed did the world of manufacturing goods truly become revolutionized and realized, as iron was a key component of machinery. These mass-produced goods would eventually be shipped from place to place across long distances. In many cases it was easier to go across a river than around it and the cast-iron bridge and locomotive soon solved this conundrum. Massive bridges also aided in transporting the coal needed for all of the newly invented steam engine machinery in major cities such as London.

ENLIGHTENMENT LEGACY

A great amount of importance was placed on humankind's intellectual ability to reason. A number of influential thinkers, or philosophers, continued the thoughts formulated during the Renaissance, and an even greater importance was placed on scientific rationalization. Enlightenment thinkers stressed logic and reason as necessary tools for promoting human equality and scientific discovery. These thinkers believed that through logic, reason, and proper education, humankind could achieve an idyllic society of eternal peace, order, and harmony. In the latter parts of the French Enlightenment, the French people pushed for the abolishment of the monarchy in order to establish a representative government.

Industrialization brought about large-scale manufacturing of a variety of goods that were normally produced on a small scale by hand in the home. The era also showcased many issues, including the atrocious living and working conditions of factory workers. Irrespective of what new invention was created, the worker in one form or the other was demeaned. But, a few individuals were voicing concerns and leading a crusade to stop the unjust treatment of the worker primarily because industrialization and globalization were part of the much larger process known as **modernization**, or developing a modern process.

Critical Thinking

Examine the excessiveness of the Rococo period.

Discuss the connection between the Enlightenment and industrialization.

Describe the major technological developments of the Industrial Revolution.

Analyze how the court of Louis XIV brought about the Age of Reason.

Explain the philosophies of Rousseau and Voltaire.

Explore how artistic expression was transformed during the Enlightenment.

Examine Swift and Hogarth contributions to highlighting inequality and injustice.

Consider how science of the Enlightenment would impact the immediate future.

ONLINE RESOURCES

Rococo Overview
https://smarthistory.org/a-beginners-guide-to-rococo-art/
Fragonard's *The Progress of Love: The Meeting* Video
https://smarthistory.org/jean-honore-fragonard-the-progress-of-love-the-meeting/
Writing Table
https://smarthistory.org/bernard-ii-van-risenburgh-writing-table/
Neoclassicism Overview
https://smarthistory.org/neoclassicism-an-introduction/
The Age of Enlightenment Overview
https://smarthistory.org/a-beginners-guide-to-the-age-of-enlightenment/
Creating Château de Versailles
https://smarthistory.org/chateau-de-versailles/
David's *Oath of the Horatii* Video
https://smarthistory.org/jacques-louis-david-oath-of-the-horatii/
Canova's *Paolina Borghese as Venus Victorious* Video
https://smarthistory.org/canova-paolina-borghese-as-venus-victorious/
Thomas Hobbes, Life and Works
http://www.bbc.co.uk/history/historic_figures/hobbes_thomas.shtml
Jean-Jacques Rousseau, Life and Works
http://www.historyguide.org/europe/rousseau.html
Voltaire, Life and Works
https://www.britannica.com/biography/Voltaire
Isaac Newton, Life and Works
https://www.newton.ac.uk/about/isaac-newton/life

Subjectivity:
Perceptions and Reality

© Gift of Mrs. Russell Sage, 1908, The Metropolitan Museum of Art

Fig. 12.1 *The Oxbow (View from Mount Holyoke, Northampton, Massachusetts, after a Thunderstorm),* oil on canvas, Cole, MET, New York City. 1836.

Knowledge Acquisition

◆ *Examine the artistic and cultural shifts made in painting, music and opera, literature, and philosophy during the early part of the nineteenth century.*

◆ *Evaluate the accomplishments made by early-nineteenth-century artists.*

◆ *Assess the impact specific writers had on early-nineteenth-century thought.*

◆ *Explore the scientific advancements of Mendel.*

◆ *Discover how Romanticism and Realism connect works of art from around the world to their own artistic, cultural, literary, and political interests.*

SETTING THE SCENE

The golden age of social, political, and economic change coincides with **indus- trialization**, or development of industry, a time when humanity moved from home manufacturing to large-scale production of goods. As the momentum behind mass-produced goods increased, so did the problems this type of production cre- ated (Chapter 11). Many problems were exacerbated by the deplorable living con- ditions of the working class. Nonetheless, the world was moving in a new direction that concluded with **globalization**, or worldwide interactions, mainly because of the cross-cultural encounters from the sixteenth through eighteenth centuries (Chapter 8). Explorers discovered new cultures and acquired new products to trade, which allowed for prosperity to flourish. Both industrialization and globalization were products of the much larger process known as **modernization**, or innovations in science and technology, with the invention of items such as the steam engine.

Victorian Age

Rapid changes in almost every aspect of daily life were the result of the Age of Industry overlapping the reign of Queen Victoria of England (r. 1837 to 1901). A significant characteristic of the era was a reaction against Romanticism, specifically in the literature English authors generated. The people were also preoccupied with Darwin's assertion regarding evolution. These assertions di- rectly influenced faith, morality, and later scientific discoveries. The middle decades of the nineteenth century witnessed British confidence ascend to its greatest heights. As considerable advancements were made in production of goods and economic gains, social stability and traditional values shifted. One facet of English life formed the basis

for symbolizing stability and tradition, the Monarchy and parliament.

A Revolution in France, Again

Life in Paris in 1848 was in a state of disar- ray, with more than a million people living in the city. People lived in danger every day because of the narrow streets, shifty passageways, and garbage and raw sewage filling the gutters. In low-lying areas of the city cesspools developed, with the smell strong enough to induce vomiting. All of this combined to create a perfect nesting place for rats with fleas that both carried deadly diseases such as cholera, dysentery, and typhoid fever. To make matters worse, the same years witnessed a food shortage, causing the agricultural economy to be thrown into a panic. The agricultural crisis, in turn, triggered bankruptcies, bank closures, plum- meting of goods prices, business failures, and rampant unemployment. Paris was ripe for another revolution.

The revolution of 1848 was supposed to bring about equality for everyone. The bourgeois in particular believed the Enlight- enment writings of John Locke and Thomas Jefferson, where government originated with the people, who then freely endorsed the ruler but had control to overthrow undesir- able leaders. The bourgeois were, in fact, capitalists who opposed any government who jeopardized their businesses or wanted to regulate their economic means. While the bourgeois primarily wanted change for their own interests, the working class wanted change as well but mainly for better living and working conditions. Coincidentally, the living conditions of the working class were, in many ways, created by the bour- geois, who were more interested in profit than safe working conditions and decent wages. Nonetheless, the working class and the bourgeois would unite to overthrow the ruling king, Louis-Philippe.

During the revolts, everyone was fighting for fairer government involvement in economic endeavors but all to a different degree and means. In June 1848, the entire crisis came to a head. Three months prior, the French government created National Workshops to provide employment, but workshop employ numbers grew from 10,000 to 120,000. The government soon realized they did not have enough work for 120,000 numbers and closed the workshops indefinitely. The 3 days that followed were the bloodiest days not just in France but all of Europe in the nineteenth century. After the revolt ended, many bourgeois believed they had narrowly survived the total dissolution of social order. The bourgeois began to foster a suspicious distrust for the working class and, as a result, life for the working class became progressively worse.

ARTISTIC MOVEMENTS

Artists of all types play an active role in promoting social change, leading to more social diversity within any given society. An artist can provide context to philosophy, religion, aesthetic theories, economics, and politics along with other social concerns.

Artists primarily record and commemorate events by giving tangibility to the unknown and to ideas and feeling within the people living in their local regions. Through an artist's works we can experience life and situations differently than we previously considered possible. Artists also help us fully understand past experiences, leading to social change and diversity.

Romanticism

The Romantic Age was an idyllic period in human history where subjective experiences and feelings were in direct opposition to the formal and objective values of Neoclassicism. People longed to return to a simpler existence. Unlike the Neoclassical movement, just a few decades earlier, Romantic artists, in particular painters, poets, and novelists, captured scenes dealing with the individual, the exotic, mysterious, and strange. The individual's imagination was a free expression of feelings that could make one feel alone but still comprising empathy for those less fortunate. The act of communing with nature regardless of whether individuals interacted with others was valued, while Neoclassical artists created work showing individuals uniting together as one.

Cross-cultural Connection

The opening decades of the nineteenth century witnessed Napoleon Bonaparte (1769 to 1821) embark on his monumentally destructive endeavors to conquer one European realm after another. He was a man of common origins who rose to power by sheer will and brute force. His dedication to equality, fraternity, and liberty, along with his ability to abolish serfdom throughout most of Europe, made him a celebrate leader. From Gibraltar, Spain to Warsaw, Poland and Naples, Italy to Hamburg, Germany he either acquired the territory or it was a dependent state. Napoleon's downfall was caused by his egoistic assumption that he was immune to defeat, until he was once again defeated on the battlefield in Waterloo by Arthur Wellesley, 1st Duke of Wellington (1769 to 1852).

James Mallord William Turner (1775 to 1851) creates an image to inspire the feeling of the overwhelming encounter with nature. Turner's use of color in rendering the lake and mountains with a hazy yet defined glow forcefully binds the entire scene. As the sun rises between the Rossberg and Mythen mountains in the background, the foreground displays nude bathing girls as villagers approach the shore and launch their boats. While paintings such as *The Lake of Zug* (fig. 12.2) provide visual input, poems inform multiple tactile senses. The opening lines of the poem "Tintern Abbey" by William Wordsworth (1770 to 1850) give the impression of a time and place to remember:

> Five years have past; five sum-
> mers, with the length
> Of five long winters! and again
> I hear
> These waters, rolling from their
> mountain-springs
> With a sweet inland murmur.—
> Once again

> Do I behold these steep and lofty
> cliffs,
> Which on a wild secluded scene
> impress
> Thoughts of more deep seclusion;
> and connect
> The landscape with the quiet of
> the sky.

In both the watercolor and the poem, there is a clear evidence of the individual being lifted atop all other experiences. Both artists, by extension, are sharing their communion with nature to wither others, thus making the experience come to life as a seamless whole, a notion best felt after reading the last few lines of the poem:

> We stood together; and that I, so
> long
> A worshipper of Nature, hither
> came,
> Unwearied in that service: rather say
> With warmer love, oh! with far
> deeper zeal

© Marquand Fund, 1959, The Metropolitan Museum of Art

Fig. 12.2 *The Lake of Zug*, watercolor over graphite, Turner, MET, NYC, New York. 1843.

*Of holier love. Nor wilt thou then
forget,
That after many wanderings,
many years
Of absence, these steep woods and
lofty cliffs,
And this green pastoral landscape,
were to me
More dear, both for themselves
and for thy sake.*

For the Romantics, individualism served as one of the basic tenets. Individualism placed value on autonomy and the benefit of the individual over the group, even over one's own nation. The individual became the primary unit within the social system and structure, an idea in opposition to the era's teaching, but the social theory behind individualism was quite simple. Each human being was unique; their actions were unique and, therefore, each social activity they partook was ultimately comprised of individual acts. In essence, what we see in the arts was the swinging of the pendulum into the realm of feelings with no limits implied, and the artistic expression was more personal than theory based.

Realism

As the nineteenth century progressed further away from the ideas of the Enlightenment and Neoclassicism, the unconstrained, emotional feelings of Romanticism gave way to a new reality rooted in unequivocal truth. All over Europe, a new reality was unfolding in regard to the conditions of the working-class. The workforce was becoming increasingly **proletariat**, or workers who do not own or control the goods they produce, a glaring opposition to the growing realization of the **bourgeoisie**

class, or those who owned businesses in which the proletariat worked. In the wake of this realization, reformist thinkers and writers across Europe reacted by writing polemical works that were meant to underscore the drawbacks of the new industrial life.

Writers were most critical of the economic crisis created by industrialization, which primarily affected the working class. In their eyes, unbridled materialism was the issue with a world that seemed life-consuming and soul-destroying. For the critics, the human heartbeat was slowly being replaced by the humming of machinery and the products they created. The Russian painter Ilya Repin (1844 to 1930) painted *Barge Haulers on the Volga* (fig. 12.3) in which one can see the effects of industrial life on the working class.

Repin depicted a group of peasant men who were fated to pull ships up the Volga River. In order to intensify the viewer's compassion toward the men, he emphasized the young male in the center. Repin cloaked the youth in brightly colored clothes, with his head lifted as a way to juxtapose him against the older, tired, and more resigned men he works alongside. The painting was a cry for action, an action against mass-manufactured goods produced, delivered, and consumed by the working class.

CREATIVE IMPULSE

Early-nineteenth-century artists and thinkers played an active role in promoting social change, leading to more social diversity within their respective societies. Artists, in particular, can provide context to philosophy, religion, aesthetic theories, economics, and politics along with other social concerns. They commentate, commemorate, and

Fig. 12.3 *Barge Haulers on the Volgai,* detail of figures, oil on canvas, Repin, The State Russian Museum, St. Petersburg, Russia. 1870 to 1873.

record events in a way that gives the events a tangible understanding to various ideas and feeling for the people beyond those living through the events. Through an artist's work we can experience life and situations differently than previously considered. Artists and philosophers of the nineteenth century helped people fully understand those ideas that led to social change they were experiencing.

Architecture and Design

England led the way in contributing to the development of a new building style called **picturesque**, or Gothic motif revival that reflected fantasy. Royal Pavilion (fig. 12.4) in Brighton, directly south of London on the coast, incorporates the visual styles of India and China with a flare of whimsy in its appearance of the new picturesque style. Designed by John Nash as the residence of King George IV, Royal Pavilion was truly a modern concept, with the exterior walls merely functioning as a screen and not as

a structural support. The interior design was dissimilar to its exterior façade. The design of the interior space combined the ornate, heavy decoration of the Baroque with the emerging Art Deco style that would dominate the latter half of the nineteenth century.

Two other monumental achievements in the new picturesque style, both built in London, were the Houses of Parliament (fig. 12.5) and Crystal Palace (fig. 12.6a). The nineteenth century proved itself to be the age of experimentation with the use of new building materials, steel, and glass. Sir Joseph Paxton was courageous in his innovation to display the archi-tectural support system of his Crystal Palace. Paxton built the Crystal Palace for the Great Exhibition of 1851 over a month period. The structure exemplified the nineteenth-century concept of state-of-the-art materials and spatial design. The overall design was created to use the newer innovation of mass production of

Fig. 12.4 Royal Pavilion, Nash, Brighton, England. 1815 to 1823.

Fig. 12.5 Houses of Parliament, Sir Charles Barry and Augustus Welby Northmore Pugin, London, England. 1839 to 1852.

the stanchions and girders along with the ability to disassembled the structure, which was then reassembled in Sydenham in 1854 (fig. 12.6b-d).

Painting and Printmaking

Caspar David Friedrich (1774 to 1840) soon realized that emotional restraint was out of fashion and that people yearned

(a)

(b)

(c)   (d)

Fig. 12.6 (a) Crystal Palace, steel and glass, Paxton, 1851. **(b)** reconstruction in progress. **(c)** interior structural support materials. **(d)** interior exhibition space. Albumen silver prints by Philip Henry Delamotte.

for powerful, life-changing emotional experiences. These experiences were sought in areas of wilderness where they could encounter the power of nature, raw and untouched by man. Friedrich, in particular, captures the very temperament of the Romantic Movement perfectly. Many of Friedrich's paintings portray a solitary figure or two enveloped by a vast,

sublime landscape, or one beyond the human mind's ability of full comprehension. *Two Men Contemplating the Moon* (fig. 12.7) reveals a favored motif of German Romantics, the moon. Friedrich often painted the moon into his work as a reference to pious contemplation.

Wanderer above the Sea of Fog (fig. 12.8) showed not only a lone man with his back

© Wrightsman Fund, 2000, The Metropolitan Museum of Art

Fig. 12.7 *Two Men Contemplating the Moon*, oil on canvas, Friedrich, MET, NYC, New York. 1825 to 1830.

to us but a scene in which the figure was engulfed by the vastness of the landscape and atmosphere around him, creating a void. Just as the Age of Reason, or Enlightenment, witnessed the beginning of the divorce of religious faith and logic, the Romantic Age would start to question religious faith with logical reasoning. In fact, the man seems to be asking the big questions in life and how, in the face of this empty vastness, does he retain his faith? It is quite possible that Friedrich would have known of and read the foremost thinker of his day, Immanuel Kant (Chapter 11), and his concepts about religious faith, logical reason, and the human mind.

Other paintings by Friedrich highlight his keen awareness to the awesomeness of nature's ability to create and destroy. In another painting, *Sea of Ice*, the focal point was unnoticed at first, a ship wrecked a little more than half way up the painting. The ship is created of wood found in nature, and

the ice, created as a result of nature's law of boiling and freezing points, has the ability to destroy the ship. The beauty in the work is in how the ice breaks and its peak rises into an opening in the sky. In an instant, the individual viewing the work would be overwhelmed with the sensation of the grandeur found in both nature and God as one entity, an immeasurable connection to the Whole.

Artists such as Eugène Delacroix (1798 to 1863) were by far more politically motivated in their works. Delacroix was a keen observer for humankind's continual quest for a more progressive age in both equality and respect for others. In *Liberty Leading the People* (fig. 12.9), Delacroix provided an element of both despair and ecstasy, mounting climax and tragic loss. The idea of using an individual's feelings originated with Neoclassical artists but perfected by Romantics to visually describe specific events that unfolded before their own eyes.

© Joinmepic/Shutterstock.com

Fig. 12.8 *Wanderer above the Sea of Fog*, oil on canvas, Friedrich. Kunsthalle Hamburg, Hamburg, Germany. 1818.

© Oleg Golovnev/Shutterstock.com

Fig. 12.9 *Liberty Leading the People (28th July 1830)*, oil on canvas, Delacroix, Louvre, Paris, France. 1830.

Global Focal Point

The **abolitionist** movement, or the ending of the transatlantic slave trade and capital slavery, took hold in the latter part of the eighteenth century and continued through the nineteenth century. In 1772, Granville Sharp (1735 to 1813) reminded and ensured those living in West Indies that they were not allowed to hold slaves as this went against English law. In the United States, the founder of the American Anti-Slavery Society, William Lloyd Garrison (1805 to 1879), was the best known abolitionist. Tensions between the North and the South mounted after the Fugitive Slave Law of 1850 was passed. After the publication of Harriet Beecher Stowe's (1811 to 1896) antislavery novel, *Uncle Tom's Cabin*, in 1852, the abolitionist cause gained wider support.

The streets of Paris were narrow before the **Haussmannization**, or the process of urbanization in Paris, that resulted as a consequence of the prior decade's revolts.

Delacroix witnessed one such revolt on the street of Paris outside his home and began painting the scene in September 1830. He employed color, light, and shadows to capture the essence of the moment. His brushwork was vigorous with implied rhythm to help balance the image. Liberty is shown striding victoriously over the rubble and corpses that form the base of the tringle she creates with the tricolor flag of France the top. Delacroix used both modern and classical references to enliven the painting. Liberty's dress is classically draped over her body but it has fallen to expose her underarm with hair. Her underarm hair is a symbol of her vulgarity, working-class status because classical artists had decreed that the skin of women should be smooth. She is in Greek profile and stands nobly resolute in her actions, with her right side illuminated and her left in darkness as she spurs them onto victory. She is an allegory surrounded by a real battle. In her right hand, she holds the tricolor flag symbolizing the people's struggle. In her left hand, she holds an 1816 infantry bayonet that gives her a contemporary look and authoritarian creditability.

The English painter J.M.W. Turner was especially skillful for in this ability to turn poetry passages and real events into visual displays of unthinkable human violence. In 1781, the captain of the Zong threw dying and sick slaves overboard to collect insurance money which was offered only if the slaves were "lost at sea." The urgency of slave traders to rid the ships of the sick and dying was not new. The Scottish poet James Thomson (1700 to 1748) fashioned a masterful poem titled "The Seasons," written over a 4-year period from 1726 to 1730. Turner used the historical events of the Zong and the following passage to paint his own masterpiece:

Increasing still the terrors of these storms,
His jaws horrific armed with threefold fate,
Here dwells the direful shark.
Lured by the scent
Of steaming crowds, of rank disease, and death,
Behold! he rushing cuts the briny flood,
Swift as the gale can bear the ship along;
And from the partners of that cruel trade

*Which spoils unhappy Guinea of
her sons
Demands his share of prey-
demands themselves.
The stormy fates descend: one
death involves
Tyrants and slaves; when straight,
their mangled limbs
Crashing at once, he dyes the
purple seas
With gore, and riots in the venge-
ful meal.*

Turner painted *The Slave Ship* (fig. 12.10) that fully enlivens the elements of Romantic painters. He additionally used disorganized diagonal lines to create the overwhelming sensations of fragmentation, which enhances the sense of horror. His ability to establish three-dimensional space was a direct result of his loose brushwork. Turner's treatment of the sea and the sky made both seem transparent, as spontaneous and energetic brush strokes flutter across the canvas. A sense of doom appeared on the horizon

as he incorporated direct and recognizable forms and subject matter.

In the newly forged country of America, English immigrant Thomas Cole (1801 to 1848) painted breathtaking landscape capturing the country's vast wilderness. His *The Oxbow* (fig. 12.1) depicted a famous bend in the Connecticut River in Massachusetts. Viewers of the painting clearly saw a distention between the land touched by man and the unsullied wilderness. Cole also painted himself into the scene, at his easel at the lower middle with his umbrella. He placed himself as the boundary between the two infinitely different terrains. A terrain to the right was perfectly defined by rows of fence and sunny fields, while the terrain to the left of him was rugged and untamed.

Realist painters used the newly forged advantage of emotional response to capture real people carrying out everyday tasks. In artistic works such as *The Stone Breaker* by Gustave Courbet (1819 to 1877) painted in 1849, the entire scene seems heavy with only

Fig. 12.10 *The Slave Ship (Slavers Throwing Overboard the Dead and Dying, Typhoon Coming On)*, oil on canvas, Tuner, Museum of Fine Arts, Boston, Massachusetts. 1840.

© Courtesy National Gallery of Art, Washington

Fig. 12.11 *The Stone Breaker,* gillotype in black on woven paper, laid down, Gillot after Courbet. National Gallery of Art, Washington, DC. after 1849.

a sliver of blue sky at the top right illuminating the predominately monochromatic brown scene. The whole composition appeared as if everything was being depressed and dragged down by the burden of manual labor. Courbet often referred to the scenes he created as being comparable to understanding absolute human wretchedness.

The astonishing aspect of *The Stone Breakers* was its size. The work was life size, more than 5 feet tall and 8 feet wide; images of this scale were reserved for historical events such as Alexandre Cabanel's (1823 to 1889) *The Birth of Venus* (fig. 12.12), not for working-class members of society. The image was a representation of the ideas behind social acceptance and how those ideas were changing. Firmin Gillot (1820 to 1872)

was so inspired by Courbet's painting that he captured the boy figure in *The Stone Breaker* (fig. 12.11) using a new printing technique called **paniconography**, or photoengraving in relief. Gillot's relief with only the boy visible emphasized the reality of hard work and the struggles of the common people, even the youth.

Courbet painted in the Realist style almost his entire career, with working-class people as his subject matter. No other artist best summarized the new feeling among the emerging Realist painters than Courbet did with the following passage:

It's the whole world coming to me to be painted on the right, all the shareholders, by that I mean friends, fellow workers, art lovers. On the left is the other world of everyday life, the masses, wretchedness, poverty, wealth, the exploited and the exploiters, people who make a living from death.

Earnest Meissonier (1815 to 1891) was a Realist painter and illustrator who captured the spirit of military and historical events with an enlivened quality. He was known for his accurate attention to every detail within his painting. Between 1861

and 1875, Meissonier undertook painting one of Napoleon Bonaparte's paramount victories in *1807, Friedland* (fig. 12.13). In preparation for the final painting, he produced hundreds of studies in both drawing and sculptured models. The painting was to be 1 in a series 5 that illustrated Napoleon life, only one other painting was ever completed. A successful Irish-American department store tycoon, Alexander T. Stewart (1803 to 1876), purchased the painting in 1876 for $60,000. The sale of the painting only

© Gift of John Wolfe, 1893, The Metropolitan Museum of Art

Fig. 12.12 *The Birth of Venus*, oil on canvas, Cabanel. MET, NYC, New York. 1875.

© Gift of Henry Hilton, 1887, The Metropolitan Museum of Art

Fig. 12.13 *1807, Friedland*, oil on canvas, Meissonier, MET, NYC, New York. c. 1861 to 1875.

added to Meissonier's achievements and wealth, as he was already reported to be wealthier than the King of France.

For most artists, the cost of living was not easily affordable or comfortable in the heart of major cities, like Paris, unless they were a part of the bourgeoisie class. For this reason, in 1848, artists Jean-François Millet (1814 to 1875) and Theodore Rousseau (1812 to 1867) moved to the small town of Barbizon, 30 miles outside of Paris. Along with two other artists they started painting everyday images of real people, living very real lives. After leaving Paris, Millet's favorite subject matter became peasant life. His work *The Gleaners* (fig. 12.14) was a 10-year study of rural working-class people.

Millet depicted three women in the rhythmic act of bending over, picking up scraps of wheat, and straightening up again. In the background, men on horseback oversaw men working the harvest for an absentee landlord. In the image you can see the social structure, but Millet has decided to highlight the poorest of the poor, the women in the foreground. One art critic,

Paul de Saint Victor 1827 to 1881), stated that Millet's "three gleaners have gigantic pretensions, they pose as the Three Fates of Poverty... their ugliness and their grossness unrelieved." In one fell swoop, regardless of the work's immediate reaction, Millet and other artists created images exposing the unjust socio-economic environment the working-class individuals were obliged to live in. The following year he produced *Woman with a Rake* (fig. 12.15) similarly portraying the tough working and living conditions of the poor working class of the French countryside.

Photography

A new method for chronicling the passage of human activity and events emerged in the 1830s and this was photography. The word was derived from the Greek words *photos*, meaning light, and *graphein*, meaning to draw. Early experimentation by Nicéphore Niépce (1765 to 1833) produced a type of image referred to as a **heliography**, or sun drawing. His technique used light-sensitive solution of bitumen and lavender oil to coat a plate before exposing it to sunlight.

© Oleg Golovnev/Shutterstock.com

Fig. 12.14 *The Gleaners*, oil on canvas, Millet, Musée d'Orsay, Paris, France. 1857.

© Gift of Stephen C. Clark, 1938, The Metropolitan Museum of Art

Fig. 12.15 *Woman with a Rake*, oil on canvas, Millet. MET, NYC, New York. c. 1856 to 1857.

He then used a camera obscure (Chapter 10) fitted with a heliography plate to produce the first photograph, *View from the Window at Le Gras*, in 1826 with an exposure time of 8 hours. The image is currently located in the collection of the Grensheim Collection in the Harry Ransom Center at the University of Texas in Austin, Texas. While the first true photographic image was indeed innovative, the heliography technique was highly technical yet paved the way for later success.

In 1835, 2 years after the death of Niépce, a professional theatrical scene painter, Louis-Jacques-Mandé Daguerre (1787 to 1851), unearthed the ability of mercury vapor to develop a latent image on a plate of iodized silver. He also reduced the exposure time to 30 minutes, but the image darkened until it became indistinguishable. Over the next 2 years he toiled at making the image

permanent, until he discovered that fixing the image with salt created a lasting impression. The daguerreotype was born. Daguerre's new invention spread quickly around the world after it was introduced in a public presentation in Paris in 1839. The uniqueness was in how each highly polished silver place created an exceedingly detailed, three-dimensional image. In 1844, Daguerre likeness was captured in a rare portrait, *Louis-Jacques-Mandé Daguerre* (fig. 12.16), either by the artists Pierre-Ambrose Richebourg (1810 to 1893) or by Daguerre himself.

Within little time the use of a portable means for quick recording became popular with archeologists such as Girault de Prangey (1804 to 1892). Between 1841 and 1844, Prangey produced over 900 daguerreotypes as he toured the areas around the Eastern Mediterranean to study Islamic architecture. He had a particular fascination with the

© Gilman Collection, Gift of The Howard Gilman Foundation, 2005, The Metropolitan Museum of Art

Fig. 12.16 *Louis-Jacques-Mandé Daguerre*, daguerreotype, Richeboug, c. 1844.

© Purchase, Mr. and Mrs. John A. Moran Gift, in memory of Louise Chisholm Moran, 2018, The Metropolitan Museum of Art

Fig. 12.17 *Baalbek*, daguerreotype, Prangey, 1843.

ancient city of Baalbek in Lebanon where he photographed *Baalbek* (fig. 12.17). Prangey's expedition was possibly a precursor to a later project by the Ottoman government to reclaim the city's origins.

In America, the partnership of Southworth and Hawes in Boston produced the finest quality daguerreotype portraits in the country. The portrait studio had a diverse clientele of leading artistic figures, intellectual thinkers, and prominent politicians. The image *Miss Hodges of Salem* (fig. 12.18) hung in the front room of the public gallery. Who Miss Hodges was is lost to history. Her

Fig. 12.18 *Miss Hodges of Salem*, daguerreotype, Southworth and Hawes, c. 1850.

portrait, however, attests to not only her photogenic qualities but also the studio's ability to produce desirable portraits.

A more controversial application of the daguerreotype was the production of nude photography. Two artists, Félix-Jacques-Antoine Moulin (1800 to 1875) and Bruno Braquehais (1823 to 1875), established themselves as artists willing to produce images the government deemed obscene. Moulin's daguerreotype *Two Standing Female Nudes* (fig. 12.19) seemed more aligned with art than **erotica**, or arousal of sexual desire. Nonetheless, in 1851, his works were confiscated, he was imprisoned for 1 month, and fined 100 francs. Braquehais produced the daguerreotype *Reclining Female Nude as Danae* (fig. 12.20) that was more closely associated with erotica images considered pornographic. His photos used boudoir props and highly provocative poses that were typically hand-colored. In

Fig. 12.19 *Two Standing Female Nudes*, daguerreotype, Moulin, c. 1850.

Fig. 12.20 *Reclining Female Nude as Danae*, daguerreotype with applied color, attributed to Braquehais, c. 1850s.

comparing the two works, Moulin's young women appear completely at ease even to the point of resembling Cabanel's *The Birth of Venus* (fig. 12.12).

Music and Opera

A key figure in the transition from the Classical to the Romantic era was Ludwig van Beethoven (1770 to 1827, fig. 12.21) creating notes for human feelings. His music showcases his life's journey with his earlier highly structured works and later compositions filled with personal emotions. Beethoven's

Third Symphony, *Eroica*, originally in honor of Napoleon, was his first work to mark his personal transition to the more expressive style. The symphony dramatically introduces its theme with a climatic end to fully establish its Romantic mood. The second movement used strong repetitive beats to imitate the sound of military drums to signify the main theme, a funeral march. The movement concludes with violins suggesting the passage of time. The entire movement is an expression of a forlorn despair. In the third movement, the mood Beethoven created was more relaxed with the injection of **scherzo**, or a quick and lively type of musical beat. The finale pulled together the symphony's themes to sensationalize Beethoven's own struggle with his tumble into despair and art being his means for triumph.

As a combination of narrative, visuals, and music, opera was perhaps the most representative art form of the Romantic Age. The stories unfold in dimly lit, theatrical settings, with the lovers often times dying at the end. Opera was the nineteenth-century equivalent to twentieth-century film, a magnificent spectacle that attracted large audiences combining multiple displays of arts into a single, exhilarating event.

One of the most remarkable operas of all time, certainly the longest artwork in the Western civilization, the *Ring* cycle, was composed over a 26-year period by

Societal Emphasis

Prostitution had been legal in Paris until 1946, with most of the larger brothels closing in 1925, yet pornographic images were illegal shortly after they were first produced in the late 1840s. The cause for their illegal status rests in the depiction of gay and lesbian sexual pleasures. In nineteenth-century Paris, homosexual nudes were not only viewed as abnormal displays of sexual activity but they disregarded the patriarchal order. The images further blurred the line between the male and the female divide of active and passive.

Fig. 12.21 *Beethoven* black and white photo of original oil on canvas, Stieler, The Bridgeman Art Library, NYC, New York. 1820.

Richard Wagner (1813 to 1883), a German composer. Wagner used the opera to convey a romantic saga with an emphasis on German history and heroism over conflicts between good and evil with a setting separate from reality. In true tragic form, nearly all important characters ultimately died, even the gods were ironically offered as sacrifice at their own altars by the end. Wagner's opera would influence later literary works by J.R.R. Tolkien (1892 to 1973).

Literature

Ralph Waldo Emerson (1803 to 1882) was a Unitarian minister in Concord, Massachusetts who encouraged people to seek their own path in finding spirituality. He was heavily influenced by the writing of British author Samuel Taylor Coleridge (1772 to 1834) when he wrote *Nature,* published in 1836. His book became the intellectual beacon for a group of Concord locals, mostly ministers, called the "Transcendental Club." **Transcendentalist** philosophy considered the alienation of urban work life in sharp opposition to their belief in the restorative capacities found in the natural world. For transcendentalist, the American wilderness inspired a sense of be able to communing with nature. Emerson was shaped by the nation's emphasis of the individual and individual liberty. These writers were free to think for themselves and their imaginations were equally free to discover who they were in nature. Transcendentalists thought that the human spirit possessed a oneness with nature. Emerson believed that a direct experience with nature united the individual with God. The experience was a way of transcending knowledge on the basis of **empirical evidence**, or verifiable observation, rather than pure logic or theory. Emerson wrote:

> To the attentive eye, each moment of the year has its own beauty, and in the same field, it beholds, every hour, a picture which was never seen before, and which shall never be seen again…... The shows of day, the dewy morning, the rainbow, mountains, orchards in blossom, stars, moonlight, shadows in still water, and the like, if too eagerly hunted, become shows merely, and mock us with their unreality.

The words expressed by Emerson in *Nature* were aligned with the Romantics' sentiments about feeling emotion, no matter the emotion.

Charles Dickens (1812 to 1870), an English writer, emphasized an entirely different aspect of human life. His works *A Christmas* and *A Tale of Two Cities* showcased the conditions, corruption, destitution, and urban blight of working-class Londoners. His novels more importantly underscored the results of a free system of economic enterprise that caused a vast number of laborers to live near the factories they worked. Reforms to living conditions were slow, but novels of those such as Dickens helped bring these issues to the forefront. His works collective are referred to as **literary realism**.

Jane Austen (1775 to 1817) was another English novelist celebrated for her decidedly modern treatment of the characters she created. Austen's novels enlivened the notion that middle-class people were ordinary to become timeless classics. She defied the conventional novel standards, or **novel of manners**, where every aspect within a scene was finely detailed. Each of the four novels, *Sense and Sensibility* (1811), *Pride and Prejudice* (1813), *Mansfield Park* (1814), and *Emma* (1815), published during her life, was turned into cinematic greatness in the latter part of the twentieth century.

Gustave Flaubert (1821 to 1880), a French author, also produced a glimpse into the reality of human life but that of a bored, materialistic bourgeois housewife. *Madame Bovary*, originally titled *Provincial Customs*, was an installment publication that appeared in the *Revue de* from October 1st to December 15th of 1856. Flaubert's writings were more pointedly a direct attack on Romantic sensibility in exchange for Realist novels. The main themes enveloping the lead character, Madame Bovary, were adultery and overindulgence of material goods leading to

Innovation and Progress

Every aspect of industry witnesses new advancements in machines and tools for labor. The milling machine brought about the ability to manufacture parts using a rotary cutting edge. The parts were made to exact tolerance that was interchangeable in a single product.

her and then her husband's ruin. The French government subsequently placed Flaubert on trial for obscenity, for which he was later acquitted. The events intensified the public's interest in the story.

Leo Tolstoy (1828 to 1910) was one of two Russian novelists who were masters of Realistic fiction. The other was Fyodor Dostoyevsky (1821 to 1881). Tolstoy was born into an aristocratic family and studied oriental languages at university but departed dropped out and returned to his family estate before earning a degree. His greatest novels were *War and Peace*, set during the reign of Napoleon, published in 1869, and *Anna Karenina*. *War and Peace* beautifully surveyed the role lofty-minded men play in the progression of historical events. The novel further explored human nature, destiny, and social complexities with a focus on Russia while narrating the life of several Russian families. Tolstoy articulated a written illustration of the Russian attitude of and toward marriage. His ability to contrast opposing aspects of nature and the characteristics of people and their behavior in a vivid manner was unmatched. He praised the simple life and intuition over civilized learned analysis.

Philosophy

A German philosopher, George Wilhelm Friedrich Hegel, progressed dialectic logic from thesis to antithesis with a reality he called the Absolute Spirit. For Hegel, the human mind was Absolute. As a result of the Enlightenment and the growing Romantic movement, the certainty found in logical reason was increasingly being used to question traditional forms of authority, both secular and religious. The argument humankind was having revolved around the necessity of political and/or religious authorities telling individuals how to live, or even worse, what to believe. If we possessed the ability to figure "things" out by ourselves, why would we allow others to rule us?

Hegel, however, believed that art celebrated the physical forms of the Absolute and that Christianity was the best of all of the world's religions. His belief was founded on the fact that God took a physical form as Jesus and that God was both finite and infinite. Hegel perceived the Absolute's ability to be both as attaining the supreme amalgamation of the known and the unknown world. He viewed these events as an ordered, rational process. Humankind's own history of evolution was a rational process that led to greater and ever greater freedom. He was extremely influential with a very diverse following, from fundamental Christians to atheists. Both Karl Marx and Friedrich Engels were notable leftist Hegelians.

The Danish philosopher Søren Kierkegaard (1813 to 1855) disagreed with Hegel's abstract philosophical thoughts. He asserted that Hegel ignored the distinctive qualities associated with a person's cognizance. His thought was that every individual had an exclusively subjective viewpoint he termed the **existential individual**. He also stressed how an individual's ethical nature was responsible for the decisions they made and for maintaining those commitments. Every decision a person made established their authenticity. He asserted that humankind's moral choices should consist of respect for others, honorable actions, and trust in the nonphysical world outside of material existence.

Friedrich Wilhelm Joseph Schelling (1775 to 1854), a little known German philosopher, was a tutor for an aristocratic family until 1798 when he was offered a professor position at the University of Jena. At Jena University, he helped Hegel obtain a position as private lecturer. Schelling is often viewed as the bridge between the idealism of Kant and Hegel. His *System of Transcendental Idealism* of 1800 and *Philosophical Investigations on the Nature of Human Freedom* of 1809 espoused his concepts of the complementary nature of his transcendental and nature philosophies. Each publication influenced subsequent philosophies and writers. His first book provided the name for an intellectual group that met and formed the "Transcendental Club." The latter publication revealed his tendencies toward spirituality and is viewed as a precursor to the ideas of **existentialism**, or individual existence, freedom, and choice, where one tries to make rational decisions in spite of the irrationality of the world.

Science

Charles Darwin (1809 to 1882) was the son of an English physician and grandson of Josiah Wedgwood (Chapter 11). He spent 3 years studying medicine at the University of Edinburgh and another 3 years at Cambridge studying theology. After his graduation, at the age of 22, Darwin set on a 5-year voyage around the world as a naturalist on H.M.S. Beagle before entering into a life of ministry. During his voyage, he collected fossil remains, finches, and other specimens. He was especially impressed with the striking adaptations found in the animals and plants he collected and with the progressive changes found in the different species of a given genus as the expedition moved along the South American coast. In the Galapagos Islands, he discovered many species of a one genus confined to a single island, yet resembling other species on other islands, and all of them resembled species on the mainland.

After he returned to England, he examined the modification of all the species he collected. Over a 20-year period he analyzed his collected data, performed experiments, read published articles, and formulated a possible mechanism to explain how species

were modified. He stumbled across a publication by Thomas Malthus (1766 to 1834) titled *Essay on Population*. Malthus's concern resided in the increase in human population. This prompted him to suggest that when a population increases to a number that outstrips its resources, resulting in not enough food for everyone, a struggle for existence ensues.

Darwin was familiar with the struggle for existence that occurred everywhere in nature. He reasoned that in such situations, favorable species were preserved and unfavorable ones destroyed. The resulting factor was the formation of new species. In 1859, he published *The Origin of Species by Means of Natural Selection or the Preservation of Favored Races in the Struggle for Life* in which he put forth his theory of evolution, but the work of Gregor Mendel (Chapter 13) was unavailable at the time.

Technology

Many systems were used to transmit messages over long distances, but the discovery and harnessing of electricity made **telegraph** (fig. 12.22), or coded transmission of information, possible. The word *telegraph* was derived from the Greek words *tele*, meaning distant, and *graphein*, meaning to write. The use of telegraph lines spanned the continents of Europe and North America. By 1866, the lines on both continents had

Fig. 12.22 Telegraph instrument, brass, c. 1837 to 1844.

been joined via the first transatlantic cable. The new method was far superior to the older methods of smoke, fire, and drums.

SUBJECTIVITY LEGACY

Industrialization that began in the eighteenth century was in full swing as the nineteenth century progressed. Individuals who wanted to generate real social change let go of the early Neoclassical and Romantic notions and took up portraying reality through Realism. Writers and artists were most critical of the economic crisis created by industrialization, knowing that it primarily affected the working-class people. Artists such as Courbet, Millet, and Repin used their talents to showcase the depravity and despair of the socio-economic situation most individuals were unfortunate to be born into and die in.

Critical Thinking

Examine the stylistic differences and similarities between Romanticism and Realism.

Describe the major philosophic tendencies of the early nineteenth century.

Analyze how Romanticism paved the way for Realism.

Examine how literature impacted the idea of social status and other relationships.

ONLINE RESOURCES

Romanticism Overview
https://smarthistory.org/a-beginners-guide-to-romanticism/
Realism Overview
https://smarthistory.org/a-beginners-guide-to-realism/
The First Photography
http://www.hrc.utexas.edu/exhibitions/permanent/firstphotograph/
Daguerreotype and *Paris Boulevard*
https://smarthistory.org/daguerre-paris-boulevard/
Houses of Parliament Video
https://smarthistory.org/barry-pugin-parliament/
Delacroix's *Liberty Leading the People* Video
https://smarthistory.org/delacroix-liberty-leading-the-people/
Turner's *Slave Ship* Video
https://smarthistory.org/j-m-w-turner-slave-ship/
Caspar David Friedrich, Ideal Modernism
https://smarthistory.org/friedrich-monk-by-the-sea/
Courbet's *The Stonebreakers*
https://smarthistory.org/courbet-the-stonebreakers/
Millet's *The Gleaners* Video
https://smarthistory.org/millet-the-gleaners/
Emerson's Poetry
https://www.poetryfoundation.org/poets/ralph-waldo-emerson
Hegel's Absolute Idealism Philosophy
https://www.britannica.com/topic/Absolute-Idealism
Morse Code and the Telegraph
https://www.history.com/topics/inventions/telegraph

CHAPTER

Modernity: Glimpses of Reality

13

Fig. 13.1 *Irises*, oil on canvas, Van Gogh, Getty, Los Angeles, California. 1889a

© Everett – Art/Shutterstock.com

Knowledge Acquisition

◆ *Examine the artistic and cultural shifts made in painting, music and opera, literature, and philosophy during Modernity.*

◆ *Evaluate the accomplishments made by nineteenth-century artists.*

◆ *Assess the impact specific writers had on late-nineteenth-century thought.*

◆ *Explore the scientific revolutions created by Darwin and Pasture.*

◆ *Discover how Modernity connects works of art from around the world to its own artistic, cultural, literary, and political interests.*

SETTING THE SCENE

The pace of life quickened, with tension and unrest increasing in many European nations, including Britain and Ireland. Approximately 70 million people emigrated to other countries, mainly to North America as well as Siberia and Latin America, to escape certain destitution and death. France did not equally participate in the mass migration of its people from their homeland. The government had adopted birth control practices to lessen the family burden in changing times, which led to the population barely replacing itself. But, because of advancement in medicine, the French population grew. The industrious technology boom of prior decades continued. And, working-class people strove to establish increased worker rights and monetary rewards they witnessed business owners enjoying. The circumstances brought about an exhilarating and daunting era.

Social Darwinism

The English sociologist and philosopher, Herbert Spencer (1820 to 1903), developed the theory of **Social Darwinism** that was first coined by Joseph Fisher in his 1877 article "The History of Landholding in Ireland." The theory was used as a means for explaining how a society was meant to function on the basis of Charles Darwin's (1809 to 1882) scientific finding in *On the Origin of Species by Means of Natural Selection, or the Preservation of Favored Races in the Struggle for Life.* Spencer later used the word *race* in Darwin's title to play nicely into his ideas, which allowed him to make a connection between people's ethic origins and their survival. The connection, species survival, and the human races that Spencer created were not the intended meaning of Darwin's published title. Proponents of Social Darwinism, however, continued to suggest that those humans most fit to survive

should and those less equipped should not be aided in overcoming their challenges or social deficiencies.

The theory of Social Darwinism was applied both to social contexts and to large-scale government actions. Colonial imperialism in the Americas and Africa was justified under this theory. As the theory suggested, it was through genetic superiority and better environmental adaptations that the people of European nations come into powerful positions. The theory was further used to justify the abuse of African and Native American populations by Europeans, as the "superior" population was meant to be dominant. Warfare, slavery, and the colonization of more land by force were acceptable under this theory.

A half-cousin of Darwin's, Sir Francis Galton (1822 to 1911), used the theory to create a new "science" called **eugenics**, Greek for "well-born." He aimed at riding society of the undesirables to improve the human race. He maintained that the social institutions of welfare and mental asylums provided less productive members within a society the ability to reproduce at higher rates than its more productive members. At the turn of the twentieth century in the United States, the movement gained traction with 32 stated passing laws that forced sterilization on more than 64,000 people considered unfit to have children. Nazi Germany drew inspiration specifically from California's laws on forced sterilization to create a pure gene pool. The theory was eventually undermined in the mid-twentieth century and lost popular support.

Political Developments

Communism, or a political theory based on communal life and governance, developed in the mid-eighteenth century, was formulated on the thoughts of Karl Marx (1818 to 1883) and Friedrich Engels (1820 to 1895). The

Cross-cultural Connection

The notion of depicting the human forms has fascinated humanity since our early ancestor created the first portable statues such as the *Venus of Willendorf* (fig. 1.7). Culturally, there are various reasons to sculpt the human figure throughout each era for societal needs. In Europe, human figures concentrated on naturalistic interpretations of human actions. In West Africa, sculptures (fig. 13.2) denoted a partnership between the sculptor and an initiated priest, or **nganga**. Once the sculptor completed the wood receptacle, the nganga filled the receptacle with **bilongo**, a powerful medicine. The medicine transformed it into an armament for curing affliction, reconciling disputes, preserving peace, and admonishing transgressors. **Mpemba**, the white clay covering the face, represented the land of the dead where the people's ancestral spirits resided. Each nail or blade fixed to the receptacle indicates that the piece was used on behalf of the community or an individual.

Fig. 13.2 *Power Figure: Male (Nkisi),* wood, iron, glass, terracotta, shells, cloth, fiber, pigment, seeds, beads, Kongo peoples, Angola or Democratic Republic of the Congo. MET, NYC, New York. Nineteenth century.

© The Muriel Kallis Steinberg Newman Collection; Gift of Muriel Kallis Newman, in honor of Douglas Newton, 1990, The Metropolitan Museum of Art

theory was derived from examining the relationship between business owners and the working classes' interaction with one another. Their collaboration became the working model for communist rule, but their ideas were squarely socialist. Marx was a member of the working-class man, an editor of a German newspaper, while Engels was the heir to his father's textile company in England.

Marx and Engels' joint thoughts were a result of their opposite backgrounds, which helped change the course of the socio-economic and political environment around the world. They did not originate the ideas behind communism, communal property, or its elementary social ideals. Instead, they used and modified their theory

from other theories by French socialists and German philosophers such as Georg Hegel (1770 to 1831) and Ludwig von Feuerbach (1804 to 1872). Marx pushed the philosophical theory even further by reinterpreting and enhancing a variety of early political economic writing by Adam Smith (chapter 11), Thomas Malthus (1766 to 1834), and David Ricardo (1772 to 1823).

ARTISTIC MOVEMENTS

Later-nineteenth-century innovators followed in the footsteps of the predecessors by continuing to stress those ideas for which they had passion. The subject matter was even more personal and provided an undisturbed glimpse into familiar circumstances. The additional camera advancements challenged the long-held tradition of what art was and who was an artist. Painters began to seek new and creative ways to engage their audiences, initially with failed results.

Impressionism

Impressionism was considered the first distinctly modern movement in painting. A small group of **avant-garde**, or experimental ideas, artists developed the style in the 1860s in Paris and then it spread throughout Europe and the world. Its origins spring from artists whose paintings were rejected from the **salons**, or official government-sanctioned exhibitions. The rejection stemmed from the fact that they produced works that were not highly refined or detailed. Instead, Impressionists endeavored to seize the momentary impression a scene produced. They valued the impressions an object generated as the eye fluttered across that moment. Most Impressionist artists began painting in **en plein air**, or outdoor painting, to accomplish this effect, instead of indoor painting (within their studios.)

The name Impressionism was derived from a painting by Claude Monet (1840 to 1926) titled *Impression, Sunrise* painted in 1872 that deputed at the first Impressionist exhibition in 1874. The painting's title motivated the critic Louis Leroy (1812 to 1885) to coin the term for a mocking review published in *Le Charivari*, an illustrated magazine in Paris. During the 1860s, nearly half of all artworks submitted to the juried show, Salon de Paris, hosted by the Académie des Beaux-Arts were rejected. Rejected artists petitioned for a Salon des Refusés.

In late 1873, a group of like-minded artists formed the Cooperative and Anonymous Association of Painters, Sculptures, and Engravers and planned an exhibition independent from the Salon for April 1874.

The main artists were Edgar Degas (1834 to 1917), Claude Monet, Berthe Morisot (1841 to 1895), Camille Pissarro (1830 to 1903), Pierre-Auguste Renoir (1841 to 1919), and Alfred Sisley (1839 to 1899). When the exhibition closed on May 15, a month after it opened, Paris witnessed the first avant-garde art movement to directly challenge the entire official art world. The Impressionist style, as a formal movement, lasted only 15 years but became the predecessor to all subsequent artistic styles that wanted to cut across the grain of established norms. While the subject matter and style of later-nineteenth-century artists varied, the idea of capturing the essence of the moment began by the Impressionists remained.

Post-Impressionism

Post-Impressionism comprises a varied and distinctive range of artistic styles but shares a universal enthusiasm that counters the visual effect of the Impressionist movement. Stylistic differences were gathered under a common notion within Post-Impressionism that ranged from a scientific inspiration in works by Georges Seurat (1859 to 1891) to lush symbolic work by Paul Gauguin (1848 to 1903) to psychic breakdowns in works by Vincent van Gogh (1853 to 1890). The stylistic changes within the movement allowed for a new era to be ushered in that permitted a more accessible window into the artist's mind instead of just a window into the world everyone lived. Later artistic groups would be influenced by the far-reaching aesthetic impacts of the Post-Impressionists during the beginning of the twentieth century.

CREATIVE IMPULSE

Individuals who wanted to generate real social change let go of the past Neoclassical, Romantic, Realism notions and took up portraying the glimpses of life they witnessed around them. Writers and artists became critical of the economic crisis created by industrialization, knowing that it primarily affected the working-class people. People of all backgrounds banded together to produce emotion-charged creation rooted in reality and everyday life that depicted **modernity**, or the quality of being modern.

Architecture and Design

New experimental designs were crafted in architecture just prior to the turn of a new century that accommodated an architect's ability to showcase their creativity. The new style was called Art Nouveau, French for New Art, and premiered in the 1890s in Brussels with the creation of Tassel House by Victor Horta (1861 to 1947). The style was more decorative with swirls, twirls, and curl forms that were delicate and sensuous, taking on an almost organic feel. The interior of Tassel House (fig. 13.3) showcased the use of metal as both structural support and attractive ornamentation. The building ceiling exemplifies the undulating curvilinear shapes of the style.

In Spain, the style became popular when Catalan architect Antoní Gaudí (1852 to 1926) introduced Art Nouveau into the design of Basílica de la Sagrada Família (fig. 13.4) in 1894. Gaudí acquired the commission for the design of the Sagrada Família in 1883, which he worked on for 23 years until his untimely death in 1926. His concept for the basilica was a cross between the Gothic and Byzantine cathedral traditions. He wanted to create a symbiotic blending of nature-inspired forms and Christian iconography. The exterior towers, for example, mimicked the orderly symmetry observed in nature with specific significance. The central tower was dedicated to Jesus, with the four towers around it symbolizing the four Gospels of the Christian Holy Bible, those pertaining to Jesus's life and teaching. Mary's tower, mother of Jesus, resided above the apse (chapter 6) crowned with a star to indicate her crowning by God upon her assumption into Heaven. The 12 remaining towers represented Jesus's 12 Apostles who witnessed his actions.

© Botond Horvath/Shutterstock.com

Fig. 13.3 Tassel House interior, metal, wood, and concrete, Horta, Brussel, Belgium, 1893.

Fig. 13.4 Basílica de la Sagrada Família, stone, Gaudí, Barcelona, Spain. 1894 to present.

As Art Nouveau introduced new aesthetical qualities to the form and shape of building, other architects realized significance of the new building materials. Alexander Gustave Eiffel (1832 to 1923), a French engineer, designed a skeletal-shaped structure that rose 984 feet high above the city of Paris. The Eiffel Tower (fig. 13.5) was built between 1887 and 1889 for the 1889 Exposition Universelle to commemorate the 100th anniversary of the French Revolution. In total, there are 18,000 specially designed and calculated pieces that were traced to an accuracy of a tenth of a millimeter, or roughly 0.004 of an inch. Chroniclers of the period referred to the tower as a "marvel of precision", while others vehemently hurled insults at the tower as "a half-built factory pipe," a "truly tragic street lamp,"

Fig. 13.5 Eiffel Tower, 984' tall, metal, Eiffel, Paris, France. 1887 to 1889.

and the "new Tower of Babel." Eiffel was, however, granted a 20-year permit to help recoup his expenses since he paid for 80 percent of the tower's construction. In 1909, after much complaint regarding the tower's monstrous appearance and uselessness, the city tried to dissemble it. But, Eiffel cunningly struck a deal and financed experiments of sending and receiving telegraphy beginning in 1898, which proved to have strategic military use during World War I.

Sculpture

Much of the truly awe-inspiring studio artworks created during the nineteenth century were on canvas or paper with two major exceptions. Edgar Degas, an Impressionist painter, dabbled in expressing his idea in three-dimensional form. The only sculpture he ever exhibited was *Little Dancer Aged Fourteen* (fig. 13.6) at the sixth Impressionist exhibition of 1881. His model was Marie von Goethem, a **petits rats de l' opéra**, or opera rats, at the Paris Opera. Opera rats were young, pretty but poor ballet students who scurried around the opera stage and were often preyed upon by their male "protectors." Degas's sculpture captures the essence of the dancers' predicament. The dancers earned a small wage to help support their family, while they learned the craft. Von Goethem, and other petits rats de l' opéra, struggled in potential ascent to the top in order to perform on stage for higher wages.

Critics were candidly unreceptive toward Degas's sculpture when it first appeared. They protested against her ugly, up-turned pug nose and striking realism to what she represented. His critics did recognize his ability to create a radically different work that broke away from the stereotypical cold, inanimate, sculptural form. His ballerina was enlivened with a

Fig. 13.6 *Little Dancer Aged Fourteen,* pigmented beeswax, clay, metal armature on wooden base, Degas, National Gallery of Art, Washington, DC. 1878 to 1881.

© Courtesy National Gallery of Art, Washington

brilliant simplicity, exposing the difficulty of her situation—a complexity of presenting the delicate tension between rendering beautiful art and expressing life's hardships. While the sculpture was disapproved of when it was first unveiled because of its stark realism, it became a symbol of his ability to be forward-thinking. Regrettably, Degas's collection of figurative sculptures from his studio was cast in bronze by his heirs after his death. The sculpture and longtime friend of Degas, Paul-Albert Batholomé (1848 to 1928), selected 72 figures for casting into 22 editions, accounting for why *Little Dancer Aged Fourteen* can be viewed at museums such as the Metropolitan Museum of Art in New York City and around the world with the original, produced by Degas, residing at the National Gallery of Art in Washington, DC.

Auguste Rodin (1840 to 1917) was a truly visionary sculptor who constantly toiled with perfecting the surface of his works to emanate energy. His style matured after 1877 as his works showed the transition from Realism to Symbolism. *Eternal Spring* (fig. 13.7) captures the essence of willful surrender by the female figure. She arches her back as her partner bends to easily kiss her, capturing the lovers' unconcealed passion for one another. He first called the work *Zephyr and Earth* and later exhibited it as *Cupid and Psyche* at the 1897 Paris Salon. In 1906, railroad investor and banker Isaac D. Fletcher (1844 to 1917) commissioned Rodin to produce a marble version for him. The work emphasized Rodin's aptitude for producing the soft play of light dancing across his figures.

With *The Walking Man* (fig. 13.8), Rodin created a sculptural hybrid of a partial figure using study pieces from pervious works. The torso was probably from an 1878 study of Saint John the Baptist Preaching that joins a pair of legs from another study. The man appeared frozen midstride with his feet firmly planted. Rodin was attempting to convey the beginning and end of the man's steps to suggest movement. As the sculpture took shape, Rodin removed any narrative connection that might suggest the figure was John the Baptist. The man's torso appears highly scarred and fragmented, indicating the freedom Rodin was employing to render the male form. The appearance of the torso also directs the viewer's attention toward the man's powerful legs. Additionally, the man's stance was not classical. Instead it was severely modern, the very embodiment of urban life.

Painting

The artist Édouard Manet (1832 to 1883) bridges the gap between Realism (chapter 12) and Impressionism. Most scholars tend to associate his works as ones that dealt

© Bequest of Isaac D. Fletcher, 1917, The Metropolitan Museum of Art

Fig. 13.7 *Eternal Spring*, marble, Rodin, MET, NYC, New York. Modeled 1881, carved 1907.

Fig. 13.8 *The Walking Man (L'homme qui marche)*, bronze, green patina, Rodin, MET, NYC, New York. Modeled 1900, cast before 1914.

with social issues and the hypocrisy of the bourgeois to which he belonged. But, his artists' companions were primarily those who painted in the newer innovative style with looser brushstrokes. *Olympia* (fig. 13.9) was originally an oil on canvas, life-size painting Manet executed in 1863. The painting was

rendered in highly precise detail with beautiful modeled hands and face of the model. Because of the painting's notoriety, Manet created an etching for mass distribution.

Contemporary audiences were shocked by Manet's *Olympia* but not because of her nudity, nor the company of her clothed maid bringing her flower. The shock lay in the confrontational gaze the audience gave and the inclusion of various details identifying her as a courtesan. These details include her bracelet, pearl earrings, the orchid in her hair, and the oriental shawl she reclined on, which were all symbols of wealth and sensuality. The dark bowtie ribbon around her neck against her pale flesh drew attention to her voluptuous yet tone figure. Manet derived inspiration for his *Olympia* from the painting *Venus of Urbino* (fig. 13.10) by the late-Renaissance painter Titian. Titian's woman gracefully covered her genital region but left it slightly open and inviting; Manet's female figure was more protective of her sexuality as she firmly pressed her hand against her thigh region in a highly concealed manner. His *Olympia* emphasized her independence and sexual dominance over men. In another display of independence, Manet replaced the little dog in Titian's image, a symbol of fidelity, with a black cat, which was a symbol of her status as a prostitute. Olympia seemed even more aloof when presented

Fig. 13.9 *Olympic (small pate)*, etching and aquatint on laid paper, state II of VI, Manet, MET, NYC, New York. 1867.

Fig. 13.10 *Venus of Urbino,* detail of women, oil on canvas, Titian, Uffizi Gallery, Florence, Italy. 1534.

with a beautiful bouquet of flowers, possibly a gift from a client.

Although philosophers and many other writers were critical of the economic crisis created by industrialization and the bourgeois, unbridled materialism became the key issue for them to target because of its life-consuming and soul-destroying effect. One intellectual thinker, Charles Baudelaire (1821 to 1867), recognized the cultural triumph of the bourgeois while at the same time believing them to be vulgar and materialistic. In his opening dedication "To the Bourgeoisie" in *Salon of 1846,* he pens these words:

> For you have need of art. Art is an infinitely precious good, a refreshing and warming draught that restores the stomach and the spirit to the natural equilibrium of the ideal. You will understand its usefulness, you bourgeois—lawgivers or business-men—when the seventh or eighth hour strikes and you bend your tired head toward the glowing embers of your hearth and the cushions of

your armchair. Then a more fervent desire, a more active reverie, would relax you from your daily grind.

In the passage, Baudelaire was openly criticizing the bourgeois for their inability to comprehend genuine artistic innovation. His writings mocked the wealthy bourgeois. Baudelaire was a supporter of works by Manet as Manet went out of his way to shock the poor, uncomprehending bourgeois, thus proving Baudelaire's point. Manet manages to shock and repulse the unintelligible bourgeois salon goers in 1863 with his painting *Luncheon on the Grass* (fig. 13.11) of 1863.

The painting was considered a **parody**, or a humorous or satirical imitation, of a classical engraving by Marcantonio Raimondi (1480 to c. 1534) titled *The Judgment of Paris* (fig. 13.12) and also drew inspiration from a work by Titian (c. 1489 to 1576) titled *The Pastoral Concert* (fig. 13.13). Manet intended the painting to represent one where the working class was judging Paris's bourgeois class. The audience was shocked by the frankness

Fig. 13.11 *Luncheon on the Grass*, oil on canvas, Manet, Musée d'Orsay, Paris, France. 1863.

Fig. 13.12 *The Judgment of Paris*, engraving, Raimondi, MET, NYC, New York. c. 1510 to 1520.

of the female nude and confrontational gaze amid her fully clothed male companions. The two male figures in Manet's image were fully engaged in a conversation just as Titian's men were, but they were at complete odds with the overall sexualized circumstances of the female nude. The female nude was unashamed of her nudity and her sexuality just as the bourgeois were unashamed of the lavish living conditions when compared with those they employed. Manet was, in reality, confronting the hypocrisy of the bourgeois with the indifference to the common people's plight.

Other artists such as Gustave Caillebotte (1848 to 1894) also highlighted the hypocrisy of the bourgeois. His painting *Pairs Streets, Rainy Day* (fig. 13.14) of 1877 showed very inconspicuously the

Fig. 13.13 *The Pastoral Concert*, oil on canvas, Titian, Louver, Paris, France. c. 1509.

Fig. 13.14 *Paris Street; Rainy Day*, oil on canvas, Caillebotte, Art Institute of Chicago, Chicago, Illinois. 1877.

travesty created by the bourgeois. Caillebotte belonged to the wealthy bourgeois class but was at odds with how they had been, and were, treating the working class. Through Caillebotte's painting, contemporary and future viewers of the work were able to understand the impact the project had on the Parisian people.

Global Focal Point

While the Gilded Age began in America and laissez-faire economics continued in France, India experienced a nationwide famine from 1875 to 1902, claiming more than 25 million lives. The imperialism the country experienced at the behest of Britain led to modernization with the introduction of the railroad and civil administration. An influx of low-cost British imports undermined India's native industries. The nation's problems were further exasperated when policies in Britain endorsed seizure of local farmland from natives and hefty taxation on local trade.

In the foreground, Caillebotte painted scaffolding that was barely visible to the left of the street lamp just under the man's umbrella, but Parisians would have recognized the scaffolding and immediately understood Caillebotte's message. The poor working-class people were being removed from the inner **arrondissements**, or neighborhoods, and moved to the outskirts of the town, into **shantytowns**, or slum settlements made of boxes, metal scraps, and wood. Baron Georges Eugène Haussmann (1809 to 1891) oversaw the project; thus, it was referred to as the "Haussmannization of Paris". The project's goal was to modernize the city by broadening its avenues and demolishing its worst neighborhoods. New gardens and a railway station that were built marked the project as the beginning of a new economic, political, and social era.

While French artists such as Eugène Delicoix (Chapter 12), Jean-François Millet (Chapter 12), and Caillebotte produced paintings that candidly exposed the difficulties of the working-class, Claude Monet took refuge in producing artworks more squarely rooted in the pleasures found in nature and leisurely pastimes. He traveled the French countryside, its urban cities, and retreated to London during the Franco-Prussian war and visited the Netherlands after his father's death in 1871. Two years later, he met Caillebotte, and the following April of

1874, the first Impressionist exhibition took place at the former studio of the notorious Parisian photographer with the pseudonym Nadar (1820 to 1910). Unlike Manet and Gustave Courbet, Impressionists were unable to obtain opportunities to gain public notoriety if they were not accepted into the official Salon exhibition. And, the *Salon des Refusés* was little more of a public spectacle than a true means for earning a living. While Caillebotte, Degas, and Morisot were financially secure, Renoir was a member of the working class, Monet and Pissarro were lower middle-class, Sisley was middle-class, and others were financially dependent on an unwilling parent.

In 1867, Monet was 26 and his lover, Camille (1847 to 1879), gave birth to their son, Jean (1867 to 1914), while he spent the summer with his family at Sainte-Adresse near the port of Le Havre. He and his friends were developing a new way of illustrating modern life. His painting *Garden at Sainte-Adresse* (fig. 13.15) depicts the garden at his aunt's villa, with his father, in the panama hat, and aunt, under the white parasol, leisurely enjoying the afternoon. Monet's decision to elevate his viewpoint emphasized the flatness of the canvases surface, which was a bold decision. He also broke the painting into three independent groupings, the garden, sea, and sky, with repeated patterns to more clearly underscore

© Everett – Art/Shutterstock.com

Fig. 13.15 *Garden at Sainte-Adresse*, oil on canvas, Monet, MET, NYC, New York. c. 1867.

modern commerce and middle-class pleasures. His use of pure colour created the intense contrast of sunlight reflecting off various surfaces throughout the painting. Monet's contemporaries found the brilliance of the colours "shocking."

Monet, Camille, and Jean traveled to the coast of Normandy in the summer of 1868. He exhibited the commissioned painting *Madame Gaudibert* that allowed some financial freedom. Monet's aunt had cut off his maintenance as a result of his continued relationship with Camille. His many unpaid bills led to a number of his paintings being impounded to settle his debt. By the summer of 1869, he and Renoir had headed to the resort town of La Grenouillére where Emperor Napoleon III and family had just visited. They realized that the location made for an ideal subject matter to produce works such as *La Grenouillére* (fig. 13.16) for a profit. Similar to his painting of *Garden at Sainte-Adresse*,

Monet employed repetition to support a compelling visual narrative.

Six years later, Monet produced a true masterpiece, *Woman with a Parasol, Madame Monet and Her Son* (fig. 13.17), which epitomized the Impressionist notion of *the glance*, that fleeting moment. The painting triumphed brilliantly in communicating the impression of an instantaneous peek into a private moment, a meandering stroll on a picturesque, sun-drenched day. The brushwork consisted of energetic splashes of color that was essential for establishing the sensation of spontaneity. Monet's rendering of the wind and sunlight likewise added a degree of movement within the painting. In areas such as Camille's scarf and the bottom half of her dress, difficulties arose when discerning where the garments ended and the wispy clouds began. Monet captured the physical embodiment of the floating clouds in the twisting folds of her dress that danced across the canvas. He merged the sunlight

© Everett – Art/Shutterstock.com

Fig. 13.16 *La Grenouillére*, oil on canvas, Monet, MET, NYC, New York. c. 1869.

© Courtesy National Gallery of Art, Washington

Fig. 13.17 *Woman with a Parasol, Madame Monet and Her Son*, oil on canvas, Monet, National Gallery of Art, Washington, DC. c. 1875.

and the breeze to form a swirling vortex in the center of the canvas. A powerful feature Monet incorporated into the painting was a forceful upward viewpoint. In viewing the figures from a lower advantage point, he outlined them against the sky, creating an intensely vigorous effect. And, by depicting only their son from the waist up, Monet conveyed a greater sense of depth within the painting. If the little boy was removed, the painting would instantly flatten, with Camille appearing to float on top of the grass tightrope with the parasol carrying her away. Monet also anchored the figures firmly with color and lines. The green of the hillside bound forcefully with the green parasol. The parasols' handle created a strong line that led the eye up to the green of the parasol and then drew the viewer down to the corresponding green of the hillside. Monet triumphed successfully with a compelling contrast between the whirling wind and light, the fixed footing of the hillside that connected the painting seamlessly.

Mary Cassatt (1844 to 1926) exemplified her amazing talent and devotion to capturing the essence of intimate moments. She is often referred to as the painter of "Mother and Child," which highlights the domestic and social life of upper middle-class women because this was the world she had access to. She was mostly "self-taught" by studying in the museums after studying at the Pennsylvania Academy from 1861 to 1865. Cassatt regularly exhibited portraits of fashionable women in the Salon starting in 1872. Degas invited her to join the Impressionist movement in 1877. His influence was one of vision, compositional devices, color range and texture, even his subject matter. She was heavier handed than Degas and was able to capture greater three-dimensionality and more graceful dispositions. Her style continued to evolve and moved away from Impressionism to a

simpler approach to painting. By 1886, she had no longer identified herself with any particular art movement because she had been experimenting with various techniques.

The painting *Lady at the Tea Table* (fig. 13.18) was to be a tribute to the Riddle family. While in London, the Riddles hosted the Cassatt in a hotel as their guests. Mary Dickinson Riddle's daughter, Annie Scott, had sent the Cassatt family the Japanese porcelain tea set featured in the painting as a gift. For these two acts of kindness, Mary offered to paint Mrs. Riddle along with the tea set as a gesture of appreciation. In addition, Cassate's sister, Lydia, had died the prior year and Cassatt had not painted much since that time. The portrait was her first full work since her sister's death. Cassatt made sure to pay careful attention to the facial features, the shape of the eyes, nose and mouth, and the play of light over her subject's aging skin. She painted the women in her natural habitat, much as Degas had done with his models. Around this time Cassatt's works were beginning to reveal

Fig. 13.18 *Lady at the Tea Table*, oil on canvas, Cassatt, MET, NYC, New York. c. 1883 to 1885.

signs of growing Japanese art influence, having an overall arrangement of flattened pattern and color, with very little modeling and more refined detail.

The painting ended up taking Cassatt 2 years to finish because of her own mother's health. The portrait was very much liked by Jean-François Raffaëlli (1850 to 1924) and Degas, who stated that the portrait was "the essence of distinction," but Mrs. Riddle and her daughter were unpleased with the portrait. They found Mrs. Riddle's nose, an attribute generally considered very beautiful, too large like a pig's snout and also believed the painting lacked sentimentality and showed a conscious avoidance of flattery. Cassatt was very vulnerable at the time, and devastated by her failure, she did not paint again for quite some time and the work remained hidden in her studio closet until 1914. Cassatt's mother wrote to her brother, Aleck, about the incident, commenting that Mrs. Riddle and her daughter were "not very artistic" as the daughter purchased a painting by Cassatt called *In the Box*, which she adored, just the prior week.

The new style promoted by the Co-operative and Anonymous Association of Painters, Sculptures, and Engravers, also known as Impressionist, laid the foundation for the artistic movements that followed, such as **Pointillism**. The term pointillism was an insult to the innovative painting technique developed by the French painter Georges Seurat. Seurat invented the unusual technique of arranging dotted brushstrokes of primary color onto the canvas without mixing them in the 1880s. He referred to the technique as **Divisionism** and believed that by placing pure color side-by-side he succeeded in producing a highly scientific method for constructing supreme optical radiance. Seurat was ahead of his time; he deemed that modern art had the potential to display contemporary life similar to classical artworks but with the use of technology.

Young Woman Powdering Herself (fig. 13.19a) was probably a study of the final portrait housed at the Courtauld Gallery in London by the same name Seurat debuted in 1890. The young woman was Seurat's lover, Madeleine Knobloch (b. 1868), an uneducated working-class women who was pregnant at the time with his child, Pierre George. Seurat painted Madeline's impending motherhood by emphasizing her shape, particularly her breasts. Here, the image is displayed twice, once enlarged (fig. 13.19b) to clearly display the individual pure color dots Seurat employed to produce the image and the size reduced to underscore the effect that stepping away from the image has on the eye's ability to render the image with depth.

Earlier works by Vincent van Gogh are rarely as appreciated as his later works, especially those produced after his father's sudden death in March 1885. *Nursery on Schenkweg* (fig. 13.20) was 1 of 20 ink drawings commissioned by his uncle, the only commission he ever received. In the drawing he produced views of the Hague, where he lived, that were sent to Marius in May 1882. In the summer of 1882, he discovered the attractive qualities of oil paint, and his brother Theo (1857 to 1891) purchased the materials for him. The financial support he received from his brother was the only way he survived as he never sold a work of art in his life. Van Gogh's first public exhibition was in 1889 at the Fifth Salon des Indépendants, an alternate salon began by the Impressionists in 1884. He entered his two paintings, *Starry Night* and *Iris* (fig. 13.1), into the exhibit. While Parisians were unimpressed, his artist-minded colleagues recognized the genius of his work.

Early in van Gogh's career he developed his hallmark **impasto**, or thick plied paint, and

(a)

(b)

© Gift of Audrey Jones Beck, The Museum of Fine Art, Houston

© Gift of Audrey Jones Beck, The Museum of Fine Art, Houston

Fig. 13.19 (a) *Young Woman Powdering Herself*, oil on wood, Seurat, MFAH, Houston, Texas. c. 1889. (b) enlarged to show individual dots of pure color and distortion of features when viewed too closely.

© Bequest of Walter C. Baker, 1971, The Metropolitan Museum of Art

Fig. 13.20 *Nursery on Schenkweg*, black chalk, graphite, pen, brush, and ink on paper, van Gogh, MET, NYC, New York. April to May 1882.

varied brushwork (13.22b and c) as observed in *Wheat Field with Cypress* (fig. 13.21a). During a voluntary stint at Saint Paul-de-Mausole asylum in Saint-Rémy-de-Provence

in the summer of 1889, his subject matter was li mited as he formed a self-imposed boundary he could not cross. The months to follow he discovered the distinctive features

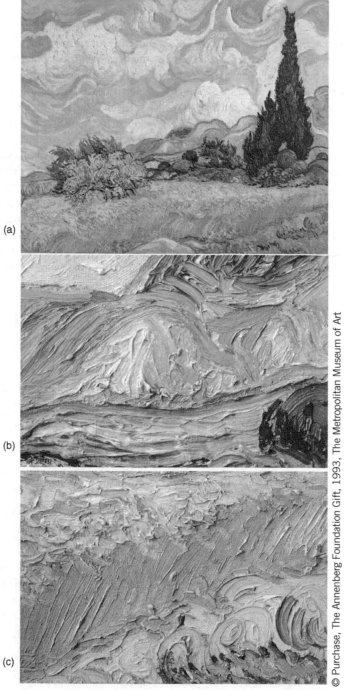

(a)

(b)

(c)

© Purchase, The Annenberg Foundation Gift, 1993, The Metropolitan Museum of Art

Fig. 13.21 (a) *Wheat Field with Cypresses*, oil on canvas, van Gogh, MET, NYC, New York. 1889. (b) detail of impasto from center of canvas. (c) detail of varied brushwork.

of the Mediterranean region, cypress trees, olive groves, and hills with sparse vegetation. Van Gogh produced a few paintings up close, with imposing cypress trees with their tops missing, but most of his images of cypress were from a distance. *Wheat Field with Cypress* was painted from a similar viewpoint as van Gogh's most famous image *Starry Night*. The cypress tree, for van Gogh, had dual symbolism of life and death as they were drenched with sunlight during the day and bathed with dark gloominess at night.

Paul Gauguin began his artistic career rather late in life after he was an established stockbroker with a wife and five children. He had a natural talent that both van Gogh and Monet recognized and encouraged

him to follow. As his interest in painting grew, he longed to portray the simplicity of the human spirit uncorrupted by the modern world. Gauguin believed Europe was insincere and conformist at its core. He decided to leave his wife and children in Paris for Tahiti. Even though the island was a French Colony filled with Europeans, he stayed and began painting that resembled the traditional Polynesian style. *Hail Mary* (fig. 13.22) was the first in a series he painted inspired by Polynesian religious beliefs. The painting's composition was based on photographs he owned of the bas-relief found at the Buddhist temple Borobudur in Java, Indonesia (fig. 13.23). In the painting, he transformed the typical Christian imagery,

© Bequest of Sam A. Lewisohn, 1951, The Metropolitan Museum of Art

Fig. 13.22 *Hail Mary*, oil on canvas, Gauguin, MET, NYC, New York. 1891.

© TheSimplegraphy man/Shutterstock.com

Fig. 13.23 Stone bas-relief visually depicting the life of Buddha, Borobudur Stupa, Java, Indonesia, c. eighth to ninth century CE.

mother and child, into a tropical delight. At Mary's feet, he painted fruit laid out of a **fata**, or a Polynesian platform used to make an offering to the gods, and to her right a blue- and gold-feathered angle. Mary and Jesus were the only figures to be graced with halos, another traditional type of depiction found in Christian artworks. Gauguin may have physically left France and painted in the Polynesian style, but he incorporated typical Western iconography into his work.

Not all late-nineteenth-century artists wanted to shock the public with paintings that were completely distorted in one way or the other. Paul Cézanne (1839 to 1906) believed that the Impressionist style should be "solid and enduring, like art in the museum." To accomplish his ideal museum style, he discarded the little dabs of color he used in *The Fisherman (Fantastic Scene)* (fig. 13.24) for block colors. His choice of subject matter also shifted from scenes of modern life to primarily still life, *Still Life with Apple and Pot of Primroses* (fig. 13.25) and landscape paintings. No other subject matter was more suited for academic painting than these two were, except historical scenes. One painting Cézanne produced that evokes a sense

of history with a powerful land motif was *Mont Sainte-Victoire and the Viaduct of the Arc River Valley* (fig. 13.26).

In Norway, Edvard Munch (1863 to 1944) produced works that shocked viewers more than 100 years ago. His art was highly personal and expressed his inner most feelings of anxiety, fearful panic, seclusion, and carnal pleasures. In 1893, he painted the wildly imaginative *The Scream* and then produced lithograph prints by the same name (fig. 13.27). Munch was plagued by agoraphobia, panic attacks, and hallucinations brought on by excessive drinking. He later explained how the idea for the painting came to him. He and two friends were walking along the riverside in Norway's capital, Christiania (now Oslo). The sun was setting and the clouds turned blood red; he began to feel ill and exhausted. He believed he could hear a scream passing through nature. The resulting painting had loud and piercing colors with think band that appear to represent sound waves. On the back of the painting, he included a telling quote regarding his own mental state, "Could have only been painted by a madman." Munch was a restless innovator and

Fig. 13.24 *The Fisherman (Fantastic Scene),* oil on canvas, Cézanne, MET, NYC, New York. 1874 to 1875.

Fig. 13.25 *Still Life with Apple and Pot of Primroses,* oil on canvas, Cézanne, MET, NYC, New York., 1890.

fully recognized the oddity of his finished works. He also fully acknowledged that his anxiety and fears was "a ship without a rudder."

Music and Dance

One of the most celebrated composers of the late nineteenth century (and today) was Pyotr Ilyich Tchaikovsky (1840 to 1893). He was born in Russia, but his music had a distinctive European flair. Two of his works, *1812 Overture* and *The Nutcracker,* were especially appreciated by Americans. His visit to America exposed the people to his *1812 Overture,* which was a commissioned work to celebrate the victory of Russia over Napoleon 70 years earlier. Tchaikovsky's incorporation

Fig. 13.26 *Mont Sainte-Victoire and the Viaduct of the Arc River Valley*, oil on canvas, Cézanne, MET, NYC, New York., 1882 to 1885.

Societal Emphasis

Working-class women, black and white, in America felt a kind of dissatisfaction over the inconsistent and constrained application of the word *democracy* to them. The post–Civil War era witnessed more women becoming public figures for social reform. Women of the Suffrage wanted the right to vote, while those of the Temperance movement pursued moderation in the consumption of alcohol or cessation. The greatest advancement by far was in the ability of women to become educated, and as a result, both teaching and nursing schools opened nationwide. And by 1900, more than 80 percent of the colleges, universities, and professional schools across the nation had been admitting women.

of booming cannons, fireworks, and ringing bells were all too familiar to Americans and their Fourth of July celebrations, which was a main reason for his popularity.

A decidedly unique synthesis of music emerged in the New Orleans known as **jazz**. New Orleans was possibly the most cosmopolitan city in America by the end of the nineteenth century with a combination of cultures such as African American, Caucasian, Creole, French, Haitian, and Spanish. The bars, dance halls, streets, and brothels were the places where this new form of music developed. Jazz was inspired by traditional drum beats and dance from Africa countries and the Caribbean. The music is characterized by a steady rhythm played against **syncopation**, or accented off-beats.

Ragtime piano music surfaced and was a precursor to jazz. The musical stylization was one where the musician played classical

Geschrei

Fig. 13.27 *The Scream*, lithograph, Munch, MET, NYC, New York. 1895.

and popular melodies in a syncopated-like approach. But, the trick was in the hand work by the pianist. The right hand played the syncopated rhythm, while the left hand kept a steady marched tempo. The style evolved from the pianist playing honky-tonk along the Mississippi and Missouri rivers. The "King of Ragtime" was Scott Joplin (1867/8 to 1917). Joplin settled in Missouri in 1895 and began studying music at the George R. Smith College of Negroes. By 1899, his performance style had been popularized.

Literature

Rudyard Kipling (1865 to 1936) was born in India to British parents and educated in England after the age of 5. He wrote poems, short stories, and novels including *The Jungle* Book. He received the Nobel Prize for Literature in 1907, the first Englishman to earn the merit. From 1898 through 1899, Kipling's poem "White Man's Burden: The

United States and The Philippine Islands" was published in various magazines. The poem asks people to

Take up the White Man's burden—
Send forth the best ye breed—
Go bind your sons to exile
To serve your captives' need;
To wait in heavy harness,
On fluttered folk and wild—
Your new-caught, sullen peoples,
Half-devil and half-child.

Take up the White Man's burden—
In patience to abide,
To veil the threat of terror
And check the show of pride;
By open speech and simple,
An hundred times made plain
To seek another's profit,
And work another's gain.

Take up the White Man's burden—
The savage wars of peace—
Fill full the mouth of Famine
And bid the sickness cease;
And when your goal is nearest
The end for others sought,
Watch sloth and heathen Folly
Bring all your hopes to naught.

Take up the White Man's burden—
No tawdry rule of kings,
But toil of serf and sweeper—
The tale of common things.
The ports ye shall not enter,
The roads ye shall not tread,
Go mark them with your living,
And mark them with your dead.

Take up the White Man's burden—
And reap his old reward:
The blame of those ye better,
The hate of those ye guard—

The cry of hosts ye humor
(Ah, slowly!) toward the light:—
"Why brought he us from bondage,
Our loved Egyptian night?"

Take up the White Man's burden—
Ye dare not stoop to less—
Nor call too loud on Freedom
To cloak your weariness;
By all ye cry or whisper,
By all ye leave or do,
The silent, sullen peoples
Shall weigh your gods and you.

Take up the White Man's burden—
Have done with childish days—
The lightly preferred laurel,
The easy, ungrudged praise.
Comes now, to search your
manhood
Through all the thankless years
Cold, edged with dear-bought
wisdom,
The judgment of your peers!

The poem can be interpreted in multiple ways from a variety of perspectives. The most common interpretation suggested to the readers of the poem was to sympathize with the idealized role of the paternalistic benefactor Europeans believed themselves to be in the areas they integrated into their growing empires. The poem consists of multiple stanzas that encouraged readers to assume their duty and do what was required to help the clearly less fortunate individuals living in the colonized areas of their empire. However, it was evident that the writer did not see a reciprocal role for members of the other culture.

The duty of the readers or people to whom the poem was directed, a white person of privilege, was clear. They were to fight the wars for, provide food for,

and heal, those residing within their territories. A clear, underlying assumption was that there was neither gratitude nor reciprocity expected from the peoples coming to live under the growing empire. In fact, according to Kipling's poem, the "White Man" was to expect this: once all this work was accomplished for the betterment of others, the recipients of this assistance would squander it and be left with unfulfilled hope. The viewpoint of the imperial powers acting as guardians or helpful father figures to the people they were taking over, which was nearly opposite to Spencer's theory of Social Darwinism, was also prevalent during the same time period. Each suggested a way to deal with the peoples within the growing empires of the day, but neither suggested that the conquered peoples should have an integral role in the process.

Kate Chopin (1851 to 1904) was an American novelist and short story writer born in St. Louis, Missouri. Her novels included the radical notions of female freedom and imbued the growing feminist movement within America. She was slow to gain popularity for her writing, with her first novel At Fault written in 1890 registering little attention. The publication of The Awakening in 1899 garnished more attention but was generally condemned for its candid sexual honesty. The novel also showcased an interracial marriage, with the main character, Edna Pontellier, abandoning her family and committing suicide. Chopin portrayed a vivid narration of what becoming "awaken" meant. She asked readers to contemplate whether living a simple, sheepish life existence was better than the ultimate destruction. Her novel was most notable for taking the reader into the realm of uncertainty of comprehending whether the events occurred or not.

Philosophy

Karl Marx and Friedrich Engels were the intellectual thinkers who represented both the working class and bourgeois. Marx was a working-class man, an editor of a German newspaper, while Engels was the heir to his father's textile company in England. In 1848, they would collaborate and write the *Communist Manifesto*, combining their voices against the deplorable working and living conditions of the working class. In the manifesto they attested to the following:

> The modern bourgeois society that has sprouted from the ruins of feudal society has not done away with class antagonisms. It has but established new classes, new conditions of oppression, new forms of struggle in place of the old ones . . . . . . The proletarians have nothing to lose but their chains. They have a world to win. WORKING MEN OF ALL COUNTRIES, UNITE.

Marx and Engels' joint thoughts were a result of their opposite backgrounds, which helped change the course of the socio-economic and political environment around the world. They did not originate the ideas behind communism, communal property, or its elementary social ideals. Instead, they used and modified their theory from other theories by French socialists and German philosophers such as Georg Hegel (1770 to 1831) and Ludwig von Feuerbach (1804 to 1872). Marx pushed the philosophical theory even further by reinterpreting and enhancing a variety of early political economic writing by Adam Smith (chapter 11), Thomas Malthus (1766 to 1834), and David Ricardo (1772 to 1823).

Marx nor the previously mentioned philosopher and economists were the first to condemn the immorality of a capitalist pursuit for economic gain. Anti-capitalist sentiments are found in the Judeo-Christian traditions. In multiple locations within the Jewish Torah and Christian Bible, verses criticize various actions such as greed, materialism, and selfishness. In the *Book of Amos*, God warns the Jews about such actions by saying the following:

> Give ear to this, you who are crushing the poor, and whose purpose is to put an end to those who are in need in the land, Saying, When will the new moon be gone, so that we may do trade in grain? and the Sabbath, so that we may put out in the market the products of our fields? making the measure small and the price great, and trading falsely with scales of deceit; Getting the poor for silver, and him who is in need for the price of two shoes, and taking a price for the waste parts of the grain.

The economic and social utopias of Marx and other nineteenth-century thinkers were aimed at discarding traditional values. They believed that there was no need for money, prices, wages, profits, interest, land-rent, calculation of profits and losses, contracts, banking, insurance, lawsuits, etc. Marx and his later followers believed that if the economic situation around the world changed, especially of that of the working class, then other social injustices would also disappear. Social problems such as class conflict, political oppression, racial discrimination, gender inequality, and religious bigotry would naturally resolve if the root causes for these were eliminated.

Friedrich Nietzsche (1844 to 1900) dedicated his first major work, *Birth of Tragedy from the Spirit of Music*, to the German composer Richard Wagner (chapter 11). In the work, he used juxtaposition between Apollo and Dionysius to explore and explain a need for both in order to yield a remarkably moving opera. The Apollo created the beautiful world of the ideal form, while Dionysius heightened the senses. Nietzsche believed in Wagner's compositions and he conveyed a seamless connection between art, dance, music, and song in a theatrical setting. He was directly challenging Socrates' call for rational thought when handling human affairs by outlining their disordered relationship and play of Apollo and Dionysius.

Nietzsche's later books *The Gay Science* (1882), *Beyond Good and Evil* (1886), and *Thus Spoke Zarathustra* (1882 to 1893) rejected the notion of organized religion. *The Gay Science* was controversial for his greatest proclamation that "God is dead," a deliberately provocative statement. Given his candid opinion about God's existence, little surprise should abound when he regarded organized religion as a means for exposing humanity to a slavish type of moral existence. His assertion was that Christian morality created a destructive society of sheep willing to follow a moral code against human nature. He considered "the herd" of sheep to be nothing more than a "great-unwashed mass." He called out for a Superman figure

who did not bow down before the any church philosophy or other authoritarian figures. Nietzsche's Superman was not confined to established values. While he did not believe that a Superman had lived yet, he did assert that Jesus, Socrates, Shakespeare, and Napoleon were role models for a future Superman.

Science

The world of science was humming along like every other sector of early-nineteenth-century life. An Austrian monk, Gregor Mendel (1822 to 1884), laid the foundational understanding for the science of genetics. In 1854, he was permitted to undertake the arduous task of hybridization at the monastery. His goal was to trace the hereditary transmission from one generation to another, studying specific observable characteristics to understand the mechanism that nature used to multiply species. Through a number of experiments over a 2-year period, he was able to discern that one characteristic was dominant and the other recessive. By starting with the parental (P) generation of two pure breeds for a characteristic, he produced the first generation (F_1) that was always identical to one of the pure breeds (fig. 13.28). After the second generation (F_2) the

Innovation and Progress

The year is 1886. The ingredients are caffeine, sugar, and vegetable extra. The man is Dr. John S. Pemberton (1831 to 1888), a pharmacist in Atlanta, Georgia. Pemberton had spent hours developing various treatments for human aliments. Another of his passion was to formulate flavors to make medicine concoctions more appealing to the taste buds. After mixing the ingredients together, he added carbonation and had the local "soda jerk," William Venable (1831 to 1888), try the drink. Venable enjoyed the mixture so much that he bought it on a continual basis along with Pemberton's other customers. Later, Frank Robinson (1845 to 1923), a partner of Pemberton's, suggested Coca-Cola. The following day they produced a decorative script of the name. The script and product remain unchanged.

MENDELIAN INHERITANCE

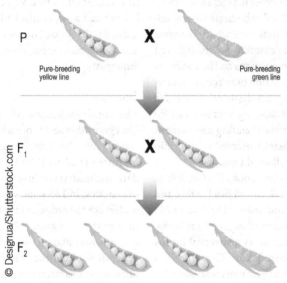

Fig. 13.28 Visual depiction of Mendelian genetics.

mathematical breakdown of offspring was always nearly ¾ resembled one pure breed and ¼ resembled the other pure breed. Mendel's results proved that specific characteristics were governed by inheritance. His successors would rediscover his 1865 paper "Experiment on Plant Hybrids" in the 1900s and advance the study of genetics. Subsequent concepts such as the law of segregation and law of independent assortment were concluded.

Technology

The means for preserving wine was known by the Chinese as early as 1117 and was documented by Japanese monks, who made a series of notations between the fifteenth and seventeenth centuries. The process was unknown in the West until the French chemist and microbiologist Louis Pasteur (1822 to 1895) demonstrated that spoilage of wine and beer was preventable. Pasture performed experiments to establish the temperature and time needed to destroy *Mycobacterium tuberculosis* and other heat-resistant microorganisms. The process of pasteurization (fig. 13.29) was so successful that it was named after Pasture.

MODERNITY LEGACY

The device of Social Darwinism, its use in imperialism, and the reaction to the growth of empires boiled down to the social evolution seen in the eighteenth and nineteenth centuries. Irrespective of how an individual reacts to these theories and ideas, they are part of our collective history and cultural thought. Each helps explain much of the social unrest seen around the world today, but they also point to a society influx— former imperialist countries started to see

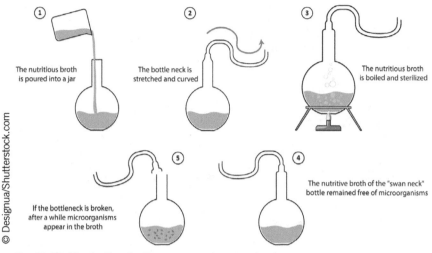

Fig. 13.29 Illustration for the process of pasteurization.

the unrighteousness of their past deeds and the people in imperialist countries started demanding change. In many ways, these theories and ideas have prompted the evolution seen within many societies since the 1860s. Even in our present day, our society is evolving to bring forth equality for every human being on earth, regardless of what society humans choose as their identity.

Those wanting to generate real social change let go of the past Neoclassical, Romantic, Realism notions and took up portraying the glimpses of life they witnessed around them. Writers and artists were most critical of the economic crisis created by industrialization, knowing that it primarily affected the working-class people. The philosophers Marx and Engels collaborated and coauthored a manifesto titled the *Communist Manifesto*, ushering in a new era of the dynamics between the people within a society and the government ruling over them.

Critical Thinking

Examine the stylistic differences between Impressionism and Post-Impressionism.

Evaluate the ideas of Social Darwinism.

Describe the major philosophical tendencies of Modernity.

Analyze how Impressionism naturally morphed into the Post-Impressionism style.

Examine how literature impacted the idea of ethnic identity.

Explain how artistic expression was transformed during the age of Modernity.

ONLINE RESOURCES

Impressionism Overview
https://smarthistory.org/a-beginners-guide-to-impressionism/
Post-Impressionism Overview
https://www.metmuseum.org/toah/hd/poim/hd_poim.htm
Social Darwinism
https://www.history.com/topics/early-20th-century-us/social-darwinism
Development of Communism
http://www.newworldencyclopedia.org/entry/Communism
Basílica de la Sagrada Família
http://www.sagradafamilia.org/en/architecture/
Degas's *Little Dancer Aged Fourteen*
https://www.nga.gov/collection/highlights/degas-little-dancer-aged-fourteen.html
Rodin's *The walking Man*
https://smarthistory.org/rodin-walking/
Manet's *Olympia* Video
https://smarthistory.org/edouard-manet-olympia/
Caillebotte's *Paris Street; Rainy Day* Video
https://smarthistory.org/gustave-caillebotte-paris-street-rainy-day/
Cassatt's *In the Loge* Video
https://smarthistory.org/mary-cassatt-in-the-loge/
Seurat's *Bathers at Asnières* Video
https://smarthistory.org/georges-seurat-bathers-at-asnieres/
Cézanne's Painting Style
https://smarthistory.org/an-introduction-to-the-painting-of-paul-cezanne/
Munch's *The Scream*
https://smarthistory.org/munch-the-scream/
Kate Chopin, Life and Works
http://www.katechopin.org/biography/
Friedrich Nietzsche, Life and Works
https://www.iep.utm.edu/nietzsch/
Gregor Mendel Life Changing Discovery, Inheritance
https://www.nature.com/scitable/topicpage/gregor-mendel-and-the-principles-of-inheritance-593

Modernism: An Age of Transfixing Occurrences

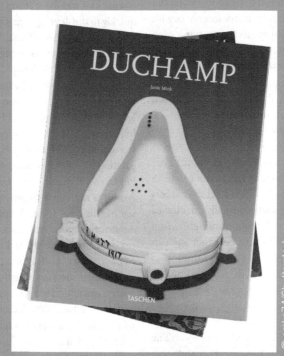

Fig. 14.1 *Fountain*, porcelain, Duchamp, TATE, London, England. 1917, replica 1964.

© emka74/Shutterstock.com

Knowledge Acquisition

◆ *Examine the artistic and cultural shifts during the early twentieth century.*

◆ *Evaluate the principal artistic accomplishments of Fauvism, Expressionism, Cubism, Futurism, Dada, and Surrealism made during the early twentieth century.*

◆ *Assess the impact of key historical and philosophical events and figures.*

◆ *Understand how political governance shapes a nation and its people.*

◆ *Discover how Modernism connects works of art from around the world to the interests of those living.*

SETTING THE SCENE

The early twentieth century was an age of unbelievable forward movement that transfixed the people with its multitude of inventions and improvements. Transportation clipped along at a fast pace from the automobile to railway and air travel to jet propulsion. The age was driven by electronic interfaces with continued developments in communication using the telephone, telegraph, radio, and eventually television to showcase the wonders of the human advancement. Inventors were the heroes of the era. Thomas Edison (1847 to 1931), Henry Ford (1863 to 1947), Orville (1871 to 1948) and Wilbur (1867 to 1912) Wright, and scientists such as Albert Einstein (1879 to 1955), Enrico Fermi (1901 to 1954), and Werner von Braun (1912 to 1977) entertained us, gave us greater access to the universe, and eventually enabled us to land a man on the moon and return him safely to earth. Perhaps no other age can tout a math formula related to motion as its motto, $E = mc^2$, where energy is equal to the mass multiplied by a constant squared. And, what other constant than the speed of light should be used to demonstrate the amount of energy trapped in an object. The age of motion was here and humanity was in wonder at its ability to transform every aspect of life.

Modernism

Although the image of a Wright brothers' flight (fig. 14.2) was documentary rather than artistic, photos and films of the first plane flights embrace the three great influences of the twentieth century; energy, motion, and pictures. The Wright brothers expanded upon the hang glider technology of Otto Lilienthal (1848 to 1896) with motorized power that was triggered by electromagnetic sparks and used wind tunnel technology to improve wing lift to create flight. They documented the event on what became the principal art form of the twentieth century, motion picture film. Energy in the form of electricity and flight as a result of motion were perhaps the two most important motivators of the era, and picture film was the art form that responded quickly to the developments related to these science-based phenomena.

The early part of the twentieth century was still steeped in European culture, but two world wars would cause the United States to become the economic and cultural leader. America produced highly original brands of art, architecture, and film. While the archetypes of most twentieth-century painting, sculpture, literature, and architecture began in Paris and other European cities, America managed to push the boundaries of the new style. A combination of American experimentalism and European modernistic thought led to a rejection of past artistic endeavors. Newer artistic movements such as Cubism, Fauvism, and Surrealism ended with the suffix "ism," and all expressed a dislike for, or an antithesis to, the past. **Tonality**, or a relation between notes played, fell out of fashion in music and was replaced by music with an **atonality**, or lacking in tonal clarity. Photographic perspective declined in painting and was replaced by non-representational forms of art. The development of new building materials led to architectural designs based upon function rather than form.

World War I

World War I, "the war to end all wars," began on July 28, 1914 after the Austro-Hungarian Empire declared war on Serbia. A seemingly minor conflict between two countries soon involved Germany, Russia, Great Britain, and France. Each was drawn into the war

© Everett Historical/Shutterstock.com

Fig. 14.2 Flight at Huffman Prairie Dayton Ohio, November 16, 1904.

because of **treaties**, or obligatory contracts, requiring one nation to defend another. In late 1914, Germany tricked Russia into believing that the Ottoman Empire attacked it. Consequently, the year of 1915 was directed by the Allied forces, mainly France, British Empire, and Russian Empire, acting against the Ottomans.

By 1916, **trench warfare**, or fighting from a dug-in position, had dominated the battlefield. Soldiers from either side directed attacks at each other with machine guns, heavy artillery, and chemical weapons. While soldiers died by hundreds of thousands of millions in these brutal conditions, no substantial success or advantage was gained. In 1917, the United States entered the war after multiple ship attacks in the Atlantic and Russia withdrew to an extent after the Bolshevik Revolution led by Vladimir Lenin (1870 to 1924). By 1918, a deadly outbreak of influenza had caused mass casualties on both sides and ended the war in the latter part of fall.

Months of negotiations led to a series of agreements called the Treaty of Versailles that formally ended the Great War. The treaty

eventually failed after 20 years of challenges. Germany was judged responsible for the war; the nation was disarmed and made to execute reparations over a 50-year period. The Germans eventually abandoned the payments and rejected the treaty terms altogether. Between 1935 and World War II, Adolf Hitler (1889 to 1945) disregarded every aspect of the treaty by reintroducing military service, annexed the German border region of Bohemia, and laid claim to Poland. A series of continued events led to the start of a second world war.

World War II

The second major world war was fought in Europe between September 1, 1939 and May through September 1945 when the war in the Pacific ended with the surrender of the Japanese. The Allies liberated the countries conquered by the Axis powers, and they were horrified by the results. They were especially disgusted when they saw how the Nazis had placed the Jews in concentration camps. The Allies planned to invade Japan in late 1945, but on August 6, 1945, an atomic bomb was dropped on Hiroshima. Three days later,

Cross-cultural Connection

Prior to the Nazis' adopting the swastika as their national symbol, the symbol was used widely throughout the ancient and modern world for prosperity and good fortune (fig. 14.3). The word is derived from Sanskrit meaning "conductive to well-being." Hindus, Jains, and Buddhists still use the symbol. For Hindus, a further distinction is made between the right- and left-hand swastika. The right-hand, or clockwise direction, is considered a solar symbol tracing the daily course of the sun. The left-hand, or counterclockwise rotation, stands for night and is associated with the terrifying goddess Kālī and magical practices.

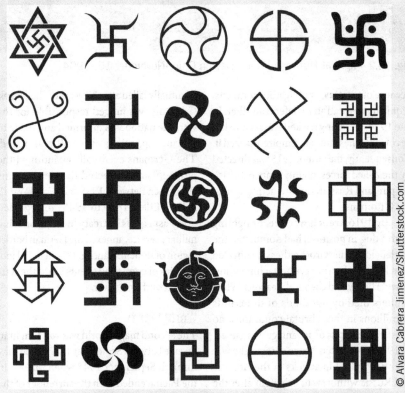

© Alvara Cabrera Jimenez/Shutterstock.com

Fig. 14.3 Swastikas from various cultures and religions.

another bomb hit Nagasaki. The Japanese surrendered on August 14. Seventeen million lives were lost during World War II, many of the casualties being civilians. Around six million Jews were starved, tortured, or killed in the concentration camps. The Union of Soviet Socialist Republics controlled much of Eastern Europe, with Germany divided into East and West. War criminals were tried for crimes against humanity and the

United Nations was formed in an effort to prevent future wars.

WORLDWIDE PROGRESSION OF ECONOMICS AND POLITICS

One of the most hotly debated components to incase the governance of a nation resides in the type of economic structure it will embrace. The primary reason for the importance placed on this component is that a nation's economic practice will directly influence its political policies and relationship with other nations. Of the three most widely used economic systems, capitalism (Chapter 9) is the oldest and was developed during the High Renaissance to replace the Medieval feudal system. The system reigned supreme for almost 400 years and was the mechanism that allowed for massive social and governance changes witnessed over that time frame. Because of the perceived slow pace these changes were taking, communism (Chapter 13) was introduced to prompt a better understanding of the business owner and worker relationship. The system eventually ushered in considerable advancements in workplace conditions. The newest economic system, socialism, was developed after World War 1 by a Russian leader, Vladimir Lenin.

Capitalism

Capitalism is an economic system with political implications where private citizens are allowed to possess and govern the use of their property according to their interests. As a general rule, this is where the unseen influence of pricing directs the supply and demand of goods within markets to the best interest of the public at large. The individual has the majority voice when it comes to what products will be promoted or fail, with government playing a less direct role.

In capitalist societies, the individuals require the government to simply maintain a sense of harmony, fairness, and impartiality, and acceptable tax policies.

Communism

The ideology behind **communism**, or a political theory based on communal life and governance, is founded on the philosophy of Marx and Engels. Their core principles regarded communal ownership where all property, produced goods, and income would be guided, controlled, and standardized by conditions outlined in a country's governmental economic plan. In theory, communism was supposed to create a classless society because everyone was primarily interested in the betterment of the community as a whole. Regardless of how committed Marx was to the idea of overthrowing capitalist governments, and more pointedly bourgeois, he did not fully form the Communist Party that is known today.

Vladimir Lenin, a bourgeois class Russian from Simbirsk, was the system's initiator. His new form of governance emphasized that a truly communist society could be achieved only through violence. Workers not only needed to unite but they needed to overthrow the capitalism bourgeois in order to establish a dictatorship for and by the proletariat. The future communist society rested on a romanticized society of communal goods founded on an authoritarian hierarchical structure. The ideology was in strong opposition to capitalism, as the communists believed that its governance did not produce a favorable end life for the working class. Communists of Lenin's era took revolutionary actions against capitalism to annihilate the idea of a private citizen. The state would possess and govern the use of private property in accordance with its interests.

Socialism

Inaccurate notions are widespread that the philosophies behind **socialism**, or an economic and political theory supporting collective or government ownership of the production and distribution of goods, were derived from the works of Marx and Engels. Marx did write a few pages regarding socialism, but he did not dive into the hows of the inner workings of the system. For Marx, the system was a good ethical outline for a society. Lenin was the true architect of what is now referred to as socialism. Lenin was the first leader to face the task of trying to reorganize an economic system without the propelling force of an incentive-driven market or compensation based on supply and demand. In Lenin's opinion, he could dissolve the long-standing financial association of goods with profit, then the profit-driven world would become less complex and the mechanism behind the markets would disappear. Lenin became the first person to put Marx's basic theory into partial application.

Lenin also believed that only the first four rules of arithmetic, adding, subtracting, multiplying, and dividing, were needed to make an economy work. Within 4 years after the 1917 revolution that installed Lenin into power, the Russian economy became so chaotic that production fell by 14 percent. In 1921, Lenin was compelled to create the New Economic Policy, which was a fragmented restoration of capitalism with an incentive-based economy. In early 1924, Lenin died and Joseph Stalin (1878 to 1953) came to power, and Lenin's unique blend of socialism and capitalism ended in 1927. Stalin instituted a new form of governance known as "forced collectivization" that allowed the Russian economy to leap into the ring with other powerful industrial nations. Under Stalin and his successors, a hierarchical style of command emerged.

ARTISTIC MOVEMENTS

Life clipped along at a swift pace and changed rapidly in the early decades of the twentieth century. Artists felt compelled to express the way people perceived the ideals and goals of modern civilization. Considerable amounts of experimentation and exploration within the realm of science prompted artists to redefine their roles as well. A litany of artistic movements were produced as artists strove to understand their new position in an ever-changing world.

Fauvism

An art critic named Louis Vauxcelles (1870 to 1943) viewed a 1905 exhibition that included works by painters Henri Matisse (1869 to 1954) and André Derain (1880 to 1954) at the salon d'autome in Paris. In the middle of the room was a sculpture by Donatello. In a reaction to the exhibition, Vauxcelles claimed that Donatello was surrounded by *les fauves*, or wild beasts. The Fauvist painters were influenced by the summer they spent in the South of France at Collioure. The artists experimented with the usage of bold, non-naturalist color palette that was often applied directly from the tube with little to no blending as seen in Derain's *The Turning Road, L'Estaque*. The movement lasted only 2 years for artists who painted on canvas, but the style continued to be fashionable in decorative art of vases.

Expressionism

Expressionists such as Ernst Ludwig Kirchner (1880 to 1938) sought to illustrate the subjective reality of a person's emotions in response to events and objects as perceived in *The Visit – Couple and Newcomer* (fig. 14.4). The artworks were primarily paintings and woodcuts with a high degree of emotional distortion, exaggeration, and pure fantasy in order to vividly express the intensity of emotions. Emotional connotations ranged from anxiety, repulsion, and displeasure to

Fig. 14.4 *The Visit – Couple and Newcomer,* oil on canvas, Kirchner, NGA, Washington, DC. 1922.

© Courtesy National Gallery of Art, Washington

annoyance and hostility. The movement was notable for its stark and brazen visual intensity with the use of jagged and distorted lines.

Cubism

A revolutionary new approach to representing the reality of an artist was credited to the artistic innovations and talents of Pablo Picasso (1881 to 1973) and Georges Braque (1882 to 1963). Picasso began painting *Demoiselles D'Avignon* (fig. 14.5) in 1907. The term for the movement originates from Louis Vauxelles when he saw a painting by Braque in 1908 and commented on everything being reduced to geometric lines or cubes. The new style was also influenced by the recent exploration and discovery of African and Oceanic masks. Other influencing factors possibly included the sixteenth-century painter El Greco's *Opening of the Fifth Seal,* Cézanne's *Les Grandes Baigneuses,* and

Fig. 14.5 *Les Demoiselles D'Avignon,* oil on canvas, Picasso, MoMA, NYC, New York. 1907

© Oscity/Shutterstock.com

Matisse's *Le Bonheur de Vivre* (fig. 14.6). Picasso's painting was a milestone and named the most influential modernist painting of the past 100 years in 2008.

Fig. 14.6 *Les Grandes Baigneuses (The Large Bathers),* oil on canvas, Cézanne, Barnes, Philadelphia, Pennsylvania. C. 1898 to 1905.

Futurism

An entirely Italian art movement began in 1909 by poet Filippo Tommaso Marinetti (1876 to 1944) when he published his poem *Manifesto of Futurism* in *Le Figaro,* a Paris newspaper. Marinetti coined the word Futurism to signify that contemporary artists should abandon past art style and embrace societal changes. The essence of the movement was to capture the dynamic energy of the modern world found in speed, energy, and the power of machines. Futurists reveled in new technology, while also applauding open defiance and violence. Artists such as Umberto Boccioni (1882 to 1916), Carlo Carrà (1881 to 1966), Giacomo Balla (1871 to 1958), and Gino Severini (1883 to 1966) published their own manifestos in 1910 regarding painting. They exalted creative uniqueness, especially based on futurist notions, and articulated hostile contempt for classical art traditions.

Vorticism

Vorticism was uniquely British, with its agent for dissemination being the London-based magazine *Blast.* Vorticism was similar to Futurism in its embrace for all the advancements of the machine age. Celebrated

painter Wyndham Lewis (1882 to 1957) and the poet Ezra Pound (1885 to 1972) founded the movement just prior to the start of World War I. While the Futurist movement eventually spread to other parts of Europe, Vorticism continued as a purely London-based movement. In literature, the vocabulary became mechanical like the speech of factory or shipyard workers. Pound viewed Vorticism as "interested in the creative faculty as opposed to the mimetic." His poem "April" vividly demonstrated the notion of creating an image and not merely mirroring directly what can be seen:

Three spirits came to me
And drew me apart
To where the olive boughs
Lay stripped upon the ground:
Pale carnage beneath bright mist

In the poem, Pound transports readers to another realm with a mystical feeling where both clarity and haziness reside. He lures his readers into this brief occurrence by constructing a circle around him that then pulls the readers closer and closer to a single moment, the moment where the realization of death by winter cannot be forgotten by the fresh hotness of the coming spring. The poem seemed to foreshow the "pale carnage" of World War I created by the "bright mist" of gun fire. After this war, Vorticists grappled with the role the machines they celebrated played in the death of millions.

Constructivism

A synthesis of ideas within Cubism and Futurism had culminated to produce the movement of Constructivism in Russia by the late 1910s. Artists of the movement such as Ukrainian-born Vladimir Tatlin (1885 to 1953) resolved to "construct" their art from modern materials such as glass, plastic, and steel. The purpose of producing an artwork was more than to simply make a theoretical account of events. The artists of the movement believed that painting as an art form was dead, but they derived their inspiration from the geometrically constructed cube-like works of Picasso.

Constructivists primarily harnessed their talents for the creation of works in architecture, ceramics, fashion design, and graphics. Tatlin was so very dedicated to the movement that in 1927 he constructed a glider he called *Letatlin* (fig. 14.7). The

glider resembled a giant insect made of a combination of organic, rawhide, cork, word, and whale bone, and modern materials like steel cable. Even though Tatlin never flew the glider, it held his curiosity during the latter part of his life. But, his creation challenged humanity by asking "what does it mean to be human?" at a critical moment in human history.

Suprematism

The movement started in association with Constructivism in Russia with an emphasis on adapting the abstract to the canvas. While the movement had its roots in Cubism, it was the first to employ only geometrical shapes to illustrate an abstract thought. A quote by Kazimir Malevich (1879 to 1935) inspired the movement's name with the purpose of distilling rare emotions using basic shapes and a limited color palate. Malevich's *Suprematist Composition: White on White* (fig. 14.8) embodies the spirit of Suprematism. The work was considered perplexing for its abstract quality of a cool white square traced in pencil, tilted to the right atop a warm white square. The heart of the work rested in the political atmosphere of Malevich's time. He strove to unearth a

© Anton Martynov/Shutterstock.com

Fig. 14.7 *Letatlin*, rawhide, cork, steel cable, wood, and whale bone, Tatlin, Air Force Museum, Russia. 1929 to 1932

Fig. 14.8 *Suprematist Composition: White on White*, oil on canvas, Malevich, MoMA, NYC, New York. 1918.

new process to convey spiritual freedom in the more repressive years when Stalin was in power.

The October Russian Revolution spurred Malevich to create a new visual language for a new world. At first glance, *White on White* appeared rather dull as it lacked character, depth, and color. Malevich rejected the use of conventional artistic techniques for the inimitable quality of pure geometry and clean simplistic. Upon closer inspection, the painting reveals strong brushwork that brightens its barren appearance. He chose to paint white over a white canvas as a symbol of the timeless tranquility of floating in any place and time. When it was unveiled in Berlin at the 1927 Große Berliner Kunst-Ausstellung

exhibition, art critics declared the piece "not art."

De Stijl

Pure abstraction was the intention of De Stijl's founders, Theo van Doesburg (1883 to 1931) and Piet Mondrian (1872 to 1944). Members of De Stijl, Dutch for "The Style," believed that Picasso and Braque were ineffective and limited in their attempt to create nonrepresentational art. De Stijl artists used straight lines, simple geometric forms, and primary or neutral (black, gray, and white) colors to convey their ideas. Mondrian was the most notable of the De Stijl painters. His painting *Composition with Blue, Yellow and Red* (fig. 14.9) was reduced to a severe purity of only line and color.

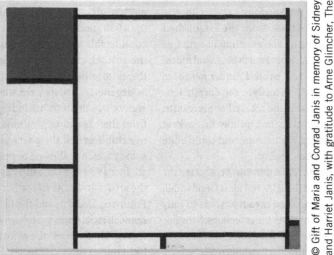

© Gift of Maria and Conrad Janis in memory of Sidney and Harriet Janis, with gratitude to Arne Glimcher, The Museum of Fine Arts, Boston, Massachusetts

Fig. 14.9 *Composition with Blue, Yellow, and Red*, oil on canvas, Mondrian, MFAB, Boston, Massachusetts. 1927.

Dadaism

The word *dada* had no meaning and was used to denote the meaninglessness of everything including art. These avant-garde artists were viewed by the general public as antagonistic and provocative. As World War I ramped up, even life became meaningless. Dadaism expressed the futility that these artists felt as a bleak mood settled over the world. In music, composer Arnold Schoenberg (1874 to 1951) wanted to represent the notion of **serialism**, or a 12-tone row. He wanted to prove that the composition had the ability to be played as if it was regular music. The poet Tristan Tzara (1896 to 1963) published a collection of poems in his *Dada Manifesto on Feeble Love and Bitter Love* from 1920:

"XIII" by Tzara
DADA is a virgin microbe
DADA is against the high cost of living
DADA
limited company for the exploitation of ideas

DADA has 391 different attitudes and colours according to the sex of the president
It changes – affirms – says the opposite at the same time – no importance – shouts – goes fishing. Dada is the chameleon of rapid and self-interested change. Dada is against the future. Dada is dead. Dada is absurd. Long live Dada. Dada is not a literary school, howl

Surrealism

The French poet, magazine publisher, and art collector, Andre Breton (1896 to 1966) was the founder of the Surrealist movement because of his interest in mental illness and the working of the unconscious mind. In 1924, Breton published the *Manifeste du surréalisme* (*Surrealist Manifesto*), where he defined Surrealism as "pure psychic automatism … the real process of thought. It is the dictation of thought, free from any control by the reason … or moral preoccupation."

The goal of the Surrealists was to liberate their imaginations from the established norms of beauty and experiment with free association. Another French poet, Paul Éluard (1895 to 1952), wrote *L'Amour fou* (*Mad Love*) in 1937 to analyze the correlations between dreams and reality. For Surrealists, there were two distinct realities that were at juxtaposition of each other but could unite to create a new reality.

The Surrealist movement reflected the subconscious thoughts and ideas found within the artist and used dream analysis to fully visualize the artist's inner feelings. Salvador Dalí (1904 to 1989) and Max Ernst (1891 to 1958) were the foremost Surrealist artists. When these artists exhibited their works, they seemed nonsensical and absurd with the illusion of being trapped in a nightmare. Artists of the movement were influenced by the writings of Sigmund Freud (1856 to 1939) and Carl Jung (1975 to 1961) about the subconscious mind. While Dalí is regarded as the quintessential Surrealist, other artists were making headway with their own conceptual impressions of alternate realities.

DEGENERATE ART

The Nazi Party adopted the term Degenerate Art in the 1920s to describe virtually all modern art. As the party rose to power in the 1930s under the direction of Hitler, a considerable amount of art was banned on the grounds that it was not German, and therefore Jewish, in nature. Artists branded as degenerate artists were subjected to a variety of sanctions, including dismissal from their teaching positions, forbidden to exhibit or sell their artworks, and, in some cases, not allowed to produce art at all. In a 1934 speech, Hitler asserted, "All the artists and cultural blather of Cubists, Futurists, Dadaist, and the like is neither sound in racial terms not tolerable in national terms." He declared the artistic works to be in one of three categories. First, works that were intent on dissolving traditional values. Second, works that ran counter to Hitler's notion of nationalism and his ideal "races". Third, works that were believed to be a general adulteration of culture and its "loftiest goal" of creating a civilized people. On May 10, 1933, universities across Germany burned more than 25,000 books deemed not German, including works by Albert Einstein, Sigmund Freud, Ernest Hemingway, Hellen Keller, Jack London, Upton Sinclair, and H.G. Wells (fig. 14.10). Authors whose books were not burned were offended.

The term, Degenerate Art, was also the title of a 1937 exhibition arranged by the Nazi

Global Focal Point

Western civilization became even more fascinated with indigenous tribes after Sigmund Freud published *Totem and Taboo* in 1913. The work further explained sexual growth (away from incest), behavior toward the opposite sexed parent (Oedipus complex), and religious evolution (from animism to one God). Each chapter outlined a different aspect of these developments, with the last chapter presenting a conclusion Freud applied to all cultures. He theorized that all cultures, regardless of their advancements, originated from an Oedipus complex society, which was the basis of all religion. He also proposed that the end of religion would signify the end of all forms of conflict.

Fig. 14.10 Book burning in Berlin on May 10, 1933 at the Opernplatz (public square).

Party in Munich. The exhibition comprised of modernist artworks haphazardly hung on the wall with descriptions ridiculing the art. The purpose was to provoke feelings against the modernists' works and the creators. The exhibition later traveled to other cities around Germany and Austria. Hitler, as dictator, gave final approval on all matters of art. The theory of degeneracy aided the Nazi Party in consolidating public support for their anti-Semitic views. To support the theory and mount the exhibition, the Nazi Party seized over 5,000 works of art and featured 650 in the exhibition. Weeks after the exhibition's opening, Joseph Goebbels (1897 to 1945) organized a second and more thorough seizure of artworks. More than 16,558 works were confiscated from their owners, resulting in the event being referred to as Rape of Europa by author Lynn H. Nicholas.

After the exhibition concluded, all works were auctioned to the highest bidder to fund the Nazis' war efforts. The paintings were sorted and sold at auction in Switzerland.

Museums around the globe acquired the works and private collectors too. Nazi officials also procured some works for their own collections. The very works that were deemed unfit for the German people were to hang in their homes as showpieces. A confiscated self-portrait of van Gogh sold in 1939 to Dr. Frankfurter with a winning bid of $40.00. In March of 1939, the Berlin Fire Brigade burned nearly 4000 works deemed to have little value on the international market.

In America, life hummed along with little concern for matters occurring in Europe, let alone Germany. The painter Norman Rockwell (1894 to 1978) began painting the cover for *The Saturday Evening Post* in 1916. By 1963, he had amassed a collection of 323 covers for the magazine. But, some of the most influential works that he created for *The Post* were four paintings executed in 1943, known as the *Four Freedoms* (fig. 14.11)—*Freedom of Speech, Freedom of Worship, Freedom From Fear,* and *Freedom From Want.* They were based on a January 1941 State of the Union address by Franklin

Fig. 14.11 *Four Freedoms*, originally oil on canvas converted to stamp, Rockwell, Norman Rockwell Museum, Stockbridge, Massachusetts. 1943

D. Roosevelt (1882 to 1945). Roosevelt's address outlined the essential human right that should be university protected; freedom of speech, worship, fear and want. Each appeared on the cover of the magazine over four consecutive weeks along with an essay for prominent thinkers of the day. To raise money for the war efforts, the United States Department of the Treasury and *The Post* sponsored a touring exhibition of the paintings. Over $132 million were raised through the exhibition revenue and the sale of war bonds. In 1994, the four images were turned into a stamp and sold to collectors and to those needing to mail a letter!

CREATIVE IMPULSE

Ezra Pound captured the determined and infectious focus of artists to shake up the artistic world in "Make it New." Artists of the early twentieth century were rebellious, yearning for radically different approaches to illustrate their modern civilization. They viewed European culture as complacently debased and bound by artificialities that consumed daily life. Artists followed in the footsteps of Paul Gauguin (Chapter 13) to explore alternate lifestyles, especially primitive cultures. Traditional religious beliefs and societal moral norms were rejected. Scientific discoveries and technological advances zipped along at lightning speed that the cultural identity of the early twentieth century was almost redefined on a daily basis. Every day had the potential for a new invention or theory to emerge and those from the day before were considered obsolete.

The notion of newer advancements continually on the horizon left society with an uneasy ability to commit to a single philosophy. No less than 10 artistic/philosophical movements were developed over the first half of the twentieth century, several lasted only a few years, while others endured a bit longer. The psychoanalyst Sigmund Freud and theoretical physicist Albert Einstein (1879 to 1955) fundamentally transformed humanity's perception of reality. Freud asked people to search their inner person and examine the repressed self. Einstein helped society realize more than just its occupied material world; he drew attention to new mechanical forces of the universe.

Architecture

The need for additional commercial space drove the experimental designs perceived in nineteenth-century architecture. Cramped urban cities were a playground for innovative architects such as William van Alen (1883 to 1954) and his Chrysler Building (fig. 14.12) design began in 1928 and completed in 1930. Architecture during the early twentieth century experimented with the juxtaposition of new materials such as steel, steel-reinforced concrete, aluminum, and plastic.

Along with the new materials came an interest in simplification of form and external decorations. The tendency toward reduction was found in buildings of the *Bauhaus School*

Fig. 14.12 *Chrysler Building*, van Alen, New York. 1928 to 1930

in Weimar, Germany, that promoted the idea of "form follows function." In America, the idea of function was translated into the practical design of the skyscraper. Skyscrapers are essentially steel cages on which walls and windows are hung—an architectural style that allows city buildings to rise up 100 stories tall and beyond. The city of Chicago was one of the first beneficiaries of new building techniques because, as a trade and business center, it re-created itself after the Great Fire of 1887. Located in the central city, the offices of Sullivan and Adler were suitably placed for Louis Sullivan (1856 to 1924), the father of modern architecture, who created skyscrapers in the cities of the Midwest.

An architect at Sullivan and Adler firm, Frank Lloyd Wright (1867 to 1959), became internationally celebrated for his creativity in both domestic and commercial designs. Wright was one of the first architects to develop new architectural ideas including organic architecture, open planning, full fireproofing, full air-conditioning, and indirect lighting and heating. *Heurtley House* (fig. 14.13) in Chicago was designed to use a **cantilever principle**, or a roof and gables canted out from a giant steel beam. The house resembles a sculpted box that causes viewers to focus more on its overall design than surface decoration. The house's dominant horizontal feel suggests fluidity.

In 1935, Wright's designs for *Falling Water* (fig. 14.14) moved toward a more organic blending of structure with nature. When the sun begins to set and the interior lights are turned on, *Falling Water's* interior resonates with the foliage that surrounds the house. The dramatic rigid structural rooflines project from a vertical support terrace that reflects a similar structure of rock ledges below. Wright designed two roomy terraces on either side of the living room and a large terrace above it. The horizontal elements help balance the seemingly continuous perpendicular lines

Fig. 14.13 *Heurtley House*, Wright. Chicago, 1910.

© Thomas Barrat/Shutterstock.com

Fig. 14.14 *Falling Water*, Wright, Mill Run, Pennsylvania. 1935

© Sean Pavone/Shutterstock.com

created by the towering structure to the left. The many horizontal and vertical lines of the house are comparable to the rock formations, ground, and trees, with the water first moving horizontally and then vertically as "falling water." The falls visibly break at an angle, creating an illusion of water flowing out from beneath the middle of the house. The sound of the flowing water fills the house continuously. The house does not have a grand front entrance. Instead, the continuity of internal and external is emphasized in keeping with the theme of a harmonious and natural relationship to the setting. Did Wright plan the house with this particular view in mind?

Theaters in the early modern era attempted to emulate the grand opera houses of Europe in order to give prestige to American drama and music halls. Typical playhouses' entrances were decorated in the **Beaux-Arts style,** or academic neoclassicism, with magnificent marquees. The façade was impressive to emphasize the social aspect of "the arrival" in the same fashion as people of the nineteenth century arrived at opera houses in Europe. Doormen greeted patrons on arrival before they entered elegantly barrel-vaulted lobbies with suspended electrical chandeliers.

Buildings such as the *Lyceum Theatre* (fig. 14.15) in New York were constructed of gray limestone with six ornate Corinthian columns. The internal space featured a foyer with two grand staircases and marble floors. Eventually, steel reinforcements were used in later theaters to enable the balconies of the auditorium to be cantilevered over the main floor and eliminated the need for vertical posts that might interfere with sight lines. Box seats were also cantilevered to provide a better view and main floors were inclined downward. All these improvements were important physical developments that limited the awkward placement of seats found in European opera houses.

The interiors of theaters were decorated in **Art Nouveau style**, or decoration with floral, vine, leaf and textile patterns, and gold gilding (fig. 14.16). Elaborate plaster relief carvings adorned the edges of balconies, ceiling fixtures, and the stage arches. Early advertisements and programs contained elaborate Art Nouveau motifs to complement the theater interiors. Box seats were typically framed by Greco-Roman pilasters and main floor seats usually had leather coverings with iron frames. Later theater developments included a number of comfort accommodations for patrons such as nurseries for children, and lobbies sometimes housed goldfish, swans, and ducks swimming in fountains.

Sculptures

Early-twentieth-century sculpture drew its inspiration directly from the fast-paced world the artists lived. Artists like Umberto Boccioni (1882 to 1916) placed a tangible notion of what the futurist movement was with his *Unique Forms of Continuity in Space* (fig. 14.17a and b). The sculpture accentuated the notion of vigorous movement and dynamic energy that underscored the potential mechanical workplace in which the

Fig. 14.15 *Lyceum Theatre*, architects Herts and Tallant, impresario Frohman. 1903

© Tupungato/Shutterstock.com

its fixation on the historical past. Sadly, in 1916, Boccioni was killed while fighting on the battlefield.

The sculptural form of Dadaism took **ready-mades**, or everyday objects, and destroyed their function with a witty, yet hidden commentary by the artist. Marcel Duchamp disregarded the conventional aesthetics of object to inaugurate this artistic upheaval opposing the established norms. For example, his first ready-made was a bicycle wheel mounted atop a stool to erase the two objects' former use and craft a purely decorative sculptural piece. A later ready-made Duchamp titled *Fountain* (fig. 14.1) took a men's urinal and turned it 90 degrees for gaining entry into the Society of Independent Artists' inaugural exhibition in 1917. The Society was founded with a goal similar to that of the Parisian Salon des Indépendants; the Society of Independent Artists sought to have a jury-free, prize-free exhibition. To test the principles of the Society, Duchamp created *Fountain* and submitted it under the name R. Mutt. But, the jury rejected the

Fig. 14.16 Ceramic tile and/or wallpaper example in the Art Nouveau style.

© Helen Lane/Shutterstock.com

figure might occupied. A momentum of the wind and speed of daily life propelled the figure forward and pulled it backward simultaneously. The Great War, World War I, began a year after Boccioni produced the sculpture. Like most futurists, he believed that the technology of modern warfare and open conflict would drag Italy out of

© Bequest of Lydia Winston Malbin, 1989, The Metropolitan Museum of Art

(a)   (b)

Fig. 14.17 (a) *Unique Forms of Continuity in Space*, front, and **(b)** *Unique Forms of Continuity in Space*, back, bronze, Boccioni, 1913, cast 1950.

submission on the grounds that *Fountain* "may be a very useful object in its place, but . . . by no definition, a work of art."

Romanian-born Constantin Brâncuși (1876 to 1957) obtained a position under the direction of Auguste Rodin in 1907 but soon parted way with Rodin. He stated, "I felt that I was not giving anything by following the conventional mode of sculpture." He eventually became engrossed with the Parisian avant-garde style of Marcel Duchamp, Henri Matisse, and Amedeo Modigliani (1884 to 1920), which he befriended. After World War I, in 1935, the National League of Gorj Women commissioned Brâncuși to create three sculptural monuments to honor the soldiers who defended Târgu Jiu, Romania, in 1916 against the Central Powers.

The first piece titled *The Table of Silence* (fig. 14.18) was designed to include a central table with 12 chairs resembling hourglasses. The table was symbolic of the one the defending soldiers gathered around to plan their battle against the enemy. The hourglass shape of the chairs marked the passage of time, similar to a sundial. The

second monumental sculpture, *The Gate of the Kiss* (fig. 14.19), resembled an ancient Roman triumphal arch (Chapter 5). Brâncuși filled the gate with symbols. Each column side had two half circles that served as a symbol for a kiss with the gate, marking the transition of life over death. The final sculptural piece he created was *The Endless Column* (fig. 14.20) that stood over 98 feet tall and made of 17 and a half rhomboidal shapes made of zinc, brass-clad, and cast-iron modules erected on a steel spine. Brâncuși considered *The Endless Column* to represent the "spiritual will" and sacrifice of the heroes. The original design for the column was based on a 1918 oak sculpture that the artist believed suggested the possibility of infinite expansion.

Painting

An artistic group known as the Blue Riders founded in 1911 developed the use of color in a nonrepresentational manner. Vasily Kandinsky (1866 to 1944) was the most prominent member of the group. Originally, he studied and lectured law at the University

Fig. 14.18 *The Table of Science*, limestone, Brâncuși, Târgu Jiu, Romania. 1938

© Radu Bercan/Shutterstock.com

Fig. 14.19 *The Gate of the Kiss*, limestone, Brâncuși, Târgu Jiu, Romania. 1938

© Adriana Sulugiuc/Shutterstock.com

Fig. 14.20 *The Endless Column*, zinc, brass-clad, and cast-iron modules erected on a steel spine, Brâncuși, Târgu Jiu, Romania. 1938

of Moscow. He declined a teaching position from the university in 1896 to study art in Munich. By 1901, he had been teaching at the art school of the Phalanx, a group he cofounded. His painting style was meant to represent ideas not from the material world (fig. 14.21) but from the elements of art such as colors, lines, and shapes. His style of painting was considered among some of the first abstract artworks to be created. His works subsequently influenced the art world of the early twentieth century.

Kandinsky's artistic creations directly impacted the art world and helped instigate new theories. His works were formed around the ideas that sounds could be seen through colors and lines and a consideration that abstract shapes were themselves a form of art. He proposed the notion of how colors and abstract shapes could form a universal language for communicating ideas across multiple generations without the concept

Fig. 14.21 *Sketch 160A*, oil on canvas, Kandinsky, MFAH, Houston, Texas. 1912.

of a specific time. When scientists split the atom, Kandinsky was impressed and believed that their innovation provided him with the courage to cast off the ideals of past traditional painting methods for his own. He felt obligated to represent the material world in new and interesting ways. Kandinsky is credited with being the first true abstract artist.

Perhaps one of the most interesting ideas about time and motion in the early twentieth century were produced by the painters Georges Braque and Pablo Picasso. While Cubism was not acclaimed as the most beautiful painting styles, it did defy the use of the medium in a profound way. Braque and Picasso were specifically challenged by sculptors who believed painting was an inferior art form to sculpture. Sculptures took this particular stance on the grounds that they were able to show all sides of an object. The painters attempted to overcome

the canvases' two-dimensional limitations by showing all sides of an object at once on a flat surface. In effect, they were trying to defy the concept of space. A typical Cubist painting such as *Violin and Candlestick* from 1910 by Braque tried to show the front, side, and top of an object all at once. The resulting fragmented pieces in another image titled *Still Live with a Bottle of Rum*, created by Picasso in 1911, spread across the painting with the appearance of a broken mirror design. The paintings give a sense of puzzle with all sides of an object shown in an analytical Cubist fashion.

One of Picasso's primary patrons was the poet Gertrude Stein (1874 to 1946). She purchased a number of his works for her apartment. One painting in particular was a portrait of her. When it was noted that the portrait did not look like her, Picasso reportedly said, "It will." Picasso may have become famous for his experimental style of painting, but it was Stein who contributed to his fame by developing a literary counterpart referred to as Cubist writing.

Marcel Duchamp (1887 to 1968) was first a Cubist who became a Dadaist after he painted *Nude Descending a Staircase (No. 2)* (fig. 14.22). The painting reduced the time-honored female number to nothing more than a series of static, fractured, and mechanized single-shot movements. The monochromatic color palate was typical of Cubist during this time, but Duchamp moved beyond the ideals of Cubism. He was attempting to depict the energy and motion of the human form as it passed through a given location. His inspiration for the painting is found in the time-lapse photographs of Étienne-Jules Marey and Eadweard Muybridge (1830 to 1904). In particular, Muybridge's *Animal Locomotion*

Fig. 14.22 *Nude Descending a Staircase (No. 2)*, oil on canvas, Duchamp, Philadelphia Museum of Art, Philadelphia, Pennsylvania. 1912

series from the 1880s depicted a series of 24 images of a seminude woman descending stairs from multiple angles.

Duchamp planned to exhibit the painting in the Salon des Indépendants exhibition in Paris, but it was rejected by the hanging committee. Two of his brothers who were on the committee informed him of the rejection decision on account of the fact that "a nude never descends the stairs, a nude reclines." In 1913, Duchamp created a flurry of debate when the painting was displayed at the International Exhibition of Modern Art held at the National Guard 69th Regiment Armory in New York. Art critics perceived the work to be an incoherent mess. Duchamp was delighted when he heard of the scandal his painting created; 2 years later he moved to New York.

Georgia O'Keeffe's (1887 to 1986) artwork was first introduced to the photographer Alfred Stieglitz (1864 to 1946), whom O'Keeffe married in 1924, by a friend. A year later, in 1917, Stieglitz organized a one-person exhibit for O'Keeffe. During the exhibition, she discovered that her style of painting was more original than she first realized. When she began painting in the Southwest, she felt a harmony she rarely actualized while living in New York. A characteristic feature of her paintings was to enlarge flowers and other objects in an unrealistic proportion as seen in her works *Grey Lines with Black, Blue and Yellow*, *Pelvis II*, and *Red Hill and White Shell*.

Mexican muralist Diego Rivera (1886 to 1957) painted scenes from the lives of the many underprivileged and hardworking people in Mexico and the United States. He was a socially motivated and political activist painter, which led to difficulties in obtaining support for his work, given its controversial nature. His *Detroit Industry Mural* (fig. 14.23a and b) depicted the working man of the assembly line in the Ford plant

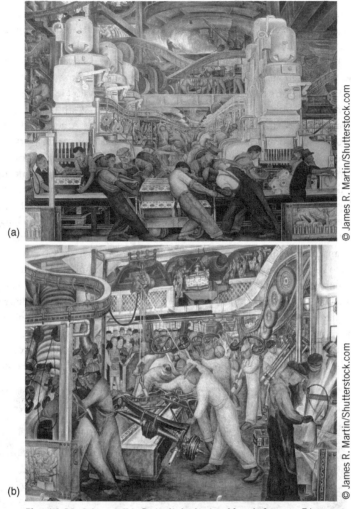

(a)

(b)

© James R. Martin/Shutterstock.com

Fig. 14.23 (a) and (b) *Detroit Industry Mural,* fresco, Rivera, Detroit Institute of Arts, Detroit, Michigan. 1933

in Detroit. The fresco illustrated an entire day in the life of assembly plant workers, demonstrating how the workers made cars using steel, processing, and drilling the metal. Even the punching of the time clock and lunch break were included in the large wall scene.

The mural program created by the Worker Project Administration (WPA) saw the flourishing of talented artists such as Thomas Hart Benton (1889 to 1975) and Aaron Douglas (1899 to 1979). In 1935, the WPA created specific programs to focus on 300 years of African-American accomplishments. One such program hired Douglas to paint a series of four panels depicting African-American history and life from Africa to America. The mural series, *Aspects of Negro Life,* was painted on the walls of the New York Public Library in Harlem.

At the age of 23, Salvador Dalí departed for Paris, where he met artists Joan Miro (1893 to 1983) and Pablo Picasso. His artistic career was highly influenced by these artists. He became obsessively committed to painting in a way that drew from his imagination while still using recognizable imagery. His figures were based on realistic objects, but the end composition evolved and morphed into something entirely different.

Dalí was one of the leading Surrealists for his use of ideas drawn from deep within his subconscious. His style was inspired by the developments of Freudian psychology and linked closely with post–World War I developments and research associated with new methods of dream interpretation. The style of Surrealism that Dalí created had a unique appearance and Dalí himself was not known to verbally explain his creations. He once told a reporter that he did not want to say much about his art, because if he had intended to explain his work, he would have become a poet instead of a painter. Two of Dalí's most memorable paintings pertained to melting watches and mountains entitled

The Persistence of Memory. The other was his interpretation of *Leonardo da Vinci's Last Supper.* Dalí's distinctive analysis and unique perspective made him a trailblazer of the Surrealistic style.

Paul Delvaux (1897 to 1994), a Belgium Surrealist, first studied architecture and painting at the Académie des Beaux-Arts in Brussels. His earlier works were Post-Impressionist and Expressionist in style until he discovered the works of Salvador Dalí and fellow Belgian René Magritte. He developed a unique style of Surrealism in the mid-1930s after a trip to Italy, where he was greatly influenced by sixteenth-century Italian Mannerist (Chapter 9) painters. Delvaux's technique as seen in *Proposition Diurne (La femme au miroir)* (fig. 14.24) was hyperrealist with extraordinary precision. True to the Surrealist ideals of two realities, the man and the woman occupy the same space and merge to initiate a combined reality. Both appear to be in a dream world, with

Fig. 14.24 *Proposition Diurne (La femme au miroir)*, oil on canvas, Delvaux, MFAB, Boston, Massachusetts. 1937.

the nude woman being the personification of idealization. Her interests are consumed with examining reflection, but the mirror is as empty as the expression on her face.

Photography

The **New Deal**, or a series of public projects aimed at financial reform in the United States, contributed to the photographic documentation of migrant workers and poor farmers. The hardship endured during the **Dust Bowl**, or areas of land in Oklahoma, Kansas, and northern Texas affected by soil erosion, and the Louisville flood were both famously captured by female photographers Dorothea Lange (1895 to 1965) and Margaret Bourke-White (1904 to 1971). Lange was most notably for portraying the rough living and working conditions of the Dust Bowl and Great Depression. The photograph known as the *Migrant Mother* (fig. 14.25) was one in a series Lange shot of Florence Owens Thompson (1903 to

Fig. 14.25 *Migrant Mother*, gelatin silver print, Lange, MoMA, New York, New York. 1936

1983) and her children during February or March of 1936 in Nipomo, California. The photo was taken at the conclusion of a month-long trip around the state for the Resettlement Administration. Lange made five exposures from the same direction as she moved closer. She asked no questions. The mother provided her name and age, 32. She also communicated to Lange that her family was living on frozen vegetables and birds her children killed. The women continued to tell Lange that her husband had left to sell their automobiles tires to purchase more sustainable food for the family. When the photograph was published in a local newspaper it became an iconic image depicting the difficulties many families faced of the 1930s.

Music and Dance

One of the most interesting concepts from the beginning of the twentieth century was the idea of **simultaneities**, or artworks' ability to possess two or more contradictory characteristics at the same time. The style was the preferred approach for the American composer Charles Ives (1874 to 1954) to create his music. But, the style was best expressed in the music of Igor Stravinsky (1882 to 1971) who composed pieces in several keys at once.

In spring 1913, Stravinsky's *Rite of Spring* premiered alongside a performance of *Les Sylphides* ballet accompanied with music by Frédéric François Chopin (1810 to 1849) at the *Théâtre des Champs-Élyseés* in Paris, France. The combination of the composition and dance was one of the great debacles in dance history. Ballet was one of the highest art forms in the West at the time, because of the influence of the French academy. By far, ballet is one of the most difficult art forms to perfect. Students devote their entire lives to the genre, drilling dance figures such as *présenté la jambe, pirouette,* and *pas de bourrée couru.*

Audiences eagerly anticipate watching dancers draw designs in the air while accomplishing magnificent athletic turns. One evening about 100 years ago, the premiere of *Rite of Spring* commenced and everyone witnessed the elegant dancing of *Les Sylphides* and heard the tonal music of Chopin that accompanied it.

French audiences were famously open-minded about artistic genres, and perhaps they tolerably anticipated this performance even though they knew *Rite of Spring* would not have the elegant figuration of a classical ballet. The resulting music was jarring, the folk outfits were too dissimilar from the classical ballet dress, and the dancing was radically different than established norms that the audience began yelling at the performers and made whistling noises. People slapped one another in the face and verbal riots broke out. The juxtaposition of inharmonious music, non-traditional dance, and a story where a tribal girl dances herself to death was too uncomfortable for the audience. Riots spilled out into the street and the police were called, resulting in over 200 people being arrested. Stravinsky and Sergei

Diaghilev (1872 to 1929) the production's **impresario**, or financial organizers, were forced to escape quickly from the *Théâtre des Champs-Élyseés*.

Stravinsky was experimenting with new ideas for musical expression, an idea of playing two unrelated keys simultaneously where each key followed an independent path. In effect, his idea was somewhat similar to how a 3D movie would be viewed without wearing 3D glasses. In music, the procedure is called **polytonality**, or the simultaneous use of two or more keys. His musical composition was one of the earliest techniques to separate the genteel nineteenth-century musical sound from the harsh, experimental twentieth-century sound. Never before had any artist or musician broken so radically with tradition. The polytonal chords were appropriate to the primitive activities described in the story of *Rite of Spring*, but they sounded more like a musician hitting the keyboard of a piano with the fist. Such sounds become perfectly acceptable in the latter part of the twentieth century, but people in the early twentieth century did not fully appreciate and accept such musical possibilities.

Societal Emphasis

Between World War I and World War II, a crisis that began in America reflected not only the constraints of capitalism but more pointedly the lingering troubles of Europe since the 1850s. The issues were further compounded with low consumer spending, international trade problems, and inflation. On October 24, 1929, Black Thursday, a wave of skittish speculation caused investors to trade 12.9 million shares and shares continued to plummet until 1932. Bankruptcy rates mushroomed in all countries that had financial ties with America. Forty million people were jobless and **on the dole**, or receiving benefits from the government. Although industry was spared, farmers burned crops to maintain higher prices while people starved. Social and political unrest was widespread. The New Deal helped America climb out of the crisis, while other countries like Italy, German, and Japan viewed war as the only logical solution.

Louis Armstrong (1901 to 1971) began learning how to play the **cornet,** or an instrument similar to the trumpet that plays the same notes but is slightly shorter, when he was 5 or 6 years old. He worked, trying to make money, and dropped out of school when he was in elementary level. He always liked listening to music and wanted to play the cornet. Eventually, he saved up to $5.00 and bought a cornet at a pawn shop. He did not take lessons but taught himself instead.

Armstrong's style was his own, which made him popular around the world. In interviews later in his life, he talked about the bad incident of being sent to reform school that turned into something good, a turning point in his life. He learned to read in reform school, and later said how important that education was to his life. In 1922, he left for Chicago with his cornet in one hand and a trout sandwich that his mother had made for him in the other. He was off to change the world of music, and he changed the world of jazz. He exercised a major influence on other players and musicians and made a lasting impact on the way musicians improvise.

Theater

Originally, films were presented as novelties in larger theaters and, therefore, were considered secondary to plays and burlesque spectacles. Film later replaced theater as the main form of entertainment. Theaters of Modernism attempted to emulate the grand opera houses of Europe in order to give prestige to American drama and music halls. Productions consisted largely of stage furniture, with **flats**, or stage scenery on a board, and drops. Dressing rooms, often located below the stage, were crowded with low ceilings, but some included modern amenities such as lavatories and dressing tables. Touring companies hauled their own backdrops with painted scenes that were lifted up and down as needed during a production. Theaters that accommodated wealthy patrons had luxuries such as three main drops, a velvet curtain, a canvas drop for advertisements, and a movie screen.

Electric lighting was controlled from backstage, often involving thousands of lights. Most early American theaters contained no heating or cooling systems, but different colored lighting helped patrons imagine that the temperatures were more comfortable than it really were. Lighting technicians changed the aisle footlights from red in the winter to green in the summer to suggest warmer or cooler temperatures, respectively. In the 1930s, theater owners proudly announced they had air-conditioning, but in actuality

Innovation and Progress

Teddy bears (1902), paper towels (1907), zippers (1913), toasters (1919), band-aids (1920), ballpoint pens (1935) duct tape (1942), Tupperware (1945), bikini swimsuits (1946), Velcro (1948), and LEGOs (1949) all emerged in the first half of the twentieth century. While each impacted society in a profound way, none was as significant as the serendipitous discovery of penicillin by Alexander Fleming in 1928. Penicillin was one of the first antibodies discovered and is still used globally to combat common bacterial infections. The antibody was revolutionary in fighting the spread of the venereal disease syphilis that was ubiquitous since the Renaissance.

they only had a water cooler that blew air around the auditorium.

Film

Perhaps the art form best adapted to the concept of motion in the twentieth century was film. Originating in the scientific experiments of Eadweard Muybridge (1830 to 1904) and Étienne-Jules Marey (1830 to 1904), and without prior examples to rely on, reject, or improve, motion pictures adopted the conservative traditions of nineteenth-century opera and drama that were already economically feasible. The motion pictures were initially treated as a novelty with a potential for scientific documentary, as seen in Muybridge's *Animal Locomotion. Volume V, Male (Pelvis Cloth)*, which commenced in 1872 and completed in 1885 (fig. 14.26). Film became increasingly popular as an entertainment form when it was able to present narratives using **jump cuts**, or abrupt scene transitions, and parallel story development. The new use of film meant viewers were able to see events unfold in time by experiencing two strands of the same story at once.

In addition to saving viewer time, film had the ability to increase the advantage point of the viewer by showing objects at various angles and in motion at different speeds. With the addition of sound track,

dialogue, music, and **sound effects**, or Foley arts, the art form engaged multiple senses, sight, and sound. The first publicly projected films appeared in the late 1890s. In Pittsburgh in 1905, Nickelodeons presented the first narrative films. By 1907, more than two million Americans had visited one of these storefront theaters that sometimes showed films to the accompaniment of improvised piano music.

As technology continued to develop throughout the twentieth century, numerous projecting, editing, and stage effects improved film reality. Sound, color, wide screen, lens effects, editing, location staging, synchronized sound and image, and sound effects all contributed to the improvements. Existing theaters in America were converted to all the aforementioned developments in film.

Technology in Film

A whole series of inventions led up to the "talkies." One of the earliest talking films was the 1915 film *Thomas Edison Talking Picture* that lasted only 6 minutes, but stimulated much interest and curiosity. An Edison phonograph was linked to a kinetoscope on the floor of the theater auditorium. A reviewer from *Variety* who saw and heard one of Edison's *Kinetophones*

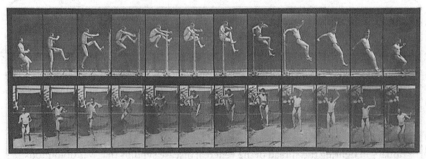

Fig. 14.26 *Animal Locomotion. Volume V, Male (Pelvis Cloth)*, photogravures, Muybridge, 1880s. (MET# 1991.1135.5)

in 1915 wrote, "The talking, instead of enhancing the picture, simply annoys." By 1923, however, the *Kinetophone* had been replaced by films that contained both the soundtrack and the image.

One of the famous lines from of a silent film came from the mouth of Al Jolson in the 1927 film *The Jazz Singer*, who said at the end, "You ain't seen nothing yet," in a silent film alternating synchronized music and speech. Most of the early film effects were borrowed from Broadway stage productions; it made sense that most of the early films were musicals. Theaters paid as much as $20,000, almost $300,000 in today's currency, to convert to talking movies. The adaption of silent film to taking movie was an indication that public taste had shifted from stage shows to Hollywood film.

Even though the Great Depression was close at hand, talking film took over as the principal form of American entertainment. Stage productions that took place in movie theaters thereafter were simply a novelty. The war years brought in a steady stream of soldiers and their lovers to the theaters, but the craze of drive-in movies after the war caused old movie palaces to fall into disuse. At the end of their run, many American theater palaces ended up showing X-rated movies rather than new Hollywood productions. Once the talkies became popular, a whole list of highly influential films developed in the twentieth century. Films with the quality of *Gone with the Wind*, *Wizard of Oz*, or *Fantasia* from 1939 were beloved by audiences then, and now.

Film continued to develop throughout the twentieth century. It was largely untouched by the abstract issues of other artistic genres. But, at the same time, it remained the most experimental art form in terms of technology. Two genres in particular allowed for the most diverse forms of experimentation,

Horror and Science Fiction films. In both, audiences expected unusual characters, film techniques, music, and sound effects.

Literature

A few individuals of the early twentieth century were exceedingly creative with the ability to express society's uncertainty through their writing. Three poets, Robert Frost (1874 to 1963), William Butler Yeats (1865 to 1939), and T. S. Eliot (1888 to 1965), had the unique ability to eloquently capture the diverse range of feelings in Western civilization. Frost took heed of the national sentiments his fellow Americans held in the first decade of the twentieth century. His poem *The Road Not Taken* of 1915 cemented his original, modern idiom with a distinct candor that reflected the **imagism**, or a movement that pursued clarity with detailed text, employed by Ezra Pound. Frost's poem reads as follows:

Two roads diverged in a yellow wood,
And sorry I could not travel both
And be one traveler, long I stood
And looked down one as far as I could
To where it bent in the undergrowth;
Then took the other, as just as fair,
And having perhaps the better claim,
Because it was grassy and wanted wear;
Though as for that the passing there
Had worn them really about the same,
And both that morning equally lay
In leaves no step had trodden black.

*Oh, I kept the first for another
day!
Yet knowing how way leads on
to way,
I doubted if I should ever come
back.
I shall be telling this with a sigh
Somewhere ages and ages hence:
Two roads diverged in a wood,
and I—
I took the one less traveled by,
And that has made all the
difference.*

Frost's poem is often misinterpreted as an anthem for can-do individualism but was intended as a commentary on self-deception. People tend to cultivate a life predicated on unknown illusion of what might happen. Humankind continually searches for that one moment, that one decision that made all the difference for a better life. Instead, the poem was intended to illustrate that either road will produce a favorable outcome but with a different ending. In 1949, on Frost's 75th birthday, the U.S. Senate passed a resolution in Frost's honor that stated, "His poems have helped to guide American thought and humor and wisdom, setting forth to our minds a reliable representation of ourselves and of all men."

In 1920, William Butler Yeats (1865 to 1939) wrote his own poem, *The Second Coming,* reflecting the attitude of the early twentieth century. He was stunningly violent in the use of chilling imagery and formalized verbiage. Yeats wrote the poem in 1919 after World War I:

*Turning and turning in the widen-
ing gyre
The falcon cannot hear the
falconer;
Things fall apart; the center cannot hold;*

*Mere anarchy is loosed upon the
world,
The blood-dimmed tide is loosed,
and everywhere
The ceremony of innocence is
drowned;
The best lack all conviction, while
the worst
Are full of passionate intensity.
Surely some revelation is at hand;
Surely the Second Coming is at
hand.
The Second Coming! Hardly are
those words out
When a vast image out of Spiritus
Mundi
Troubles my sight: a waste of des-
ert sand;
A shape with lion body and the
head of a man,
A gaze blank and pitiless as the
sun,
Is moving its slow thighs, while all
about it
Wind shadows of the indignant
desert birds.
The darkness drops again but
now I know
That twenty centuries of stony
sleep
Were vexed to nightmare by a
rocking cradle,
And what rough beast, its hour
come round at last,
Slouches towards Bethlehem to
be born?*

The poem was about more than a just bird that flew over the area he lived and no longer listened to his master. The opening lines of the open were used to create a complex visual depiction of apocalyptic times. Yeats was capturing more than the political turmoil and unrest of the world. The poem divulges his anxious concerns for the social evils of Modernism, the fractured traditional family values, the demise of religious faith, and a general sense of discarding old systems with nothing to replace them.

T.S. Eliot assembled the greatest eulogy for the death of Western culture stretching back to ancient Greece and the beauty of yesteryears. He reasoned that the decline originated with the constant dumbing down associated with excessive alcohol consumption, the rise of atheism, and general laziness. His 1921 poem *The Waste Land* provided him an outlet to express his despair that is sensed in the opening lines:

April is the cruelest month, breeding
Lilacs out of the dead land, mixing
Memory and desire, stirring
Dull roots with spring rain.
Winter kept us warm, covering
Earth in forgetful snow, feeding
A little life with dried tubers.

The opening line was a direct reference to the Anglican burial service performed so frequently during World War I and afterward. His vast knowledge of the classics and philosophy stemmed from his Harvard education. The poem, when read in its entirety, exudes his scholarly education and conveys the message that being versed in five languages and knowing the scope of Western history has merit.

Eliot's poem was written in elevated language that referenced literature and cultures from around the world, even very obscure ones. First-time readers are puzzled by the how hard the poem is to read. But, that was Eliot's goal. He wanted people to think and possibly even go to a library to learn what they did not know. A second reason the poem is a difficult read was how Eliot shifted between different characters and scenes.

Philosophy

The existential individual viewpoint fashioned by Kierkegarrd (Chapter 12) was applied to early-twentieth-century thought. Karl Jaspers (1883 to 1969) coined the term **existentialism**, or analysis of a human's life. Jaspers was a trained medical doctor with a focus in psychiatry who transitioned into the field of philosophy over a 9-year period. The switch was part coincidental and part passion, and the medical faculty was fully staffed, but the philosophical department needed an experimental psychologist. Jaspers believed that philosophy was a subjective interpretation of the Being, as described by Aristotle, and endeavored to propose standards of value and dogmas of life that were generally rational. After the events of World War II he and his Jewish wife endured, and he wrote *Die Schuldfrage* (*The Question of the German Guilt*) in 1946 to condemn those who participated in or tolerated Nazism.

The French essayist, novelist, and playwright Albert Camus (1913 to 1960) used the hardship of his childhood years to publish a collection of essays in 1937 titled *L'Envers et l'endroit* (*The Wrong Side and the Right Side*). His 1942 essay, *Le Mythe de Sisyphe* (*The Myth of Sisyphus*), best explained the existentialist viewpoint. The essay developed a supportive evaluation of **nihilism**, rejection of all religious and moral principles, and considered the nature of the absurd. He further reasoned that life was meaningless even though humans continue to seek meaning to inexplicable questions. He used the Greek myth of Sisyphus, fated by Hades to eternally roll a boulder up a hill to watch it roll down, as an allegory for humankind's ceaseless struggles against the fundamental absurdities of existence. While human life ends in death, Sisyphus has no option expect for to object to his punished by celebrating it. Camas believed that a jubilant acceptance of life's struggles in spite of certain defeats allowed a person to obtain contentment, find a sense of individuality, and, most importantly, surmount the nothingness of life.

Sigmund Freud was captivated by the human mind and its unconscious portion. He likened the human mind to an iceberg (fig. 14.27) where the conscious portion was the tip of the iceberg seen above the surface of the water. But, the larger portion that drove our thoughts and actions in ways we were unaware, was hidden. He was curious to discover why people do things that seem to make no sense and create unnecessary problems? According to Freud, our unconscious mind was driven largely by our sexual and aggressive nature. These feelings and urges were normally repressed as a person followed society's **social norms**, or informal guidelines that govern behavior. But, the repressed unconscious mind must release these feelings and urges in some form. According to Freud, a person's buried emotions do not go away; instead they lay dormant and will surface when least expected, with potentially humiliating consequences.

Freud postulated two techniques to handle the unconscious mind, dream analysis and free association. In dream analysis, the patient and the doctor discuss the dreams and then try to interpret their meaning. While a person sleeps, the mind is busy processing all lived experiences and is dealing with unresolved issues. Some symbols with a dream are obvious and others are obscure. Freud believed that "every dream is a wish" and most of our repressed wishes are quite unusual. Free association allows for the patient to recline and chat away about whatever comes to the mind. The doctor then uses the ramblings of the patient to find meaning and unlock the mysteries of the unconscious mind.

Freud also developed the three components of an individual's personality and five stages of psychosexual development. A person's personality comprises the Ego, Id, and Superego (fig. 14.27). The Ego is considered the central organized self that a person is most aware of and the world sees. The Id is deemed the primal side of a person that forms the unconscious mind. The Superego is regarded as the ethical component that was instilled by a person's parent and society. Freud's five stages of psychosexual development are the Oral, Anal, Phallic, Sexual, and Genital Stages.

Science

Science was the vehicle that set the early twentieth century into a frenzied rat race with monumental discoveries that changed the world. German-born Albert Einstein is one of the most celebrated scientists of the twentieth century. His 1905 theories about relativity laid the foundation for multiple new branches in physics. The significance of his Special Theory of

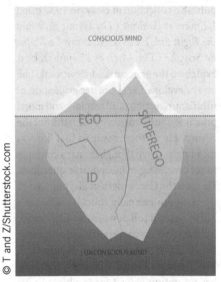

© T and Z/Shutterstock.com

Fig. 14.27 Freud's iceberg analogy of the conscious and unconscious mind.

Relativity is comparable to Copernicus's (Chapter 10) heliocentric planetary theory. In 1916, Einstein proposed the General Theory of Relativity that was central to understanding the universe. Through his work, the development of atomic energy was discovered. He and a multitude of talented scientists helped transform the political balance of power in the twentieth century toward American democracy and away from the fascist Germany and Italy.

The British physicist Sir Charles Chadwick discovered the neutron in 1932. Over the next 3 years, the Italian scientists Enrico Fermi developed the math required to explain the phenomena of subatomic particles and discovered *nuclear reactions* brought about by slow neutrons. Fermi was awarded a Noble Prize in 1938 and Mussolini allowed him to collect his prize in Sweden. After the ceremony, he and his Jewish wife, Laura, defected to the United States where he continued his research. Fermi became an American citizen in 1944 and moved to Los Alamos, New Mexico, where he worked on the Manhattan Project.

In 1935, Japanese physicist Hideki Yukawa (1907 to 1981) proposed a new theory on nuclear force he called U-quantum that was not discovered until 1947 by British physicist Cecil Powell (1903 to 1969). The theory suggested that atoms contained strong and weak nuclear forces that held their protons and neutrons together. Given the new proposal about how an atom's nucleus was held together, Austrian physicists Lise Meitner (1878 to 1968) and Otto Robert Frisch (1904 to 1979) along with a German chemist Otto Hahn (1879 to 1968) investigated the way in which an atom would split, or cause **nuclear fission**. The culmination of all the aforementioned discoveries led to the creation and detonation of Trinity, the Manhattan Project atom bomb (fig. 14.28a-d).

Many other notable discoveries occurred in science. The first gene was mapped to a chromosome in a *Drosophila melanogaster* (fruit fly) by the American evolutionary biologist and geneticist Thomas Hunt Morgan (1866 to 1945) in 1910. Edwin Hubble (1889 to 1953), an American astronomer, had described the nature of galaxies by 1923. Hubble and fellow colleague Milton Humason (1891 to 1972) proposed Hubble's Law. In 1929, Hubble used the lab to establish the theory Universal Expansion. This theory was the first evidence for the Big Bang Theory proposed by a physics graduate student, Ralph Alpher (1921 to 2007), and his PhD advisor, George Gamow (1904 to 1968), in 1948. As World War II raged on in Europe, American agricultural scientist Norman Borlaug (1914 to 2009) created the "Green Revolution" to alleviate hunger around the world. He experimented with creating disease-resistant strains of wheat that could survive harsh climates.

Technology

Early forms of computer use were developed as military message machines such as the Telex messaging network. Telex messaging originated from the early period of the German Third Reich and served as a worldwide text messaging system into the 2000s. Belgian Paul Otlet (1868 to 1944) had a goal of collecting, organizing, and sharing information with people around the world. Author H. G. Wells (1866 to 1946), "The Father of Science Fiction," wrote a collection of essays titled *World Brain* that resembled the World Wide Web that prompted others to explore such concepts. American engineer Vannevar Bush (1890 to 1974) conceptualized the idea of indexing, archiving, cross-referencing, and retrieving information with a device he called Memex in 1945. His idea foreshadowed the creation of hyperlinking information within a Web

(a) 0.025 sec after detonation

(b) 2 sec after detonation

(c) 4 sec after detonation

(d) 9 sec after detonation

Fig. 14.28 First atomic explosion on July 16, 1945 in Alamogordo, New Mexico. Photographs at (a) 0.025,- (b) 2,- (c) 4,- and (d) 9-second intervals after the initial Trinity detonation of the Manhattan Project.

page. By 1949, British mathematician and logician Alan Turning (1912 to 1954) had been quoted in the *London Times* with the belief "I do not see why it (the machine) should not enter any one of the fields normally covered by the human intellect, and eventually compete on equal terms."

The age of technology that gave birth to the modern computer had arrived. The first fully automated calculator, Mark 1 (fig. 14.29), was designed by Harvard graduate student Howard H. Aiken (1900 to 1973) in 1937 and financed by the International Business Machine Corporation. The device weighed more than 11,000 pounds with 500 miles of wires and was delivered to

Harvard in 1944. Mark 1 houses an internal clock to synchronize its system. The purpose of the device was to solve mathematical problems for the U.S. Navy Bureau of Ships that normally required groups acting as human "computers."

MODERNISM LEGACY

By examining developments in painting, literature, and music, one can imagine the turmoil and complexity that arose during Modernism. The many artistic styles were directly related to current events and reflected the turmoil and despair that were felt by many people. The styles that emerged from

© Everett Collection/Shutterstock.com

Fig. 14.29 Mark 1, October 1944, Harvard University.

that period had major repercussions upon the artic world. Twentieth-century art forms reflected the lifestyle changes of people trying to keep up with the quickened pace of life in a mechanical age. Advancements in the field of communications ushered in a new way of thinking about the world and humanity's role in it. Expansive new methods of communication meant more freedom for some people, but others felt these new developments challenged old, traditional values. Artists reveled in producing works from these new viewpoints. The entire progress of the early twentieth century witnessed a broader global awareness among people from many different countries and cultures. Films played a greater role in creating a "global community."

Critical Thinking

Examine the difference between the artistic movements of the early twentieth century.

Evaluate the ideas of the political and economic systems of capitalism, communism, and socialism.

Describe the major technology advancement of the early twentieth century.

Analyze how each successive art movement led to the next.

Examine the impact film had on society.

Illustrate how artistic expression was transformed during the early twentieth century.

ONLINE RESOURCES

Abstract Art Explanation Video
https://smarthistory.org/case-for-abstraction/

Fauvism Overview
https://smarthistory.org/a-beginners-guide-to-fauvism/

Expressionism Overview
https://smarthistory.org/expressionism-intro/

Futurism Overview
https://smarthistory.org/italian-futurism-an-introduction/

Dada Overview
https://smarthistory.org/introduction-to-dada/

Surrealism Overview
https://smarthistory.org/surrealism-intro/

Chicago Style Building
https://smarthistory.org/sullivan-carson-pirie-scott-building/

The Chrysler Building
https://smarthistory.org/van-alen-the-chrysler-building/

Wright's *Fallingwater*
https://smarthistory.org/frank-lloyd-wright-fallingwater/

British Art and Literature During WWI
https://smarthistory.org/british-art-and-literature-during-wwi/

Art in Nazi Germany
https://smarthistory.org/art-in-nazi-germany/

Picasso's *Portrait of Gertrude Stein* Video
https://smarthistory.org/picasso-portrait-of-gertrude-stein/

Malevich's *Suprematist Composition: White on White* Video
https://smarthistory.org/malevich-white/

Mondrian's *Composition with Red, Blue, and Yellow*
https://smarthistory.org/mondrian-composition-ii-in-red-blue-and-yellow/

Duchamp's *In advance of the Broken Arm*
https://smarthistory.org/art-as-concept-duchamp/

Dalí's *The Persistence of Memory* Video
https://smarthistory.org/salvador-dali-the-persistence-of-memory/

Sigmund Freud, Life and Works
https://www.pbs.org/wgbh/aso/databank/entries/bhfreu.html

The Atomic Bomb History
https://www.history.com/topics/world-war-ii/atomic-bomb-history

History of the Computer
http://www.computerhistory.org/timeline/computers/

Post-Modernism: Ramifications of World Wars

Fig. 15.1 *Spoonbridge and Cherry*, stainless steel and aluminum painted with polyurethane enamel, Oldenburg and van Bruggen, Minneapolis, Minnesota. 1988.

© photo.ua/Shutterstock.com

Knowledge Acquisition

◆ *Examine the artistic and cultural shifts made during the post-modernism era.*

◆ *Evaluate the principal accomplishments made during the post-modernism era by artistic expressions.*

◆ *Explore how each subsequent artistic movement paved the way for the next.*

◆ *Assess the impact of key artistic, historical, and philosophical figures.*

◆ *Discover how post-modernism connects works of art from around the world to its own artistic, cultural, literary, and political interests.*

SETTING THE SCENE

Prior to modernism, the world was explained in one of two methods, religion or science. The world that humankind created and inhabited was relatively simplistic. Artists of all varieties produced traditional works that were accepted by the general public on their merits and quality. As modernity settled into the lives of the later-nineteenth-century society, avant-garde artists yearned to create glimpses of reality. They experimented with time-honored techniques for expressing their ideas. The world these avant-garde artists knew changed drastically and newer forms of creative expression soon eclipsed their experimental methods. Modernism was, in all reality, a rejection of the idea that religion could explain much about the newer innovations that science developed. For modernist thinkers, religious faith was a coordinated structure that held humanity back from crafting authentic progress. Modernism witnessed the production of artworks solely for creating them and using them to explore who humanity was. Modernists looked inward to understand the world around them. Post-Modernism flat out rejected this belief.

POST-MODERNISM

Sentiments of the late twentieth century in the West are best characterized by the philosophy of postmodernism. Society had developed a general sense of skepticism and suspicion of reason. Society became acutely sensitive to the role ideology played in preserving economic, political, and social equity. While post-modernist thinkers were aware that all aspects of thought were relative, they did not believe that any one aspect provided a grand theory for human interactions. The movement and time period tend to be highly self-reflective and ironic

to the point of extreme sarcasm. Often, the artworks were absurd because life seemed illogically absurd.

RAMIFICATIONS OF WORLD WAR II

Prior to World War II, the so-called Third World was under colonial rule. The war that the Allies (Great Britain, France, Russian Empire, and United States) mounted against the Axis Powers (Germany, Italy, and Japan) was economically and strategically exhaustive. The resources that were needed to prevail on **D-Day**, or the invasion of France by the Allied forces on June 6, 1944, (fig. 15.2) affected each country involved. Economic hardship combined with nationalistic wars for independence in colonial-held territories led to decolonization. During the latter part of the 1940s, both the British and Dutch planned for decolonization in certain territories, even though the Cold War of the 1950s polarized the world. Decolonization efforts triggered extensive complications as tribe leaders fought for power, oppressive dictators surfaced, human rights were negated, and famine flourished. People yearned for the freedom they believed would accompany the removal of other nations ruling over them. Decolonized territories soon learned that freedom was not synonymous with economic stability. As unrealistic expectations continued to surface, violence sprang from their dissatisfaction.

RAMIFICATIONS OF THE COLD WAR

The 45 years after World War II (1946 to 1991) witnessed two Allies, the United States and the newly formed Soviet Union, pursuing a "peaceful coexistence" as each sought to protect their influence over the other and the world. Germany was divided into East and West and the Soviet Union concealed itself behind an Iron Curtain (fig. 15.3). The height of

Fig. 15.2 Omaha Beach after D-Day, June 7-10, 1944, Normandy, France.

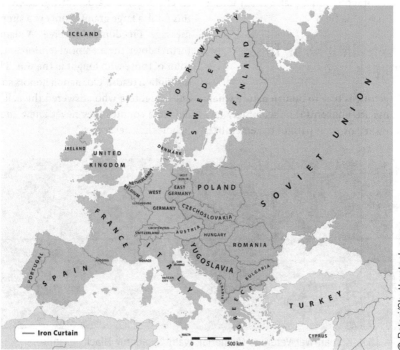

Fig. 15.3 Iron Curtain Cold War era on Europe's political map, 1945 to 1991.

open, yet peaceful hostility was reached between 1946 and 1962. The mood shifted between 1950 and 1953 with an antagonist military campaign in Korea. Relations began to warm but quickly eroded after the French were defeated in Vietnam and the region destabilized. The United States sought the creation of a military post in South Vietnam as it had in South Korea.

The latter part of the 1960s saw the rise of Arab nationalism in the Middle East. The Arabs' loss of strategic roads and defeat in the 1967 along with the death of Egypt's President Nasser in 1970 initiated a return of fundamental religious leadership. Protests turned to hostile violence after multiple attempts to develop Arab nations to equivalent standards of the West failed. Local hostilities flourished into the terror attack that led to the events of 9/11 on the World Trade Center towers, the Pentagon, and a plane crash into a Pennsylvania field.

RAMIFICATIONS OF THE KOREAN WAR

Forgetting is true to human nature when events are uneventful or seemingly unnecessary or even painful to remember.

The Korean War was not necessarily uneventful, unnecessary, or painless but was relegated to a forgotten status. The war unfortunately followed closely on the heels of World War II. Sentiments toward involvement in other nation's conflicts were waning. Fewer troops were killed than in the prior war, and the Korean War simply faded into history.

Forty-two years to the day after the war ended with 54,246 dead Americans and 8,000 listed as missing in action, the Korean War Veterans Memorial (fig. 15.4) was dedicated on July 27, 1995 in Washington, DC. The memorial was designed by the Cooper-Lecky architect firm, sandblasted murals were completed by Louis Nelson (b. 1936), and 19 stainless steel statues were created by Frank Gaylord (1925 to 2018). The site also includes a pool of remembrance, an honor roll at its entrance, and a dedication stone. At this pool, a large granite conveys a simple message "Freedom Is Not Free." A plaque further down the memorial reinforces the valor of those who fought in the war. The inscription reads, "Our nation honors sons and daughters who answered the call to defend a country they never knew and a people they never met."

© Giuseppe Crimeni/Shutterstock.com

Fig. 15.4 Korean War Veterans Memorial, wall: "academy Black" granite, Cooper-Lecky, photographic murals: sandblasted, Nelson, Statues: stainless steel, Gaylord. Washington, DC. 1995.

RAMIFICATIONS OF THE VIETNAM WARS

Wars tend to promulgate mixed emotions with a forlorn hopelessness for the victors and the defeated alike. Wars have never resulted in an end-all solution to disputes between nations. Vietnam's conflicts with foreign people date to its recorded beginning in second century BCE. The nation's current political problems arose in the eighteenth century under Chinese rule. The problems continued under French control until the nations efforts failed and resulted in France's defeat on May 7, 1954. Open conflict between North and South Vietnam resulted in Vietnam being allowed to self-govern for the first time.

The 1954 Geneva Peace Conference provided citizens to move freely between the two areas, north and south, for a 300-day period. Estimates suggest that more than 120,000 Catholics fled south to escape any potential persecution by the communist leader Hồ Chí Minh (1890 to 1969). The US government funded the relocation program to the south controlled by Ngô Đình Diệm (1901 to 1963) in 1954. The United States next provided South Vietnam with military supplies and eventually with military advisors in 1955 and then troops by November 1963. American involvement in the war between North and South Vietnam lasted until troops withdrew and a peace treaty was signed in 1973.

In 1979, decorated Vietnam War Veteran, Jan C. Scruggs (b. 1950) founded the Vietnam Veteran's Memorial Fund (fig. 15.5) that raised over $8 million in private donation in 2 years. His purpose for raising the funds was to erect a physical memorial dedicated to the brave American men and women who fought in the war. A competition encouraged the public to submit their design, resulting in the receipt of more than 1,400 submissions. Each submission was given a number with no name provided. The winner of the competition was a 21-year-old

Fig. 15.5 Vietnam Veterans Memorial, black granite, Lin, Washington, DC. 1982.

Yale University undergraduate, Maya Lin (b. 1959) in 1981. Her concept for the memorial was a V-shaped opening in the earth resembling an open, abrasive gash. The opening further elicits a somberness for the 58,318 soldiers who perished in battle with the use of dark granite.

CIVIL RIGHTS MOVEMENT

In the 1954 landmark U.S. Supreme Court ruling, Brown v. Board of Education, the courts decided that "separate but equal" was "inherently unequal." The court found segregation at all types of schools to run counter to the Fourteenth Amendment. The following year (December 1, 1955), Rosa Parks (1913 to 2005) refused to move to what was called "the Negro section of the bus." Dr. Martin Luther King, Jr. (1929 to 1968) called for a boycott of all municipal buses; the boycott lasted a year. Eight years after the Parks incident, racial tension mounted in Birmingham, Alabama. African Americans protested the cities' lack of desegregation. The black community called for boycotts of businesses that maintained "separate but equal" business practices. The city responded by halting

its distribution of food to the needy. King, leader of the Southern Christian Leadership Conference, decided that Birmingham would be their battleground for civil rights reform. In the Spring of 1963, he mounted multiple marches to picket segregated businesses. American discontent with status quo, especially within younger generations, was at an all-time high. In 1963, Bob Dylan (b. 1941) deliberately wrote "The Times They Are A-Changin" song in an attempt to create an understanding for the newest evolution of human society. The album was released the following March and became the anthem for his generation.

ARTISTIC MOVEMENTS

The years following World War II cemented the world's understanding regarding the freedoms enjoyed by Americans. Freedom of thought, expression, and individuality traversed the nation and then the globe as never before. Artists were frustrated by the perceived moral indifference of certain people and disgusted by the mind-numbing qualities of others. While they understood and identified with them as the governing characteristics of existentialism, they did not want them to

Societal Emphasis

The youth in America were consumed by the rebellious nature of the post-modern movement and the violence of multiple wars. In August 1969, the Woodstock Music Festival was organized by Artie Kornfeld (b. 1942), Michael Lang (b. 1944), John Roberts (1945 to 2001), and Joel Rosenman (b. 1942) as an investment opportunity. The festival took place on the Yasgur's dairy farm in Bethel, New York over a 3-day period. The audience was diverse and reflected the changing times. People were happy to have an escape from the controversy of the Vietnam War and the unrest that followed the Civil Rights Movement. The iconic film that recorded the event and the event's name "An Aquarian Experience: 3 Days of Peace and Music" summed up festivalgoers' sentiments perfectly.

dominate their artistic creativity. Works by Hans Hoffmann (1880 to 1966), Franz Kline (1910 to 1962), Willem de Kooning (1904 to 1997), and Jackson Pollock (1912 to 1956) traced their roots to Cubism, Kandinsky's virtually abstract canvases, and Surrealist artists' keen awareness of self-psychoanalysis. The artworks created by Abstract Expressionist artists were used by the United States State Department to stage an ambitious touring exhibition around Europe. Its purpose was to parade the ideals of an America with a free spirit, rampant with innovation. The world of art moved from Europe, especially Paris, to New York City. Artistic movements and media employed evolved rapidly.

Abstract Expressionism

The avoidance of recognizable forms was a hallmark of the Abstract Expressionism movement. The style developed in the United States after World War II until half-way through the 1960s. The artworks showcased the individual liberties that artists were afforded in America. Artists such as Clyfford Still (1904 to 1980) and Willem de Kooning (1904 to 1997)

envisioned that their works would reflect the "stream of consciousness" idea enjoyed by early-twentieth-century authors such as James Joyce (1882 to 1941) and Virginia Woolf (1882 to 1941). Joan Mitchell was a leading Abstract Expressionist during the 1960s who painted enormous works such as *La Grande Vallée* (fig. 15.6) a detailed view of the massive work. Her paintings consisted of overlapping lines, roiled color, and unrecognizable shapes. Mitchele once stated that "painting was like music – it is beyond life and death. It is another dimension."

The style of Abstract Expressionism varied widely among the artists' group in this category. The Abstract Expressionist Jackson Pollock (1912 to 1956) referred to his works as "action painting," where he dripped paint onto a canvas. He believed that his "drips" were a powerful, spontaneous expressions of who he was, rather than simply being a chance accumulation of paint on canvas. Mark Rothko (1903 to 1970) developed an entirely different style of Abstract Expressionism known as "color field painting." Rothko repudiated being labeled or having to adhere

Fig. 15.6 *La Grande Vallée* (detail), 1 in a suite of 21-painting, oil on canvas, Mitchell, MFAB, Boston, Massachusetts. 1962.

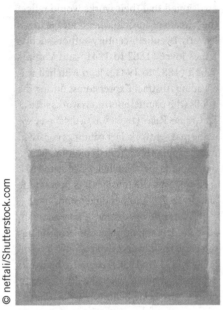

© neftali/Shutterstock.com

Fig. 15.7 *Orange and Yellow*, oil on canvas, Rothko, Albright-Knox Art Gallery, Buffalo, New York. 1956.

to any one artistic style. In *Orange and Yellow* (fig. 15.7), Rothko used vibrant colors with unfinished edges to suggest dynamic energy. His works aimed at eliciting an emotional reaction, as he once stated, "I am not interested

in the relationship between form and color." He believed that his works were profound expressions of humankind's basic emotions such as sorrow, elation, and fate. He encouraged viewers to stand exactly 18 inches from the canvas, close enough to engage the work and also be overwhelmed by it.

Op Art

For century, artists had been intrigued by the concepts of depth perception and optical illusion that could be artistically created on a two-dimensional plane. By the 1950s, their obsessions with these concepts had combined with newer technology and psychology, which blossomed into Optical Art, or Op Art. Their artworks employ repeated abstract patterns that reveal contrasts between the foreground and background. The Hungarian-French artist Victor Vasarely was the leader of the Op Art movement. Originally, Vasarely worked in black and white starting as early as 1937 with *Zebra* but transitioned to vibrant color to produce his disorientation to mind-disturbing painting (fig. 15.8). The works, for the most part, were painted to create an optical illusion when viewed because of the use of geometric forms.

© Dedo Luka/Shutterstock.com

Fig. 15.8 Op Art exhibition at the Vasarely Museum, Pecs, Hungary.

Hard Edge

The psychiatrist and art critic Jules Langsner (1911 to 1976) began noticing a new style of painting emerging in the late 1950s in California. The style developed out of the abstract tendencies of "color field painting" but employed cleaner lines and contrasting colors. Artists sought to avoid the soulful expression found in Abstract Expressionist works. They opted to unite the composition, color, and smooth surface into a seamlessly executed painting much like Mondrian (chapter 14) had. Furthermore, they detested the scores of less talented gestural abstraction artists who simply copied the "action painting" style with little regard for its true existential meaning.

Pop Art

In 1964, the sociologist Marshall McLuhan (1911 to 1980) coined the term, "The medium is the message." The phrase insinuated that media, primarily television, was a new form of **medium**, or a material used to create a work of art. A few years later he playfully changed the word *message* to *massage*, implying that the media massaged their beliefs into its audience. He further commented that "mass communication" provided by television was a one-directional medium conveyed to a passive audience unable to respond. He believed that the media existed only to "invest our lives with artificial perceptions and arbitrary values." In short, media created a society filled with desires that were all-consuming for what a person did not have.

McLuhan's sentiments were echoed in the work of American and Britain artists of the 1960s. They revolted against traditional approaches to creativity. Pop art emerged as a response to popular culture advancements in mass media. Newly graduated art students sought to connect their artistic creations to their daily lives. Many of these young artists did not relate to works found on the walls of the great fine art museums around the world. They were not motivated by artworks considered classical masterpieces. Instead, they turned to comic books, contemporary music, advertising, and Hollywood movies for inspiration. Everyday objects used for entertainment were more exciting and significant to these artists.

Claes Oldenburg (b. 1929) and his wife Coosje van Bruggen (1942 to 2009) collaborated extensively to create some of the most iconic pop art sculptures. Their larger-than-life sculptures *Spoonbridge and Cherry* (fig. 15.1), *Shuttlecock* (fig. 15.9), and *Flying Pins* (fig. 15.10) exemplify the concept of "realist" art that represented reality in terms that everyday people could understand.

Minimalism

Frank Stella (b. 1936) is credited with launching the artistic movement known as Minimalism. His works were predicated on the theories developed by hard-edge artists. Each movement asserted that the basic principle and elements of art were necessary to the overall design of an artwork. Minimalists also pondered over the essence and qualities of what made a piece of work a work of art, much like Duchamp (chapter 14). Minimalists, however, pushed the boundary by questioning what was minimally necessary to constitute a work of art. Pop art suggested that creating copies of everyday popular items in various media were themselves works of art. For them, their art was a commodity if someone purchased it or art if someone valued its existence. Minimalists opposed this idea and stressed the importance of a work's aesthetic quality and its simplicity as seen in Stella's *Hyena Stomp* (1962) and *Harran II* (1967) oil on canvas. Stella's creativity was not only confined to painting on canvas. He also extended his Minimalist ideas onto a 1975 BMW 3.0 CSL automobile

Fig. 15.9 *Shuttlecocks*, aluminum and fiber-reinforced plastic with painted polyurethane enamel, Oldenburg and van Bruggen, installed, Kansas City, Missouri. 1994.

Fig. 15.10 *Flying Pins*, steel, fiber-reinforced plastic, polyvinyl chloride foam with polyester gelcoat and polyurethane enamel, Oldenburg and van Bruggen, Eindhoven, Netherlands. 2000.

(fig. 15.11) for the BMW Art Car Project introduced by French racecar driver and auctioneer Hervé Poulain (b. 1940).

Conceptual Art

While Minimalists tried to redefine the aesthetical qualities of what made a piece of work a work of art, conceptual artists, also referred to as Neo-Dadaist, returned to Duchamp's ready-made idea for inspiration. Robert Rauschenberg (1925 to 2008) spent decades as a political and social activist before returning to his studio to focus on a single material for an extended period of time. His choice was cardboard. The material was readily abandoned after it fulfilled its intended transportation duty, making it easily obtainable. His *Plain Salt (Cardboards)* created in 1971 allowed him to bring a sense of dignity to an ordinary material, while conceding to its lackluster commercial use. In a later conceptual display of originality, Rauschenberg

produced a series he termed *Bicycloid*. His *Bicycloid IV* (fig 15.12) creation consisted of a vintage bicycle outlined with neon-tubing to emphasize the objects overall visual aesthetics and was then mounted on an aluminum base.

Photorealism

The movement Photorealism, also called Superrealism, began in the 1960s in America. Artists Chuck Close (b. 1940), Ralph Goings (1928 to 2016), and Audrey Flack (b. 1931) endeavored to reproduce photographic images with camera-like quality. Photorealism artists were drawn to the everyday subject matter of commercial life, much like pop art and minimalism. Artists of the movement normally projected a photographed picture onto the canvas and airbrushed the image into picture perfect, high-gloss reproduction. The resulting image was almost indistinguishable from the photograph used to make the painting.

Fig. 15.11 1975 BMW 3.0 CS, painted in a black and white grid, Stella, BMW Group, Munich, Germany. 1975.

© Eric Broder Van Dyke/Shutterstock.com

Fig. 15.12 *Bicycloid IV*, bicycle with neon-tubing and aluminum base, Rauschenberg, Tokyo, Japan. 1994.

Fig. 15.13 *Do Women have to be Naked to Get Into the Met Museum?*, poster, Guerrilla Girls, MFAB, Boston, Massachusetts. 1989.

Feminist Art

Art historian Linda Nochlin (1931 to 217) questioned the ability of modern society to recognize female artists in her essay titled "Why Have There Been No Great Women Artists?" in 1971. In the essay, she examined factors leading to the inability of talented women to attain the same artistic accolades as those of their male counterparts. Judy Chicago (b. 1939), in reaction to the growing feminine movement, created the iconic exhibition *The Dinner Party* in 1979. The installation was a triangular table set for 39 of the most prominent, creative female figures throughout history, with another 999 names inscribed in gold on the white tile floor. In 1985, the American female art activist group, Guerrilla Girls, was formed. This group was outraged to discover the exhibition "An International Survey of Painting and Sculpture" mounted by the Museum of Modern Art featuring 169 artists with only 13 women included. One of the most iconic posters they displayed in 1989 was titled *Do Women have to be Naked to Get Into the Met Museum?* (fig. 15.13) The group has since widened its focus to include multiple aspects of perceived social injustice.

Land or Site-Specific Art

Land or site-specific art drew inspiration from both Minimalism and conceptual art. Artists of the movement take the location into consideration when conceptualizing the artwork. Works of art designed specifically for a location, such as Smithson's *Spiral Jetty* (fig. 15.14) and Christo Javacheff (b. 1935) and Jeanne-Claude's (1935 to 2009) *The Floating Piers* (fig. 15.15),

would lose its meaning if removed and are referred to as "installation art or land art."

CREATIVE IMPULSE

Literary rejection was not a novel concept in the years following World War II. In fact, the concept was developed at the turn of the twentieth century by modernist artists such as Duchamp, Kandinsky,

Fig. 15.14 *Spiral Jetty*, rock and dirt, Smithson, Great Salt Lake, Utah. 1970.

Fig. 15.15 *The Floating Piers*, yellow fabric, Christo and Jeanne-Claude, Lake Ieso, Italy. 2014.

Malevich, and Mondrian. Modernists yearned to express their worldview devoid of illustrating a historical or cultural event via text. Early post-modernists, Mitchell, Pollock, Rothko, Stella, and Vasarley, used lines, colors, and patterns to evoke a feeling and impart a reaction. But, their works left viewers confused as they did not see a story to help them understand the message. When audiences view Millet's *The Gleaners* (fig. 12.14), they can fashion a story about the three figures. In Stella's works, there was no story to create because Stella stated:

> My painting is based on the fact that only what you can see there *is* there. It really is an object…What you see is what you see

For post-modern artists, to accept the past was to realize the present and seize the future.

Architecture

The transition from modernism to post-modernism began in the 1970s as architects started to reject the clean lines of the preceding decades. Post-modern architects freely borrowed from all styles and used opposing elements as their hallmark. True to the ideals of pop art, the *Centre Pompidou* (fig. 15.16) designed by Richard Rogers (b. 1933) and Renzo Piano (b. 1937) makes ordinary aspects of a building unexpected focal points. The façade of the Centre resembles a building still under construction with scaffolding. The escalators and air ducts, traditionally hidden from view, are displayed on the outside of the building. The entire structure is painted in bright colors. The plastic-covered escalator looks like a giant caterpillar. The structures provide a playful happiness in contrast to its more serious surroundings of Gothic cathedrals and French-style buildings.

© Roka/Shutterstock.com

Fig. 15.16 *Centre Pompidou*, steel, cables, nuts, and bolts, Rogers and Piano, Paris, France. 1971 to 1977.

Another non-traditional architectural building to emerge was the *Dancing Hall (Fred and Ginger)* designed by architects Frank Gehry (b. 1929) and Vlado Milunić (b. 1941) in the Czech Republic (fig. 15.17). The original dance hall was destroyed by bombs in 1945. The style is known as **deconstructivist**, or new-Baroque, because of its overall unusual shape. The architects used a static and dynamic contrast between the seemingly "dancing" figure on the left and the "standing" figure on the right. Milunić, who initially designed the façade, and Gehry, an invited collaborator, wanted to maintain Milunić original symbolic design that commemorated Czechoslovakia transition from a communist regime to a democracy.

At roughly the same time as Gehry was collaborating on the *Dancing Hall,* he designed the *Guggenheim Museum Bilbao* in Spain (fig. 15.18). Gehry used organic shapes

usually used by sculptors to turn the building into one that blurs the distinction between a sculpture and a building, prompting one to ask "Can architects be sculptors too?" At first glance, the museum's design resembles a ship to possibly pay homage to the Nervión River it calls "home." Then, on closer inspection, the structures bear a resemblance to shiny fish swimming in the river. The museum's overall unique design, like the Guggenheim in New York, may compete with its interior exhibitions for viewers' attention.

Sculptures

Numerous sculptors turned to abstraction at the turn of the century, including Isamu Noguchi (1904 to 1988), Henry Moore (1898 to 1986), and Constantin Brâncuși (1876 to 1957). Among them, Alexander Calder (1898 to 1976) was concerned with motion in his works. As the inventor of the **hanging mobile**, or a kinetic sculpture taking

© Vladimir Sazonov/Shutterstock.com

Fig. 15.17 *Dancing Hall (Fred and Ginger),* glass, concrete, steel, Gehry and Milunić, Prague, Czech Republic, 1992 to 1996.

© Manuel Ascanio/Shutterstock.com

Fig. 15.18 *Guggenheim Museum Bilbao,* glass, limestone, and titanium, Gehry, Bilbao, Spain. 1991 to 1997.

advantage of the equilibrium principle, he designed sculpture to react to wind currents and produce multiple views of the same artwork.

Calder's kinetic sculpture such as *Carmen* (fig. 15.19) was quite a different type of free-standing sculpture with a number of viewpoints. One could take a number of photographs of free-standing sculpture, but there is no fixed version of a mobile. Its shapes change as the artwork is blown by wind. Motion is an inherent part of the hanging-mobile art form.

Henry Moore (1898 to 1986) attended the Royal College of Art in London. He became interested in art from the Prehistoric era after vising Stonehenge located in Wiltshire, England. Stonehenge intrigued him at that time and stuck with him throughout his career, influencing him in two ways. In his works, he wanted to have an evident connection with ancient civilizations, and second, he wanted to be able to do large-scale

pieces. *Large Reclining Figure* (fig. 15.20) reflected his purposeful selection of organic shapes designed to imitate the natural beauty of the human form, as well as his interest in the art of the Mayan and African cultures. Moore continually valued the art of ancient cultures and wanted to tie the past to the present.

Painting

Jackson Pollock (1912 to 1956) was in his prime, only 44 years old, when he died in an automobile accident. Pollock had a somewhat troubled youth, during which the problems that eventually caused his death first began. The primary problem seems to have been alcoholism stemming from the continual movement of his family since childhood. At age 18, Pollock moved to New York and studied with Thomas Hart Benton, a regionalist painter at the Art Students League. He was hired during the Great Depression

© Manuel Ascanio/Shutterstock.com

Fig. 15.19 *Carmen*, aluminum sheet, iron sheet, and paint, Calder, Lawnton, PA, 1974.

© Ron Ellis/Shutterstock.com

Fig. 15.20 *Large Reclining Figure*, lead maquette, Moore, Kew Gardens, London, England. 1984.

to work for a federally funded program in which artists were hired to paint murals in public buildings. He managed to produce one major work suitable for installation approximately every 6 weeks. He realized at that time that he had to do something about his drinking problem, and he sought help through psychotherapy.

The years between 1948 and 1952 were when most of the paintings known as his "drip" or action painting were accomplished. Convergence (fig. 15.21) demonstrates Pollock's experimentation with paint thrown from buckets or dropped to create lines on canvas that failed to become shapes. The lines intersected and still remained visibly, distinguishable lines. His idea was to play with his own subconscious feelings. Some canvases were so large that he actually walked onto the canvas and threw paint down in streams of lines onto its surface. The finished product was a mixture of several colors of lines in layers of textures. Each was vibrant and full of patterns that seem to defy known definitions of art.

To Pollock, this was his expression. His drip paintings were a significant style that advanced the art world.

Printmaking

The newer technology of **photopolymer** or solarplate printing eliminated many of the problems associated with traditional printmaking such as the use of harsh chemicals. Starting in the 1960s, newspapers used polymer plates instead of traditional metal plates. The use of polymer plates prompted Dan Welden to start "experimenting with light sensitive polymer plates" in order to find an easier alternative to metal plate etching. He discovered that if the polymer plate was exposed to sunlight, a high-quality intaglio like plate was created. By 1972, the process for solarplate printing had been born. Welden's method was a faster, non-toxic approach to creating an edition than traditional etching and relief printing.

Many of the techniques for producing an artwork with this process are the same as those for the traditional method. However,

Fig. 15.21 *Convergence*, enamel on canvas, Pollock, Albright-Knox Art Gallery, Buffalo, New York. 1952.

© neftali/Shutterstock.com

the beginning methods may vary from person to person and from work to work. There are three common elements artists use when producing a solarplate print. These are (1) a transparency or translucent film, (2) a solarplate, and (3) sunlight/ultraviolet exposure. The variation in the beginning step depends on the artist's preference.

Andy Warhol (1928 to 1987) entered the Carnegie Institute of Technology in Pittsburgh after graduating high school. He received considerable attention from the film industry for his off-the-wall ideas. His film about a person sleeping gained him artistic recognition, and he continued to make films and create art. In time, Warhol worked on perfecting his skill at printmaking. He began using ink and silk to produce silk screens. Warhol produced silk screens of Marilyn Monroe (1926 to 1962), a film icon who rapidly rose to fame. He also created a series of silk screens of Campbell's soup cans and *Mao Tse-Tung* (fig 15.22).

Another innovative development was when Romare Bearden (1911 to 1988) used his collage works to produce prints. Originally, Bearden's artworks were inspired by the use of fragmented rhythms of jazz. He used magazine clippings to assemble the identity and life of black America as seen in images his 1964 collage images *The Train* and *The Dove*. Both collage works used a cut-and-paste technique with gouache, pencil, and colored pencil on board to create a unique artistic expression.

Graffiti

As an art form, graffiti was started by a Greek American teenager in 1972, who **tagged**, or signed, his work TAKI183 to denote his name and street address. By 1975, the youth in the Bronx, Queens, and Brooklyn began spray-painting colorful murals onto the side of trains after breaking into the train yards. Soon, galleries and art dealers around the world were displaying and selling graffiti art. The New York City Transit Authority was less than excited about the open displays of trespassing and vandalism. They placed dogs in the train yards, put up barbed-wired fences, removed the paint with acid, and stationed undercover police at the yards. Today, graffiti artists are provided an outdoor exhibition space (fig. 15.23) in Queens, New York to showcase their talents on a building known as "5 Pointz."

© Radu Bercan/Shutterstock.com

Fig. 15.22 *Mao Tse-Tung (series)*, screenprint on paper, on display in 2015 at the Albertina Museum, Vienna, Austria. 1972.

© starmaro/Shutterstock.com

Fig. 15.23 "5 Pointz" graffiti building in Queens, New York.

Music, Dance, and Theater

Musical theater with dance became a popular genre in the late twentieth century. Both Leonard Bernstein (1918 to 1990) and Andrew Lloyd Webber (b. 1948) created sensational musical theatrical pieces. Bernstein was successful in introducing a generation of young people to *The Young People's Guide to the Orchestra* (1945) through his lectures. His work in popular musical theater pieces such as *West Side Story* (1957) reinvented Shakespeare's *Romeo and Juliet*. Webber is one of the most prolific composers of musical production with the longest-running Broadway shows such as the rock opera *Jesus Christ Superstar* (1970) based on the last 7 days of Jesus's life. His 1981 production *Cats* (fig. 15.24a and b) is based on the poetry of T.S. Eliot (chapter 14).

Radio Music

Music heard on the radio was not new to the post-modern world. The first transmission of music over the radio was in 1906 by a Canadian experimenter named Reginald Fessenden (1833 to 1932). Radio grew during World War I and witnessed its golden age between 1930 and 1955. But, the 1960s witnessed new initiatives with the development of **frequency modulation** radio that had a constant amplitude for better sound quality.

Quality radio paralleled the emergence of **rock and roll**, or strong beat music with vocals, of the late 1950s. Early rock artists changed the world with their new beats and expressive lyrics. Elvis Presley (1935 to 1977) set the tone for rock and roll music. He had an elastic voice and good looks. His first appearance on *The Ed Sullivan Show* (a television show, fig. 15.25) on September 9, 1956 was electric, as women in the audience went crazy for his movies. People wanted more Elvis Presley. His songs were outrageously different and ranged widely from gospel to romance to simply emotion charged. More than 4 decades after his death people still admire his talents.

(a)

(b)

© kojoku/Shutterstock.com

© JStone/Shutterstock.com

Fig. 15.24 (a) and (b) *Cats*, musical theater, Webber, New York, New York. 1981.

Cross-cultural Connection

George Harrison, a member of The Beatles, traveled to India in 1966 to study the **sitar**, or a plucked stringed instrument, with Pandit Ravi Shankar (1920 to 2012). While there, Harrison met Maharishi Mahesh Yogi (1918 to 2008) and transformed his life with meditation, which helped him stop using the drug lysergic acid diethylamide. Three years later, Harrison performed the Beatles single "Hare Krishna Mantra." As a result of his experiences with Hinduism, Harrison believed that "life on Earth is but a fleeting illusion edged between lives past and future beyond physical mortal reality."

Fig. 15.25 Elvis's appearance on *The Ed Sullivan Show*, 1956.

If Elvis put rock and roll into motion, a British rock band, "The Beatles" (fig. 15.26), ramped it into high gear in the early 1960s. Band members included John Lennon (1940 to 1980), Paul McCartney (b. 1942), George Harrison (1943 to 2001), and Ringo Star (b. 1940) all born in Liverpool, England. In 1964, their music reached America, causing *Beatlemania*. Their music was originally regarded as a juvenile genre, but Lennon and McCartney quickly evolved the band's music to become more sophisticated and varied. For young listeners, "The Beatles" were more than just musicians. They represented the hedonistic and experimental pleasures of the new **counterculture**, or a way of life opposed to social norms. The band reinvented the meaning of rock and roll as a cultural force. But by the spring of 1970, "The Beatles" had formally disbanded.

Later music genres developed, such as heavy metal, pop rock, and hip-hop or rap. Of these newer developments, hip-hop was a distinctive style of music that originated in the economically depressed South Bronx area of New York City. The area was predominantly African American at the time. Pioneering hip-hop **deejay**, or a person who conducted the program, DJ Kool Herc, also known as Clive Campbell (b. 1955), used two turntables to meld fragments of older songs and popular songs together for a continuous flow.

The first successful hip-hop group was the "Sugarhill Gang" with its 1979 song *Rapper's Delight*. From this, other groups began to emerge, such as "Grandmaster Flash and the Furious Five" (fig. 15.27), whose album *The Message* was a social platform describing inner city poverty. The group influenced later rappers such as "Public Enemy" and "N.W.A."

Film

In 1959, Alfred Hitchcock (1899 to 1980) made the film *North by Northwest* about a twice-divorced, sleekly handsome debonair mistaken for someone else. One famous scene

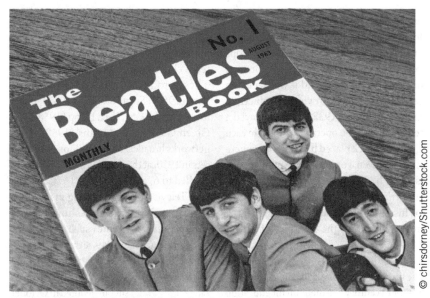

Fig. 15.26 "The Beatle Monthly Book," August 1963.

© chirsdorney/Shutterstock.com

Fig. 15.27 Grandmaster Flash and the Furious Five (Scorpio, Mele Mel, Kid Creole, and Rahiem), Rock and Roll Hall of Fame induction. March 12, 2007.

© Everett Collection/Shutterstock.com

was of the crop duster airplane swooping down upon Cary Grant (1904 to 1986) in a field out in a barren area with no crops to be dusted. In 1960, Hitchcock directed and produced *Psycho*, and it was seen as a departure from his previous production. Anthony Perkins (1932 to 1992) played a demented son who operated a motel. In each film, Hitchcock placed himself somewhere in a scene, even if only for half a minute, such as when he got on a bus at the beginning of *North by Northwest*. He was best known for his ability to create suspense, making an audience enjoy the emotions of terror.

Television

The history of the television dates to the early twentieth century as a medium for education and mass communication. Broadcasting of television programs existed prior to World War II but was suspended during the war and

did not resume until 1948. Once broadcasting resumed, television was instrumental in marketing the plethora of new products and retail chains that developed in the 1950s. These products included Kraft Minute Rice (1950), Sugar Smacks (1953), Crest toothpaste (1955), Hula Hoop (1958), and Green Giant canned beans (1958). Four networks broadcast to 3.1 million television sets in 1950; at the decade's end, the number swelled to 67 million.

Television programming in America transitioned from **variety shows**, or live entertainment, to genres such as westerns and game shows. In 1949, **sitcoms**, or situation comedy, emerged as weekly, 30-minute shows with a reappearing cast. The *I Love Lucy* (fig. 15.28) sitcom debuted in October 1951 starring Lucille Ball (1911 to 1989) and her husband Desi Arnaz (1917 to 1986) and it ushered in a revolution in American

© catwalker/Shutterstock.com

Fig. 15.28 Commemorative stamp; Season 2 Episode 1, Continuous Flow in the Candy Factory. 1952.

television. The show's popular appeal was attributed to the main character, Lucy, who wanted to be more than a housewife. She wanted a career and this idea resonated with female viewers.

On September 26, 1960, the first ever presidential debate was broadcast between Senator John F. Kennedy (1917 to 1963) and Vice President Richard M. Nixon 1913 to 1944) in black and white. The debate was simultaneously broadcast, or **simulcast**, on the three networks with an estimated audience of 70 million. Television allowed for important political questions to be discussed in more than the 30-second commercials that candidates previously used. Controversy quickly erupted over the television broadcasting of the debate. People who listened to the debate on the radio believed Nixon to be the more qualified and articulate candidate. Television watchers believed Kennedy was more suited for the presidency. A large number of viewers saw, for the first time, the appearance of each candidate. Kennedy appeared tan, younger, and dressed in a dark suit, while Nixon seemed haggard in his gray suit with hastily applied makeup to conceal his facial stubble. (Watch video clips of the Kennedy/Nixon debate found in the "Online Resources.") To this day, these sorts of subtle visual nuances are carefully controlled by the candidate's debate preppers.

The years and decades to follow witnessed a number of mostly sitcoms aimed at entertaining and transforming American minds. Each show's writers were on the cutting edge and challenged the American perception of life within different demographs. These shows tackled every topic from politics to race relations and social mores to family values. These sitcoms included "My Three Sons" (1960), "The Brady Bunch" (1969), "All in the Family" (1971), "The Waltons" (1971),

"Sanford and Son" (1972), "The Jeffersons" (1975), "Eight Is Enough" (1977), "Family Ties" (1982), "The Cosby Show" (1984), "Married with Children" (1986), "The Wonder Years" (1988), "Roseann" (1988, 2018), "Seinfeld" (1989), "The Simpsons" (1989), "Ellen" (1994), "Friends" (1994), "Modern Family" (2009), and "Black-ish" (2014).

Literature

Post-modern America was consumed with science fiction, or sci-fi, and fantasy genera. Both allowed the mind to explore the unthinkable or unattainable aspect of the world and human nature. Russian-born American author and biochemist Isaac Asimov (1920 to 1992) was a prolific writer of sci-fi. His two most notable volumes were the Foundation and robot series. The Foundation trilogy was a collection of stories written between the tumultuous years of 1942 and 1949 and brought together from 1951 to 1953. The series mimics the fall of the Roman Empire but is set in the last days of his fictional Galactic Empire. One of the main characters Hari Seldon, a mathematics professor, develops psychohistory to help predict future events in probabilistic terms. His psychohistory algorithm predicted the fall of the Galactic Empire, and the "Foundation" team strove to shorten the galactic dark age from 30,000 to 1,000 years. The trilogy *Foundation* (1951), *Foundation and the Empire* (1952), and *Second Foundation* (1952) was the first example of a sci-fi collection to use the "Science Fiction Cosmology" later identified by Donald A. Wollheim (1914 to 1990) in the 1950s. For experienced sci-fi readers, the "cosmology" only needs to be hinted at for them to piece together the story's background details and possible future. Asimov received 14 honorary doctorate degrees, the Humanist of the Year award in 1984, and numerous other awards.

Global Focal Point

Christo and Jeanne-Claude's work titled *The Umbrellas* was unveiled in 1991 on opposite sides of the Pacific Ocean, California and Japan, with a cost of $26 million. They used yellow and blue to symbolize the cultural difference but umbrellas to acknowledge their global interdependency. These two locations were the places where the electronic revolution had sprung. The artists sought to accentuate the differences of the landscape. Christo and Jeanne-Claude negotiated with 452 landowners in Japan, while in America they only needed to negotiate with 26 landowners to gain permission to use their land for the project. While Japan's land usage was cramped, California's was open and owned by far fewer individuals. Their decision to use umbrellas underscored the fact that no matter how different they were culturally, both used the umbrella for protection and shelter form the rain and the sun.

Columbian novelist Gabriel García Márquez (1927 to 2014) wove together a utopia in the fictitious town of Macondo in Colombia with his *One Hundred Years of Solitude* of 1967. Márquez used the novel to present the many different national myths within Columbian history as told by seven generations of the Buendía family. The novel traces important Columbian historical events such as political reformations for and against Liberal colonial life, arrival of the railway to very remote areas, the introduction of the United Fruit Company, the advent of cinema and the automobile, and a military massacre of striking workers. Márquez overlaps myth with reality while exploring the fluidity of time and the families' proclivity toward incest on account of their remote location of solitude. The novel earned Márquez a Nobel Prize for Literature in 1982.

American author David Foster Wallace (1962 to 2008) wrote *Girl with Curious Hair*, a collection of short stories, in 1989. Each story provided a unique examination of American life from its fascination with celebrities to Wallace's apprehension about contemporary trends in fiction. The last short story "West ward the Course of Empire Takes Its Way" was Wallace's comprehensive response to John Bath's (b. 1930) *Lost in the Funhouse*, written in 1968, and a precursor to his 1996 novel *Infinite Jest*. The book is set in a future where the United States, Canada, and Mexico comprise the Organization of the North American Nations, and year numbers are replaced by corporate products such as Year of the Trail-Size Dove Bar. The book contains four major interwoven narratives that are connected in the file *Infinite Jest*, or "the Entertainment." The novel touches on a variety of topics from multiple forms of addiction, family relations, mental health including suicide, film theory, and national identity. Wallace based part of the novel of the play *Hamlet* with a link to the *Odyssey* and *The Brother Karamazov* by Russian author Fyodor Dostoevsky (1821 to 1881). The file *Infinite Jest* featured in the novel has been equated to the 1969 Monty Python sketch "The Funniest Joke in the World." The book is classified as an **encyclopedic novel** on account of its experimental use of endnotes, resulting in a length of 1,079 pages. In 2005, *Time* magazine listed it as one of the 100 best English-language novels published between 1923 and 2005.

Philosophy

Two philosophers, Jean-Paul Sartre (1905 to 1980) and Simone de Beauvoir (1908 to 1986), were on the cutting edge of Modernism. While both were active during the Modernism period, their profound impact on post-modern society pushes them into the post-modern classification. Sartre, like Camus (Chapter 14), was another French existentialist with slugfest political thought, who even praised the Soviet Union's actions during the Cold War. Unlike Camus, he refused the Noble Prize in literature when it was offered to him. In his 1943 essay, "Being and Nothingness," he viewed humanity at its best when rebelling against the aloofness of society. He believed that humankind was "condemned to be free" and a person's actions should not reside in self-victimization or blaming others for their problems. In his 1944 play, *No Exit*, he explored the dynamics between three individuals, a man, lesbian, and a vacuous beauty, trapped in a nicely furnished room. Each one likes the opposite, who in turn does not like them. Sartre created an atypical love triangle. At the end of the play, the man concludes that "Hell is other people!"

Simone de Beauvoir was Sartre's life-long intimate companion, even though they both maintained independent lives. Their relationship knowingly challenged the bourgeois belief in respectable relationship values. She wrote four volumes of memoirs that illustrated and championed the unrestricted nature of their relationship. In her 1949 book, *The Second Sex*, she worked toward deflating what she termed "the myth of feminity." She argued that most women were "very often very well pleased with her role as *Other*" to have a secondary status next to men. De Beauvoir stated:

> Man-the-sovereign will provide woman-the-liege with material protection and will undertake the moral justification of her existence; thus she can evade a once both economic risk and the metaphysical risk . . . This is an inauspicious road . . . But it is an easy road; on it one avoids the strains involved in undertaking an authentic existence.

Her book outlined the need for women to create an authentic existence separate from their male counterparts. She is credited with further prompting the growing feminist movement.

Science

If the modernist world of the early twentieth century was dominated by discoveries in physics, the post-modernist world gravitated toward the biological sciences to illuminate its understanding of humankind. The first vaccination for polio was developed in 1952

Innovation and Progress

Electronic media transformed society ever since Thomas Edison's (chapter 14) first audio recording. The advancements in film and the digital age of the Internet each impacted the arts differently. Nam June Paik (1932 to 2006), a Korean-born artist, made video a useful medium form with his *Video Flag* installation from 1985 to 1996. The installation featured 70 video monitors, four laser displayers, a computer, timers, and electrical devices to operate it.

by Jonas Salk (1914 to 1995) and first used in 1955 after 3 years of placebo-controlled testing in Canada, Finland, and the United States. The year 1953 saw major advancements in the structural appearance of DNA as a double helix by James Watson (b. 1928) and Francis Crick (1916 to 2004) with the assistance of Rosalind Franklin's (1920 to 1958) x-ray diffraction picture. In 1958, the first understanding of the protein structure as three-dimensional was published by Sir John Kendrew (1917 to 1997). Nine years after unlocking the structure of DNA, Crick and three of his colleagues, Sydney Brenner (b. 1927), Leslie Barnett (1920 to 2002), and Richard Watts-Tobin, proposed **codons**, or three nitrogenous bases, that code for a single amino acid.

By 1970, the scientists David Baltimore (b. 1938), working independently, and Howard Termin (1934 to 1994), along with Japanese virologist Satoshi Mizutani, had unlocked the mystery of **reverse transcription**, or the reversal of normal DNA transpiration found in RNA viruses. In 1977, Fredrick Sanger (1918 to 2013) and his colleagues, Walter Gilbert (b. 1932) and Paul Berg (b. 1926), introduced the "Sanger method" used to accurately and rapidly sequence portions of DNA. The discovery earned the three a Nobel Prize in Chemistry in 1980, for Sanger a second one. After 40 years of gigantic leaps forward in biological science, the Human Genome Project was launched in 1990 and was estimated to take 15 years to fully unlock the secrets of humanity's DNA. The project concluded in April 2003, which coincided with the 50th anniversary of Watson and Crick's publication of the DNA structure.

Technology

The 1950s and 1960s were fueled by humankind's fascination with hurling a human into space. As the Cold War affected many aspects of everyday life, the two opposing

Superpowers wanted to be the first to claim space as their own. In 1957, Russia launched the first man-made object, **Sputnik** meaning "traveler," into space. The object was also the first satellite to orbit earth. Not to be outdone by Russia, the United States launched its own satellite, Explorer I, in 1958. The "space race" intensified over the next few years. Then in 1961, President Kennedy boldly, and very publicly, announced that the United States, "should commit itself to achieving the goal, before this decade is out, of landing a man on the Moon and returning him safely to the Earth." On July 16, 1969, three astronauts, Edwin "Buzz" Aldrin (b. 1930), Neil Armstrong (1930 to 2012), and Michael Collins (b. 1930), attempted the first lunar landing with success. Armstrong was the first man to walk on the moon as he famously said, "one small step for man, one giant leap for mankind." The United States had effectively "won" the race, with Americans landing on the moon. The Russians made four failed attempts between 1969 and 1972 and never put a man on the moon.

The rise of the personal computer created by Steve Jobs (1955 to 2011), Steve Wozniak (b. 1950), and Ronald Wayne (b. 1934) ushered in the Information Age of the 1980s to the present day. The three men co-founded the company Apple on April 1, 1976 with a computer designed and hand-built by Wozniak. Personal computers were of little use to the ordinary person until the invention of the World Wide Web by Sir Timothy Berners-Lee (b. 1955) by 1989. The early days of the Internet used scientists to communicate with other scientists. Also, the Internet was controlled by the US government until 1984, making it only possible for Berners-Lee to propose the global Internet after that time.

Wozniak's first computer, Apple I, was available for purchase in July 1976 with a market price of $666.66, or inflation adjusted to $2,957.66 in 2018. In 1984, Apple launched the first personal computer, Macintosh (fig. 15.29), sold without a programming language. Sales for the device were good, but the high price and limited range of software damped its appeal to the masses. By the 1990s, Apple products had been in decline and the company restructured its product line. The company regained its profitability in the late 1990s but became exceedingly successful with the launch of the iPhone in 2007.

POST-MODERNISM LEGACY

While most accounts of post-modernism place its emergence in the 1970s, the world after World War II was forever changed.

Concepts of what was considered an acceptable "norm" were challenged. People fostered different opinions regarding human beings' relationship with one another. Questions ran rampant, some of them being "Who am I?," "How did I get here?," and "How can I make my life useful?" Artists were paving the way for society to seek alternate avenues for answering these questions. Religious faith in the West collapsed even more as the decades rushed by and people settled into the new way of life. The 1970s gave way to the digital dot-com era powered by the newer form of mass communication, electronic mail or e-mail. The many advantages of the Information Age were realized through the process of globalization via globalism but so were the pitfalls of a world consumed with fastness.

Fig. 15.29 Apple Macintosh, 1984.

© Taner Muhlis Karaguzel/Shutterstock.com

Critical Thinking

Examine the differences between the artistic movements of the later twentieth century.

Evaluate the ramifications of World War II, Cold War, and Vietnam War.

Describe the major technological advancements of the later twentieth century.

Analyze how each successive art movement led to the next.

Examine the impact film and television had on society.

Illustrate how artistic expression was transformed during the later twentieth century.

Online Resources

Abstract Expressionism Overview
https://smarthistory.org/abstract-expressionism-an-introduction/
Pop Art (Contemporary) Overview
https://smarthistory.org/contemporary-art-an-introduction/
Minimalism Overview
https://smarthistory.org/an-introduction-to-minimalism/
Conceptual Art Overview
https://smarthistory.org/conceptual-art-introduction/
Vietnam War Overview
https://www.khanacademy.org/humanities/us-history/postwarera/1960s-america/a/
the-vietnam-war
Lin's *Vietnam Veterans Memorial* Video
https://smarthistory.org/maya-lin-vietnam-veterans-memorial/
Gehry's *Guggenheim Bilbo*
https://smarthistory.org/frank-gehry-guggenheim-bilbao/
The Berlin Wall, A Symbol of the Cold War
https://smarthistory.org/the-berlin-wall/
The Case for Mark Rothko and His Art
https://smarthistory.org/the-case-for-mark-rothko/
The Importance of Jackson Pollock Art
https://smarthistory.org/why-is-that-important-looking-at-jackson-pollock/
The Case for Andy Warhol and His Art
https://smarthistory.org/case-for-andy-warhol/
Oldenburg's *Lipstick*
https://smarthistory.org/oldenburg-lipstick-ascending-on-caterpillar-tracks/
Smithson's *Spiral Jetty* Video
https://smarthistory.org/robert-smithson-spiral-jetty/
Calder's *Mobile* Video
https://smarthistory.org/alexander-calder-mobile/
Characters of Musical *Cats*
https://www.catsthemusical.com/characters
The Music of Elvis Presley
https://www.elvisthemusic.com/
Explore Songs by The Beatles
https://www.thebeatles.com/explore-songs

Watch an Episode of *I Love Lucy*
https://www.cbs.com/shows/i_love_lucy/
Jean-Paul Sartre, Life and Works
https://www.nobelprize.org/prizes/literature/1964/sartre/biographical/
Race to the Moon
https://video.nationalgeographic.com/video/00000144-0a34-d3cb-a96c-7b3dfba00000

Globalism:
Redefining Social Norms

Fig. 16.1 *Stop and Search (Girl and a Soldier)*, stencil and spray paint, Banksy, Bethlehem, Israel. 2007.

© Murrissey72/Shutterstock.com

Knowledge Acquisition

◆ *Examine the artistic and cultural shifts made during the first few decades of the twenty-first century.*

◆ *Evaluate the principal accomplishments emerging in a global era.*

◆ *Discover how artists of the global era connect their works to cultural, political, and social interests.*

SETTING THE SCENE

The twenty-first century commenced on January 1, 2001, a year after the mad panic to reconcile the **Year 2000 bug**, Y2K or Millennium Bug, before the supposed digital "end of the world." Exactly 254 days into the twenty-first century on September 11, 2001 (9/11), Americans received what felt like a rippling shockwave of the "end of our world" as they knew it. The event also made people globally standstill in spine-chilling numbness. The devastating event killed nearly 3,000 people with three attacks simultaneously planned by **terrorists**, or people who unlawfully incite violence primarily against civilians for political purposes. The attacks were carried out by hijackers who used commercial airplanes to target the World Trade Center Towers in New York City and the Pentagon in Washington, DC. A third airplane, United Airline Flight 93, was more than likely on its way to the U.S. Capitol Building, but was stopped in its mission as passengers fought back and crashed the plane into a field in Pennsylvania. Today, a multiacre memorial (fig. 16.2) resides at the location where the "Twin Towers," or the World Trade Center Towers, were originally located. The memorial stands as a tribute to the past and hope for the future. The two large, black squares are the largest man-made waterfalls in America, with each nearly 1 acre in size.

Almost 5 years after the events of 9/11, Hurricane Katrina devastated portions of New Orleans when more than 1,800 lives were lost as a result of a category five hurricane and levee failures. Neither of these events compared with the deadliest loss of life generated by a tsunami that struck off the coast of the Indonesian island of Sumatra in the Indian Ocean. More than 225,000 people perished across dozens of countries on December 26, 2004.

© BrandonKleinVideo/Shutterstock.com

Fig. 16.2 Aerial view of the 9/11 Memorial in New York City.

The close of the first decade did not end in utter disarray. On November 4, 2008, the American people elected the first African American, Barack Obama (b. 1681), as the 44th President of United States. Two women, Elena Kagan (b. 1960) and Sonia Sotomayor (b. 1954), were appointed to the Supreme Court of the United States. In other world news, China became an economic power and the Olympic Games returned to its birthplace, Athens, Greece, in 2004. The world watched as 33 Chilean miners trapped underground for 69 days were miraculously safely rescued.

Other developments in the first part of the twenty-first century were that of cross-cultural exchanges of ideas and new invention. The twenty-first century witnessed growth in the development of fine arts, new forms of architecture, and a broader availability of the Internet and other forms of communication. The Internet opened up different social network platforms such as Facebook, Flickr, Instagram, LinkedIn, Meetup, Pinterest, Tumblr, Twitter, Wattpad, Weibo, Yammer, YouTube, and so many others.

Globalism and Globalization

The terms globalism and globalization signify complex changes of international interaction that date to the early 1600s in accordance with global exploration and cross-cultural encounters (Chapter 8). **Globalism** is based on interconnected, multinational economic pacts that bring world businesses and cultures into a mutually beneficial relationship. However, intertwining of business relationships is governed by each nation's government's **doctrines**, or a set of policies that guide a government's actions, with other nations. Doctrines are the mechanism that allow for one nation to become involved in the affairs of another. Thus, these doctrines create international coalitions for or against a particular global situation. The origins of **globalization**, or internationally operating markets, are traced to the Roman Empire (Chapter 5) and the Han Dynasty from 200 BCE to 400 CE. Both impressive civilizations used elaborately built roadways to transport products and their ideas. Modern globalization grew out of the 1980s' emergence of a single "world market" that connected banking and financial operations on an international scale. But, the term can be applied in a multitude of ways such as cultural globalization. **Cultural globalization** has created a world that brings people around the world together. Thomas L. Friedman (b. 1953), author of *The World is Flat*, wrote that globalization creates a "flat" world through the use of technology and various communication platforms. He also asserted that this *flatness* leads to social and economic implications. One such implication of technology has resulted in English as the main communication format for global business, commerce, and Internet exchange.

Arab Spring

A wave of prodemocracy protests first began in Tunisia on December 17, 2010 when a young street vendor, Mohamed Bouazizi (1984 to 2011), protested the confiscation of his vegetable cart by a policewoman. The policewoman had determined it to be an unlicensed cart. A government official tried to halt the unrest with violence. Later that day, Bouazizi went to the provincial headquarters to mount a complaint, but they refused to meet with him. He returned within minutes and poured gasoline over himself and lit himself on fire. Bouazizi did not die immediately but lingered in pain until January 4, 2011 when he passed away.

Massive protests broke out in Egypt, where President Hosnī Mubārak (b. 1928) lost military support after 30 years in office. Mubārak's senior military officers assumed power. The Arab world was encouraged by

© ymphotos/Shutterstock.com

Fig. 16.3 Capital of Yemen, Sanaa, witnessed a wave of violent and nonviolent protests.

the rapid success in both Tunisia and Egypt. Protests for prodemocracy were held in Yemen (fig. 16.3), Bahrain, Libya, and Syria. Unlike the success in the other two nations, the latter countries experienced a prolonged series of bloody struggles between the opposing people and ruling regimes. Each country's protesters had a different set of political and economic demands and obstacles to overcome before authentic change can be obtained.

Of the nations that began protesting for prodemocracy, Syria was most troubled by an ongoing civil war. As of 2018, more than 400,000 people have died, with more than 6 million displaced inside Syria and 5 million being refugees living outside Syria. The massive amounts of refugees flooding into many European nations have sparked a worldwide debate over nationalism—who should and should not be allowed to enter a nation? People have either forgotten or become unaware that revolutions, and war in general, are not resolved by peaceful

negotiations or at the speed at which technology is developed. Western civilization must recall the amount of planning and the fighting that occurred during both the American and French Revolutions (Chapter 11). While specific dates are placed on their supposed beginning and end, multiple other battles occurred decades later. Are we witnessing a Syrian Revolution and other Arab nations' revolutions in a lifetime? Does Western society believe that because it went through the pains of destruction and rebuilding, other nations are exempt from this process? Each nation must forge its own path, but in a globalized world, how is this accomplishable?

Climate Change Debate

Throughout Earth's history, climate has changed radically from a snowball Earth where every inch was covered in ice to having a tropical rainforest at the Artic Pole. In just the past 650,000 years, the globe attests to seven cycles of glacial advance and retreat. The last of these cycles ended more than

7,000 years about, which marked the beginning of the Earth's current climate. Current climate shifts away from severe cycles gave birth to human civilization (Chapter 1). Multiple factors are known to control the Earth's global climate, such as sunspots, solar winds, Sun cycles, Milankovitch Cycles, Chandler wobble, and seasonal cycles, which have no human involvement. Milankovitch Cycles were described by Serbian civil engineer Milutin Milanković (1879 to 1958) to explain variations in Earth's orbit in connection with climate patterns on Earth. The Chandler wobble was hypothesized by American astronomer Seth Chandler (1846 to 1913) to explain the precessions of the equinoxes. The precession of the equinox provide the overall axial tilt combine with the wobbliness of the Earth over a 25,772-year period.

While humankind cannot control certain aspects of the globe's overall climate, it can alleviate the overall strain it places on the environment as a whole. The National Aeronautics and Space Administration (NASA) has collected data from around the globe attesting to the damaging effects

of heat-trapping greenhouse gases such as carbon dioxide. To date, NASA has compiled a list of specific evidence that denotes how rapid the globe's climate is changing. The evidence is, first and foremost, an increase in the planet's average temperature by 1.6°F since the latter part of the nineteenth century. According to worldwide records, the year 2016 was the hottest on record. Other evidence points to a rise in ocean temperatures along with retreating glaciers and shrinking ice sheets. The most pressing evidence to accompany both the retreat of the glaciers and shrinking ice sheets was an 8-inch rise in global sea levels over the last century. While the evidence suggesting global climate change is man-made and staggering, the issue facing future generations is how to offset centuries of resource mismanagement. The debate remains as to what new innovations will the young minds of future generations around the world develop to rectify the health of their home planet? Or, will humanity continue down a path of denial and only seek to inhabit other celestial bodies such as Kepler-186f (fig. 16.4)?

Fig. 16.4 Kepler-186f, the first Earth-size planet in the habitable zone.

© Egyptian Studio/Shutterstock.com

Gender Revolution

While most people do not balk at living in a binary gender society, a growing sector does. Their inability to be confined to either male or female has steered the newest generations, Millennials and Gen Z, to question gender identity and sexual orientation. The statement "True Love Transcends Gender" summarizes the changing landscape of gender identity and acceptance in contemporary Western society. For example, a 2016 survey launched by the combined efforts of The Australian Sex Party and Queensland University of Technology in Australia provided participants with 33 different gender identity options. Beyond man, women, and transgender, these identities also include **cisgender**, or gender in accordance with the birth sex, and **none gender** or **gender non-conforming** for those individuals who did not want to identify with a specific gender. The list also includes a plethora of genders where people considered themselves a mix of both male and female, such as **genderfluid, demigender, pangender, bigender**, and **androgyny**. The two major identity groups were **third gender**, or neither male or female, and **trigender** where the person shifts between male, female, and third gender.

The idea of gender has recently moved into the realm of a person petitioning the court for a legal reconciliation of what they believe or feel their gender is. On an emotional level, the request seems valid and logical. This sort of legal change of gender raises fundamental questions about who we are at a biological level. Does society no longer abide by the rules of nature and genetics? If one can legally change one's gender, why can one not change one's age to reflect how old one feels? Or even one's ethnic or racial identify to conform with the group one feels most connected to on a cultural basis?

Same-Sex Marriage

The practice of two individuals of the same-sex marrying has ranged from a celebrated union to being a criminal act. While there are still people who perceive same-sex marriages as against traditional values, Western Europe and the United States have both legalized and sanctioned such marriages. The first country to provide couples of the same-sex legal married status was the Netherlands in 2001, closely followed by its southern neighbor Belgium in 2003. Other nations such as Germany (2001), United Kingdom (2005), Ecuador (2008), Liechtenstein (2011), Croatia (2014), and Italy (2016) provide same-sex couples a legal statue raging from a civil union to a registered partnership. A nation's acceptance of same-sex marriages resides in the fact that governments cannot dictate who can and cannot love one another. A principal question that arose during the wake of increased same-sex marriages or union legalizing was, what line can society not cross when it comes to *love*? Does society need to accept *love* relationships between minors and adults, given that same-sex relationships were once also against the law? Or even polygamy relationships on the basis of *love* and religion that have also been deemed unlawful?

CREATIVE IMPULSE

Throughout human history, humankind has felt obliged to explore its creativity and document its experiences. The twenty-first century is marked by shifts in our perception of art and its usefulness as a communication tool. Humanity lives and breathes visual input, and this input shapes our thoughts and perceptions of reality more profoundly than the written words. The famous phrase "a picture is worth a thousand words" has hard-to-trace origins but accurately summarizes the growing use of images as a powerful means for cultural, political, and social revolutions.

Architecture

Architects of the twenty-first century are heavily invested in creating unique structural forms. Some architects lean toward an organic fusion with the landscape, while others construct builds that appear to float at first glance. The French architect Paul Andreu (1938 to 2018) designed the National Grand Theatre, Center for the Performing Arts (fig. 16.5), for the city of Beijing. Locals refer to his building simply as "the egg." The structure was constructed of glass and titanium with an interior height soaring to 151 feet. "The egg" rests of an island with an artificial pond surrounding it. Visitors gain access to the building's interior via a 197-foot underground passageway. In total, the theater holds three performance areas for operas, concerts, and theater plays along with public spaces for lounging and dinning. Performance goers not only look forward to being entertained but also relish taking

in the structure's overall aesthetic qualities. Since a portion of the building is transparent, passersby are able to see performance in the evenings. When viewed at night or day, the reflection of the egg-shaped dome in the pond makes it seem whole.

Italian architect Renzo Piano (b. 1938), known for his 1970s' collaborative design of the *Centre Pompidou* in Paris, applied his high-tech vision of public spaces with the design of *Centro Botín* in Northern Spain (fig. 16.6). The building soars 20 feet above the ground with a central open area perched between two expansive wings. However, the central opening was a response to local concern that the building would block the bay view. Other inevitable debates were mounted as the project continued, such as traffic flow. But locals now believe that the project has improved the city by creating a new tunnel for vehicles that frees the areas for pedestrians, reducing both air and noise pollution.

© EQRoy/Shutterstock.com

Fig. 16.5 *National Grand Theatre ("The Egg")*, glass and titanium, Andreu, Beijing, China. 2001 to 2007.

© Omaly Darcia / Shutterstock.com

Fig. 16.6 *Centro Botín*, steel and glass, Piano, Santander, Spain. 2012 to 2017.

Piano once stated, "from the very beginning, I wanted the building to fly." The building does indeed appear to be an object inflight with a portion of its back half hanging over the Atlantic Ocean bay of Santander, Spain. The two wings were designed for different purposes. The larger wing houses an 8,200 square feet gallery space on two levels and the smaller side holds a 300-seat auditorium and workshops. The project's private benefactor, the Botín Foundation, provided a substantial sum of almost $100 million to bring Piano's design to fruition and beautify the birth city of Emilio Botín (1934 to 2014), the name sake of the foundation and center.

Sculptures

British assemblage artists and painter Damien Hirst's (d. 1965) works address an assortment of provocative views on beauty, mortality, death and rebirth, and technology since the mid-1980s. Hirst's work forces people to grapple with uncomfortable topics. Early

installations included live maggots and beautiful butterflies that reflected humans' inability or unwillingness to face their own mortality. The creation of his 2003 installation in Kyiv, Ukraine featured the sculpture *The Promise of Money* (fig.16.7) that questions more than mortality. The work highlights human experiences; it further questions why certain taxidermy displays are welcomed and others are shunned. Hirst's work pushes the boundaries of acceptability, while underscoring political and religious issues relevant to the region to which the work was originally displayed.

American sculptor Richard Serra (b. 1938) began his artistic endeavors in the late 1960s working in the aftermath of the Minimalism and Abstract movements. His most famous work is the 1981 *Titled Arc* (fig. 16.8) located in lower Manhattan's Federal Plaza. The work prompted numerous discussions regarding the commissioning, installation, and removal of public art. His 2007 creation *Titled Spheres* for Toronto's

© Slavko Sereda/Shutterstock.com

Fig. 16.7 *The Promise of Money* with the artist, resin, cow hair, sling, chain, hook, blood, Iraqi money, and mirror, Hirst, PinchukArtCentre, Kyiv, Ukraine. 2003.

© Shawn Goldberg/Shutterstock.com

Fig. 16.8 *Tilted Spheres*, steel, Serra, Terminal 1 at Pearson International Airport, Toronto, Canada. 2007.

Pearson International Airport continues the dialogue of the necessity for public art. Regardless of the debate, his works are inviting. Each is massive and offers viewers the ability to engage them by walking into, though, and around them.

Painting, Printmaking, and Photoshop

The artistic approach to creating science-based art to this point has used medium techniques hundreds of years old. This section explores new technology with the aid of older traditions. These traditional methods of producing print editions required a mastery of image inversion and cutting or etching skills. These methods leave little room for error. If an error is encountered, the entire work could be ruined. The newer technology of photopolymer or solarplate printing eliminates many of these issues (Chapter 15).

The technique used by K. M. Jantz (b. 1978) to create solarplate prints starts by painting the image onto a one-eighth-inch thick plywood board covered in gray high-gloss exterior latex paint. Two separate boards are used to create the final product. One board contains the pathogenic image *HTLV-1* (fig. 16.9), while the other board contains the historical/scientific image *Skeleton and Lymphocyte* (fig. 16.10). The use

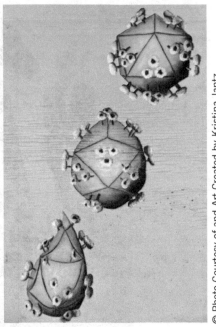

Fig. 16.9 *HTLV-1*, oil paint over high-gloss paint on plywood, Jantz, Houston, Texas. 2010.

© Photo Courtesy of and Art Created by Kristina Jantz

of two boards is an easy and fast way to paint only one pathogenic image that can then be multiplied with the use of Adobe Photoshop. Once the two boards are created, a high-resolution digital image of at least 300dpi is captured. The captured manipulated images

Fig. 16.10 *Skeleton and Lymphocyte*, oil paint over high-gloss paint on plywood, Jantz, Houston, Texas. 2010.

© Photo Courtesy of and Art Created by Kristina Jantz

produce an idealized final image *Skeleton/ Lymphocyte and HTLV-1, Red Green Blue (RGB)* (fig. 16.11).

Solarplate printing requires a full-size positive transparency for image transfer. Therefore, once the idealized final image is completed, the black, gray, and white values are amplified to maximize their transfer to the plate. If not enough difference between these colors is achieved once the image is converted from RGB mode to black and white, the final print image will not have enough highlights and shadows. To accomplish a good mix between highlights and shadows, additional digital manipulation is needed after the images are photoshopped

together. Once the highlights and shadows are maximized, the image is converted from RGB (fig. 16.11) to gray scale and saved as a jpeg. The gray scale jpeg is then used to create a right-reading photo, emulsion sideup transparency for producing the solarplate-etched print.

The final work titled *The Reason* (fig. 16.12) was based on an individual who immensely inspired the artist. The work focused on the viral infection know as human T-lymphotropic virus (HTLV-1), which causes Adult T-cell leukemia. The virus was the first human retrovirus (before HIV) to be discovered in 1980 and was found to be endemic in Japan and South America.

© Photo Courtesy of and Art Created by Kristina Jantz

Fig. 16.11 *Skeleton/Lymphocyte and HTLV-1, RGB,* Photoshop digital image, Jantz, Houston, Texas. 2010.

© Photo Courtesy of and Art Created by Kristina Jantz

Fig. 16.12 *The Reason,* solarplate etching, Jantz, Houston, Texas. 2010.

The virus was known to be thousands of years old and probably originated with the paleo-Mongoloids who migrated to Japan and South America before the Colonial era, or roughly 10,000 years ago. Isolate bone-marrow DNA from mummified remains in northern Chile were determined to be carriers of a specific type of HTLV-1. These mummified remains and the odd mutation HTLV-1 caused in the T-lymphocyte sparked an idea for a solarplate composition.

The Reason brings together the traditional, ugly outcome of viruses, which was death, and their beautiful nature not seen by the naked eye. The virus in reality attacks T-lymphocytes, causing them to take on the appearance of a flower. These "flowers" grow in the infected individual's body just as real flowers grow after a spring shower. The morbid, graphic detailing of the skeleton was something seen in anatomy and physiology classrooms. The skeleton figure in the print was partly inspired by a real Chilean mummy and also by Vincent van Gogh's *Skull of a Skeleton with Burning Cigarette* painting in 1886. Van Gogh's skeleton has a stark reality that can be quite moving, which was the intended feeling being conveyed in *The Reason*.

Graffiti

British graffiti artist Banksy, an anonymous street artist, creates a not so subtle tongue-in-cheek spray paint and stenciled works. There is suspicion that Robin Gunningham (b. 1973) from Yate, England is Banksy or the artist is possibly from a group of seven artists who work as a team. No matter who Banksy is, the works produced range from social irony to political dark humor (this can be seen in the work *Stop and Search [Girl and Solider]* (fig.16.1) and from humanitarian messages for kindness to ultrasatirical criticisms of human stupidity (this can be seen in the work *Go Back to Africa, Migrant* (fig. 16.13). But, Banksy can also display witty spoofs on normal human curiosity in *Boyish Mischeif* (fig. 16.14).

Literature

By the twenty-first century, humankind had lived through and documented its share of life-changing events. Books such as *The Road*

Fig. 16.13 *Go Back to Africa, Migrant*, stencil and spray paint, Banksy, Essex, England. 2014.

© photogeoff/Shutterstock.com

Fig. 16.14 *Boyish Mischief,* stencil and spray paint, Banksy, Somerset, England. 2015.

(2006) by Cormac McCarthy (b. 1933) and *The Hunger Games* (2010) by Suzanne Collins (b.1962) resonate with humankind's bleak optimism for contemporary times. Even though the books are written for different points of view, third and first, respectively, the trials the main characters undergo are undoubtedly harsh and gruesome. Both authors present readers with unfathomable situations that become animated and relevant through how the characters muddle through them to the end.

In 2007, Dominican American, creative writing professor at the Massachusetts Institute of Technology, Junot Díaz, emerged onto the literary scene in 2007 with his debut novel *The Brief Wondrous Life of Oscar Wao.* Díaz won the National Book Critics Circle award and the Pulitzer Prize for his saga tell of an immigrant family. His book scrutinizes the difficulties of more than Oscar's family relocates to New Jersey. The book analyzes the themes of both national and racial identity

but also probes into the typical masculinity assumptions placed on Latin Americans. While the book tackles a few hot topics people in the twenty-first century are still grappling with, the amount of footnotes, numerous narrators, and language shifts from English to Spanish may leave readers a bit overwhelmed. Nevertheless, Díaz's book helps all Americans understand their self and the diversity of American culture as never before.

Philosophy

British-born American philosopher Kwame Anthony Appiah (b. 1954) immigrated to America in the 1980s. He has enjoyed a long career as a professor of philosophy, African studies, and African American studies at multiple Ivy League universities such as Yale University and Princeton University. His earlier philosophical writing concentrated on politics and African identity in the West. In his 2006 book, *The Ethics of*

Identity, Appiah surveyed prominent thinkers throughout the ages and across cultural divides to discover if humanity is constrained by socially accepted identities or if they enable individual liberty. Appiah's chapter titled "The Ethic of Individuality" embarks on an analysis of John Stuart Mill's (1806 to 1873) essay On Liberty. After a lengthy summary and personal debate, Appiah offers the conclusion that an individual may find "inherent value not in diversity...but in the enterprise of self-creation." For this, he asserts that Mill's basic tenet of "liberty" resides in the fact that "only free people can take full command of their own lives." To his credit, Appiah sees in the personal growth of an individual rather than their outward appearance or circumstances in which they reside a better source for identity.

In 2007, Appiah turned his attention to the art world for a brief moment to espouse his thoughts of world heritage in *Cosmopolitanism: Ethics in a World of Strangers*. After a lengthy introduction to the book, which covers cultures and people from the fourth century BCE to the year of the book's publication, he asks some of the most relevant questions of humanity's contemporary era. Who, exactly, owns cultural artifacts? Does an artifact's nation of origin or the individual who rescued it from almost certain destruction matter more? These are the questions asked regarding the arguments between Italy and the city of Florence over Michelangelo's *David* (Chapter 9) and of Greece and England over stone reliefs form the Parthenon. More importantly, does the Artists Rights Society, only founded in 1987, have the ethical right to require their permission to reproduce a work of art that anyone can freely take a picture of and post to a royalty-free domain?

On the heels of Appiah, Lewis Hyde (b. 1945) explored the idea of communal space such as the Internet in his 2010 publication *Common as Air: Revolution, Art, and Ownership*. He asks questions regarding ownership of ideas and content in books, films, and online. The rapid exchange of ideas and files through various forms of technology raise the question of digital piracy and content thievery or manipulation. Hyde concludes that no one can really own knowledge and that creativity belongs to humanity as a whole. But, this debate over ownership will continue until resolved by various legal outcomes around the globe.

Technology

Only a few decades into the twenty-first century can humanity attest to its many astonishing developments that permeate into almost every aspect of societal interaction. Technology has continued to zoom along ever so rapidly that technology unveiled one day is practically obsolete the next. In 2007, Steve Jobs (Chapter 15) revealed the launch of the first **iPhone**, or a device combining a computer, music storage, camera, and cellular phone, that promised to revolutionize the phone industry. The iPhone and similar devices are collectively referred to as "**smartphone**." Our reliance on these devices has made scholars question if they are in actuality making people "smarter," as their names imply. These questions arise as a result of the fact that society, for the first time in history, has the whole of human history at its finger tips in our smartphones. But, how accurate are blogs and articles written by impassioned people?

GLOBALISM MOVING FORWARD

Humanity is only a few decades into the twenty-first century with "a bag of mixed results" to show for all our efforts of constructing and sustaining a society filled with equality, justice, and liberty for all. Equality is not always given freely and, therefore, must be clarified when inequalities arise. Justice is not always granted simply because we believe ourselves to be an open-minded people, instead there are instances when it must be legally obtained. Liberty is not for the weak-hearted, as the price for obtaining it is sometimes deadly. The remaining years of the twenty-first century will unfold in dramatic procession just as every other moment humankind has encountered. As we move through our daily existence, we make choices. Some choices are random, others are deliberate. Each person should strive to live a life filled with a hopeful intent that will help transform the next generation into a society with the ability to live in harmony.

Critical Thinking

Examine the differences between the artistic movements of the early twentieth century.

Evaluate the ideas of the political and economic systems of capitalism, communism, and socialism.

Describe the major technological advancements of the early twentieth century.

Analyze how each successive art movement led to the next.

Examine the impact film had on society.

Illustrate how artistic expression was transformed during the early twentieth century.

Online Resources

Arab Spring Overview

https://www.npr.org/2011/12/17/143897126/the-arab-spring-a-year-of-revolution

Gender Revolution Overview

https://www.sbs.com.au/guide/article/2018/07/25/wrap-your-head-around
-gender-and-sexual-identity-gender-revolution-katie-couric

NASA Explains Climate Change Causes

https://climate.nasa.gov/causes/

NASA Discovers First Earth Like Habitable Planet

https://exoplanets.nasa.gov/resources/1063/nasas-kepler-discovers
-first-earth-size-planet-in-the-habitable-zone/

Serra's _Band_ Video

https://smarthistory.org/richard-serra-band/

Christo and Jeanne-Claude Projects

https://smarthistory.org/christo-and-jeanne-claude-the-gates/

Damien Hirst, Sculptor and Painter

https://www.theartstory.org/artist-hirst-damien-artworks.htm

Discovery the Works by Banksy

http://www.banksy.co.uk/

Kwame Anthony Appiah, Life and Works

http://appiah.net/